A Bitter Peace

The New Cold War History
John Lewis Gaddis,
editor

Pierre Asselin

A Bitter Peace

Washington, Hanoi, and the Making of the Paris Agreement

The University of North Carolina Press
Chapel Hill and London

© 2002 The University of North Carolina Press

All rights reserved

Manufactured in the United States of America

Designed by Cameron Poulter

Set in Meridien by Keystone Typesetting, Inc.

The paper in this book meets the guidelines
for permanence and durability of the Committee on
Production Guidelines for Book Longevity of the
Council on Library Resources.

Library of Congress Cataloging-in-Publication Data

Asselin, Pierre.

   A bitter peace : Washington, Hanoi, and the making of
the Paris agreement / Pierre Asselin.

     p. cm. — (The new Cold War history)

Includes bibliographical references and index.

ISBN 0-8078-2751-7 (cloth: alk. paper)

ISBN 0-8078-5417-4 (pbk.: alk. paper)

   1. Vietnamese Conflict, 1961–1975—Peace.

2. Vietnamese Conflict, 1961–1975—Diplomatic history.

3. United States—Foreign relations—Vietnam (Democratic Republic)

4. Vietnam (Democratic Republic)—Foreign relations—United States.

I. Title. II. Series.

DS559.7 .A87   2002

959.704′31—dc21

2002005685

cloth   06 05 04 03 02   5 4 3 2 1

paper 06 05 04 03 02   5 4 3 2 1

Contents

Maps and Illustrations

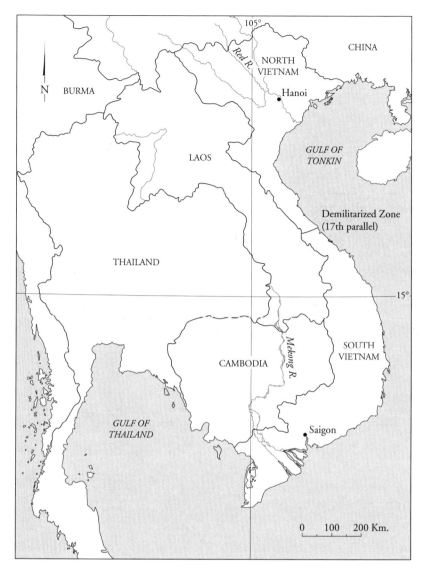

Indochinese Peninsula, 1954–1975

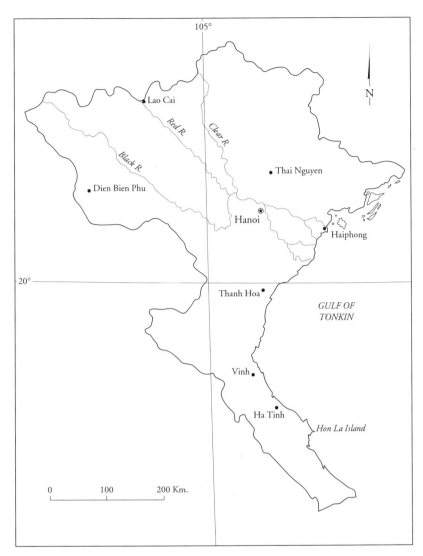

North Vietnam, 1954–1975

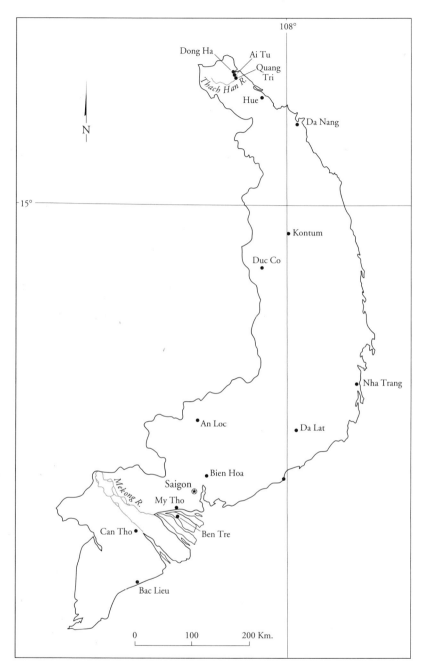

South Vietnam, 1954–1975

Preface

On 24 January 1973, Henry Kissinger, President Richard Nixon's na-
tional security adviser, confirmed the imminent signing of the Paris Agreement, ostensibly ending the Vietnam War. When later asked how the agreement had been agreed upon and what it meant, Kissinger replied, "These facts have to be analyzed by each person for himself."[1] This study is a response to that reply. It is about the diplomatic effort to end American participation in the war in Vietnam, a conflict known in Vietnam as the Anti-American Resistance and in the United States as the Vietnam War. Relating the diplomacy that created the agreement and led to the American withdrawal from Vietnam, this study discusses the making of the Paris Agreement by tracing the positions of Washington and Hanoi during their negotiations in France and the strategies each used to achieve its purposes during five years of secret and private diplomacy.

The principal aim of this *histoire évènementielle* is to explain the circumstances that doomed the peace promised by the agreement. As this study demonstrates, Washington and Hanoi signed the Paris Agreement acrimoniously and with the understanding that its implementation would be highly problematic. Fading prospects of victory after 1968, perpetuation of the military stalemate through mid-1972 despite efforts to break that stalemate, and difficulties on the domestic front convinced both sides that the signing of an agreement in January 1973 was the most expedient solution under the circumstances. Washington and Hanoi thus acted in collusion and agreed to vague and largely unworkable positions because finalizing an agreement was more important than peace itself. Since the agreement constituted a timely necessity, the two sides ignored it once it had served certain immediate, cynical purposes. For Washington, those purposes included securing the release of American prisoners, withdrawing from Vietnam without formally capitulating, and preserving American credibility in the Cold War; for Hanoi, they included forcing the withdrawal of American forces, saving the socialist revolution in the North, and improving the prospects of reunification.

The United States elevated diplomacy over military activity as the more likely vehicle to prevent defeat in the aftermath of the Tet Offensive; and after 1969, the Nixon administration emphasized diplomacy to the point that it manipulated the ground and air wars in Vietnam to serve the purposes of the negotiations in Paris. In Hanoi, the process was more gradual but the outcome similar. The leadership initially assigned diplomacy a tertiary role below that of military and political activity in South Vietnam but reversed that order of priorities after the 1969–70 *période creuse*. At its Eighteenth Plenum in 1970, the Central Committee of the Vietnamese Workers' Party (VWP) raised the diplomatic mode of struggle, and thus the Paris peace talks, to a par with the military and political modes. During the ensuing two years, however, Hanoi wavered between serious negotiation and intensified military activity. Ultimately, the failure of the 1972 Spring Offensive convinced Hanoi that military victory was elusive and perhaps impossible, and success through diplomacy quite likely.

By mid-1972, both Washington and Hanoi saw diplomacy as the best means of ending their war on the most favorable terms they could hope to achieve. Contrary to the assumption or conclusion of many Western writers, the negotiations were not secondary to the ground and air wars. On the contrary, the negotiations in Paris eventually dictated battlefield activities by both sides, and as that occurred the ground and air wars became secondary to diplomacy.

Because the Paris Agreement was signed by both sides under extreme duress—that is, as a result of military and other circumstances they could not control—it was doomed to unravel. The situation in South Vietnam after January 1973 remained unpalatable to all three Vietnamese parties. Saigon was indignant that North Vietnamese forces stayed in the South after the cease-fire; the Provisional Revolutionary Government of the Republic of South Vietnam (PRG)—the political arm of the National Liberation Front (NLF) after 1969—resented that the current regime in Saigon remained; and Hanoi spurned any solution that did not provide for the timely reunification of the nation. The war had lasted too long and been too costly for the parties to accept the kind of peace promised by the agreement, mainly one that did not guarantee the fulfillment of their respective ambitions. Thus, neither side honored the spirit nor the letter of the agreement beyond its most immediate purposes.

North Vietnamese–American relations during the Vietnam War went through a distinct evolution. Between the introduction of American ground forces in March 1965 and the Tet Offensive in early 1968, there was infrequent diplomatic interaction between Washington and Hanoi. Each was too preoccupied with fighting the war to think of negotiating

an end to it. In the aftermath of the Tet Offensive, the two sides conducted public and then private talks, but for more than a year and a half
the talks produced nothing but the Johnson administration's decision to
end the bombing of North Vietnam. Then, in early 1970 commenced a
period of sustained diplomatic interaction that produced few results. In
the summer of 1972, however, the talks began to bear fruit and culmi-
nated in the signing of the Paris Agreement. As Washington and Hanoi
moved closer to agreement, Saigon and the PRG became increasingly
intractable. Saigon, in fact, prevented an agreement from being signed in
late October 1972. This last period, from mid-1972 to early 1973, is the
focus of this study.

This focus accentuates two important realities scholars have ne-
glected. The first is that North Vietnam was as active a player in the war
and throughout the negotiations as the United States was. This study
demonstrates that the agreement of 1973 represented the culmination of
a process during which the Nixon White House and the Hanoi politburo
under VWP general secretary Le Duan made a series of compromises
prompted by specific circumstances that led each party to conclude that
an agreement was preferable to continued stalemate on the battlefield.
While the Saigon government and its opponents in the PRG/NLF never
directly participated in the secret and private discussions, their pressures
on Washington and Hanoi, respectively, combined with the dynamics of
American and North Vietnamese politics to make them influential factors in the negotiations. Thus, the two South Vietnamese parties figure
prominently in this study.

The second reality this study accents and other studies have ignored is
the centrality of diplomacy in the Vietnam War. The outcome of the
war—and of the Vietnamese Revolution—was not determined on the
battlefield but at the negotiating table. There, conditions were created
and the stage was set for the conclusion of the war. The Paris Agreement
changed the balance of forces in the South as it precipitated the completion of the American withdrawal and permitted North Vietnamese troops
to remain. The fall of Saigon occurred in the propitious context created
by the agreement; this study explains how that came about.

Chapters 1 and 2 describe the diplomatic situation from the Tet Offensive of 1968 to the middle of 1972, during which time the peace negotiations made no consequential progress because neither side was willing to
compromise on substantive issues. In mid-1972, however, the discussions
entered a new phase that lasted seven months and produced the agreement that Kissinger announced the signing of in January 1973. That
period is the body of the study, Chapters 3 through 6. Despite temporary

ups and downs, the negotiations throughout this time were sustained and ultimately fruitful due to the determination of both sides, finally, to obtain an agreement. In fact, by late 1972, signing an agreement had become an end in itself for both Washington and Hanoi. Chapter 7 considers the last round of negotiations in January 1973 and the finalization of the agreement and includes a discussion of Nixon's efforts to get South Vietnamese president Nguyen Van Thieu to accept the agreement, which compromised South Vietnamese interests, as Thieu clearly understood. The epilogue summarizes the consequences of the accords, especially their breakdown in South Vietnam, considers the fall of Saigon in 1975, and assesses fundamental aspects of North Vietnamese–American diplomacy.

This study does not consider the semipublic talks that paralleled the private negotiations. Begun in 1968, attended by all four factions, and continued until the signing of the Paris Agreement, these talks were largely cosmetic and conducted mainly for propaganda purposes. They captured media attention but contributed nothing to the final agreement.

Note on Translations and Vietnamese Names

Translations from French and Vietnamese are my own. For the sake of clarity, I have excluded all Vietnamese diacritical marks. As is standard in Vietnam, Vietnamese personal names are used where the entire name is not. In Vietnamese, the personal name is last. For example, Le Duc Tho (surname "Le") is "Tho." Exceptions to the rule include Ho Chi Minh, commonly called "Ho," and Le Duan and Truong Chinh, who are always referred to by their full names.

Note on Chinese Words

All Chinese words, including personal and geographical names, are in Pinying, unless they appear as part of a quotation, in which case the original wording was kept.

Acknowledgments

Contributions from several individuals and institutions have made the completion of this book possible. First, I wish to thank John Lewis Gaddis and Edwin E. Moïse for taking the time to read the manuscript. Their critical comments and suggestions significantly enhanced its quality. Since this work started out as a doctoral dissertation, I am also much indebted to the members of my dissertation committee for their assistance and guidance. I owe my largest debt of gratitude to Idus Newby. His ideas on converting the dissertation into a publishable manuscript were immensely constructive. Additionally, his wisdom, dedication, and exceptional editing skills greatly improved the readability of the narrative. Tim Naftali offered inspiration, encouragements, and incisive comments. Truong Buu Lam and Margot Henriksen provided important input and much-needed support. Special thanks to Stephen O'Harrow, friend and mentor, for suggesting that I exploit Canadian archival materials and for allowing me to turn his classes into a forum to discuss the American intervention in Vietnam.

A historical narrative is only as good as the sources on which it is based. While researching this work, I incurred numerous other debts of gratitude. For his indispensable service, I thank William Joyner, archivist at the Nixon Presidential Materials Project at the National Archives and Records Administration in Maryland. Bill guided me to the documents that became the foundation of this study. I also wish to acknowledge the staff of the Asia Division at the Library of Congress in Washington, D.C., for their help in locating valuable Vietnamese-language materials. In Canada, I am indebted to George Lafleur and Lori Baker of the Canadian National Archives, and Greg Donaghy and Ted Kelly of the Historical Section of the Department of Foreign Affairs and International Trade, who on very short notice pulled and allowed me to read dozens of files that have yet to be formally declassified. My thanks, too, to Michel Gauvin, former chairman and member of the International Commission of Control and Supervision (1973–75) (ICCS), for taking the time to clarify the historical record.

The quantity of valuable information I gathered during my seven-month stay in Vietnam in 1996 and during shorter visits in 1998 and 1999 exceeded my expectations. That was in large part due to the assistance of numerous individuals. Among them, I wish to thank Professor Phan Huy Le for his precious advice and countless letters of introduction and Nguyen Van Phong, his assistant. At the Hanoi National Library, I am indebted to Duong Thi Hong and Pham Thi Dung for navigating me through their collection. The staff at State Archives Center 3 in Hanoi committed their expertise to the work. Trieu Van Hien, head of the Document Conservation Department at the Revolution Museum in Hanoi, and Pham Mai Hung, its director, were generous with their time. I am indebted to Luu Van Loi, former assistant to North Vietnamese foreign minister Nguyen Duy Trinh and author of several works on Vietnamese foreign policy, for meeting with me to discuss Vietnamese-American relations and his role in the negotiations.

For their financial contributions, I wish to express my appreciation to the Fonds de la Formation de Chercheurs et l'Aide à la Recherche in Québec City, Canada; to the Hawaii Council for the Humanities in Honolulu; and to the College of Arts and Sciences, the history department, the Center for Southeast Asian Studies, and the Research Council of the University of Hawaii at Manoa.

At the University of North Carolina Press, I wish to express my utmost gratitude to Lewis Bateman, who first considered the project; to Charles Grench for supporting it through its most crucial stages; to Alison Waldenburg, Ruth Homrighaus, and Amanda McMillan, for their professionalism and efficiency; and to Mary Caviness, my editor, whose diligence and remarkable capacity to see the not-so-obvious significantly improved the language and accuracy of this book.

Behind every effort of this magnitude lie special contributions. Yves Frenette remains the individual who has had the most profound impact on my academic *cheminement*. During those formative years at Glendon College in Toronto, Canada, his door was always open, and I remain grateful for his help and encouragements. Peter Worthing, a former colleague in the history department at the University of Hawaii and a former teammate on the Hawaiian Hockey League 1995 Champion Northwest Airlines Wings, was a good friend who gave me great advice. Special thanks to Hy Van Luong and the late Huynh Kim Khanh for opening my eyes to important realities of Vietnamese history; to Tom Tynan and John Keyes, with whom my interest in Vietnamese-American relations began to grow; to Gary Hess for his comments on an earlier draft of the text; to Shel Hershinow for his guidance and help on the title of the book; to Matthew Martin for reading and editing portions of the manuscript; to Phi

Hong Nhung for her friendship; to Sylvester Stallone and his "Rambo" for spurring my interest in Vietnam; to Pierre-Marie for looking out for me; to Nathalie Vézina, whose support, assistance, and commentaries were essential for the completion of my dissertation; and to my family—Marie-France, Fernande, and Jacques—for its love and constant support. I am also grateful to the Montemayor family in Silver Spring, Maryland, and the Vézina family in Québec City, Canada, for their hospitality. Lastly, my appreciation goes to the lovely and scintillating Grace Cheng, whose comments and encouragements during the revision of the manuscript proved invaluable.

All contributions aside, I alone accept responsibility for any shortcomings in this work.

I dedicate this book to my mother, who taught me the importance of education.

Abbreviations

ACC	Army Central Committee	xix
ARVN	Army of the Republic of (South) Vietnam	
B-52	American strategic bomber	
CIA	Central Intelligence Agency	
COSVN	Central Office for South Vietnam	
CP.50	Hanoi-based advisory committee for the Paris peace talks	
DIA	Defense Intelligence Agency	
DMZ	Demilitarized zone. Demarcation separating North and South Vietnam at the seventeenth parallel established in 1954 by the Geneva Accords	
DRV/DRVN	Democratic Republic of (North) Vietnam	
FPJMC	Four-Party Joint Military Commission	
GNP	Gross National Product	
GVN	Government of (South) Vietnam	
ICCS	International Commission of Control and Supervision (1973–75)	
ICSC	International Commission for Supervision and Control (1954–73)	
IGC	International Guarantee Conference	
JCS	Joint Chiefs of Staff	
JEC	Joint Economic Commission	
JGS	Joint General Staff	
KCP	Kampuchean Communist Party. Maoist nationalist organization officially called Angka Padevat (Revolutionary Organization). Under Pol Pot's leadership, dubbed the Khmer Rouge	
MACV	Military Assistance Command, Vietnam	
MIA	Missing in action	
MiG	North Vietnamese (Soviet-made) jet fighter	
NCNRC	National Council of National Reconciliation and Concord	
NLF	National Liberation Front of South Vietnam, commonly known as Viet Cong	
NSC	National Security Council	
NVA	North Vietnamese Army	
OPIC	Overseas Private Investment Corporation	
PAVN	People's Army of (North) Vietnam	
POW	Prisoner of war	
PRC	People's Republic of China	

PRG	Provisional Revolutionary Government of the Republic of South Vietnam
PRP	People's Revolutionary Party. Southern branch of the VWP in North Vietnam
RVN	Republic of (South) Vietnam
SAM	Surface-to-air missile
TPJMC	Two-Party Joint Military Commission
UN	United Nations
USSR	Union of Soviet Socialist Republics
VC	Viet Cong. Abbreviated from *Viet Nam cong san* (Vietnamese Communist). Officially recognized as the National Liberation Front of South Vietnam
Viet Minh	Vietnamese nationalist paramilitary front formed in 1941. Short for Viet Nam Doc Lap Dong Minh (Vietnamese Independence League)
VNAF	(South) Vietnamese Air Force
VWP	Vietnamese Workers' Party. North Vietnam's Communist Party

A Bitter Peace

CHAPTER ONE

The First Round
1968–1971

By 1968, the United States had been heavily involved in Vietnam for   1
nearly three years. The Vietnamese, on the other hand, had been at war
for most of the prior three decades. After World War II, the French attempt to reinstate the colonial regime in Indochina had degenerated into
a "dirty war" that reached its denouement in 1954 at Dien Bien Phu. The
flawed peace of Geneva and the French withdrawal that followed did
little to end the bloodshed. In fact, the ambiguity of the Geneva Accords
encouraged a new civil war. After 1954, the Vietnamese divided themselves into those who wanted a Communist regime that was inward-
looking and fiercely nationalist and those who preferred a Western-
oriented polity and economy.

These differences produced special difficulties in southern Vietnam,
where the divisions were acute and the resulting tensions soon led to
armed insurgency and brutal repression. By the mid-1960s, the Saigon
government and military were incapable of suppressing the insurgency.
Their appeals to Washington in the Cold War context resulted in American military intervention, which soon became massive. Although the
decision to intervene on such a scale was Lyndon Johnson's, it was the
predictable culmination of years of increasing American involvement in
Vietnam. Between 1960, the last year of Dwight Eisenhower's presidency, and the assassination of his successor, John F. Kennedy, in 1963,
the number of American advisers assigned to the Army of the Republic
of (South) Vietnam (ARVN) rose from 875 to 16,263. Since the situation showed no signs of improvement from the American standpoint,
Kennedy's successor, Lyndon Johnson, continued the escalation and, in
March 1965, authorized a massive buildup of American forces in South
Vietnam.[1]

Concurrently, Johnson authorized sustained naval and aerial bombardment of North Vietnam. From Washington's perspective at the time,
the insurgency in South Vietnam was not an indigenous movement but
foreign aggression. A 1961 white paper produced by the Kennedy admin-

istration had concluded that the main opposition group in the South, the National Liberation Front of South Vietnam (NLF), was in fact "Hanoi's creation." It was thus "neither independent nor southern," nor did it seek "what most men would consider liberation." Since the NLF was an arm of Hanoi in the South, the United States had to take action against the North.[2] In another white paper in 1965, the Johnson administration maintained similarly that North Vietnam was "carrying out a carefully conceived plan of aggression against the South." The American purpose in Vietnam, Johnson himself contended, "is to join in the defense and protection of freedom of a brave people who are under attack that is controlled and that is directed from outside their country."[3] Thus emerged a consensus in Washington favoring sustained bombing of North Vietnam until Hanoi reached a "threshold of pain" and ceased subversion in the South.[4]

The air campaign against North Vietnam, code-named Rolling Thunder, had three objectives: to reduce North Vietnamese contributions to the insurgencies in South Vietnam and Laos; to bolster morale among South Vietnamese; and to escalate the pressure until North Vietnam decided that supporting the insurgencies was too costly. The Johnson administration believed that bombing the North would stop the infiltration of men and supplies into the South and, in conjunction with the deployment of American ground forces, decimate the insurgency there.[5]

In January 1959, in response to mounting tensions and appeals from insurgents in the South, the Central Committee of the Vietnamese Workers' Party (VWP[6]) had approved the pursuit of armed and violent struggle there to precipitate the collapse of the Saigon regime and bring about the reunification of the nation.[7] Thereafter, the Democratic Republic of (North) Vietnam (DRVN) began the infiltration of troops and supplies into the South via the Ho Chi Minh Trail, a network of roads that ran through Laos and Cambodia. In December 1960, it encouraged the creation of an indigenous southern maquis—the NLF—"to rally all patriotic classes and sections of the people" opposed to the Americans and their "puppets" in the Saigon government.[8] Though the NLF was more nationalist in character than it was communist, its leaders worked closely with Hanoi and were autonomous only to the extent the northern leadership allowed them to be.[9]

In 1965, after the United States began its direct military commitment, the VWP organized and coordinated an effort it called officially the "Anti-American Resistance for National Salvation" (*cuoc khang chien chong My cuu nuoc*). This Resistance consisted of three modes of struggle (*dau tranh*). The military struggle aimed, through a strategy of continued attrition in South Vietnam and active resistance in the North, to render enough of the enemy's forces combat-ineffective to produce demoralization and capitulation. Known as *lam chu de tieu diet dich, tieu diet dich de lam chu*, which meant "control to annihilate the enemy, annihilate the enemy to control," that strategy paralleled the strategy of "search and destroy" adopted by the Americans in South Vietnam after 1965.[10] The political struggle, the second mode, entailed propaganda activity among the South Vietnamese people to recruit and retain partisans. Lastly, the diplomatic struggle consisted of engaging the enemy in public fora and through the media to increase the pressure on Washington to pull its forces out of Indochina. It also meant negotiating secretly with the enemy at an opportune time to ratify the gains achieved through the political and military struggles and expedite the withdrawal of American forces.[11]

North Vietnamese policymakers, specifically VWP general secretary Le Duan and the rest of the VWP politburo, initially considered diplomacy the least promising of the three modes of struggle. Despite the new context and enemy, they continued to favor armed struggle.[12] Achieving the Vietnamese Revolution's basic objectives—liberating the South (*giai phong mien Nam*), building socialism in the North (*xay dung chu nghia xa hoi mien Bac*), and unifying the nation—was their overriding concern. Given the nature of those objectives, they sought not compromise with the American aggressors and their Saigon collaborators but decisive victory on the battlefield.[13] Lessons learned from the past reinforced that way of thinking. After the overwhelming victory at Dien Bien Phu, Hanoi had decided not to press the fight against France but to participate instead in the Geneva Conference on Indochina. That strategic blunder meant continued foreign interference in Vietnam. After 1965, the VWP politburo intended not to repeat the mistake, that is, not to betray the revolutionary effort again by negotiating an end to a war it could win through sufficient sacrifice and continued effort.[14] Accordingly, it refused to make diplomacy a primary arena for dealing with the United States, insisting instead that the only acceptable settlement was one amounting to American capitulation. The DRVN first proposed the bases for such a settlement in 1965, when it demanded the withdrawal of American and other foreign forces from Indochina, the removal of the existing regime in South Vietnam, and the replacement of that regime with a coalition government that included pro-Communist and pro-Hanoi representatives. These demands were the Three Aims of the Anti-American Resistance, immutable foundations for achieving the fundamental objectives of the Revolution.[15] Fortunately for Hanoi, after 1965, both Beijing and Moscow provided massive aid to help the Resistance.[16]

In these early years of the war, Washington was as ambivalent toward diplomacy as Hanoi. In fact, the Johnson administration considered negotiation with Hanoi undesirable. As a recent study points out, Johnson felt that the credibility of America and of the Democratic Party was at stake in Vietnam. Fearing personal and national humiliation, Johnson rejected negotiations, opting instead for an increased military effort as the most promising means of succeeding in Vietnam. Johnson, the recent study notes, had earlier mourned the "loss" of China and now had no intention of losing South Vietnam.[17] Another factor that encouraged the Johnson administration to dismiss diplomacy was the potentially negative impact negotiations would have on Saigon. Substantive discussions with North Vietnam while the military situation was unsatisfactory might antagonize Saigon and risk "destroying the South Vietnamese government altogether."[18] Washington, too, had a blueprint for acceptable settlement: it comprised fourteen points and was first presented to the foreign minister of Poland by veteran diplomat Averell Harriman, in December 1965. Predictably, that blueprint was incompatible with the Three Aims.[19]

Since neither party was prepared to compromise, or even to negotiate seriously, a diplomatic impasse ensued. Contacts between the two sides were informal, sporadic, and inconsequential. Between 1964 and 1967, Washington and Hanoi had five direct and indirect contacts.[20] As long as both parties felt the war would be lost or won militarily, their diplomatic efforts concentrated on mustering foreign support by manipulating world opinion. In January 1967, the Thirteenth Plenum of the Central Committee of the VWP confirmed the secondary role of diplomacy in the war effort. "The military and political struggles in the South," it resolved, "are essential factors in bringing about victory on the battlefield and creating a foundation for victory on the diplomatic front."[21] Party propagandists would thereafter "denounce still more strongly the savage acts of aggression conducted by the American invader, and denounce its scheme to bring peace with bombs."[22] The Johnson administration adopted a similar stance, seeking, with moderate success, international support of its crusade in Southeast Asia.[23] Between 1965 and 1967, diplomacy failed "because each nation refused to give way on the basic issues."[24]

In early 1968, NLF forces and their North Vietnamese allies launched Tet Mau Than, the Tet Offensive. That singular development broke the military stalemate that had persisted since 1965. The resulting urban warfare and the shock waves it generated forced both parties to realize that military victory was highly problematic under current or foreseeable circumstances. Although Hanoi and the NLF scored important psychological gains over Washington and Saigon, their casualties were nearly ten times as high. That frightening cost proved that conditions were not ripe for toppling the Saigon government militarily.[25] In the United States, the mere fact of a widespread enemy offensive shattered the myth that allied armies were winning the war and fueled domestic opposition to the conflict.[26] On 25 March 1968, a group of retired American officials and military officers known as the Wise Men met in Washington to discuss American involvement in Vietnam. They concluded that the involvement would never achieve its objective and recommended de-escalation. That recommendation encouraged Lyndon Johnson's decision to seek new serious negotiations with Hanoi.[27] In a well-publicized television speech on 31 March, Johnson announced that his government sought and would work to achieve a diplomatic solution to the war. He also announced he would not run for reelection and ordered an immediate end to the bombing of North Vietnam above the twentieth parallel.[28]

In the past, the VWP politburo had rejected American offers for direct negotiations. This time, however, its answer was different. "It is clear that the American government has not seriously and fully met the just demands of the Democratic Republic of Vietnam government, or of progressive public opinion in the United States and the rest of the world," read its response to Washington on 3 April. "Nevertheless . . . the Democratic Republic of Vietnam government declares that it is prepared to send representatives to meet and to determine with American representatives the unconditional cessation of the bombing and all other acts of war against the Democratic Republic of Vietnam to start the negotiations."[29] The need to relieve the stress on the political and military fronts below the seventeenth parallel and the effects of the war on North Vietnam itself spurred Hanoi's acceptance of Johnson's offer to negotiate. After the Tet Offensive, as DRVN special adviser to the Paris talks Le Duc Tho admitted later, resistance forces in the South were so crippled that "we needed to sit and talk."[30]

On 13 May 1968, the first encounter between representatives of the DRVN and the United States took place at the International Conference Center of the Hôtel Majestic in Paris. Averell Harriman, a veteran of diplomatic summits since World War II and onetime ambassador to the Soviet Union, headed the American delegation. Joining Harriman were former under secretary of defense Cyrus Vance, former Eisenhower aide

Andrew Goodpaster, Vietnam specialist Philip Habib, and National Security Council (NSC) staffer William Jorden, who acted as press spokesman. Former foreign minister Xuan Thuy headed the North Vietnamese
delegation assisted by Ha Van Lau, former director of operations of the
General Staff of the People's Army of (North) Vietnam (PAVN) and a
participant in the 1954 and 1961–62 Geneva Conferences on Indochina
and Laos, respectively. Accompanying Thuy and Lau were Phan Hien,
director of the press department of the Foreign Ministry; Nguyen Minh
Vy, director of the General Department of Information; and Nguyen
Thanh Le, deputy editor in chief of the daily *Nhan dan* (The People), the
central organ of the VWP, who was press spokesman for the delegation.
The presence of these representatives of propaganda branches of the
VWP and government made it clear that Hanoi was not ready for serious
negotiations.[31]

At the opening of the session, Harriman and Thuy shook hands. That
gesture was positive and the dialogue that followed it sustained, but the
meeting itself was unproductive. Each side accused the other of responsibility for the war. Harriman lectured Thuy at length on the rights of the
South Vietnamese people, emphasizing that North Vietnam had no busi-
ness attempting to subvert a popularly elected government or waging
war to spread communism. Thuy in turn denounced America's aggression in South Vietnam and its violations of DRVN sovereignty by aerial
and naval bombardment. No settlement was possible as long as the aggression continued, he said; in fact, the United States must halt the aggression before serious talks could occur. Though the meeting ended on a
sour note, Thuy and Harriman agreed to hold future discussions. Those
discussions, too, were fruitless. This was due partly to the fact that the
meetings were public. Neither party was willing to compromise, or even
discuss compromise, in public, even on trivial matters, fearing loss of
public support or of future flexibility. On the contrary, both parties articulated intransigent positions, and the talks quickly degenerated into predictable and unproductive routines. From the divergent perspectives of
Washington and Hanoi alike the only merit of the talks was the propaganda value of what their own representatives said.[32]

The lack of results prompted both sides to look for another, less conspicuous forum for dialogue. On 3 June, Foreign Minister Nguyen Duy
Trinh, who was also a member of the VWP politburo, advised Thuy's
delegation to "continue to effect well the public struggle and prepare to
talk behind the scenes—while talking in public—at a favorable moment."
Less than two weeks later, Trinh again advised, "We advocate private
contacts to investigate [the other side's intentions], not yet to bargain."

In the meantime, Washington was instructing its envoys along the same lines. Having given up hope of military victory, the Johnson administration could not afford to prolong the talks indefinitely. Accordingly, on 12 June, William Jorden invited Nguyen Thanh Le to dinner, where he broached the possibility of private talks. Within days, Ha Van Lau, deputy chief of the Vietnamese delegation, agreed to meet privately with his American counterpart, Cyrus Vance.[33]

The meeting occurred on 26 June at the residence of the Vietnamese delegation in Virty-sur-Seine. After opening salutations, Vance told Lau that Washington would end the bombing of North Vietnam if Hanoi stopped infiltrating men and supplies into the South, ceased attacks on civilians in urban centers, and respected the demilitarized zone along the seventeenth parallel as a boundary between the two Vietnams. Lau rejected the offer on the spot, and after two hours of discussion, the meeting adjourned. When the two men met again in mid-July, Vance repeated the conditional cease-fire proposal and Lau again rejected it. The "circumstances" in Vance's proposal made the bombing halt conditional, Lau explained, and that violated the negotiating principles set forth by Hanoi. According to those principles, the bombing halt must be unilateral and unconditional and was a precondition to negotiation itself. Since this was the chief impediment to substantive discussions, Vance and Lau met again on 4 and 19 August to find a way around it. At the latter meeting, Vance suggested for the first time that substantive bargaining would necessitate the participation of the Saigon government. Saigon's participation would not imply recognition of that government by Hanoi, but it was necessary for meaningful negotiation. As a reciprocal gesture, Washington would allow delegates from the NLF or another organization of Hanoi's choosing to join the discussions, even though Washington would not thereby acknowledge the legitimacy of the organization. Lau agreed to consider the proposal.[34]

In Saigon, South Vietnamese president Nguyen Van Thieu thought the Americans were "naive" for pursuing expanded peace talks. He understood that the participation of his government would entail the participation of the NLF. That meant Saigon would have to negotiate with the NLF, thus giving the organization legitimacy. From the time he assumed the presidency, Thieu's position was that the NLF was a creation of Hanoi with no legal standing in the South. To do as the Americans wished and negotiate with NLF representatives would not only give the "Viet Cong" equal status with Thieu's own regime but constitute "the first step" toward the creation of a coalition government and "the end of democracy" in the South. However, because he believed Hanoi would not accept the proposal for quadripartite talks since it did not recognize his government, Thieu never formally communicated his objection to the proposal to Washington.[35]

At the next private session, on 8 September, Xuan Thuy, Le Duc Tho, and Averell Harriman joined Lau and Vance. Special Adviser Tho, a member of the VWP politburo and the head of the VWP Organizational Committee, did most of the talking, criticizing the United States for its aggression. Though this meeting accomplished nothing, the presence of Tho and the heads of both delegations attested to the increasing importance the two governments placed on the private talks. In sessions attended by the same men on 12, 15, and 20 September, the two sides reached their first agreements. They agreed that the Geneva Accords on Indochina in 1954 and on Laos in 1962 were suitable foundations for negotiating peace in Indochina. They also narrowed their differences over the participation of representatives of the Saigon government and the NLF in the talks. To encourage Hanoi to withdraw its troops from the South, Harriman proposed a simultaneous withdrawal of American and DRVN forces. He also proffered American assistance for postwar reconstruction in both Vietnams and the rest of Indochina. Still, the negotiators made no progress on the crucial matter of ending the bombing of North Vietnam.[36]

On 3 October, the Vietnamese delegation received new instructions from Foreign Minister Trinh. "Under the present situation, our course of action is to find out how to compel the Americans to de-escalate [their war] in order to defeat them and guarantee the implementation of our political tasks," Trinh wrote. "We must fully use the trend in American policy, use the contradictions between American ruling parties [Democratic and Republican], and use discreet tactics to pressure the Johnson administration into making another important de-escalation, ending the destruction of the North, and finding an honorable way to get out of the war." If Hanoi succeeds in "forcing the Americans" to do what it wanted them to do, Trinh continued, "it will be an important strategic victory for us. The period between now and the American presidential election [of 5 November 1968] is an opportune time to pressure the United States to de-escalate [the war]."[37]

At that juncture, the VWP politburo's strategy was to keep the talks going in hopes that Washington would construe that as a friendly gesture and use it as an occasion to de-escalate the war and make new concessions at the bargaining table, in an effort to appease antiwar sentiment in the United States.[38] Hanoi understood that, though not a candidate himself, Lyndon Johnson wanted to help the election chances of fellow Democrat Hubert Humphrey. The politburo thus felt little pressure to negotiate seriously, and stalled the Paris talks. At sessions on 11, 15, and 17 October, Thuy and Tho remained intransigent, waiting to see if Washington would make concessions to improve the election prospects of Democrats. To encourage Johnson to do that, Xuan Thuy on 26 October agreed to include the NLF and the South Vietnamese government in the negotiations. Thuy presented this as a concession to the Americans. Four days later, the ploy paid off. Harriman told Thuy, "The President is going to issue an order in the early evening of October 31, namely 7 or 8 o'clock Washington time, . . . to stop all air, naval and artillery bombardments and all other acts involving the use of force against the entire territory of the DRVN. Those orders will be effective twelve hours later."[39]

Thuy had hesitated before consenting to quadripartite talks because Hanoi was seriously concerned that the participation of Thieu's government might complicate the negotiations and delay the withdrawal of American forces.[40] Ultimately, however, the North Vietnamese renounced their original position for three reasons. First, Washington would not end the bombing unless it got satisfaction on the issue. Second, the inclusion of the NLF in the negotiations would enhance its legitimacy. Third, since the United States considered expanded talks favorable and Thieu objected to negotiating with the NLF, the issue could "drive a wedge" between the Americans and their South Vietnamese allies.[41]

Hanoi's assessment of the divergent positions of Washington and Saigon proved correct. Upon hearing the news that the DRVN had accepted the American proposal to expand the talks, Thieu became furious. As stated earlier, he never expected the North Vietnamese to accept the proposal. As it turned out, however, Hanoi not only conceded, but its acceptance came at the worst possible time. With the American presidential election just days away, Johnson and the Democrats would seek to capitalize on that breakthrough and increase the pressure on both Hanoi and Saigon to accept a negotiated settlement. Unprepared and unwilling to face that possibility, Thieu undertook initiatives of his own to guarantee the safeguard of his regime and the sovereignty of South Vietnam. These included undermining Johnson's efforts to end the war and supporting the candidacy of Hubert Humphrey's rival, Richard Nixon.[42]

The United States ceased bombing North Vietnam on 1 November. As Xuan Thuy stated in Paris, Hanoi considered the cessation to be "unconditional" (*khong dieu kien*) and to imply that the United States agreed to stop "all other acts of war" against North Vietnam.[43] Vietnamese sources support that statement.[44] American negotiators, however, affirmed otherwise. They maintained that the cessation was contingent upon unwritten "understandings" that the DRVN would respect the demilitarized zone (DMZ) separating the two Vietnams; that North Vietnamese and NLF forces in the South would cease indiscriminate rocketing and shelling of major population centers; and that the United States could continue to bomb the North's supply corridor in Laos—part of the Ho Chi Minh Trail—and fly reconnaissance missions over the North. Nothing in the documentary record indicates that Hanoi ever agreed to these understandings. In fact, when Harriman told Thuy on 30 October that the United States would end the bombing the next day, he stated no conditions. Nonetheless, the United States insisted that the understandings were binding since Hanoi had "assented by silence" to them.[45]

Hanoi interpreted the cessation to mean that Johnson was desperate to end the war, and it thereafter remained intransigent in the negotiations. "In order to arrive at a political solution concerning Vietnam," the VWP politburo decreed on 2 November, "the United States must renounce its interventionist and aggressive schemes in Vietnam, and respect the individual rights of the Vietnamese people. As long as the United States attacks Vietnam, the Vietnamese nation will continue fighting until total victory [*thang loi hoan toan*] is achieved."[46] This decision manifested a desire to exploit the political weakness of the Johnson administration and to enhance the confidence the bombing halt had generated in Hanoi. Diplomacy, the politburo had come to see, might produce victories unattainable on the battlefield.

Without the commitment of the Vietnamese factions, the talks foundered. Several authors attribute the failure of the negotiations of late 1968 to presidential hopeful Richard Nixon, who induced Saigon's obstinacy. In the final weeks of the 1968 presidential campaign, Nixon intermediaries approached the South Vietnamese in an apparent attempt to sabotage the peace talks and undermine Hubert Humphrey's presidential candidacy. Through Anna Chennault, the widow of World War II hero General Claire Chennault and vice chair of the Republican National Finance Committee in 1968, Nixon informed Thieu that Saigon would get a substantially more favorable settlement with a Republican in the White House. Accordingly, Saigon should decline offers from the Johnson administration to engage in serious negotiations with the North Vietnamese before the American election. While the episode may attest to Nixon's duplicity, Thieu was his own man in the negotiations and, as related earlier, had reasons of his own to reject Johnson's plan. Thus, there exists little evidence that Nixon's maneuver was "probably decisive in convincing President Thieu to defy President Johnson" and the cause of the failure of the round of talks under way in late 1968.[47] In his insightful study, William Bundy, Johnson's assistant secretary of state for

East Asian Affairs, fittingly concludes that "no great chance was lost" because of Nixon's interference.[48]

Once the bombing ceased, DRVN authorities embarked on a massive campaign of reconstruction. The aim was to redevelop and recentralize the economy.[49] In an effort to minimize the effects of the bombing, Hanoi had in 1965 mandated economic decentralization and encouraged localized production.[50] Large "national factories" were cannibalized before the Americans could destroy them, and their components were used to set up hundreds of ateliers, or workshops, dispersed throughout the North. Each province thus became "a strategic unit for production and for combat."[51] Between 1965 and 1967, centralized industrial output declined 30 percent while handicraft and regional production increased substantially.[52] By 1968, several provinces were self-sustaining in subsistence goods and services.[53] Decentralization was not limited to the economic sphere. A typical village now possessed its own medical clinic, school, and militia, and each district its own hospital, secondary school, and larger military unit.[54]

Although successful in minimizing the impact of the American bombing, decentralization did not grow the national economy. That troubled DRVN leaders. Since the Third VWP Congress in 1960, the government had considered the building of socialism in the North to be a pressing, essential task. The Anti-American Resistance had strained that task and made it more difficult, but the task itself remained to be done. In fact, in VWP thinking, the consolidation of a strong socialist "rear base" (*hau phuong*) in the North was "the most deterministic aspect" in realizing the objectives of the Vietnamese Revolution.[55] "We must consolidate the North to make allowances for progress in the South," VWP leaders had resolved in 1963.[56] "Strong roots, healthy tree" (*Goc co manh, cay moi tot*), they added subsequently to illustrate the importance of a strong rear base.[57] "We must continue to build socialism in the North and support its every aspect," observed Prime Minister Pham Van Dong, "for the sake of the people of South Vietnam, for the liberation of South Vietnam, and for the reunification of the country."[58]

The slogan of the effort was the same as that used at the outset of the war in 1965, *vua san xuat vua dau tranh*, "producing while struggling."[59] Its paramount economic goal was developing the central industrial base. To achieve that goal, industry had to be recentralized and the economic orientation of the country changed from agriculture to heavy industry. The nation had to modernize, in other words, and to do so rapidly if the state was to prosper and socialism to flourish. "Our main task for the future," Ho Chi Minh had said in 1960, "is to evolve from a backward agrarian country into a socialist society without undergoing the phase of capitalist development."[60] The American military intervention had stalled the plan to accomplish that, but the Hanoi leadership revived those plans when sustained bombing ended. The faith in Marxism-Leninism was unshaken. "The most indispensable foundation for socialism is heavy industry," VWP general secretary Le Duan said, reminding the party faithful of Lenin's words. "Whoever forgets this is not a Communist."[61]

On a less ideological level, the economy had to be strengthened because the DRVN could not depend forever on assistance from the Soviet Union and on the People's Republic of China (PRC). Dependence was contrary to Vietnamese pride and the national ethic. It carried with it dangers to the credibility of the party and the government. The legitimacy of both of those entities derived from the fact that their principal figures were revolutionaries who sacrificed in the name of the nation. Their long and heroic fight against Japanese imperialism and French colonialism was still an example to everyone. Their heroism had been self-reliant, their victories products of their own independence and determination. The American, Soviet, and Chinese assistance from which they had benefited during that fight was appreciated in private but never acclaimed in public. Now, in the Anti-American Resistance, the DRVN received untold quantities of outside assistance, but continued dependence on foreign largess would lead eventually to a loss of legitimacy, and with it the fruits of the Revolution.[62]

The reconstruction effort proceeded smoothly at first. It was soundly orchestrated and effectively implemented, and the masses were enthusiastic about it. The bombing of the DRVN had been unprovoked and illegitimate in the eyes of the average North Vietnamese. It was therefore easy for Hanoi to cast the United States in a neoimperialist role and mobilize the masses behind the Resistance. One anthropologist has noted that as the frequency and intensity of American air operations mounted between 1965 and 1968, "the solidarity among villagers increased in support of the war effort, both in terms of resources and manpower."[63] The guiding principle of the VWP in those years was, "Let the entire people fight the enemy and take part in the national defence."[64] Even schoolchildren participated in the effort. By late 1965, their curriculum included filling bomb craters and performing other passive defense tasks.[65] Women were also mobilized. In March 1965, the Central Committee of the Women's Union launched the Three Responsibilities campaign: producing, working, and substituting for male combatants; encouraging male family members to join the war effort; and preparing to fight if necessary.[66] By the end of 1968, women made up 75 percent of the workforce. In local self-defense units and militias, more than half the members were women.[67] By 1967, women also comprised 48 percent of the members of People's Village Councils (the arm of the VWP at village level), compared to 21 percent in 1965 and 16 percent in 1961.[68] Under the circumstances, Hanoi was confident that the reconstruction effort would succeed and precipitate the victory of the Revolution.

On 20 January 1969, Richard Nixon became president of the United States. As Lyndon Johnson's successor, he inherited a tormented America as well as the war in Vietnam. The situation in Southeast Asia had not improved for the United States since Johnson had curtailed the bombing in the preceding March and ended it in November. Those acts had made possible the dialogue with Hanoi, but the dialogue had gone nowhere and the prospects for substantive progress were dim. The Johnson administration's efforts to break the military deadlock in South Vietnam through "escalation" and then end the impasse in Paris through "de-escalation" of the air war against North Vietnam had accomplished little. The Tet Offensive discredited escalation, and the inability of the bombing above the seventeenth parallel to halt the flow of men and supplies into the South signaled a similar failure in the North.[69]

Interpreting his election as a mandate to end the intervention in Indochina on acceptable terms, Nixon made the chief goal of his foreign policy a "fair negotiated settlement that would preserve the independence of South Vietnam."[70] He had outlined that goal in accepting the Republican presidential nomination in August 1968. "The first priority foreign policy objective of our next Administration," he promised, "will be to bring an honorable end to the war in Vietnam."[71] To accomplish that, dialogue was indispensable. "After an era of confrontation, the time has come for an era of negotiations. Where the world's superpowers are concerned, there is no acceptable alternative to peaceful negotiations."[72] Though he intended to make resourceful use of diplomacy to achieve his goal, Nixon never had a "secret plan" to end the war.[73] That phrase was, as White House aide Peter Rodman said, a "journalistic cliché."[74] Nixon's intention was to emulate French president Charles de Gaulle, who had extricated France from Algeria "carefully" over a four-year period. De Gaulle had insisted that France must "emerge from its travails with its domestic cohesion and international stature intact" and withdraw its forces "in a manner reflecting a national decision and not a rout." Nixon hoped to follow that example in extricating American forces from Indochina.[75]

From the outset, Nixon busied himself and his aides plotting negotiating strategies and substantive positions. In early spring, he ordered the Vietnam Ad Hoc Group of the NSC to devise strategies for dealing with such key issues as the DMZ, troop withdrawal, and prisoners of war (POWs). The resulting document weighed the possibilities of Hanoi accepting various proposals and offered options for dealing with Thieu in the likely eventuality of bilateral secret negotiations with the DRVN.[76] Nixon and his aides understood they would have to extricate American forces sooner or later, but they believed they could do so without damaging American credibility as a superpower. The manner in which they ended the intervention, they believed, was more important than peace itself. The country's global clout, as well as the very fabric of American society, hung in the balance. A swift collapse of South Vietnam due to a too precipitate American withdrawal would imperil Washington's efforts to shape the international order after the war. "The impact on friends, adversaries and our own people would be likely to swing us from post World War II predominance to post Vietnam abdication," National Security Adviser Henry Kissinger said discussing this problem. "An ignominious rout in Vietnam would leave deep scars on our society, calling into question the heavy sacrifices" already made in the war "and fueling the impulses of recrimination." It would also aggravate the already threatening crisis of authority in the nation. "For the future of our own people as well as for international reasons," Kissinger concluded, "it is essential that we leave Vietnam as an act of governmental policy and with dignity, not as a response to pressures and in the form of a collapse."[77]

After Nixon's election, the discussions between Harriman and Thuy ceased. The two men last met on 14 and 17 January 1969, but only to assess the state of their talks and bid each other farewell. Neither knew Nixon's thinking on substantive issues, but both understood that no settlement was possible until the new administration was in place. The public sessions, however, continued. After the North Vietnamese accepted the American proposal for quadripartite talks in October, preparations for those talks began. They turned out to be unexpectedly difficult. The two sides could not even decide what to call the expanded talks, which would involve the United States and three Vietnamese factions. Hanoi wanted to call them "four-party talks" to augment the stature and legitimacy of the NLF; Washington countered with "two-sided discussions." Finally, they agreed that each side could call them whatever it wanted to. They also disagreed over the shape of the table or tables around which the negotiators would sit. DRVN negotiators proposed a square or lozenge-shaped table, with each of the four delegations on its own side. The United States wanted instead a two-sided arrangement, the Americans and South Vietnamese on one side, and the other two parties on the other. This difference took three months to resolve. On

15 January, both sides accepted a Soviet recommendation to use a large round table for negotiators and two small rectangular tables situated on opposite sides of the round table for note takers.[78] The ensuing quadripartite talks began on 25 January. Like the preceding bilateral public discussions, they produced no substantive results, though they did, in weekly sessions, give the parties a forum for denouncing each other and exalting themselves. "I have concluded that these plenary sessions are not in our interest," Nixon wrote in November noting their sterility. "I want a plan developed to get us out of them—or to reduce the number; they have been used for a year to repeat old arguments."[79] Nixon subsequently decided not to cancel the public talks but to use them to publicize Washington's concern over the fate of American servicemen detained by enemy forces in Indochina.[80]

In February, Nixon directed Henry Cabot Lodge, Harriman's successor as head of the American delegation in Paris, to contact his DRVN counterpart about reopening the private talks.[81] Hanoi eventually accepted the offer, but before doing so, the VWP politburo convened to assess the diplomatic struggle, still geared toward mustering international support for the Three Aims. The politburo decided that the diplomatic effort could best serve the Resistance and the Revolution by compromising American activities in Indochina. That meant capitalizing on the contradictions within the enemy camp to force Washington to reduce the intensity of the war.[82]

Henry Cabot Lodge and Xuan Thuy met privately on 8 and 22 March, and again on 7 May. In these meetings, each man candidly stated the position of his government on the preconditions necessary for a cease-fire. The two sides differed on a number of issues, the most important of which were the presence of North Vietnamese troops in the South and their status following a cease-fire and the political future of the Republic of (South) Vietnam (RVN). Washington demanded that North Vietnamese forces in the South withdraw simultaneously with an American withdrawal. Hanoi rejected that demand and denied the presence of PAVN units in the South. North Vietnamese personnel in the South, it maintained, were volunteers amalgamated into NLF units over which Hanoi had no jurisdiction. Washington also insisted that the political future of South Vietnam was a matter for the South Vietnamese to decide. Nixon's negotiators wanted a peace settlement that dealt with military matters only and left political matters to be worked out later.[83]

The drafting of two separate agreements—one covering military issues, the other political matters—was known as the "dual track" approach. First proposed by Averell Harriman and Cyrus Vance, that approach was delineated by Kissinger in *Foreign Affairs* in January 1969 and embraced by the Nixon administration until September 1972. According to that approach, the United States stood a better chance of ending its military commitment promptly and honorably by negotiating an agreement with Hanoi that covered military issues only. A satisfactory agreement would leave the GVN intact and effect a cease-fire and exchange of prisoners. Once the cease-fire was in place, the Vietnamese parties would resolve their political differences through negotiations among themselves. It was more reasonable, the Nixon administration felt, for the Vietnamese to negotiate their own future than for Washington to negotiate the fate of South Vietnam with Hanoi.[84] Besides, making Saigon a responsible party in negotiations with Hanoi would simplify the task of American negotiators in Paris and exonerate the United States in the event that the talks stalled and hostilities resumed and the Saigon regime eventually collapsed.

Hanoi rejected the dual-track formula, insisting that the war would continue until all political questions were resolved in an agreement with the United States. For Washington, that insistence augured ill. An agreement on political as well as military matters would require negotiating the future of South Vietnam, and thus the involvement of Saigon in the negotiations and Thieu's endorsement of the resulting agreement. "The Republic of Viet-Nam naturally should have the central role in any development relating to the events in Viet-Nam," Thieu stated publicly in April 1968.[85] Those requirements constituted formidable hurdles to success for the United States. The Nixon administration knew Saigon distrusted the DRVN and would refuse to negotiate earnestly with the NLF over the fate of South Vietnam. "Every South Vietnamese with a working knowledge of Communist tactics and strategy," wrote former South Vietnamese ambassador to the United States Bui Diem, "was convinced there was not a single chance for serious negotiations."[86] Even if Saigon agreed to negotiate with the two Communist entities, the talks would be long and difficult. Hanoi would never accept the political status quo in the South, and Saigon would agree to nothing that jeopardized the future of the Thieu regime. In the remote chance that a reasonable agreement could be negotiated, Nixon estimated that Thieu would finally reject it. Any agreement would compel Thieu to accept some political compromises and sanction the withdrawal of American forces, both of which he adamantly refused to do.[87] Moreover, Thieu insisted that the GVN would accept no peace agreement that allowed North Vietnamese forces to stay in the South after a cease-fire. "Many times we have made it clear that we want nothing more than the withdrawal of North Viet-Nam's aggression troops and an end to their subversion and terrorism in

South Viet-Nam," Thieu declared at his inauguration in October 1967.[88] Thus, unless Hanoi desisted from its political—and military—efforts in the South, political negotiations would place the United States between the proverbial rock and the hard place. The fighting would persist while the political negotiations stalemated, and the repatriation of American forces and prisoners would be delayed indefinitely. With these considerations in mind, American negotiators urged the North Vietnamese to begin negotiating a military agreement and leave political issues to be resolved after a cease-fire.

On the last day of May, Lodge met with Le Duc Tho, the VWP politburo emissary in Paris. The two men first reviewed the positions of both sides and then discussed a Ten Points program the NLF representatives had presented in the public talks on 8 May and an Eight Points proposal advanced by Nixon in a television speech on 14 May. They made no progress.[89]

After this series of meetings, Washington consulted Thieu concerning the opening of new talks. At Midway Island in early June, Nixon asked Thieu his opinion on possible secret negotiations between Washington and Hanoi. Whereas previous negotiations had been private, their existence had not been kept secret. Now, Nixon was proposing to hold negotiations whose existence would not even be known to members of his administration—much less to Congress and the American public—except for those few key personnel who would be directly involved in those negotiations. That formula, Nixon believed, would prove more conducive to constructive bargaining than previous arrangements. Unaware that Nixon had already laid the groundwork for such negotiations, Thieu gave his assent. In return, Nixon promised Thieu that the United States "would raise only military issues" in those negotiations but "would be willing to listen to proposals on political issues concerning South Vietnam." Under no circumstances, Nixon assured Thieu, would American negotiators "reply to political proposals without consulting the GVN." Nixon also pledged that Washington "would consult with the GVN" on all matters of substance raised in the secret talks and "would keep the GVN fully informed" on the talks.[90]

Two other important exchanges transpired at Midway. First, Nixon revealed that he intended to begin a gradual withdrawal of American troops from Vietnam and asked Thieu to consent to that. The South Vietnamese had anticipated that move and agreed to it. "We felt comfortable with our own strength," a Thieu aide explained later.[91] Though he expressed no objection at the time, Thieu was vexed that the withdrawal was a "conceptual fait accompli" in Washington before he was apprised of it. Second, Thieu reiterated the conditions for peace his government had stated in July 1968: reestablishment of the seventeenth parallel as the demarcation between the two Vietnams; respect for the territorial integrity of South Vietnam; compliance with the principles of noninterference between the two Vietnams; withdrawal of all North Vietnamese forces from the South; cessation of hostilities throughout Vietnam; and effective international supervision of the cease-fire and guarantees for the post-cease-fire period. Thieu requested and received from Nixon a public statement that Washington would not agree to a coalition government in the South. Each man left Midway with guarded optimism about the future.[92]

To enhance its status within South Vietnam and in the international arena, the NLF in June created the Provisional Revolutionary Government of the Republic of South Vietnam (PRG). The new entity was the product of an organizing congress held in Tay Ninh province, South Vietnam, from 6–8 June to create a "legal" revolutionary government and raise the diplomatic struggle to a new level. The PRG was a coalition comprised mainly of members of the NLF and the People's Revolutionary Party (PRP), the southern branch of the VWP in North Vietnam. At the head of the organization was the Council of Elders, which included NLF president Nguyen Huu Tho and other senior members of the PRP and NLF. The "cabinet" of the new provisional government included Huynh Tan Phat (chairman), Duong Quynh Hoa (health), Luu Huu Phuoc (information and culture), Can Van Bon (economy and finance), Truong Nhu Tang (justice), and Nguyen Thi Binh (foreign affairs). Binh soon thereafter became the PRG/NLF representative at the quadripartite public negotiations in Paris. Washington interpreted the creation of the provisional government as a ploy by Hanoi to undermine the Thieu regime and increase the pressure for a settlement.[93]

The GVN responded in early July by announcing a Six Points proposal for a general election in the South. The proposal called for the participation of all political parties and groups, including the NLF, which renounced violence; the creation of an impartial commission to conduct the election and an international body to oversee it; talks between the GVN and the opposition to set the timetable and modalities of the election; and agreement by all parties to accept the results of the election and to forego reprisals and discrimination afterward.[94] Implicit in the proposal was the withdrawal of North Vietnamese forces from the South before the election. "The South Vietnamese government could not possibly hold open elections," a Thieu aide commented, "while its life was being threatened by an enemy army operating on its territory."[95] The GVN never implemented the proposal, using it instead to gain public sympathy while increasing the pressure on Hanoi to withdraw its forces from the South.

Before he became president, Nixon had opened a secret channel of his own with Hanoi, the existence of which was unknown even to his secretaries of state and defense. On 22 December 1968, a month before his inaugural, Nixon dispatched Henry Kissinger to meet Raymond Aubrac, a Frenchman who had befriended DRVN president Ho Chi Minh when Ho had been in Paris in 1946 negotiating the political future of Vietnam. Kissinger had first met Aubrac in 1967. After learning Aubrac knew Ho intimately and would help the two sides reach a settlement, Kissinger informed the State Department. When Aubrac and a friend flew to Hanoi in July of that year, Washington designated Kissinger as their American connection. Though the mission was futile, it marked Kissinger's debut in North Vietnamese–American diplomacy. Now, Kissinger's assignment was to apprise Aubrac of Nixon's views on negotiating with North Vietnam, so Aubrac could transmit those views to Hanoi. Kissinger told Aubrac that Nixon wanted a settlement reflecting the political and military realities in Vietnam and would negotiate in good faith to achieve such a settlement. Aubrac reported this to Hanoi, which replied through Mai Van Bo, head of its commercial delegation in France, that the DRVN was eager for substantive talks to resume as soon as possible.[96] This positive response kept the contact alive, and on 14 June 1969, Aubrac met the DRVN chargé d'affaires in Laos and gave him a message from Kissinger. "The President," Kissinger had written on 22 May, "would like to exploit channels outside the current framework of the negotiations. Conceivably, delegates from the United States and Vietnam could meet outside the Paris framework to discuss the general principles of a solution. If the special negotiators from the United States and the Democratic Republic of Vietnam can achieve an agreement on principles, then the final technical negotiations could shift back to Paris."[97]

A month later, on 15 July, Nixon himself met Jean Sainteny, a Frenchman who had played a pivotal role in the mid-1940s in Indochina, where he came to know a number of Vietnamese revolutionaries, including Ho Chi Minh. Nixon gave Sainteny a letter addressed to Ho in which he urged Ho's government to begin serious discussions to end the war. Toward that end, Nixon proposed that Xuan Thuy meet Kissinger. Nixon also asked Sainteny to tell Hanoi that if the present impasse in the negotiations continued beyond 1 November 1969, he would resort to measures "of great consequence." Three days later, Sainteny gave Nixon's letter to Thuy and with it an oral statement of Nixon's intentions.[98]

The overtures signaled Nixon's strong desire to negotiate. Since that portended the possible end of American intervention, the VWP politburo instructed Thuy to meet Kissinger and discuss the opening of "backchannel" talks. Hanoi recognized that Nixon would find it difficult to escalate the war once such negotiations were under way. On 4 August, Thuy and Kissinger met secretly at Sainteny's Paris apartment. With Kissinger was General Vernon Walters, the military attaché in Paris, and with Thuy were Mai Van Bo and Nguyen Dinh Phuong, who took notes and translated the conversation. For three and a half hours, Thuy and Kissinger discussed the conditions of an acceptable peace agreement. The differences between the two sides remained dramatically large. Kissinger wanted an Indochina-wide cease-fire, the DMZ recognized—and respected—as a political border between the two Vietnams, and a prisoner exchange. Xuan Thuy, on the other hand, wanted the current Saigon regime deposed and a coalition government substituted for it, and unilateral and unconditional withdrawal of American troops from Vietnam. Since these positions had been elaborated before, their repetition here dramatized the fact that a year and a half of negotiation had achieved nothing but the cessation of American bombing of the North. Still, Kissinger insisted that the backchannel talks take place. "In order to accelerate the negotiations," he told Thuy, "the President of the United States is prepared to open another, secret channel with Vietnam . . . [and] to appoint a high-ranking representative of competence to have productive discussions. . . . If this channel is opened, the United States will adjust its military activities to create the most favorable circumstances to arrive at a solution."[99] Thuy agreed to the formula Kissinger suggested, and thereafter, the secret channel became the forum for serious negotiations.[100]

Despite the opening of the new channel, no end to the war was in sight, since neither Washington nor Hanoi was ready to compromise on anything important. The situation in South Vietnam was not rosy for either side in the late summer and early autumn of 1969, but neither felt that it was bad enough to make substantive concessions necessary or even attractive. Hanoi still thought the war was winnable, while the Nixon administration thought it salvageable. Neither government was yet desperate, though neither was sure enough of the other's strength and will to know what, if any, concessions it would be advantageous to negotiate at the moment. Thus, the two sides continued to stand by the positions articulated by Thuy and Kissinger on 4 August. The Johnson administration had effectively given up on the war and South Vietnam, but the change of government in Washington brought with it a *vent de renouveau*, which gave American negotiators time to reassess that defeatist attitude. Accordingly, the strategy of both sides was to wait and see, to continue fighting as well as talking.

On 28 November, Vernon Walters asked Mai Van Bo for another meeting between Thuy and Kissinger. Thuy declined, explaining to Washington on 12 December that Nixon's latest statement on negotiations, made in a public address on 3 November, repeated conditions for a cease-fire that Hanoi had already rejected, and there was nothing to talk about until Washington had something new to offer. "The United States is still seeking a military victory, and is not willing to settle fairly the Vietnam problem by negotiations," Thuy told the White House. "When the circumstances are favorable and the United States has something new [to offer], then perhaps the two sides will meet again."[101] This stance manifested optimism in the VWP politburo about the prospects of military victory.

Thuy exaggerated when he accused Washington of seeking "military victory," but he was correct that the Nixon administration was not eager to negotiate from the weak position it inherited from Johnson. Nixon's first priority was not ending the war promptly but improving his negotiating position by putting enemy forces on the defensive in South Vietnam. Toward that end, the White House undertook a series of initiatives to give the war a new orientation and, in doing so, to buy time with the American public and improve the diplomatic situation.[102]

A most important initiative, introduced in the spring and summer of 1969, was what the White House called the "Vietnamization" of the war. Vietnamization was a program designed to enlarge the South Vietnamese role in and responsibility for the military side of the war—the actual fighting—while simultaneously reducing the American role and responsibility and providing the South Vietnamese the military hardware and other assistance necessary to accomplish the enlarged task.[103] Toward these ends, Nixon announced on 8 June the withdrawal of 25,000 of the approximately 540,000 American troops then in Vietnam and later confirmed that the number of troops in Vietnam would be reduced by 150,000 over the next twelve months, with additional reductions thereafter.[104] At the same time, the United States pledged, and began delivering to, the RVN vast quantities of weapons and other supplies for its armed forces. Kissinger later defended this "retrenchment strategy" as the one that best "kept in relatively safest balance the three key components of America's extrication from Vietnam: sustaining America's domestic morale, affording Saigon an honest chance to stand on its own, and giving Hanoi incentive to settle."[105]

In accordance with this strategy, the value of American arms transferred to the RVN increased by $200 million in 1969, and by 1970, ARVN troops were amply equipped with small arms and had begun to receive sophisticated heavy artillery and tanks.[106] As ARVN forces became thus lavishly armed, they did more and more of the fighting, which increased the intensity of the civil war and further polarized the Vietnamese nation. In the altered circumstances, it was more difficult for Hanoi to character- ize or justify the struggle in the South as a resistance to foreign encroach- ment and domination. Because of Vietnamization, "Asians were fighting Asians, and Vietnamese killing Vietnamese," and doing so in increasing numbers.[107] That widened the rift within South Vietnamese society and between North and South Vietnam as well. Continued long enough, Vietnamization would compromise the eventual reunification of the country, the Revolution's ultimate objective. "Vietnamization did not represent the end of the war," DRVN foreign minister Nguyen Duy Trinh wrote in 1979, "but an extension of the war of aggression in South Vietnam; it was not symbolic of the American disengagement from South Vietnam but constituted a magnification of the military aggression in the South."[108] The horror at the policy and fear of its long-term consequences were such that the PRG issued a special communiqué demanding the immediate end of Vietnamization and of the attendant policy of "pacifica- tion" it made possible, which the Saigon regime was using to the serious harm of the liberation effort.[109] In 1992, one Vietnamese author sug- gested that Vietnamization had been a ploy to make the American people and world opinion think that the United States was on its way out of Vietnam, when in fact, it was intensifying the war.[110]

Extension of the Vietnamization doctrine to forces allied with the United States in Cambodia and Laos added to the strain on revolutionary forces. Communist guerrilla movements in Indochina outside Vietnam were weak and no match for regular forces equipped with American weaponry. Since the VWP believed that the success of the Vietnamese Revolution was contingent, in part, on Communist victories in Cam- bodia and Laos, it felt it had no choice but to become directly involved in the fighting there. That meant deploying PAVN units and aid scheduled for South Vietnam to Cambodia and Laos.[111] The effect was to relieve pressure on Saigon and weaken revolutionary forces in the South.[112] Growing concern over "Indochinization" (*Dong Duong hoa*) of the war prompted the DRVN in 1970 to call together representatives of the Lao- tian, Cambodian, and Vietnamese revolutionary factions to discuss coop- eration against American aggression. Hanoi thus hoped to motivate Lao- tian and Khmer revolutionaries to step up the fight against the American imperialists and their puppets.[113]

Stress on the Cambodian front increased after Washington and Saigon deployed ground forces into that country in 1970. Since 1959, North Vietnam had been infiltrating men and supplies into the South via the Ho Chi Minh Trail. Also over the years, PAVN and NLF units had sought sanctuary from ground attacks by retreating into those officially neutral countries. The objectives of Washington and Saigon in invading Cambodia were to disrupt these supply lines and rear bases and put PAVN and NLF forces there on the defensive. To facilitate the incursion, the United States may have supported the coup that overthrew the head of the Cambodian government, the neutralist Norodom Sihanouk. The coup, which took place on 17 March 1970, while Sihanouk was on his way to Beijing from Moscow after his annual obesity cure on the Côte d'Azur, brought to power General Lon Nol and Prince Sisowath Sirik Matak, both staunch anti-Communists. This coup, plus the incursion that followed and the secret B-52 bombings that preceded it, were among the most controversial enterprises undertaken the by Nixon administration to improve the military situation in Southeast Asia in order to enhance its position in the Paris negotiations. Nixon justified them as necessary to stop the aggression in South Vietnam. Among the targets of both the bombings and the incursive forces was the Central Office for South Vietnam (COSVN, or Trung Uong Cuc Mien Nam Viet Nam), the highly mutable, semiformal structure that functioned as the nerve center of insurgent forces in South Vietnam. This office also coordinated the activities of NLF units and acted as Hanoi's eyes and ears below the seventeenth parallel.[114]

A total of 31,000 American and 43,000 ARVN troops took part in the incursion into Cambodia, which had limited success. American intelligence estimated that the invading forces killed 11,349 and captured 2,328 enemy soldiers, cleared 1,600 acres of jungle, destroyed 8,000 bunkers, and captured or destroyed large stocks of weapons. The United States lost 354 men killed and 1,689 wounded, while ARVN casualties totaled 638 killed and 3,009 wounded.[115] Even though the invaders failed to "capture" the COSVN, they interrupted supply lines, forced a momentary suspension of COSVN functions, and, by American estimates, "virtually ended the NVA threat in the southern half of South Vietnam, the most populous part of the country."[116] The attack, however, had damaging reverberations in the United States. There, critics of the war denounced the incursion as a provocative and intolerable escalation at a time when Nixon was assuring the American people he was winding down the war. Student riots and the fatal shooting of four students at Kent State University on 4 May came in the wake of the incursion and symbolized the widening gap between the administration and the burgeoning antiwar movement. Such incidents prompted talk in Congress

of constitutional amendments or other measures to limit Nixon's authority to conduct the war or to impose deadlines for ending American involvement and withdrawing American forces. Particularly troubling for
the White House were the so-called Cooper-Church and McGovern-
Hatfield amendments to Defense Department appropriations bills that
would have imposed deadlines for the American troop withdrawal.[117]

Washington's policies of Vietnamization, Indochinization, and widening the war into Cambodia caused serious difficulties for North Vietnam.
By late 1970, as a recently published Vietnamese source states, "the situation of the war had deteriorated to the detriment of the revolution and
the revolutionary war. History had come to a tough period."[118] At the
same time, an intensified pacification campaign in the South impeded
proselytizing efforts there, and NLF control over the countryside decreased dramatically between 1969 and 1970. For example, by 1968, in
Region VIII in central Nam Bo (Cochinchina, or southern South Vietnam), NLF forces had "liberated" a total of 123 communes (*xa*) and
1,000 hamlets (*ap*), but at the end of 1969, only four and 312 of these,
respectively, remained in NLF hands. During that period, the number of
guerrilla fighters in western Nam Bo dropped from 85,000 in September
1968 to a little over 21,000 a year later. Incredibly, the number of soldiers
recruited by the NLF in the South fell from 16,000 in 1968 to 100 in
1969.[119] Cumulatively, the population controlled by the NLF fell from
7.7 to 4.7 million between 1968 and 1970.[120]

This concert of military and political difficulties produced immediate
shortages of adept cadres in the South, and efforts to deal with those
shortages compounded intraparty disagreements in North Vietnam. On 3
March 1970, the VWP politburo promulgated Resolution 195 NQ/TU to
"increase the quality of party members and admit Ho Chi Minh School
cadres" (*nang cao chat luong dang vien va ket nap dang vien lop Ho Chi Minh*),
and it later ordered the expulsion from VWP membership of everyone
who "worked and led poorly" or "lacked merit and motivation."[121] In the
ensuing purge, the authority of such men as General Secretary Le Duan,
chairman of the Standing Committee of the National Assembly Truong
Chinh, and Prime Minister Pham Van Dong remained uncontested, but a
number of lower-level cadres were demoted or expelled. To invigorate
the party, the leadership inducted 39,644 graduates of the Ho Chi Minh
School. Of these, 23,650 entered the armed forces, while others filled
positions vacated by death, capture, or expulsion, all of which exerted
heavy tolls on VWP operatives. In the first months of 1969 alone, the
enemy captured or killed 1,080 cadres sent from the North to the South
and broke up sixteen VWP cells.[122]

Under these conditions, the Central Committee of the VWP held its Eighteenth Plenum in January 1970. The theme of the plenum was "evaluating the development of the complexion of the war since the launching of Tet Mau Than." The delegates discussed the problems caused by Nixon's initiatives and after heated debate, concluded that the Resistance was relying too heavily on military activity. To rectify that, the VWP and government would "broaden" and "diversify" the Resistance.[123] "We . . . must answer enemy attacks not only with war and political activity," read the final decree, "but also with diplomacy."[124] This decision signaled the first abandonment of the strategy embraced at the beginning of the Anti-American Resistance and reaffirmed as recently as 2 November 1968: subordinating diplomacy to military and political activity. Vietnamization and the widened war were jeopardizing the revolutionary cause by undermining efforts below the seventeenth parallel. Under these new circumstances, Nixon would not acquiesce in Hanoi's demands as easily as Johnson had done. Thus, the VWP elevated the diplomatic struggle to the level of military and political activity. As the Tet Offensive had exposed the futility of the Pentagon's "search and destroy" strategy, which in turn persuaded Washington to press harder for a negotiated settlement, so developments in 1969 and 1970 made Hanoi realize that victory by military and political means alone might be impossible.

January 1970 thus marked an end to Hanoi's policy of "fighting while stalling," or pursuing military victory while negotiating without intent to compromise. Thereafter, the North Vietnamese coordinated diplomatic activity in Paris with military and political activity in the South. The commitment to serious bargaining in Paris was paralleled on the battlefield by a reduction of random attacks on American and South Vietnamese forces. From now on, Hanoi would emphasize the diplomatic mode of struggle—serious negotiations specifically—when the situation in the South seemed unpromising and would fight ardently when that situation improved or the negotiations stalled. By this change of policy, the VWP acknowledged that if Saigon continued to receive high levels of assistance from the United States, the balance of forces below the seventeenth parallel might remain unchanged, or even deteriorate, and the military stalemate persist indefinitely. For the future of the Revolution, Hanoi must prevent that; it must, in other words, seek a diplomatic solution to the war.

In late January, Vernon Walters asked Mai Van Bo for a secret meeting. This time, the North Vietnamese accepted the offer. When the two sides met on 21 February, Le Duc Tho was present, as well as Kissinger and Thuy. This meeting came immediately after the policy change at the

Eighteenth Plenum, and the presence of the eminent VWP politburo member was significant. Kissinger spoke first and at length on the war and the need to find a peaceful solution as soon as possible but reiterated his previous position on substantive issues rather than offering new ones. In response, Xuan Thuy repeated again that the United States must withdraw its forces unilaterally and unconditionally within five or six months and agree to a coalition government in the South that included members of the PRG and NLF but excluded the three leading members of the existing Saigon regime, President Thieu, Vice President Nguyen Cao Ky, and Prime Minister Tran Buu Kiem. During the afternoon session, Tho gave a positive assessment of the situation from the perspective of revolutionary forces, after which he and Kissinger exchanged views on other matters and agreed to meet again on 16 March.[125]

In subsequent meetings, Tho and Kissinger jockeyed with each other on matters of detail but did little to improve the prospects of a cease-fire or a comprehensive settlement.[126] The chief snag remained the terms of American withdrawal. Unwilling to forsake South Vietnam, the Nixon administration refused to set a date for completing the withdrawal of American forces until Hanoi agreed to a cease-fire, to withdraw its forces from the South, to release the POWs, and to accept the neutrality of all of Indochina in the Cold War. "If we are going to retreat regardless of what happens," Kissinger explained to Tho, "you must get used to the idea that we will do so at our own pace and one convenient for us, and apart from other issues. If you want to negotiate it, we have to settle the other terms. To retreat on a fixed deadline, we don't need an agreement with you; we can do that on our own."[127] Hanoi rejected Kissinger's terms. Constructive negotiations, it insisted, could begin only after Washington publicly announced a fixed schedule for withdrawal. Moreover, "disengagement" must apply to *all* forces, not just combat soldiers. "When we request the total withdrawal of U.S. forces," Xuan Thuy told Kissinger, "we mean that all U.S. forces, ground forces, naval forces, air forces, marine forces, military advisers, military personnel, technical personnel, war material, and military bases all be withdrawn without any exceptions and without any reservations."[128] The PRG endorsed that request and demanded in addition that the United States stop "all support and commitments" to the Thieu government.[129]

The demands of both sides were legitimate from their respective perspectives. The United States did not want to give up the diplomatic leverage its forces in South Vietnam provided nor jeopardize the release of the prisoners. The DRVN, on the other hand, wanted the troops withdrawn to strengthen its negotiating position. As they grew weary of the impasse and as battlefield conditions failed to change, both sides became less

intractable. On 7 September 1970, the DRVN agreed to couple the release of the POWs, which it had previously insisted was a matter to be
settled in the "aftermath" of the war, with the schedule of American
withdrawal. Until then, the American side had not pressed the POW
issue in the secret talks, refusing, it said, to bargain over a "humanitarian
issue." "I have not pushed this matter in this channel," Kissinger told Tho
on 27 September, "because we do not believe that this is an issue for the
kind of military and political negotiating which we wish to do in these
meetings." Washington would, he continued, regard flexibility on the
issue as evidence of Hanoi's desire to reach a settlement. "But we do not
believe that these men should become pawns in military and political
discussions, and we will not permit them to be used. I hope you have not
interpreted my failure to mention them here as a sign that we are not
vitally interested about this matter, or that I am not personally concerned."[130] Though Kissinger insisted that Hanoi not regard the prisoners
as "hostages" to American assent to a comprehensive settlement, Tho's
proposal on 7 September reflected the fact that Hanoi viewed the POWs
as America's Achilles' heel and wanted to exploit the issue. To soften the
effort to do that, Tho, at the direction of the politburo, dropped the
standing demand for reparations, though Kissinger feared the demand
would eventually resurface.[131]

In February 1971, less than a year after the incursion into Cambodia,
South Vietnamese forces with American air support carried out another
incursion, this one into Laos. This test of Vietnamization, code-named
Lam Son 719, had mixed results. Informed by spies in Saigon and alerted
by media reports of the time and location of the incursion, Hanoi sent
36,000 heavily armed PAVN regulars to greet the invaders.[132] The purpose of this exceptional effort was not only to repulse the invasion but
also to damage the RVN government politically by exposing the failure of
Vietnamization. Outgunned, outnumbered, and outprepared, the South
Vietnamese forces retreated after six weeks of fierce combat. But before
they did so, Washington and Saigon claimed, they had killed 15,000
enemy troops and destroyed Hanoi's ability to launch major assaults into
northern sections of South Vietnam from Laos. The price of this "success," however, was exorbitant. The two ARVN divisions involved sustained casualty rates of nearly 50 percent, including 2,000 dead, despite
massive support by American air units, which dropped more than 48,000
tons of bombs during the operation.[133]

On 31 May, in the aftermath of the allied incursion into Laos, Kissinger made a new set of proposals softening the American stand on several

substantive matters. The United States would agree to a date for completing the withdrawal as part of an overall settlement that included the exchange of prisoners and a cease-fire in place by all forces in Indochina.[134] The last provision implied that Washington would agree to North Vietnamese troops remaining in the South at least temporarily after a cease-fire. This was a pivotal concession, made without informing Thieu.[135] Along with the cease-fire in place, Kissinger proposed a ban on the infiltration of outside forces into the countries of Indochina, international supervision of the cease-fire, and respect for the 1954 and 1962 Geneva Accords.[136] On 27 June, Thuy and Tho responded to Kissinger's proposals, presenting a nine-point "bargaining proposal" notable not for its content but for its conciliatory nature. For the first time, Hanoi presented proposals to be negotiated rather than demands to be fulfilled. It also agreed to release the prisoners simultaneously with troop withdrawals, rather than merely to discuss that issue.[137]

Kissinger's decision to concede on the issue of North Vietnamese troops in the South was a direct consequence of the outcome of the incursion into Laos. Nixon had considered the Laotian operation of paramount importance to demonstrate the merits of Vietnamization and silence critics of the policy. In mid-February 1971, he had instructed his staff to leave no stone unturned "in order to make sure the Laotian operation works out." In the end, however, Nixon's hopes were dashed. During a 23 March meeting with Nixon, Kissinger reluctantly admitted that Laos "comes out as clearly not a success." That distressed Nixon. Three days later, on 26 March, he accepted Kissinger's recommendation to press for a settlement during the next secret meeting with the North Vietnamese.[138] Ostensibly, Nixon feared that Hanoi, inspired by recent successes, might increase military pressure on the South and pursue military victory more aggressively. That would jeopardize the talks and delay indefinitely the signing of an agreement, thus giving Hanoi more time to compromise Vietnamization and expose the frailty of ARVN forces. On account of its impact, one scholar has called the failed allied incursion into Laos "the military turning point of the entire war."[139]

Although the sessions of May and June were breakthrough sessions, the negotiations had still produced nothing substantive and the two sides remained far apart on several major issues. In the late summer of 1971, the frequency of secret meetings increased as Washington made a series of substantive concessions. On 26 July, Kissinger announced that the United States was "prepared in the next five years to provide $7.5 billion in aid to Indochina, of which $2–2.5 billion could go to North Vietnam." He also said Washington was willing to limit military aid to South Vietnam, remain neutral in political matters in Vietnam, and complete its withdrawal of troops within nine months after an agreement instead of the sixteen months proposed in May 1969.[140] A few weeks later, on 16 August, the DRVN accepted responsibility for the release of all American prisoners in Indochina as soon as Washington agreed to a date for completing the withdrawal. Vietnamese negotiators later withdrew that offer, saying it involved the authority of entities over which Hanoi had no control.[141] After an unproductive meeting on 13 September, Le Duc Tho allegedly fell ill and Hanoi failed to respond to a new eight-point proposal submitted on 11 October.

The two sides would not meet again that year. In the fall of 1971, American intelligence reported a military buildup along the northern side of the DMZ. Indeed, as Nixon had feared, what the North Vietnamese considered a "victory of strategic importance" over ARVN forces in Laos encouraged Hanoi to press further the effort to defeat Vietnamization by military means. Earlier, on 17 July, the VWP politburo had instructed its negotiators in Paris to make no new concessions to the Americans. Now, it was poised to resume the military struggle.[142] In response to this and to the shelling of Saigon by NLF troops, Nixon on 26 December implemented operation Proud Deep Alpha. Over the ensuing five days, American aircraft flew 1,025 attack sorties against supply depots, surface-to-air missile (SAM) sites, airfields, and petroleum storage areas situated immediately above the seventeenth parallel.[143] The attack was not the first one of significance mounted by the United States against North Vietnam since Nixon had come to office. In fact, during the bombing halt, the United States regularly conducted air strikes of varying intensity against the DRVN. Under the pretext that Hanoi violated the understandings of 1968, the Nixon administration sanctioned at least one air strike against the North in every month of 1969 except December, every month of 1970 except October, and every month of 1971.[144]

Nonetheless, the short but intense bombing campaign of late December incensed Hanoi to the point that it decided to suspend its secret talks with Washington. Nixon was aware that the bombing campaign risked compromising the negotiations. However, he also did not want Hanoi to think that he wanted peace at any price and was prepared to abandon South Vietnam. Thus, Washington staged a flurry of intensive strikes to hurt the North militarily but refused to protract the bombing because it harmed the prospects of the negotiations and aroused the antiwar movement at home. Nixon's "coercive diplomacy" had until then improved the American negotiating position in Paris by causing difficulties for Hanoi, but it undermined his political position at home. Cambodia and Kent State had produced public outcries in and out of Congress that continued through 1971. Publication of the *Pentagon Papers* in June renewed the erosion of public confidence in the nation's leaders by exposing the inept and duplicitous handling of the war by the Johnson administration. Soon thereafter, Congress enacted the so-called Mansfield Amendment urging the president to fix a date for completing the withdrawal of American forces from Indochina, subject to the release of POWs and accounting for the servicemen missing in action (MIA). That was a serious political blow to the White House on the eve of the year in which Nixon had to run for reelection. The more opponents of the war believed America was pulling out, Kissinger thought, "the more they are trying to impose restrictive conditions on our exit so as to claim credit for what they know we will do anyway."[145]

As troublesome as popular and congressional protests were, Nixon stuck to his plan to disengage from the war honorably and salvage South Vietnam and the Thieu government. The Mansfield Amendment had little effect on his prosecution of the war. "It is without binding force or effect," Nixon said of it. "It does not reflect my judgment about the way in which this war should be brought to a conclusion. My signing the bill that contains this section, therefore, will not change the policies I have pursued and that I shall continue to pursue toward that end."[146] This tenacity worked because Nixon retained the support of the "great silent majority" of the American public he often appealed to in explaining and defending his course of action. "North Vietnam cannot humiliate the United States," he told the public in one such appeal on 3 November 1970. "Only Americans can do that."[147] After the speech, Nixon's approval rating soared to 68 percent.[148] In thus masterfully placing his critics on the defensive, Nixon enabled his administration to withstand the controversies stirred by his conduct of the war and gave himself greater freedom to do what he thought he had to do.[149]

By the end of 1971, there was little indication that a negotiated end to the war was forthcoming. Although the two sides talked, at times seriously, they failed to make significant progress in the negotiations because neither was willing to compromise on substantive issues. Hanoi still believed it possible to achieve its objectives militarily. The Nixon administration, on the other hand, felt no strong domestic or international pressure to end the war promptly. Thus, the negotiations stalled.

CHAPTER TWO

Détente and the Spring Offensive

JANUARY–JUNE 1972

At its Twentieth Plenum in January 1972, the Central Committee of the   31
VWP decreed that the tasks of the Anti-American Resistance in the
South were to "defeat the policy of 'pacification' and crush the enemy's
plan to 'Vietnamize' the war." Accomplishing these tasks would "cause
the collapse of the puppet forces and regime while compelling the American imperialists to sign an agreement and withdraw rapidly and totally
their forces together with those from other foreign countries."[1] Since
1970, when the committee last addressed these issues at its Eighteenth
Plenum, the war in the South had taken a turn for the better. In a number of localities, revolutionary forces had regained the initiative and expanded the areas under their control.[2] The VWP now hoped to capitalize
on this turn of events.

In the North, on the other hand, the most pressing tasks of the Resistance were economic. While the VWP was concerning itself with the
situation in the South, the Central Committee of the Fatherland Front
(Mat Tran To Quoc) reaffirmed its commitment to building socialism in
the North.[3] Without economic development, Truong Chinh affirmed,
"we cannot guarantee support to other fronts." "The armed struggle in
South Vietnam is on two fronts," he emphasized, "the military front and
the production front. Nothing short of success on both of these fronts can
cause the Revolution to progress."[4] Meanwhile, the VWP Central Committee concluded that to ensure the success of the Resistance in the
South, it must, among other duties, "guarantee continued success in the
field of economic recovery and development, and achieve high levels of
socialist production."[5] The reconstruction efforts begun in 1968 were
well under way, and manufacturing as well as handicraft production had
surpassed pre-1965 levels. In 1971, the DRVN's Gross National Product
(GNP) grew 14 percent, while centrally and regionally managed con-
struction increased 23 percent.[6] Between 1968 and 1971, industrial production increased 142 percent.[7] Notwithstanding these strides, VWP
leaders reckoned that "the problem of economic management remains
our main weakness." The chief aspects of that problem were the lack of

adequate infrastructure and the difficulties of moving from "small production to large socialist production."[8] Still, the politburo expected the recent progress to continue, and optimism pervaded the ruling circles in Hanoi.[9]

In Washington, meanwhile, Kissinger worried that Nixon's commitment to his strategy for bringing the war to an honorable end was waning. He urged the president not to "bug out," telling him his instinct was that "the North Vietnamese are ready to give, so we'd be totally wrong to show any nervousness." Kissinger also suggested that should the United States offer a new peace proposal in January, as Nixon was thinking of doing, Hanoi would consider it an act of desperation and "tear it to pieces."[10] He recommended that Nixon buy time at home and abroad through a public relations campaign blaming Hanoi for the negotiating impasse and shoring up international support for its side in the war. Despite mounting clamor from the antiwar movement, Kissinger thought it imperative that the administration stay its course. Nixon had thus far done well on Vietnam, he suggested, because he had acted without regard to domestic pressures, and in so doing had turned a desperate situation into a salvageable one. If Nixon won public support for continued negotiations, the prospects for "peace with honor" were good.[11]

After some hesitation, Nixon accepted Kissinger's advice. On 25 January 1972, he told a national television audience that his administration had been secretly negotiating with Hanoi since August 1969, but to little effect.[12] "Just as secret negotiations can sometimes break a deadlock," he later explained, "I now felt that public disclosure might help to break a secret deadlock."[13] Although no longer secret, the Paris negotiations between Tho and Kissinger would remain private. Nixon also disclosed the Eight Points plan he had offered Hanoi on 11 October and to which Hanoi never responded. The plan, he said with justification, constituted the most comprehensive and balanced offer ever made in the negotiations. It called for a general, Indochina-wide cease-fire upon the signing of a comprehensive settlement, a withdrawal of all American and other foreign forces from South Vietnam within six months of the settlement, and a parallel exchange of all military and civilian prisoners. More problematically, the plan also called for an end to the infiltration of outside forces into any country in Indochina, for an international control commission to supervise military aspects of the cease-fire, and for all parties to respect the Geneva Accords of 1954 and 1962 on Indochina and Laos, respectively. Finally, the plan specified that disputes between states in Indochina be resolved by the states themselves on the basis of mutual respect for the sovereignty and territorial integrity of each other.[14]

Nixon's proposal dealt with the political future of South Vietnam in several equally problematic provisions. The people of South Vietnam would, without outside interference, decide the fate of the Saigon government in elections within six months after the settlement. The elections would be open to members of all political groups in the South and be conducted by an autonomous body representing those groups and in the presence of international observers. The autonomous body would settle disputes over the eligibility of candidates, and, to guarantee the openness of the process, the president and vice president of South Vietnam would resign a month before the elections. In the interim, a caretaker government would assume administrative duties. The United States would remain neutral during the election campaign, accept the results, and define its relationship with the new government on the basis of those results. The new government and all other governments in Indochina would adopt a neutral foreign policy consistent with the 1954 Geneva Accords, and the reunification of Vietnam would be decided by negotiation and the voluntary agreement of the people of the North and of the South. Finally, the two sides would participate in a conference of representatives of all interested governments to work out international guarantees for the agreement.[15]

The proposal included a number of new items, some of them complicated and conditional. It set a deadline of six months for completing the American withdrawal and offered bases for a comprehensive political and military settlement. If Hanoi accepted the military settlement only— the cease-fire and the prisoner release—American and other allied forces would withdraw from the South but the Saigon regime would remain in place. On the other hand, if Hanoi accepted the political agreement as well, the election provisions outlined above would kick in and the American withdrawal would have to be paralleled by that of PAVN units in the South. Nixon also proposed to tie the levels of future American assistance to South Vietnam to the levels of aid the DRVN received from its Chinese, Soviet, and other allies, and to provide several billion dollars to assist in the postwar reconstruction of Indochina, in which North Vietnam could share.

The most curious item in this complicated proposal was the evident agreement of President Thieu to resign his office a month before the proposed elections. This, however, was illusory. Though Thieu agreed to step down a month before the elections, he had no intention of otherwise playing by the rules Nixon announced, and Nixon knew it. With the complicity of Washington, Thieu covertly arranged with the official who was to replace him, the chairman of the South Vietnamese Senate, to resume presidential power on the eve of the elections. That would enable Thieu—and by extension, Nixon—to control whatever situation the elections created.[16] Despite this chicanery, Nixon's offer of assistance to the DRVN was genuine, though it, too, had an ulterior motive. By brandishing a carrot of financial assistance, Nixon hoped to buy Hanoi's assent to an agreement that otherwise had little appeal to it.

The public offer provoked immediate response from Hanoi. Within days, Xuan Thuy and Nguyen Thi Binh, who headed the PRG/NLF delegation in the public negotiations, denounced it as vague and unresponsive to the situation that would exist within South Vietnam after the cease-fire. They did not, however, reject it; and they promised to say more about it later.[17] Thuy also denounced Nixon for violating the confidentiality of the secret talks and for blaming Hanoi for their failure. Nixon's action, Thuy insisted, was an election-year ploy designed to deceive American and world opinion and to justify the horrors of Vietnamization. To substantiate these claims and to embarrass Nixon, the North Vietnamese released nine major documents relating to the secret negotiations.[18] Instead of putting Nixon on the defensive, however, these actions played into his hands, creating a sensation about the secret talks and publicizing his efforts to end the war.

On 2 February, Nguyen Thi Binh announced two concessions to help the negotiations along. The PRG, she said, now agreed to link the release of the prisoners to the withdrawal of foreign forces from South Vietnam, and to accept the resignation of Thieu rather than the dismantling of his government as a condition for the cease-fire.[19] Hanoi supported Binh's announcement to beat Nixon at his own game and had it widely disseminated. Hanoi also had its embassies around the world issue statements commending the PRG for its conciliatory gesture and its eagerness to help the peace process along.[20]

As noted above, Nixon had from the outset sought to advance the negotiations through military initiatives in South Vietnam, Cambodia, and Laos. By the middle of 1971, it was apparent that those initiatives had not produced the desired results. The White House therefore turned to diplomatic initiatives, specifically détente with the Soviet Union and rapprochement with China.[21] Aware that both Moscow and Beijing had wanted new relationships with Washington since their border clashes in 1969, Nixon hoped to use these initiatives through a policy he called "linkage" to help him solve his problems in Southeast Asia.[22]

Unlike Johnson, who had considered the real enemy in Vietnam to be China, Nixon and Kissinger understood the Vietnamese revolutionary movement to be autonomous.[23] However, they recognized that Hanoi relied heavily upon external support to sustain the war in the South.[24] As early as July 1968, Nixon had spoken of the possibility of using Soviet and

Chinese pressures to get Hanoi to agree to an acceptable end to the war. With that in mind, he launched diplomatic negotiations with the Soviet Union in Warsaw in 1970, encouraged the "ping-pong diplomacy" of 1971, and dispatched Kissinger on secret missions to Moscow and Beijing to set the stage for presidential visits to those capitals.[25] To impress the Kremlin with the seriousness of his purpose, Nixon wrote Leonid Brezhnev a terse letter warning that Washington would hold the allies of North Vietnam responsible for any designs the latter undertook to humiliate the United States.[26] The rationale behind these initiatives was unclear at the time, but Nixon later said it was mainly to spoil the relations between Hanoi and the two Communist powers and in turn to exploit the rift between Moscow and Beijing to help him end the war in Indochina by negotiating a settlement in Paris. "I had long believed," he wrote, "that an indispensable element of any successful peace initiative in Vietnam was to enlist, if possible, the help of the Soviets and the Chinese. Though *rapprochement* with China and *détente* with the Soviet Union were ends in themselves, I also considered them possible means to hasten the end of the war. At worst, Hanoi was bound to feel less confident if Washington was dealing with Moscow and Peking. At best, if the two major Communist powers decided that they had bigger fish to fry, Hanoi would be pressured into negotiating a settlement we could accept."[27]

Nixon's task was not an easy one. Throughout the American military intervention in Indochina, the USSR and China had been reliable if not unshakable allies of the DRVN. (In spite of troubles in its relationship with Hanoi in 1964, the Soviet Union had been thereafter firmly committed to North Vietnam.[28]) For the sake of socialist solidarity, they had put their differences aside and over the years sent the North Vietnamese massive amounts of military and other supplies, including technical experts and advisers, while keeping the applications of force against them by the United States within bounds. Without taking anything away from the resourcefulness of the Vietnamese, these contributions had been vital to the DRVN's success in frustrating American designs in Indochina.[29]

In opening dialogues with the two Communist giants, Nixon hoped to ease Cold War tensions while improving his political position at home and his stature as a statesman abroad. He was confident that improved relations with the Communist powers would bear important dividends in Indochina. He and his advisers believed the Soviets and the Chinese were prepared, or could be encouraged, to constrain Hanoi militarily and prod it diplomatically into more constructive relations with Washington. American analysts estimated that if Moscow and Beijing cooperated to limit arms shipments to North Vietnam, the end of the war was "likely," especially if the limitations applied to "sophisticated equipment in large enough quantities to enable North Vietnam to undertake overt large-scale operations."[30] So confident were they, in fact, that Secretary of State William Rogers told Canadian ambassador Léo Cadieux in October 1972 that he thought it improbable that the DRVN would mount another offensive against the South using Soviet-manufactured hardware. Moscow knew that that would "raise much broader issues in terms of Soviet-USA relations," Rogers said, and jeopardize détente.[31] Even if Nixon's initiatives failed to affect the levels of Soviet and Chinese aid to North Vietnam, they might at least make North Vietnamese leaders less certain of themselves, and thus more responsive to American diplomatic pressure. In addition, the more Washington befriended the rival superpowers, the less hazardous it would be to pressure Hanoi militarily. New relationships with China and the Soviet Union would relieve Nixon of the fears Johnson had had that the use of massive force in Indochina might provoke a military response from the Chinese or the Soviets, or both. In such an environment, massive bombings of the North to convince Hanoi to end the war would become a viable contingency.

The White House was certain the North Vietnamese would react to these initiatives and commissioned a study to calculate their probable responses. One early estimate was that they might attempt to subvert the upcoming summits in Beijing and Moscow by precipitating a military crisis. Using stockpiled weapons, "they might very well move to cut Vietnam in half," the estimate read, "and create a super crisis that we would have trouble dealing with."[32] Such prospects failed to stop preparations for the summits. It was Nixon's intention to be adamant on Vietnam in both Beijing and Moscow, whatever Hanoi did. The progress he had made in Vietnam, he assessed, was due to boldness and forcefulness, and he had no inclination to soften his approach now. Kissinger was more sensitive to the niceties of diplomacy. The diplomatic situation regarding the Chinese was especially precarious, and antagonizing Chinese leader Mao Zedong and Prime Minister Zhou Enlai might compromise the future of Sino-American relations.[33]

Confident that Beijing wanted a new relationship with Washington, Nixon asked his hosts in the Chinese capital between 21 and 28 February 1972 for help in ending the war in Vietnam. During the summit, he reiterated Kissinger's earlier pleas that Beijing pressure Hanoi to negotiate a settlement with Washington. Though anxious for improved relations with the United States as a counterweight to the Soviet Union, Beijing refused to commit itself. The remarks on Vietnam in the Shanghai communiqué that ended the summit were insubstantial and reflected no serious commitment on China's part to the restoration of peace in Vietnam.[34] Mao and his advisers knew that any collaboration with Washington on the peace issue would agitate Hanoi. In fact, DRVN prime minister Pham Van Dong had gone to Beijing just before Nixon to ask Mao to refuse to meet Nixon. To have endorsed Nixon's overtures on the spot after this plea from a longtime ally would have added insult to injury and left Hanoi no alternative but to embrace the Soviets. This was an outcome China was as anxious to avoid as it was to establish better relations with Washington. From the beginning of the Anti-American Resistance, Hanoi had benefited from Chinese-Soviet competition. Despite its problems with Moscow, Beijing facilitated the shipment of Soviet goods across China to the DRVN and otherwise contributed substantially to the Vietnamese war effort in order to maintain influence in Hanoi. Chinese leaders recognized that success in the war could lead to Vietnamese hegemony over Cambodia and Laos, and they refused to let the Soviet Union be the uncontested champion of Vietnamese nationalism.[35]

Nixon thus left Beijing with no promise of Chinese help in extricating the United States from the war in Vietnam.[36] However, the "week that changed the world" was not without its successes, though these became clear only later. Washington's recognition of the principle that Taiwan was part of Chinese territory prompted Chinese leaders to prod the North Vietnamese in directions Nixon wanted. Five days after Nixon left Beijing, Zhou Enlai went to Hanoi to report on the summit and "share opinions" with the DRVN government.[37] At the same time, China increased its assistance to Hanoi in an effort to encourage the DRVN to negotiate an end to the war.[38] Back in 1968, when Hanoi first entered the peace talks, Beijing had voiced its objection by scaling down its aid.[39] Now, to encourage negotiation, it did the opposite.[40] To Beijing's chagrin, this "carrot-and-stick" approach failed to move Hanoi in 1972 as it had in 1968. "Vietnam is ours," the VWP politburo told the Chinese in a blunt statement. "You have no right to discuss the Vietnam problem with the United States. . . . You already interfered in 1954, now you need not meddle in our affairs any more."[41] "In 1954," former DRVN deputy foreign minister Nguyen Co Thach explained later, "China had negotiated with France to solve the Indochina war behind the backs of the Indochinese countries. In 1971–72, we were not about to let it negotiate with the United States to solve the war in Vietnam again behind the backs of the Indochinese countries."[42]

Recognizing the importance of 1972 for Nixon because he faced reelection, Hanoi endeavored to use the calendar to advantage. In the aftermath of the "victory" over ARVN forces in Laos, the VWP politburo had debated in July 1971 the possibility of again elevating the military mode of struggle over the diplomatic one. "The time has come for us to bring about a favorable moment [*thoi co*]," the VWP Central Committee declared at that time. "We must intensify our struggle, energize our military . . . attacks. We must generalize our assaults in the South and in the rest of Indochina. It is essential that we crush America's efforts at 'Vietnamization' and defeat its plans of aggression in Cambodia and Laos to achieve a decisive victory in the year 1972 and compel the American imperialists to end the war through negotiations on our terms."[43]

After assessing the situation, the Army Central Committee (ACC) decided that the best way to force American concessions in Paris—or possibly win the war militarily—was to alter the balance of forces in South Vietnam through "an unprecedented effort." Accordingly, the PAVN planned a general offensive spearheaded by tanks and other armored vehicles to deal the enemy a crushing military blow. With only 95,000 American troops left in Indochina and the fighting ability of South Vietnamese forces still unproven without American support, the ACC was confident of success. Washington might respond with savage bombings, but strong condemnations from the Soviet Union and China would surely limit that response above the seventeenth parallel.[44] What was more, Hanoi counted on the American antiwar movement in and out of Congress to limit Nixon's response. Under such circumstances, the ACC concluded, "It is certain that our effort will be victorious . . . and will force the United States to stop its war and withdraw the totality of its troops while crippling the puppet Saigon government together with its armed forces."[45]

The politburo agreed to the offensive, which centered on an invasion into the northernmost provinces of South Vietnam, Quang Tri and Thua Thien. These provinces, planners believed, would be easier to hold after conquest than areas nearer and more important to Saigon. To facilitate the invasion, the PAVN would mount diversionary assaults in the Da Nang–Phu Khanh area, the central highlands, and southern South Vietnam.[46] The latter assaults would pin down enemy forces, thus preventing their dispatch to the principal theater of attack. Annexing the two northern provinces was the objective of the campaign, but a secondary goal was "to annihilate a maximum number of enemy forces and cripple its main force units." Success would "change the balance of forces in the conquered provinces to our benefit and usher our war of resistance into a new era."[47] Politburo approval of the plan signaled a new confidence in the military mode of struggle and the persuasiveness of military leaders in promising to deliver a potentially deadly blow to the South's ability to resist the North.[48] The politburo had concluded that the war could still be won militarily after all, and the military establishment was anxious to prove that conclusion correct. Victory, therefore, was "of utmost importance."[49]

The offensive began on 30 March 1972. On that day, five PAVN divisions consisting of 120,000 men crossed into South Vietnam from bases in North Vietnam and Laos. Included in the invading force were two armored regiments, two tank battalions, two missile regiments, more than a dozen artillery regiments, eight antiaircraft regiments, and countless specialized (sapper, commando, and transport) units. Its highly sophisticated weaponry included the new SA-7 shoulder-fired antiaircraft missile.[50] In preparation for the crossing, support units cleared 565 kilometers of new roads and repaired 600 kilometers of old ones, and 10,000 *dan cong* (conscripted laborers) working day and night placed 20,000 tons of foodstuff, weapons, medicine, and other supplies in strategic locations near the DMZ.[51] The ACC prepared the attack well, and the preparations sustained it effectively after it began.

The diversionary assaults in the Da Nang–Phu Khanh area, the central highlands, and southern South Vietnam did not surprise Washington and Saigon. This was a move they had been "concerned about and waiting for."[52] On 9 February 1972, Kissinger had even discussed such a move during a press conference at the White House.[53] The attack on the provinces of Quang Tri and Thua Thien, however, was unexpected and fierce, and it caught ARVN units off guard. Not surprisingly, the South Vietnamese sustained heavy casualties and lost key towns below the seventeenth parallel. To relieve the stress, the White House ordered massive B-52 bombings of fuel storage areas in and around Hanoi and Haiphong, the North's busiest harbor and second most important city, and against supply lines throughout Vietnam and in Laos.[54] To Hanoi's consternation, neither Moscow or Beijing reacted to this showering of violence on an ostensibly valued ally.

On 15 April, the DRVN abruptly canceled the private negotiating session scheduled for the twenty-fourth. With the situation in South Vietnam evolving in its favor, Hanoi decided to wait on military events. Despite the disappointing response of its allies to the renewed bombing, it had no incentive to negotiate. At Washington's insistence, Hanoi agreed to reschedule the canceled meeting for 2 May but in doing so warned that it had nothing new to offer the Americans.[55] In the immediate aftermath of these events, Kissinger traveled to Moscow to prepare Nixon's summit with Brezhnev. Coming on the heels of the increased violence in Vietnam, the trip was of transcendent importance for the negotiations.

On 20 April, a few hours before Kissinger's first meeting with Brezhnev, Nixon told Kissinger that his "goal in talking to [Brezhnev] is *solely* to get action on Vietnam." He added emphatically, "You should approach these talks recognizing that Brezhnev and probably [Soviet foreign minister Andrey] Gromyko as well will have as their prime aim getting you to talk about the summit. Your primary interest, *in fact your indispensable interest*, will be to get them to talk about Vietnam." Alluding repeatedly to Vietnam as his "primary interest," Nixon suggested that Kissinger be "tough as nails" with Brezhnev concerning the war and not let the Soviet leader "get away with discussions of philosophy, personalities or other summit agenda until you have reached some sort of understanding on Vietnam." In conclusion, Nixon added that "the point we both have to recognize is that we cannot have useful discussions on the other items until we get down to brass tacks on Vietnam and make some progress on that issue."[56]

Kissinger's first session with Brezhnev, on 21 April, lasted four and a half hours. Kissinger described the atmosphere of the meeting as "extremely cordial, almost effusive." He found Brezhnev intelligent "but," he told Nixon, "not in the class of other leaders we have met." Brezhnev, he concluded, was eager to meet Nixon but little interested in Indochina. During the discussion, Brezhnev read a telegram from Hanoi rejecting "in particularly insolent terms" a Nixon proposal to meet in Moscow. Nevertheless, he assured Kissinger, "We must remove all obstacles to the summit." The meeting ended on a positive note, the Soviet leader telling Kissinger Moscow would do "everything" it could to help Nixon get reelected.[57]

The next day the two men met again in an equally warm atmosphere. For half of the five-hour discussion they exchanged views on Vietnam and Nixon's desire to end the war. Kissinger presented the American position on the war and reviewed the history of the Paris talks. Kissinger's immediate concern was to get Brezhnev's help in returning the situation in Vietnam to what it had been before Hanoi's recent offensive. That entailed among other priorities getting Hanoi to withdraw the five PAVN divisions that had recently invaded the South. In return, the United States would end the bombing of the North, agree to an immediate exchange of POWs held for more than four years, and guarantee the military status quo while negotiating a final settlement. At this stage, Washington visualized a two-part peace process. The first part involved an immediate reduction of the violence and the withdrawal of foreign troops from the South, which would take perhaps a year. During that year, the two sides would make a "serious attempt" to implement the second part of the plan, which was to negotiate an end to the war. This plan reflected Nixon's desire to reduce American casualties to tolerable levels as well as his confidence in his ability to resist the pressures for an immediate end to the war.[58]

Brezhnev responded to Kissinger's presentation of this plan by saying that the pressing imperative was to end the fighting. If the United States insisted on the withdrawal of North Vietnamese troops as a precondition for negotiations, "it would mean continued warfare." The Soviet leader recommended a de facto cease-fire in place. That would preserve the current military balance in the South and avoid the problems of regroupment into separate zones. Kissinger demurred, pointing out that the United States had proposed a cease-fire in place only to have Hanoi reject it. In light of the recent invasion, he added, "we are faced with a violation of the 1968 understandings which must be restored and the status of the DMZ respected." The 1968 understandings were those "tacit" agreements reached back in the fall of that year that Hanoi would undertake no aggressive acts following the Johnson administration's cessation of the bombing of the DRVN. Brezhnev promised to do what he could, but he told Kissinger he "could not vouch for the DRV." The Hanoi politburo was its own creature, accountable only to itself. After the meeting, Brezhnev took Kissinger aside to assure him of his desire to be helpful and to "protest" that Soviet deliveries of weaponry to Hanoi "had not been excessive." He added that "the enemies of the summit in Hanoi and Peking were trying to wreck the summit" and the United States and the USSR had to "thwart them." He would do "anything" he could to de-escalate the fighting, but he could not impose his will on Hanoi. Later, Kissinger wrote Nixon of Brezhnev, "He made it clear that we would have to cancel the summit: He would not." Soviet ambassador to Washington Anatoly Dobrynin, who later joined the talks, told Kissinger that he, too, was "extremely anxious" for the summit to occur.[59]

Nixon was pleased with Kissinger's handling of the negotiations with Moscow. He was particularly happy, he cabled Kissinger, with "the effect on Hanoi of Moscow receiving you three days after we bombed Hanoi-Haiphong." However, he also had words of caution. "We cannot be oblivious to the fact that while they have agreed to send messages [to Hanoi], secretly, they will be continuing to send arms, publicly, and the latter fact will be the one our critics at home on both the left and the right will eventually seize upon," Nixon told Kissinger. "There is one hard fact that stands out—anyone who gives a murder weapon to someone he knows is going to kill with it is equally responsible for the crime. You and I have reason to believe that both Peking and Moscow would like to de-fuse the situation in Southeast Asia but cannot do so for reasons of which we are aware. On the other hand, in dealing with our own opinion at home, this sophisticated analysis makes no dent whatever." Nixon was anxious about the war because the response to the summit in Moscow, at home and abroad, depended upon his success in handling the war. "We have painted ourselves into this corner—quite deliberately," Nixon told Kissinger, "and I only hope that developments will justify the course we have followed."[60]

Despite his desire for Soviet help, Nixon's conduct of the war was unchanged. He was especially firm in his intent to be as provocative as possible in bombing the North, as the battlefield situation required. "I am convinced," he wrote Kissinger, "that we cannot pay that kind of price for the Soviet summit—much as I recognize that substantively that [*sic*] the Soviet summit is of course going to be infinitely more productive than the Chinese summit." Nixon had calculatingly jeopardized the summit by ordering bombing raids near the most populous urban areas in the North; and he was prepared to continue the raids if Kissinger's 2 May meeting with Le Duc Tho was unproductive. Renewed bombings, he told Kissinger of the Moscow summit, will "probably damage it irreparably," but "we may have no other choice if that meeting [with Tho] turns out to be a failure."[61] Kissinger agreed. Should the meeting with Tho fail to make progress, Nixon would have no choice but to order "a major onslaught on Haiphong." He told Nixon, "I am certain that Moscow will try to avoid a confrontation with us over Vietnam, though there is a limit where things will get dicey."[62]

On 24 April, Kissinger met Brezhnev again for more than four hours, this time with Dobrynin and Foreign Minister Gromyko present. Brezhnev opened the session with an emotional statement that Moscow was not behind the DRVN offensive in South Vietnam. Hanoi had been "hoarding Soviet weapons for two years," he charged, and was using them now to sabotage the summit at the behest of Beijing and its own hardliners. Moscow would proceed with the summit, however, despite "a formal request from Hanoi to cancel it." Later, Gromyko told Kissinger that Moscow had realized only recently how determined Washington was to end the war. He therefore pleaded with Kissinger to give the Soviets more time to "use their influence." To show their goodwill in the meantime, the Soviets agreed to transmit to Hanoi Kissinger's peace proposal of 22 April, despite reservations about parts of it.[63]

Though Nixon wished Kissinger had pressed the Soviets harder, even at the risk of jeopardizing the summit, he considered Kissinger's trip to Moscow successful.[64] Hanoi would feel pressure from Moscow to be more conciliatory and would take the peace proposal more seriously, and Kremlin leaders now knew that Washington was "deadly serious" about Vietnam, that "everything else is dependent on it."[65]

In late April, Hanoi offered to resume the public negotiations suspended at the beginning of the offensive, on condition that Washington stop bombing the North.[66] The White House accepted the offer but refused to stop the bombing until Hanoi ended the offensive. The North Vietnamese, Nixon told an aide, "sold that package to the United States in 1968 and we are not going to buy it again. We found then that while we talked, they continued to fight." "We are not trying to conquer North Vietnam," Nixon continued, "but we will not be defeated; and we will never surrender our friends to Communist aggression." At the same time, the White House announced the withdrawal of another 20,000 American troops from Vietnam, bringing the troop ceiling there down to 49,000 by 1 July.[67]

Meanwhile, PAVN units increased their attacks in the central highlands and southern regions and besieged the town of An Loc. Undeterred by Washington's overtures to Moscow and Beijing, they also intensified their efforts in Quang Tri, pushing back ARVN forces. Though fierce, the bombing of their supply lines had no visible effect on their performance and capabilities. Military Assistance Command, Vietnam (MACV), commander Creighton Abrams described this second phase of the offensive as an "all-out" effort. By the end of April, Hanoi had committed to the offensive six additional divisions from the North, plus another regiment, bringing the total of PAVN units in the South to eleven divisions, twenty-three independent infantry regiments, and seven artillery regiments. Despite retreating hastily in several places, South Vietnamese forces had, in Abrams's view, responded effectively under difficult circumstances. They had prevented PAVN forces from seizing any major towns or cities and shown responsibility in facing the enemy. "The combination of determined defensive and offensive operations by ARVN ground units and [tactical air and] B-52 support," Abrams concluded in late April, "has been decisive thus far." Thieu had also acted "nobly" by providing sound military and political leadership. Still, the future of the RVN remained uncertain.[68]

Faced with a desperate military situation and a diplomatic stalemate, Nixon considered blockading North Vietnamese ports and widening the bombing.[69] To him, he faced a "do-or-die proposition." The South Vietnamese had to have a chance to "win this one" for their own sake and the sake of Americans who had invested so much time, effort, and blood in helping them.[70] Knowing that what he contemplated might cause Moscow to cancel the summit, Nixon went ahead anyway. North Vietnam had invaded the South with Soviet weapons, and détente lost some of its appeal in view of the fact that the lives of Americans and South Vietnamese were being lost due in part to Soviet assistance to Hanoi. "We cannot let the Soviet Summit be the primary consideration in making this decision," Nixon told Kissinger of his plans to blockade North Vietnamese ports and intensify the bombing. "I intend to cancel the Summit unless the situation militarily and diplomatically improves by May 15 at the latest or unless we get a firm commitment from the Russians to announce a joint agreement at the Summit to use our influence to end the war."[71]

On 2 May, a few hours before Kissinger was to meet with Le Duc Tho, the city of Quang Tri fell to PAVN forces. Abrams informed Washington, adding that Hue was threatened and the RVN military leadership "was beginning to bend and, in some instances, break." The leaders were losing the will to fight, Abrams reported, and could not always be relied upon to take the measures necessary to guarantee that their men would stand and fight. Thieu had attempted to remedy the problem by restructuring the officer corps and making command changes to infuse new vigor in the troops. That had done little to improve the situation. On the battlefield, twelve of fifty maneuver battalions had incurred losses that made them combat ineffective. Meanwhile, PAVN units were attacking with increasing success and the situation in the northern region was becoming "serious." American airpower was buying time, but if ARVN units lost the will to fight, the Thieu regime itself might not survive.[72]

Against this background, Kissinger and Tho met in Paris for the first time in almost eight months. In his opening statement, Kissinger wasted no time denouncing the recent invasion of South Vietnam and the DRVN's attitude toward the negotiations. "There is no sense in talking about future agreements while your invading armies are tearing up past ones," he said, referring to the 1968 understandings. Charging the DRVN with engaging in a "talk-fight" strategy intended to deceive world opinion, Kissinger told Tho it was "difficult indeed to trust your negotiating intentions when one considers the cynical and brutal game you have been playing with your careful orchestration of military offensives and the scheduling of our private meetings." When Tho interjected that Washington had violated the spirit of the negotiations when it renewed the bombing, Kissinger replied that to end the bombing Hanoi must halt the offensive, withdraw its forces deployed after 29 March 1972, and negotiate seriously. Exuding self-confidence, Tho and Xuan Thuy rejected Kissinger's demands outright.[73]

The preliminaries over, Tho asked Kissinger if he had a new substantive proposal. Kissinger replied that the DRVN had not responded to the last proposal of 25 January. Tho answered that that proposal had been unacceptable because it left political matters to be settled after a cease-fire. If Washington wanted a settlement, he said, all it had to do was agree to "the immediate resignation of Thieu, the adoption of a policy by the Saigon administration of peace, independence and neutrality," end oppression and abolish "concentration camps" in the South, and guarantee "democratic liberties" and "freedom of the press" there "as provided by the Geneva Accords." These were the same demands the PRG had made in February. What was striking about this exchange was that Tho and Thuy offered Kissinger no counterproposal, which suggested that the recent military successes had stiffened Hanoi's resolve to win the war on the battlefield. Tho and Thuy were now as intractable as they had been during the Johnson administration. After three hours, Kissinger broke off the talks without either side asking that a future meeting be scheduled.[74]

This outcome pleased Hanoi. The VWP politburo commended Tho and Thuy for rejecting Kissinger's demands and refusing to offer a counterproposal. "We continue to successfully execute our military and political plans on the battlefield," the politburo told the two men. "Only by doing so can we have a foundation to achieve a solid solution." Hanoi then directed Tho and Thuy to hold no further private talks pending the outcome of the Moscow summit. At that point, the politburo would evaluate the military and diplomatic situations.[75]

The failure in Paris plus the Abrams dispatch discussed above caused the White House to act. To impede PAVN advances and relieve the threat to Hue, Nixon ordered more air strikes on both sides of the DMZ and in Laos, including additional B-52 bombings of the North. Nixon favored the latter because they were "exceptionally effective, the best ever in the war."[76] So overwhelming was the new round of bombings that even some of Nixon's field commanders urged him to measure his use of force. Creighton Abrams warned Washington of possibly disastrous consequences of air strikes too far North of the seventeenth parallel. However, Nixon felt the situation demanded what would otherwise be an undue application of airpower. He had to end the war in Vietnam even if it meant interrupting the thaw in the Cold War. "Honor" in Indochina meant more in the short run at least than good relations with the USSR. "The Summit isn't worth a damn," he concluded, "if the price for it is losing in Vietnam."[77] Despite this calculus, the administration faced a dilemma. Kissinger thought it was impossible to intensify the bombing to the levels Nixon was ordering and to have the summit too; the Soviets would never tolerate that.[78] Therefore, Nixon would have to weigh the advantages of canceling the summit himself or waiting for the Soviets to do so. If Washington did the canceling, it would give American and world opinion the impression that Nixon was more intent on waging war than working for peace. If Moscow made the decision, it would in all probability blame the bombing, thus ruining the chances of easing Cold War tensions and perhaps Nixon's prospects for reelection as well. While

Nixon favored announcing the cancellation, Kissinger and Haldeman urged him to go ahead with the bombing and await Soviet reaction.[79] In Nixon's inner circle, only Kissinger's deputy Alexander Haig and Treasury Secretary John Connally thought Moscow would not respond to intensified bombing.[80]

Nixon made his decision on 4 May. In an afternoon meeting with Kissinger and Haldeman, he explained that he must not and would not lose the war, that the only mistakes he had made as president were when he failed to follow his instincts to act boldly. He still regretted, for example, that he had failed to retaliate after a North Korean MiG-21 shot down an American EC-121 "spy plane" in international air space on 15 April 1969.[81] Though he was now certain the Soviets would cancel the summit, Nixon felt he had to act decisively in Indochina in order to halt the PAVN offensive if he was to have any chance to secure an honorable peace. Thus, he would go ahead with the bombing and with the blockade of Haiphong harbor and wait for the Soviets to react as they thought best.[82] Kissinger agreed. "If we bomb," he said, "we should do it totally." When Kissinger suggested that it would be preferable to blockade Haiphong first to achieve surprise, Nixon accepted the idea. Moments later, Haig, Connally, and the chairman of the Joint Chiefs of Staff (JCS), Admiral Thomas Moorer, joined the meeting. Nixon impressed upon Moorer that he, Moorer, was responsible for the success of the blockade, that if the bombing and the blockade succeeded he would save the military's honor in Vietnam, and that he should be ready to implement the blockade by 9 May. Since Nixon wanted to involve the South Vietnamese in his initiatives, he considered asking Saigon to mobilize 2,000 to 3,000 troops for an amphibious landing north of the DMZ.[83]

These decisions raised the stakes considerably for Washington, both internationally and domestically. They made it imperative that the military escalations end the negotiating deadlock, especially in light of the expected cancellation of the summit and the presidential election looming in November. In the interests of an "honorable" extrication from Vietnam, the White House had opted for a politically inexpedient solution. It opted, too, for a path of uncertainty, even potential disaster. Just as Nixon would let the Moscow summit go to have a freer hand in Vietnam, so he would risk a second term in office to obtain a settlement he and the United States could live with. This was a problematic strategy, as Nixon clearly understood. The plan "has to work," he told Haldeman; "we've crossed the Rubicon."[84] In his memoirs, Kissinger recalled the 4 May meeting in which these developments transpired as "one of the finest hours of Nixon's Presidency."[85]

In the final analysis, Nixon gave precedence to the war in Vietnam over American relations with the Soviet Union because he believed that what was at stake was American prestige and national honor. In January 1972, White House staffer Doug Hallett had written a memorandum on how Nixon might improve his public image. Among other points, Hallett recommended that Nixon say in public that "the hyper-individualistic— 'We're No. 1'—frontier American philosophy is bankrupt and outdated." When he read Hallett's recommendation, Nixon scribbled in the margin, "wrong on this—typical Ivy League."[86] Thus convinced, Nixon believed that if he "lost" South Vietnam, the repercussions would diminish the nation's greatness and harm its worldwide interests. When he later read Herman Kahn's "Four 'What Ifs' for Vietnam," a fatalistic analysis of the consequences of a hasty disengagement from Indochina that appeared in the *Saturday Review*, Nixon found it so compelling that he wrote on his copy: "K[issinger]—a brilliant analysis—Be sure to have our key people read it."[87] His favorite analysis of that subject, however, was an independent study by Walt Rostow, which he also made sure his staff read. Rostow had been chairman of the State Department Policy Planning Council under Lyndon Johnson and the architect of the air war against North Vietnam. His famous "Rostow thesis"—that the insurgency in South Vietnam could be suppressed by limited, graduated military actions reinforced by political and economic pressures on North Vietnam—had been the rationale behind the Johnson administration's Rolling Thunder bombing campaign.[88]

In formulating his analysis, Rostow described the American objective in Vietnam as "pulling back from Asia to enable Asians to take over without pulling back so fast as to cause an Asian collapse." Rostow contended that if the United States deserted South Vietnam and the Communists won there, all of the other countries of Southeast Asia down to Singapore would succumb to communism in a dominolike effect; hardliners in Beijing would be encouraged to challenge American interests wherever they could; Japan would be vulnerable to neutralist pressure or worse; countries like Germany, Japan, and India, no longer sure the United States would honor its commitments, would face pressures to develop nuclear weapons; and the United States would be abandoning a continent where in the year 2000, 65 percent of humanity would live and some of the nations would be on the threshold of technological maturity. But if the United States held its position in Indochina, Rostow argued, "the year 2000 can see on the rim of Asia 'a Great vital arc of free nations.'" Though certainly pessimistic, Rostow's analysis appealed to Nixon because it legitimized his angst and confirmed his own impressions. On his personal copy, Nixon made two notations: "the mistake this generation makes will be paid for by the next generation" and "withdraw in way Asians can take over their defense—not withdraw in way Asians will collapse."[89]

Nixon explained his decisions of 4 May in a televised address four days later. From his desk in the Oval Office, he spoke of the DRVN's "massive invasion of South Vietnam," the Soviet desire to end the war, and Hanoi's "bombastic rhetoric" in private negotiations. He had offered Hanoi "the maximum of what any President of the United States could offer," he said, listing every concession he and Lyndon Johnson had made since the beginning of negotiations in 1968. In view of Hanoi's new aggression and continued refusal to negotiate, Nixon explained, he had no choice but to act decisively. "We shall do whatever is required to safeguard American lives and American honor," he said, announcing the mining of Haiphong harbor and other North Vietnamese ports and an intensification of the air war. These initiatives would continue until Hanoi left the fate of South Vietnam to the South Vietnamese people, agreed to return all the POWs, and accepted an internationally supervised cease-fire throughout Indochina. Only these terms would "permit the United States to withdraw with honor." Once Hanoi agreed to them, American forces would complete their withdrawal from Vietnam not within six months, as Nixon had announced in January, but within four months. In concluding, Nixon spoke directly to the leaders in the Kremlin. He urged them to encourage Hanoi to pursue peace more actively and not let the United States and the USSR "slide back toward the dark shadows of a previous age." He even suggested that Moscow would be to blame if his initiatives undermined détente. "We, the United States, and the Soviet Union, are on the threshold of a new relationship that can serve not only the interests of our two countries, but the cause of world peace," Nixon told the Soviets. "We are prepared to continue to build this relationship. The responsibility is yours if we fail to do so."[90]

At the end of the first week of May, Washington set the new initiatives in motion. Revising Nixon's earlier decision, the resumption of sustained bombing, code-named Linebacker, preceded the blockading of North Vietnamese ports.[91] The tactical objectives of the bombing were to destroy North Vietnamese lines of communication, restrict the flow of supplies into North Vietnam by land, and stop the flow of men and matériel into South Vietnam in order to "choke" PAVN forces there.[92] The strategic aims were to cripple the DRVN's economy, annihilate its capacity to wage war, and break the stalemate in Paris. The prospects for achieving these goals were not unpromising. They unfolded in the context of the rapprochement with China and the détente with Moscow.

By the middle of May, it was apparent that Beijing would not jeopardize Sino-American relations over Vietnam and Moscow would not cancel the summit. Although "shocked and indignant" at the fierceness of the American response, Soviet leaders would not renounce détente for the sake of their Vietnamese allies. Brezhnev felt he had already invested too much in the summit to let it founder.[93] Moreover, Moscow had to engage Washington and thus proceed with the summit to answer China's reception of Nixon. Nixon's China trip "had major international implications in the way Washington and Moscow dealt with each other," Anatoly Dobrynin wrote later. "No longer would they regard themselves as the only two heavyweights at the opposite ends of a tug-of-war. A third force had been added to the equation, offering the other two the challenges and risks of greater maneuver."[94] Eventually, the Soviets became so eager for the summit meeting that in mid-May Dobrynin told Kissinger that Brezhnev intended to give Nixon a hydrofoil in the symbolic exchange of gifts preceding it, and what Brezhnev wanted from Nixon was "a hot sports car."[95]

In this atmosphere, American commanders had broader leeway in selecting targets than was the case in earlier bombings of the North. During Rolling Thunder, for example, Johnson rarely approved strikes on petroleum storage facilities, power plants, or airfields, for fear of killing Soviet or other foreign experts known to frequent such sites. But now, Nixon had no fear of Soviet or Chinese intervention in Indochina. Hence, though raids on Hanoi and Haiphong remained at his discretion, he imposed no restricting limitations on the men planning and executing them. "I think we have had too much of a tendency to talk big and act little," he told Kissinger of the raids. "This was certainly the weakness of the Johnson Administration. To an extent it may have been our weakness where we have warned the enemy time and time again and then have acted in a rather mild way when [the] enemy had tested us." Hanoi "has now gone over the brink, and so have we," Nixon continued. "We have the power to destroy his war-making capacity. The only question is whether we have the will to use that power. What distinguishes me from Johnson is that I have the will in spades. . . . For once, I want the military and I want the N S C staff to come up with some ideas of their own which will recommend action which is very strong, *threatening*, and effective."[96] The effect was palpable. As a later report put it, "The prevailing authority to strike almost any valid military target during *Linebacker* was in sharp contrast to the extensive and vacillating restrictions in existence during *Rolling Thunder*."[97]

Hanoi had never discounted the possibility of a resumption of the air war on a large scale. Since the middle of 1971, it had sporadically prepared for that contingency. Immediately following the politburo's decision to launch what became the 1972 offensive, Hanoi had ended the demobilization of National Defense forces and ordered new training for self-defense units against the possibility of renewed bombing.[98] It had also improved air defense capabilities, particularly around major population centers. These and other measures made Hanoi confident that the nation would respond to new bombings as it had responded to those of 1965–68. The main concern was the effects of renewed bombings on heavy industry. Sustained bombing could destroy the progress made since 1968 in reconstructing heavy industry and in so doing threaten the socialist base of the North Vietnamese state—and the Revolution. Economic growth made possible by that reconstruction was one reason the recent offensive had been possible and why it was successful, and thus why Le Duc Tho and Xuan Thuy had been able to resist American pressures in Paris.[99]

Soviet and Chinese responses to Nixon's escalations turned out to be minimal. During Nixon's visit, Brezhnev referred to the mining of North Vietnamese harbors as "barbaric" but refused to make Washington's handling of the war a summit issue.[100] Beijing, for its part, limited its response to a statement condemning the escalation.[101] The Soviets as well as the Chinese obviously valued their new rapport with Washington as much as—if not more than—the Americans. They thought of their relationship with the United States in terms of its implications for such issues as strategic arms limitation, the Cold War thaw, grain deals, and the future of Taiwan. Compared to these issues, the war in Vietnam was to Moscow and Beijing a sideshow, of secondary importance.[102] This distressed Hanoi. For most of the Resistance, Hanoi had had unwavering support from the two Communist giants. It therefore had great faith in them, and had come to rely on them perhaps too much for its own well-being. As recently as April 1972, unidentified DRVN officials had boasted that Nixon "would never dare bomb Hanoi or Haiphong for fear of Soviet reaction to such attacks." They boasted similarly that Hanoi had gone ahead with the offensive in the South confident that the Moscow summit would prevent Nixon from resuming sustained bombings.[103] Now, China and the USSR had both met Nixon and made deals with him. That surprised Hanoi and raised questions there concerning the integrity of its main allies. The prospect that the bombing might also affect the flow of goods necessary to sustain the offensive in the South and resist American pressures in Paris was not inviting.[104]

On 10 May, American naval forces mined the principal ports and waterways of North Vietnam.[105] The goal of the operation, code-named Pocket Money, was to impede the flow of seaborne supplies reaching the North. The DRVN had no choice but to close its harbors, including Haiphong. When the Americans activated the mines on 12 May, thirty-one foreign merchant ships found themselves trapped in Haiphong and twenty-three ships carrying 150,000 tons of cargo to North Vietnam had to be diverted.[106] In the first quarter of 1972, seaborne imports into the DRVN had soared to an all-time high of 580,000 tons, including 152,800 tons of petroleum. Within days after the mining, the tonnage dropped to virtually nothing. Unable to reach their destination, some ships went to China, where they unloaded their cargo for transshipment to North Vietnam by land. By 31 July, sixteen ships, including two Soviet tankers, carrying a total of 59,000 tons of goods had done that. This practice became standard almost immediately and largely neutralized the effects of the mining. Hanoi also developed a process of "lightening," off-loading the cargo of freighters offshore onto ships capable of carrying approximately 12,000 pounds each. This occurred around Vinh and Hon La Island, for example, where eight Chinese ships off-loaded cargoes between 8 May and 10 August. An estimated 75 percent of such off-loaded cargoes made it to shore. Smaller junks also created coastal supply links with China. These junks operated under cover of darkness with little danger from the Americans. The closing of Haiphong and other harbors thus delayed but failed to end the arrival of overseas cargo. This was in large part due to continued Chinese-Soviet cooperation to assist the Vietnamese Resistance. That cooperation quickly became evident in Hanoi and was a morale booster of incalculable dimensions.[107]

After the mining was in effect, some 2,200 tons of supplies crossed the Chinese border every day from Pingxiang in the northeast, plus an additional 200 tons a day from Hekou in the northwest. Of these daily totals, about 300 tons were petroleum, and despite the savage bombing of rail and road facilities, almost all these supplies eventually reached transshipment points in Vietnam. Most of the tonnage came by rail from Pingxiang, though in early June, American bombers put this line out of commission for the rest of the month. The rest came via the Hekou-Hanoi rail route through Lao Cai. When rail lines were inoperable, truck routes were used. Though trucks were slower than trains, there were fifteen to twenty roads from China into Vietnam with a combined capacity of 10,000 tons a day in the dry season and 3,000 tons a day during the monsoon season from June to September. By rail and road, hundreds of tons of supplies arrived in the Hanoi area every day. More than 2,800 trucks shuttled between Pingxiang and the border every night. On a day of unparalleled activity, American pilots reported seeing thirty or forty trucks a mile on the roads, describing the traffic as "very heavy" or "bumper-to-bumper." At the outset of this effort, Hanoi had at its disposal approximately 21,000 trucks, far more than enough to sustain projected losses in the short run. Also, three new oil pipelines from

China, with a combined capacity of 3,000 tons per day, helped the North Vietnamese effort.[108]

Early in that effort, Central Intelligence Agency (CIA) analysts concluded that with "no increase in the current level of air attacks against transportation targets north of Hanoi and similar weather conditions, it seems likely that, if anything, increased levels of resupply will be achieved in the months ahead." On the basis of this estimate, the White House ordered intensified bombings of railways and roads leading into China, including targets in the immediate vicinity of the Chinese border.[109] Technologically advanced weapons, a more sophisticated design of "smart bombs," made this possible, the precision of their electro-optical (television) and laser-based guidance systems minimizing the political as well as the physical risks from "misses" across the Chinese border or in residential areas in the cities of North Vietnam. The unprecedented accuracy of the bombing contributed much to its efficacy.[110] For example, since 1965, American pilots had flown 700 sorties against the strategically vital Ham Rong bridge in Thanh Hoa province without seriously damaging it. But on 13 May 1972, fighter-bombers using smart bombs destroyed it completely. Dozens of other bridges and tunnels throughout North Vietnam were similar victims of the new weapons, which soon crippled the North's transportation system.[111]

On 16 May, Nixon ordered new strikes on military and industrial targets in and around Hanoi, Haiphong, and Thai Nguyen. This unanticipated escalation worried Hanoi. "What took Johnson two years to undertake," observed a DRVN government report, "Nixon set out to do within ten days."[112] Just as RVN forces had been astounded by the ferocity of the invasion that began in March and still continued in May, so the new air war astonished the DRVN. It was quickly evident in Hanoi that the fierceness and pervasiveness of the attacks were eradicating the state's industrial base and destroying the fruits of the reconstruction efforts. The smart bombs and specially designed aircraft were equally deadly against the transport system and air defense units and facilities. The destruction of radar sites blinded antiaircraft batteries and neutralized SAMs. A side effect of the latter was that the missiles often fell back to earth, where they detonated and sometimes caused substantial damage. In April and May alone, that happened seventy-two times. In late May, the PAVN high command pronounced the radar situation "critical."[113]

By June, the effects of Nixon's initiatives were notable. Incessant B-52 bombings around the seventeenth parallel had sharply reduced the flow of supplies and reinforcements to PAVN units in the South, diminished their firepower and that of the NLF as well, and stiffened the resistance they met from ARVN forces.[114] By 8 June, to illustrate, the number of shells fired at the besieged town of An Loc dropped from a daily average of 8,000 to less than 300. This drastic reduction was symptomatic of the inability of the invading PAVN troops to sustain their aggressive activity.[115] This effectively blunted their invasion of the South, as the bombing of the North dealt grievous blows to economic reconstruction. At the same time, the "re-Americanization" of the war revitalized the antiwar movement in the United States. With the presidential election looming in November, Nixon had little time to deliver "peace with honor."

On 1 June 1972, the VWP politburo promulgated Resolution 220 NQ/TU stipulating that the DRVN must accelerate mobilization efforts on every front in the North to more effectively counter Washington's war of aggression in Vietnam.[116] In effect, the resolution signaled the abandonment of the military effort initiated on 30 March against the southern regime. The intensity of America's response surprised Hanoi. By late May, the bombing of the North had caused significant damage to its infrastructure, threatening the future of the DRVN. Having failed to achieve the victory expected and needed on the battlefield, Hanoi recalled the invading forces, including the armored and artillery divisions, and in late June issued orders to cease large-scale military operations everywhere and to "expand our guerrilla forces and activities."[117] "After June," PAVN general Van Tien Dung later observed, "we had to temporarily desist to consolidate, reinforce, and resupply our forces. . . . Our efforts were confused, and the enemy was capitalizing on that."[118] A prompt military victory was now out of the question.

The United States and the DRVN both undertook momentous initiatives to break the impasse in the negotiations during the first half of 1972. Washington formally engaged the Soviets and the Chinese, and Hanoi countered by launching the Spring Offensive. Had the stage been set for a breakthrough in the talks? The weeks to come would tell.

CHAPTER THREE

Serious Bargaining

JULY–SEPTEMBER 1972

At the end of June, the VWP leadership met to reorient the Resistance. In late March, the Resistance had reverted to the military mode of struggle, but after three months, it was obvious that that shift had not achieved the desired results. The enemy had suffered frighteningly heavy losses, but so had liberation forces, and the balance of forces below the seventeenth parallel was unchanged while Washington clung obstinately to the regime in the South. Moreover, the recent bombings had had "disastrous effects" on reconstruction efforts in the North.[1] After appraising the situation, the politburo decided that primary reliance on military activity was no longer feasible and now was an "opportune time" (*thoi co*) to "drive the United States into serious bargaining." More emphasis would henceforth be given to diplomacy and negotiations to end the devastating bombings and get the Americans out of the South, and thereby improve the prospects of the Revolution.[2]

Following the politburo meeting, VWP general secretary Le Duan sent field commanders in the South a series of messages summarizing these decisions and the reasoning behind them and emphasizing the need again to press the guerrilla war.[3] The "most imperative tasks" of the Resistance, he told the commanders, remained to drive American forces from Indochina, end American support for the Thieu regime and the war, and create a satisfactory government in the South. At this point, these tasks required diplomacy because further substantial losses among liberation forces would imperil the Resistance and with it the Revolution itself.[4]

This insistence on Thieu's removal and the creation of an acceptable government in the South reflected Hanoi's understanding of the American intervention as a political act. The political purpose of the intervention, a *Nhan dan* editorial commented, was to perpetuate a puppet regime that "enslaves" the South Vietnamese people.[5] It was therefore imperative that the creation of an acceptable government in the South be part of a cease-fire and peace agreement. On a practical level, DRVN leaders feared that if Thieu remained in power after a cease-fire, the White House might feel obligated to him even to the extent of intervening on his behalf, or worse, leaving a garrison of troops in the South as it had done in South Korea after the cease-fire there in July 1953. This last possibility had in fact been an obstacle in previous peace overtures. At a press conference on 2 February, the PRG representative in Hanoi had noted his party's rejection of previous American offers to end the war because they were "designed specifically to continue indefinitely the occupation of South Vietnam by American forces."[6] " 'Vietnamization' of the war or 'de-Americanization' of the war in no way means that the US will withdraw all its troops from South Viet Nam," Truong Chinh had said, invoking the Korean precedent. "Instead it will leave behind a residual force for a long-term occupation of a number of military bases to be used as bridgeheads for helping the Saigon puppet army to continue its criminal persecution and massacre of our people and turn South Viet Nam into a US neo-colony and military base."[7]

Revolutionary leaders pointed out that preserving a non-Communist regime in Saigon had been the raison d'être of American intervention in the first place and remained the rationale for continued American involvement. The chances Washington would abandon the Saigon regime were thus slim. "Did the Americans spend more than 200 billion dollars in South Vietnam and send in half a million expeditionary troops just for fun?" a newspaper editorial asked in 1972.[8] As long as Thieu was in power, the United States had leverage in Vietnam. Washington was as committed to him as it had been to the Rhee regime in South Korea. Unless negotiators got ironclad guarantees of a complete, permanent American disengagement from Indochina, Thieu's removal would remain a prerequisite for a negotiated solution.[9] This was not an idle fear. Several members of the Nixon administration, of whom Alexander Haig was the most ardent, favored a Korea-style cease-fire under which the United States would largely disengage from Vietnam but leave behind a token military force, danger to which might trigger reintervention in the future.[10]

To encourage a favorable diplomatic solution, Hanoi also decided to undertake a campaign to exploit the "contradictions" within American society and between the United States and other nations over America's role in Vietnam. Success in this enterprise would pressure Nixon to be more conciliatory and thereby improve Hanoi's negotiating position. The greater the mobilization of American and world opinion against the Nixon administration, the stronger would be the pressure to end the intervention.[11] As the mobilization commenced, VWP leaders worked to blunt the economic effects of the bombing. Despite the devastation, agricultural and especially industrial production had to be looked after. The DRVN could not afford to become dependent on outsiders for the subsistence of its people, nor could it postpone the building of socialism. The politburo thus began measuring success in the North not by the number of bombers downed but by the tonnage of food produced and goods manufactured. Signs that the bombing was destroying agricultural and industrial production would justify negotiating a settlement with the United States in order to save the Revolution.[12]

On 19 July, at a private residence in Choisy-le-Roi, outside Paris, the peace negotiators held their fourteenth secret/private meeting. Kissinger was "more cheerful" than he had been when the two sides last met, a result no doubt of changes in the war. Tho spoke first, stating that the United States and the DRVN "should settle all military and political problems and after the agreement is reached and after the signing of an agreement, then a ceasefire could take place." He suggested that that was the best way to reach an agreement, citing the examples of the Geneva Accords of 1954 and 1962.[13]

Kissinger then announced that he had a "final proposition" to make. But before making it, he lectured Tho on American understanding of the current situation. The United States, he said, wanted an equitable peace, and only the intransigence and duplicity of Tho's government stood in the way of that goal. He commended Beijing and Moscow for the maturity they showed in accepting American overtures for peaceful coexistence and wondered why Hanoi rejected a similar relationship. After Tho responded, Kissinger proposed a temporary, four-month cease-fire in place during which the two sides would negotiate the details of a comprehensive military and political settlement. An international commission satisfactory to both sides would oversee the cease-fire and implementation of the settlement. As soon as the commission was in place, the withdrawal of American and other foreign forces—excluding North Vietnamese troops in the South—would begin, as would the exchange of prisoners, both processes to be completed within four months. The settlement would also include principles to govern negotiations between the Vietnamese parties concerning the future of South Vietnam.[14]

The novel feature in this proposal was the unilateral nature of the American withdrawal, which was no longer contingent on a parallel withdrawal of North Vietnamese troops from the South. At the end of May 1971, the United States had agreed to a cease-fire in place during which PAVN forces would have remained in the South temporarily. Now, the United States was agreeing to their remaining indefinitely. That was another major concession made without consulting or informing Thieu.[15]

Tho objected to the proposal because it separated political and military issues and was too general on several points. "What you have called a modification and a specific proposal," Tho explained, "I feel is not a modification and is not specific because you still maintain a cease-fire and withdrawal of U.S. forces in four months—because previously it was four months—and release of prisoners. Regarding political questions, I have the impression I am hearing again what you have said over the past thirteen sessions. They are not even as clear as your Eight Points—for example, on the resignation of Nguyen Van Thieu and the timing of elections. So these are not as concrete and specific as your previous Eight Points."[16] Kissinger, who sat passively as Tho spoke, later told Nixon, "This was a predictable first reaction." But Kissinger was confident that the politburo would take the proposal seriously and that the coming days could bring a turning point in the talks. Should the DRVN decide to negotiate on the basis of the proposal, as Kissinger believed, a settlement could be reached within weeks, before the November election. A positive omen was that the next scheduled session of the talks was on 31 July or 1 August, marking the shortest interval ever between sessions of the negotiations between Tho and Kissinger.[17] That and the seriousness of the Tho-Kissinger exchange were signs of Hanoi's new emphasis on diplomacy.

The VWP politburo welcomed news of Kissinger's new proposal. At last, Washington was showing flexibility and signaling a desire for a prompt settlement. In a message to Hanoi, Tho and Thuy estimated that either Washington would acknowledge the failure of Vietnamization and sign an agreement "that favors us but which the Americans can accept," or Nixon would seek reelection without a settlement and prolong the hostilities to obtain concessions from the DRVN. The politburo reply was optimistic. "Within the United States, there are serious contradictions between the American people and Nixon, [and] between the Republican and Democratic Parties concerning the Vietnam problem," Hanoi told Tho and Thuy on 22 July. "In solving the Vietnam problem, the balance of forces on the battlefield is primordial; presently, however, it is very important to exploit the serious contradictions in the [presidential] election in the United States, and to use the pressure of the American people and the contradictions between the two parties. From now until the Republican Party Convention (24 August), we must consider these important principles." Tho and Thuy endorsed these views, adding that it was impossible to divine Nixon's intentions but wisest at this point to continue emphasizing the diplomatic mode of struggle.[18]

While Kissinger and Tho negotiated, the White House continued the bombing. In October 1968, Johnson had ended Rolling Thunder when serious talks began. "It has always been my theory," Nixon later wrote explaining why he thought Johnson had made a mistake, "that in dealing with those very pragmatic men—and we must respect them for their strength and pragmatism—who lead the Communist nations, that they respect strength, not belligerence but strength; and at least that is the way I am always going to approach it, and I think it is going to be successful in the end."[19] Nixon therefore felt that he needed to increase the pressure on Hanoi to exact concessions at the bargaining table and erase the impression that he was selling out Saigon. Such an impression would alienate conservative groups that constituted the base of his political support. Kissinger later wrote of this time, "Nixon saw no progress until after the election and probably did not even desire it. Even then, he preferred another escalation before sitting down to negotiate."[20]

The continuation of the bombing during the negotiations took Hanoi by surprise. DRVN officials had confidently expected that "if the U.S. returns to the Paris Conference, it will stop the bombing of North Vietnam." That this was not the case impressed on North Vietnamese leaders the strength of Nixon's resolve to end the war only on acceptable terms.[21] Of the options available to Nixon in the summer of 1972, bombing was the one surest to influence the negotiations. Between 1965 and 1968, the Johnson administration had used bombing to encourage Hanoi to be flexible in negotiating and bombing pauses to get its negotiators to the conference table.[22] With periodic pauses, Johnson had hoped Hanoi's leaders would appreciate the benefits of peace and thus cooperate in attaining a cease-fire. In the end, he succeeded only in bringing them to the negotiating table. For Nixon, bombing had a different purpose. When he renewed the air war in 1972, he was convinced that halting it would never encourage Hanoi to negotiate. To get Hanoi to the bargaining table, he would have to use punishing violence. A "fourth rate" power like the DRVN, Kissinger convinced him, must have "a breaking point."[23] Bombed long and hard enough, North Vietnam would bend and give Nixon the honorable peace he desired. That, Nixon concluded, required the unremitting application of airpower.

In midsummer, the VWP politburo responded to Washington's initiatives by attempting to exploit the "contradictions" within the United States. In an effort to widen the gap between the White House and the antiwar movement, Hanoi released stories, rapidly picked up in the Western media, of American aircraft deliberately destroying irrigation dikes used by North Vietnamese farmers. Farmers in several regions did in fact suffer great losses as a result of flooding caused by damage to irrigation systems. However, almost all of that damage was due to unusually heavy monsoon rains, which overwhelmed dikes in various states of disrepair. According to the mayor of Hanoi in the summer of

1972, dikes damaged by torrential rains in 1971 were never repaired.[24] Asked about the bombing of dikes, Nixon answered vehemently, "We have had orders out not to hit dikes because the results in terms of civil casualties would be extraordinary. As far as any future activities are concerned, those orders are still in force." He later added, "If it were the policy of the United States to bomb the dikes, we could take them out, the significant part of them, in a week. We don't do so . . . because we are trying to avoid civilian casualties, not cause them."[25] However, the American bombing did in fact damage the dike system. According to an NSC estimate, American bombers accidentally hit eleven dikes near military targets, causing "reparable" damage.[26] The flap over bombed dikes thus had little foundation in fact but considerable psychological effect. Antiwar activists accepted Hanoi's accusations at face value and reacted strongly, eroding Nixon's credibility at home and weakening the hand of his envoys in Paris.

At the end of July, despite the efforts of both parties to hasten the negotiations along, an agreement still seemed far away. The tacit agreement on the unilateral withdrawal of American and other foreign troops represented progress, but the negotiators still differed on the substance of a final agreement. The North Vietnamese insisted on a settlement whose political provisions conduced to reunification of the nation and the triumph of the Revolution; the Americans wanted a military settlement only—cease-fire, withdrawal, and POW exchange—and refused to discuss political matters beyond general elections in South Vietnam. The American position was simple, and to Washington's advantage. Under it, the United States would have no role in Vietnam after the withdrawal and prisoner exchange. It was thus absolved of responsibility for anything that happened thereafter, including the fate of the RVN.

Tho repeated Hanoi's position at the 1 August meeting at Choisy-le-Roi. During this eight-hour session, which Kissinger thought was the most interesting of their meetings yet, the two sides discussed a new Ten Points proposal by the DRVN as well as a new American proposal comprising twelve points. The American proposal again called for unilateral foreign troop withdrawals and prisoner exchanges to be completed within four months of a cease-fire and international supervision in the South after the cease-fire. It also included a new provision calling for a presidential election—rather than the general elections proposed earlier—in the South within six months after the two sides agreed on a post-cease-fire political settlement. Presumably, the new election proposal would satisfy the concerns of Hanoi and the PRG regarding Thieu while better protecting American interests in the South. The details of the political provisions would be worked out within three months following the cease-fire; and to ensure fairness, Thieu would step down two months before the election.[27]

The North Vietnamese thought this proposal indicated that the Americans were beginning to come around. They insisted, though, that the details of the political provisions be negotiated before the cease-fire. They also thought four months was too long for the troop withdrawal, suggesting one month instead. That timetable, Tho pointed out, would mean the quick release of prisoners. Hanoi also still maintained that North Vietnamese troops in the South were under NLF command and thus a matter for the United States and the PRG to resolve. To allay Kissinger's concerns regarding these troops, Tho stated that settlement of the "Vietnam problem" would facilitate settlement of other problems of interest to the United States. He did agree, however, to the parallel release of prisoners in Vietnam and the withdrawal of foreign troops, as well as to Kissinger's proposal concerning a presidential election in South Vietnam.[28]

Tho rejected the idea that the DRVN was responsible for the release of prisoners in Cambodia and Laos or for arranging cease-fires in those countries. This rejection stemmed from two factors. First, Hanoi refused to admit that it had troops or political authority in the neighboring countries. Second, and perhaps more important, Hanoi's relationship with its Cambodian allies had recently deteriorated. Since the Lon Nol coup and the American invasion of Cambodia, Hanoi and the Kampuchean Communist Party (KCP, also known as Khmer Rouge) had been at odds over issues that included the number of North Vietnamese troops in the country and the political role of deposed king Sihanouk. By 1971, the differences were so serious that the KCP Congress in September defined the entire Vietnamese nation as "the long term 'acute enemy' of Kampuchea."[29] By the end of the year, the relationship had deteriorated to the point where KCP units were kidnapping and assassinating NLF cadres. Hanoi was thus in no position to negotiate a cease-fire or to make other commitments on behalf of its Cambodian "allies." To negotiate on behalf of Laos alone might cause the Americans to discern the divide between Hanoi and the KCP and thereby undermine Tho's position at the bargaining table. The VWP politburo thus decided to keep both countries out of the negotiations for the time being.[30]

Tho then offered proposals of his own. In 1970, Kissinger had agreed that in return for a cease-fire, the United States would provide a schedule for troop withdrawals. Now, Tho no longer demanded a detailed schedule but only a date upon which the withdrawals would be completed. He also demanded that the withdrawals include technical and advisory personnel, civilian as well as military, and that the United States sever all ties with the armed forces of the RVN and cease all military aid to the GVN the moment the cease-fire took effect. Tho accepted a loosely defined international body to monitor the cease-fire and agreed to an exchange of lists of prisoners on the day the settlement was signed. But he demanded that the government created in South Vietnam after the cease-fire be permanent, not provisional, despite American objections. In exchange, the DRVN would not insist on the right to veto the composition of non-Communist segments of the coalition government. Despite its positive aspects, Tho's proposal included provisions the American side found unacceptable. It limited the cease-fire to Vietnam and the prisoner exchange to POWs in Vietnam and required the United States to pay reparations—$8 billion, Tho proposed, including $4.5 billion for North Vietnam as compensation for the bombing. Kissinger said the United States was prepared to fund a substantial reconstruction program in Indochina, but as a "voluntary undertaking," not an obligation. Also, Tho's proposal tied the release of POWs not only to the withdrawal of troops but to the withdrawal of technical and advisory personnel as well, while Kissinger insisted that the release be unconditional.[31]

Less than two weeks later, on 14 August, the negotiators met again. During the seven-hour session, Kissinger and Tho made a *compte rendu* of where they were. They now agreed on several important general items, among them a cease-fire in place; international supervision of the cease-fire; withdrawal of American and other foreign troops from South Vietnam; American neutrality in a postsettlement political process in South Vietnam that would include the participation of all political groups there, a presidential election, and Thieu's resignation two months prior to that election; guarantees of the independence and reunification of Vietnam as provided by the 1954 Geneva Accords; and respect for the 1954 and 1962 Geneva Accords on Indochina and Laos and for the independence of the states of Indochina. In substantive discussions of the details of these areas of agreement, Kissinger was especially insistent that "there is no possibility whatsoever that we will leave Indochina or will agree to any proposal while any American prisoners are left anywhere in Indochina or unaccounted for." The two men also aired their differences over the issue of American aid for postwar Vietnam. Tho would agree to no American military assistance to Saigon after the cease-fire, but Kissinger insisted on some such assistance and proposed that he and Tho come to a private understanding of the amount and kinds of assistance. Since this represented a concession on Kissinger's part, Tho agreed to consider it and make a counterproposal.[32]

On 17 August, the first day of a three-day stay in Saigon, Kissinger met Thieu. In the course of their discussion, Kissinger said of the Paris talks with Tho and Thuy, "At the next meeting I would like to accept their proposal that there be no cease-fire until *all* is done." The remark indicated that the White House wanted to break the stalemate in the talks. It had become clear to Kissinger that Hanoi would never sign a cease-fire until the two sides agreed on political matters concerning South Vietnam. He had to sell that idea to Thieu, and with it the terms of a political settlement. "We want to go to the absolute limit of what is and looks reasonable," he told Thieu, "but defend the principle that the U.S. will not end the war in which it lost 45,000 men by joining our enemy against our friend, or destroying a government allied with us for 400 prisoners of war, or even to win an election. We would rather not win the election on that basis. The history books will last longer than the election." Though he would make the offer, Kissinger continued, there was no certainty Tho would accept it. But Washington wanted "to be in a position that they have rejected our reasonable proposals." After the election, which the Republicans were now confident of winning, "We can move quickly . . . we can destroy so much that they will not be in a position to come back and harm you for a long time to come." Thieu asked Kissinger what would happen if Hanoi accepted a formulation based on Nixon's proposal of 8 May, which included an Indochina-wide cease-fire. Kissinger replied quickly, "They won't accept it. There is no possibility." Thieu then asked if the United States would accept an offer from Hanoi to exchange the prisoners in return for an end to the bombing and blockade. "I will be honest," Kissinger answered. "If they propose this during the election campaign, we will be in a very difficult position."[33]

This exchange upset Thieu. He and his cabinet had had little interest in the negotiations, which they now strongly disapproved of. But they understood that the talks had made no progress and an agreement was nowhere in sight. Now, however, Thieu sensed that Nixon and Kissinger were willing to make significant concessions at Saigon's expense to reach an agreement. That was the way Thieu read Kissinger's willingness to give in to Hanoi's demand that the final agreement arrange political as well as military matters in the South after the cease-fire. To Thieu, any political settlement palatable to Hanoi would entail compromise with the NLF and effectively end the American military commitment to Saigon and was therefore unacceptable to him. Equally disconcerting to Thieu was Kissinger's acknowledgment that Nixon might accept a DRVN offer to release the prisoners before the American presidential election in exchange for an end to the bombing and the blockade. If he did that, what would become of South Vietnam? Kissinger tried to reassure Thieu. He told Thieu and his cousin and close adviser Hoang Duc Nha that he himself did not foresee or desire a cease-fire in the near future. "I thought at first that it would be best to have a cease-fire as soon as possible because of our election," he said. "But upon reflection I have decided that it is easier if we keep up the bombing through the election, unless in your view your military situation requires a cease-fire." Kissinger also preferred that the POWs be released after the election so Nixon could continue the bombing and the blockade. To assure Thieu and Nha of the sincerity of the American commitment, Kissinger added that the United States would not end military and economic aid to the RVN before the election, and "it is out of the question that we will make any additional concession after the election." That did little to comfort Thieu and Nha, who were shocked by what Kissinger had told them.[34]

Kissinger's visit convinced Thieu that Washington was "working behind his back." Thereafter, he feared an American betrayal and became wary of American intentions. For the first time, he preoccupied himself with the talks in Paris. It was now apparent that once Nixon got a settlement he could live with, he would leave the GVN to fend for itself. Thieu was certain that no document the North Vietnamese signed would keep Hanoi from using force to reunify Vietnam as soon as the opportunity presented itself; he therefore committed himself and the resources of his government to obstructing the negotiations.[35] From then until the two sides signed the agreement in January 1973, Saigon was a thorn in Kissinger's side.

Late in August, Nixon wrote Thieu confirming his intention of settling with Hanoi and explaining the necessity of the two presidents cooperating in the process of ending the hostilities. "Our essential task now is to work closely together, on the basis of complete frankness and trust," Nixon wrote. To that effect, he instructed his ambassador in South Vietnam, Ellsworth Bunker, to work closely with Thieu and his government to ensure Saigon's "meticulous and thorough consultations with you at every stage."[36] The tone of Nixon's letter to Thieu evidenced his anxiousness to reach a settlement, extricate American troops from Vietnam, and get the prisoners back. If Kissinger's visit made Thieu wary, Nixon's letter left him stunned. The letter indicated clearly that settling was a matter of when and not if. In polite language, Nixon was pressing Thieu to give his blessing to something Thieu had every reason to fear and despise. In effect, he was demanding that Thieu behave as the puppet Hanoi and the PRG/NLF said he was. The South Vietnamese–American alliance had reached the stage of mutual mistrust.

After the private session in Paris on 14 August, a flurry of messages traveled between Hanoi and Paris. The latest American overtures meant that the talks had reached a critical juncture. Tho and Thuy concluded that it was now in the DRVN's interest to "lead the United States into real negotiations" with a view toward reaching a final agreement, even though the two envoys remained wary of Washington's intentions. "We should probe and seek to understand the intentions of the Americans, and see how much they show their cards before we show them our cards," they wrote Hanoi. "Generally speaking, we should see what they offer and play an equivalent card. However, we should also be accommodating; it is not absolutely necessary for them to concede before we concede, and at times we could also take the initiative and concede first as a means of probing [the Americans] and guide them in our direction. We should steadfastly abide by those principles and be resourceful about tactics. We could play our highest card and, depending on the situation and depending on the American reaction, play other cards."[37] Despite misgivings, Tho and Thuy were convinced the White House wanted to settle and that the timing was opportune to get the United States out of Vietnam. Even if it entailed compromising on some issues of substance, Hanoi should wait no longer. If seven years of warfare and the bombings and blockade were not incentive enough, the coming election in the United States was. If there was no agreement before the latter and Nixon won reelection, as it now looked like he would, "the situation will be rather complicated for us." Tho and Thuy thus recommended that the politburo accept Washington's minimum demands and agree to a settlement.[38]

This recommendation perplexed the politburo, which thought that Nixon wanted to win the election without an agreement. If Nixon really wanted a settlement and the politburo denied him one, and he then won reelection, the DRVN might find itself worse off than ever, as Tho and Thuy were suggesting. If, on the other hand, Nixon was prepared to forego a preelection settlement and Hanoi softened its position to offer him one, Nixon would interpret that as a sign of weakness and stiffen his own position. After careful consideration, including an assessment by CP.50, the special advisory committee on the Paris talks, the politburo decided to "press for a settlement of [outstanding] issues with Nixon before [presidential] election day in the United States."[39] The calculation of Nixon's intentions was not the only reason for this decision. Another factor was the heavy losses of men and matériel during the recent offensive.[40] American intelligence estimated that North Vietnamese forces suffered 120,000 casualties in the Spring Offensive, including 40,000 to 60,000 killed.[41] They also lost about 70 percent of the tanks deployed and countless amounts of other weaponry and matériel. A DRVN official corroborated these estimates, characterizing the losses as "extremely heavy."[42] Senior VWP historian Nguyen Khac Vien later confessed that though an agreement had not been a necessity in the late summer or early fall of 1972, "one must accept this or that according to the balance of forces."[43]

Another reason for the decision to reach a settlement was the continued success of joint American–South Vietnamese pacification efforts in the South. Since the Tet Offensive, those efforts to win the "hearts and minds" of the South Vietnamese people had been increasingly effective and had put the NLF on the defensive. The Phoenix/Phung Hoang program had been particularly successful in blunting political activity by decimating the ranks of NLF units and killing or capturing their leaders. By mid-1972, the program had led to the capture of 33,000 insurgents and to the death of 26,000 more, and 22,000 insurgents had changed sides to avoid such fates.[44] At the same time, in January 1972, the size of the ARVN increased under Vietnamization, reaching a total of 1,048,000 troops, including 516,000 regulars. These figures were more than double those of 1966.[45]

Still another reason for the decision to settle in Paris had to do with shifting attitudes in Moscow and Beijing.[46] Despite their continued assistance, Soviet and Chinese commitments to the Vietnamese Revolution had become problematical. Since the recent rapprochement with the United States, one of its ambassadors had told Hanoi in mid-June, "The Soviets are treating [us] like Arabs." Similarly, a PRG chief of mission noted that the attitudes of the Soviets and the Chinese toward Washington compounded the problem of the losses in the Spring Offensive.[47] A *Nhan dan* editorial complained that the Communist powers had sacrificed proletarian internationalism to accommodate American imperialists and their policy of reconciliation. Though that enhanced the strategic position of the Communist powers, it weakened the revolutionary movement and with it the "heroic" cause of the Vietnamese people.[48] If the war dragged on, Hanoi would sooner or later suffer from diminished support from Moscow and Beijing.

Finally, the VWP politburo decided to settle because the bombings and the blockade were taking heavy tolls. By the beginning of fall, American bombers had dropped more than 155,000 tons of explosives on North Vietnam and destroyed military and civilian facilities worth more than $100 million. Every industrial plant in the country had sustained heavy or irreparable damage, except those in the cities of Hanoi and Haiphong, as had every bridge and communication line.[49] In a number of areas, the transport situation was "critical," as sustained bombing made rebuilding or repairing impossible.[50] The costs of lost production, including the infrastructure and factories unbuilt, were even greater and more to be rued.[51]

The politburo apprised field commanders in the South of its decision in measured terms. The decision might provoke negative reactions in guerrilla units, which had not been consulted about it. Le Duan told the commanders that in spite of their dedication and heroism and their accomplishments in the recent offensive, the results were not enough to meet the "requirements" of the situation. To safeguard the future of the Revolution, Hanoi had to settle with the United States. This language absolved the DRVN of responsibility for the change; the movement in the South was responsible for the fact that a diplomatic accommodation was now necessary. "In the process of 'de-Americanization' [*phi My hoa*] Nixon has widened and intensified the war with the Vietnamization campaign and his efforts to spread the war to all of Indochina," Le Duan explained. "In the North, since April of 1972, Nixon has sowed mines in our harbors and resumed the war of destruction on a scale far surpassing that of the Johnson period. . . . The military and political struggles are crucial; however, at this juncture, we must seize the opportunity [*thoi co*] and make resourceful use of the diplomatic weapon to fight and defeat the enemy in a most meaningful way. . . . We must not only be resolute to win; we must know how to win."[52]

The units in the South accepted the decision. In the days that followed, combat operations were reduced as troops focused their efforts on political and propaganda work. They preached the need for peace and the benefits it would bring and criticized continued warfare as counterrevolutionary. The aim of the new effort was to win the masses, as the enemy had been doing through pacification, and thereby set the stage for victory after the settlement with the United States. "Now as in the future," Le Duan wrote, "we must constantly esteem and pay closer attention to propaganda activity. . . . We must make clear that the revolutionary cause is that of the masses."[53]

Since the politburo had decided on a diplomatic solution, it was mandatory that the White House make the same decision, lest Hanoi be seen as desperate. Le Duan and the politburo therefore decided to "struggle ardently to cause Nixon difficulties" in the period before the election.[54] Ideally, Nixon might lose the election, in which case the DRVN would get an easier and better settlement from the Democratic candidate George McGovern, an advocate of peace at any price. To arouse public opposition to Nixon and facilitate its purpose, Hanoi received a special envoy from McGovern and a few days later released three POWs to a delegation of antiwar Americans in Hanoi on the occasion of Vietnamese Independence Day.[55] On 11 September, the PRG issued a special statement denouncing the Nixon administration for aggression in Indochina and the Thieu regime for fascism in the South. The statement insisted that Washington allow the Vietnamese people to determine their own political future, acknowledge that "there exists in South Vietnam two administrations, two armies, and three political forces," and agree to a coalition government in the South following a cease-fire.[56]

By early fall 1972, the main impediment to further agreement in Paris was Hanoi's fear of American interference in South Vietnam after a settlement. The DRVN therefore insisted that the RVN constitution be annulled and Thieu be removed from office immediately and the PRG and the NLF be recognized as legitimate political forces and given a dominant role in a new coalition government. It also insisted on ironclad guarantees following a cease-fire that the Americans would complete the withdrawal by a specified date, never reintroduce American troops into Vietnam after the withdrawal nor resume the bombing, end military assistance to the GVN, and pay for war damages to North Vietnam. Washington refused those demands not only because they were objectionable but also because Saigon would never agree to them. The two sides did agree on international supervision of the cease-fire but remained at odds on the composition and responsibilities of the supervisory body. Hanoi wanted a body consisting of members from nations represented in the current International Commission for Supervision and Control (ICSC), Canada, India, and Poland, and from two additional countries, one selected by each side.[57] Because of the deterioration of its bilateral relations with India during the recent India-Pakistan war, Washington objected to India's participation, saying it would tilt the commission against Washington and toward Hanoi. Washington proposed Indonesia instead. In addition, the United States wanted the agreement on POWs to cover the release of all prisoners in Indochina while the DRVN continued to insist that it had no jurisdiction over those outside Vietnam. On 1 August, Hanoi had agreed to "the release of all military men and civilians of the parties captured during the war." Subsequently, it agreed to the release of prisoners captured "during the Vietnam war," thus excluding those in Cambodia and Laos.[58] Other problem areas included the fate of civilian prisoners held by

Saigon and the time limit for the American withdrawal. Washington now wanted three months to complete the withdrawal, while Hanoi thought thirty days were enough.[59]

Kissinger opened the seventeenth private meeting on 15 September by offering still another Ten Points plan, which he described as a basis for negotiation rather than a take-it-or-leave-it proposal. The White House was prepared to "work within this framework" to arrive at a prompt, equitable settlement. Tho, on the other hand, thought the proposal a step backward since it characterized South Vietnam as a sovereign nation and thus failed to respect the unity of Vietnam. He also objected that it linked American aid to Saigon to Chinese and Soviet aid to Hanoi and failed to deal adequately with political circumstances in the South after the cease-fire. But instead of responding to the new plan in detail, Tho reiterated Hanoi's expectations concerning an overall agreement. In doing so, he amended his stance on the coalition government in the South after the cease-fire. "Last time we proposed the creation of a three-party Provisional Government of National Concord [PGNC] leading to the elimination of the [PRG] and the Saigon regime the day the [PGNC] is established," Tho said. "This time we propose the creation of the above [PGNC], but the [PRG] and the Saigon regime may still exist. . . . Since the [PRG] and the Saigon regime will remain, the authority of the [PGNC] regarding the internal affairs [of the South] will be limited." Hence, according to the new formula, the PRG and the Saigon regime "will temporarily perform the task of administering the areas under their control and—it goes without saying—implement the decisions of the [PGNC]."[60]

Tho also changed his position on two other matters. He extended the troop withdrawal period from thirty to forty-five days and agreed that the money Washington was to provide Vietnam for war reparations would be considered "postwar reconstruction," provided Washington agreed to raise the total to $9 billion to be distributed equally between the North and the South. Regarding the removal of North Vietnamese soldiers from the South, he remained adamant. The soldiers were "hundreds of thousands of young southerners who had repatriated to the North in 1954 and young northerners who volunteered to go to the South to struggle." They served in NLF units under PRG commanders over whom Hanoi had no control. Saigon and the PRG would have to negotiate their status. Finally, Tho repeated, as long as the White House rejected a comprehensive settlement, no cease-fire was possible.[61]

These changes in Hanoi's position, particularly the extension of the time for troop withdrawals, appealed to Kissinger. Though Tho still insisted on a coalition government in the South, he had dropped the demand for Thieu's removal. That Hanoi dropped this previously nonnegotiable demand suggested to Kissinger that the politburo was bidding to settle before Nixon's reelection. Consequently, when Tho completed his presentation, Kissinger seized the opportunity to take the talks into a new phase and end the stalemate. He then reneged on his word to Thieu and announced that the White House withdrew its insistence that the troop withdrawals and prisoner releases be immediate while political issues were worked out. "We accept your position on the implementation of various aspects of an agreement," he told Tho. "As you know, our view has been that certain aspects of a settlement, such as withdrawals and the release of prisoners, could be carried out while other details were still being worked on. While we continue to object strongly to your holding our prisoners as hostages, we are prepared to change our position on the sequence issue as well. To show our good will and to remove your fear that we might renege on an agreement in principle," Kissinger continued, "we now agree that implementation of the withdrawal and prisoner provisions would not begin until all negotiations are completed and an overall agreement is reached."[62]

The concession satisfied Hanoi's most basic demand. It put the politburo in a position to assure American disengagement from Vietnam and achieve its minimum political demands before surrendering its basic bargaining chip, the American POWs. It assured Hanoi, too, that there would be no Korea-style armistice and no American forces in South Vietnam after the settlement. "No one naively believes," the VWP had earlier reported, "that if there is a cease-fire, if the Americans withdraw their troops and if the captured soldiers are released, the Vietnamese people will be able to solve their own political problem, as Nixon boasted." Without the kind of agreement Kissinger's concession now made possible, the United States would have remained in a position to maneuver in favor of the Saigon regime in the postwar South. That was why Hanoi and the PRG had always wanted more from a cease-fire agreement than an exchange of prisoners and a withdrawal of American troops. "To cease-fire or to release the captured soldiers are only concrete acts," Hanoi explained, "the political objective is the only problem of decisive significance."[63] These specifics aside, this session showed that the White House wanted to end the war before the election. Aware of this, the politburo could reciprocate without seeming desperate.

Immediately following Kissinger's concession, the Vietnamese delegation displayed an "extreme eagerness to settle quickly" and did so in what Kissinger described as "their most conciliatory tone to date."[64] Le Duc Tho even insisted on a timetable for concluding the negotiations, an unprecedented act. Estimating that a final agreement could come "within weeks," he expressed a "strong desire" to meet again as soon as possible, and on successive days. "Do you really want to bring this to an end now?" he asked Kissinger. After Kissinger answered affirmatively, Tho added, according to Haldeman and Kissinger, "Okay, should we do it by October 15?" To this, Kissinger answered, "That'd be fine." The two men then shook hands and, again according to Haldeman and Kissinger, Tho said, "We have finally agreed on one thing, we will end the war on October 15."[65]

Vietnamese sources indicate that Kissinger, not Tho, proposed the deadline.[66] The contradiction is interesting. Vietnamese and American sources on the secret/private negotiations, including those written by participants in the negotiations, differ considerably in their interpretations of issues and proposals brought before the negotiators. In the presentation of factual matters, however, they are remarkably congruent. Details in one side's sources are occasionally missing in the other's, but, overall, the substance of the two sets of records corresponds.[67] That is what makes the difference over the matter of the deadline important. The memorandum of the conversation between Tho and Kissinger on this point was evidently sanitized before it was declassified. It is therefore impossible to state for certain which side's sources are telling the truth. Whatever the case, the fact that Vietnamese and American sources are contradictory on this factual point and not on others illustrates the importance of this point in the negotiations. For the first time, one side conceded that it wanted to end the war by a specific date. Until then, neither Hanoi nor Washington had made such a concession since eagerness to end the hostilities suggested vulnerability in its negotiating stance. Whoever suggested the 15 October deadline was obviously concerned about the upcoming presidential election in the United States and evidently wanted to take advantage of the pressure created by that approaching event to hasten the end of the war. Regardless of who set the deadline and why, its fixing was enough to prompt one side to deny, long after the war ended, that it made the concession implicit in it.

On the day the two sides agreed to end the war by mid-October, Kissinger showed Tho the results of recent polls of American attitudes toward the war and Nixon's reelection to convince the VWP politburo that a quick settlement was in its interest.[68] He wanted to persuade Hanoi that its chances of settling the war favorably would diminish after Nixon's reelection. He also offered to work with Tho to complete the settlement before the election. Throughout the negotiations, Kissinger had presented Nixon as unpredictable in an effort to keep Tho and the politburo off guard. According to Kissinger's portrayal, Nixon was a "madman" who did whatever he pleased and served no master save ambition.[69] Elected on a peace platform, he had prolonged the war, invaded Cambodia and Laos, and staged savage bombing campaigns against the North. He also changed the nation's relations with its archenemies, the Soviet Union and China, and in ways decidedly advantageous to his purposes in Vietnam. To top this off, he was going to be reelected by a landslide. In the face of such representations, Hanoi prepared itself to sign an agreement that delayed the realization of its revolutionary objectives. By September, according to Truong Nhu Tang, the "overriding aim was to get the United States out of Vietnam on the best basis possible, and keep her out," for that was the best way under the circumstances to secure the future of the Revolution.[70] Now that the White House was prepared to disengage from Vietnam, Hanoi was optimistic.

The assessment that Kissinger's concession meant the White House wanted to end the war promptly was not inaccurate. The November election was looming, and Nixon had not fulfilled his promise to end American involvement in Vietnam. Hoping to capitalize on this failure, Nixon's Democratic opponent, George McGovern, was campaigning on a promise of peace at any price. That rallied antiwar protesters to his side, but McGovern remained well behind Nixon in public opinion polls. By September, it was not McGovern that worried Nixon but the reaction in Congress after the election. This gave him a strong incentive to settle soon, but not necessarily before the election. The administration and its allies in Congress had spent the past year fending off antiwar legislation. In 1972, members of Congress introduced thirty-five resolutions to limit or end American military involvement in Vietnam. Thirty-one senators, including George McGovern, called for unconditional disengagement from Indochina. The longer the war dragged on, the more difficult the fight over such measures was. The House of Representatives regularly rejected legislation to force the administration to disengage from Vietnam, but by decreasing margins. On 24 July, the Senate approved by five votes the so-called Cooper-Brooke amendment, a measure calling for American withdrawal in return for the release of the POWs, but defeated by the same margin a measure to make the withdrawal contingent on Washington and Hanoi agreeing on an internationally supervised cease-fire.[71] To Nixon and his aides the war with Congress was, in the language of the day, unwinnable. In 1972, Democrats controlled both houses of Congress, the Senate by a margin of 57 to 43, and the House of Representatives 243 to 192.[72] At the same time, the Watergate scandal was beginning to worry Nixon and erode his political strength. On 12 September, the White House learned that a grand jury would indict the "plumbers" arrested for breaking into Democratic Party headquarters on behalf of some of Nixon's political operatives.[73]

More significantly, Nixon now believed the military situation in Vietnam made a settlement possible. The armed forces of the RVN had stopped the Spring Offensive with American air support, recaptured Quang Tri, and largely restored the situation before the offensive; and the North was visibly suffering from the bombing and the blockade. Now was the time to let the South Vietnamese assume responsibility for their future. Also, the phased withdrawal of American troops begun in August 1969 left less than 40,000 of them in Vietnam in September 1972, and if Nixon kept delaying an agreement, he risked losing the leverage this dwindling presence represented.[74] Once the last Americans withdrew, he would have no chance for an agreement.

In agreeing to a settlement before a cease-fire, Washington opened a door for Hanoi. If it played its cards carefully, Hanoi could get a satisfactory political settlement and assurances against future American intervention. This prospect made an early settlement appealing to DRVN leaders. Kissinger knew this as well as Tho, so he cabled Ellsworth Bunker in Saigon to tell Thieu that an agreement was likely. He also directed Bunker to impress on Thieu the importance of a united front between Saigon and Washington. "It is . . . important that Thieu understand that in the sensitive period facing us, his discernible attitude on the negotiations could have a major influence on Hanoi's strategy," Kissinger wrote. "If Thieu is genuinely worried that we might settle permanently, he must understand that the appearance of differences between Washington and Saigon could have the practical consequence of influencing Hanoi toward a rapid settlement in the secret talks so as to exploit what they might perceive as a split between the U.S. and the GVN and the resulting political disarray." Accordingly, Kissinger concluded, "it is essential that Thieu stay close to us so that we demonstrate solidarity to Hanoi."[75]

Because the media had learned where the private talks were occurring, Kissinger and Tho shifted the next meeting to a secluded private residence at Gif-sur-Yvette. There, on 26 and 27 September, the two delegations met for a total of eleven and a half hours, the first two-day session in the history of the talks. Buoyed by prospects of a favorable agreement, Tho and Thuy showed "the same sense of urgency for an early end to the war that they did on September 15."[76] For the second time in as many meetings, they presented a new comprehensive proposal, something that usually took them six months. Kissinger found parts of the new proposal unacceptable but saw in it a number of political provisions that "might signal a possible opening." Tho assured Kissinger there were no American prisoners in Cambodia and promised to "work out arrangements with our friends" of the Pathet Lao, the Laotian revolutionary/Communist front, to release the ones they held, "if you settle the political issues and pay damages." Admitting for the first time to the presence of North Vietnamese troops in those countries, Tho assured Kissinger that Hanoi would withdraw those troops after the cease-fire. He refused, however, to put that in writing "because this involves the sovereignty of these countries" and "we can't in the place of Laotians and Cambodians lay down an international guarantee for their countries." Kissinger then spoke briefly about the need to end the war, and the two sides agreed to meet again on 7 October.[77]

The late-September sessions affirmed Kissinger's conviction that the Vietnamese were eager for a settlement. Returning to Washington, he conveyed this conviction to Nixon, Haig, and Haldeman and discussed with them a new proposal he wanted to make to Tho. The novel feature in the new proposal called for creating a new government in South Vietnam through a democratically elected constituent assembly rather than a presidential election.[78] Despite his pledge to Thieu and Nha to make no agreement with Hanoi before the American election, Kissinger told Nixon and his advisers that if all went well, "we can move to an announcement of the settlement sometime between [the] 20th and 30th of October" and the settlement "would take effect with the cease-fire in place and a start of the release of prisoners in November."[79]

Nixon, however, had reservations. Kissinger was suggesting that the United States propose to Tho the dismantlement of the Thieu regime. Though Kissinger assured him that his staff had plans to reinstate Thieu later, Nixon questioned the merits of that proposal. According to Haldeman, Nixon had gone into the meeting "prepared to tell Henry we couldn't make a deal" within the next month. But Kissinger insisted that he could not maintain his position in the talks indefinitely and that a breakthrough in the negotiations was more likely before than after the election. When the breakthrough came, the White House would have the "honorable settlement" it wanted, one, Kissinger said, that did not sell out South Vietnam. The potential snag was Thieu. Neither of the four men felt there was "much more than about an even chance" of Thieu "going along with" what Kissinger was negotiating in Paris. "We're in the ironic position of wanting to continue the talks as long as possible if we're not going to settle," Haldeman wrote in his diaries, "but wanting to complete them as soon as possible if we do, because the closer the settlement comes to the election, now, the more it'll look like a political ploy,

which it is in no way, but it will be hard to sell that if we have to announce the settlement just before the election. Even so, it's worth doing
as long as it doesn't involve the fact or appearance of a sellout, and they
feel that can be avoided." In the end, Nixon gave Kissinger a free hand to
reach a settlement before the election on the terms Kissinger had just
proposed.[80]

Kissinger sent Thieu a much more pessimistic assessment of the talks
than the one he gave Nixon. "Looking at the immediate future," he
wrote Thieu, "we see practically no possibility of a settlement between
now and November unless Hanoi totally reverses its position. What we
must look to now is how best to insure that we keep [the] situation under
control in this interval and best position ourselves for post-November
strategy."[81] This was quite different from Kissinger's report to Nixon of a
"possible opening" in the talks and of Hanoi's "sense of urgency for an
early end" to them. Perhaps Kissinger was preparing the grounds for the
surprise announcement he hoped to make of a completed agreement. Or
perhaps he reasoned that if he and Nixon presented Thieu with a fait
accompli, it would be difficult for Thieu to denounce the text or refuse to
sign it. In any case, the less Thieu knew of the prospects for a settlement,
the less chance he would have to jeopardize the negotiations.

Since he could not keep Thieu in the dark indefinitely, Kissinger dispatched his chief aide, Alexander Haig, to Saigon. Haig arrived in Saigon
on 29 September and met with Thieu three days later. He reviewed the
negotiations and told Thieu the substance of what Kissinger would propose at the next session, including the proposal to create a new government in Saigon through a constituent assembly. Haig assured Thieu that
this posed no risk to Thieu. By avoiding a presidential election and manipulating the constituent assembly, Thieu could guarantee his and his
administration's survival. That was unconvincing to Thieu, who was baf-
fled by Washington's sudden resolve to negotiate a settlement on Hanoi's
terms and, more important, to accept the creation of a new government
in Saigon. He voiced his indignation in a letter he gave Bunker on 4
October. The American proposal, he pointed out, was tantamount to
surrender. "Everything will disappear," Thieu wrote Nixon of the effect
of the proposed plan on Saigon, "the president, the constitution, the
general assembly, even the government itself." Haig returned to Washington without Thieu's agreement to Kissinger's proposal, but before he
left Saigon he told Thieu that "the United States would conclude no
agreement with Hanoi without prior consultation."[82]

Thieu's reaction alarmed Kissinger, who continued to hope for a preelection agreement. It did not, however, trouble Nixon, who concluded

that a preelection settlement was not desirable if it meant a confrontation with Thieu. "Any interpretation of a sellout" before the election, he figured, "would hurt us more than it helps us."[83]

Hanoi had a more difficult time preparing for the next negotiating session. Despite the offer of 15 September, Kissinger still rejected most of the political provisions in the last DRVN proposal and had made no counterproposals to those provisions. That surprised Tho and Thuy, who were unsure of what to make of it. The two men were certain the White House wanted a settlement before the election. The three sessions in July and August had convinced them of that, and the session on 15 September reaffirmed that judgment. But with the election only a little more than a month away, Kissinger had not budged. Tho and Thuy did not realize that Kissinger was probing their own intentions before getting Nixon's assent to finalize an accord.

The VWP politburo met on 30 September to assess the situation. The members concluded from Tho and Thuy's reports that "it is obvious that the Americans do not intend to sign an agreement to end the war before the election but only want to use the negotiations to win the election." Yet, deferring a settlement was not to their advantage. "After the election," Tho and Thuy believed, "it will be difficult to compel the Americans to make additional concessions to those we can secure before the election; and there is even a possibility that the United States [and its Saigon] puppets might rescind matters [both sides] agreed to before the election." They concluded, therefore, that they had no choice but to force Nixon into an early agreement. To do that, Tho and Thuy would have to set aside "complicated matters," which meant sacrificing their position on some important principles. The Revolution would lose more from prolonging the Resistance than agreeing to an immediate settlement. They would therefore accept the lesser evil.[84] The CP.50 had prepared for this eventuality. Apprised of the politburo's decision, the group soon had a draft settlement that embodied the minimum terms the DRVN would accept. The politburo approved the draft, which Luu Van Loi, an assistant to Foreign Minister Nguyen Duy Trinh, delivered to Tho and Thuy in Paris. "This agreement," according to the accompanying instructions, "is mainly aimed at ending the American military involvement and providing for a number of principles regarding the internal problems of South Vietnam."[85]

Détente, the American rapprochement with China, and the disastrous outcome of the Spring Offensive disabused Hanoi of the idea that military victory was possible under current circumstances. In the United

States, the escalation of the war prompted by the North Vietnamese invasion increased antiwar sentiment in and out of Congress. Ultimately, both Washington and Hanoi saw diplomacy as the best means of ending the war on the most favorable terms they could hope to achieve. Between July and September 1972, the two sides effectively sustained the negotiations, in the process removing several obstacles to agreement. The stalemate in the negotiations thus broken, a settlement seemed imminent.

CHAPTER FOUR

From Consensus to Discord

OCTOBER 1972

Before the next meeting in Paris, the VWP politburo cabled Tho and 79
Thuy concerning the terms of the new draft proposal. The settlement, the
cable said, must guarantee the rights of the South Vietnamese people as
recognized in the 1954 Geneva Accords; end all American and other
foreign military involvement in South Vietnam, including the withdrawal of all foreign troops; recognize the existence of two governments,
two armies, and two zones of control in South Vietnam; and compensate
Vietnam for war damages.[1] In further instructions on 4 October, the
politburo told Tho and Thuy, "We should attempt to end the war before
the American election, defeat Nixon's plan to extend the talks to win
the election, continue Vietnamization of the war, and negotiate from a
strong position." To achieve that objective, the two men had to get Kissinger to sign an agreement that at the minimum provided for a cease-
fire in place and the withdrawal of American forces. "We cannot resolve
certain issues because the situation does not yet permit that," Hanoi
continued. "Even if we continue to negotiate after the American election
we still will not succeed, unless there is a change in the balance of forces
in the South. However, if we succeed in ending the [American] military
involvement in the South, we will have conditions to resolve those issues
later and win bigger victories in the struggle with the [Saigon] puppets."[2]

Soon thereafter, Hanoi informed Washington of its desire to conclude
the talks. "The DRVN side believes that the meetings in the three coming
days are extremely important and the time has come to decide the course
of the negotiations," Hanoi told Washington. "Either the two sides find
agreement on the main issues raised so they can respect the time limit
fixed by the two sides to end the war and sign a comprehensive agreement by the end of October 1972 or earlier; or the two sides do not reach
an agreement, the negotiations are deadlocked, the war continues, and
the United States assumes responsibility."[3] Nixon's reaction to this was
enthusiastic; the message confirmed what Kissinger had recently told
him of Hanoi's intentions to settle.

Because Alexander Haig's discussions with Thieu took longer than expected, Washington asked that the negotiating session scheduled for 7 October be postponed for a day so Haig could accompany Kissinger to Paris. During the morning session on 8 October, Tho and Thuy repeated their customary demands on political matters. Frustratingly for them, Kissinger let them talk, saying only that he was prepared to sign an overall agreement but there was a limit to what Washington could tolerate and Saigon would accept. At the afternoon session, Tho presented a draft of the first complete agreement ever submitted by either side. Titled "Agreement on Ending the War and Restoring Peace in Viet-Nam," the draft contained important concessions on political matters. Hanoi no longer demanded the removal of Thieu, the creation of a coalition government, or the right to veto the composition and constitution of the Saigon government during the transition period. In return for these concessions, the draft proposed the formation of an "administrative structure" called the National Council of National Reconciliation and Concord (NCNRC) to oversee implementation of the agreement in the South after the cease-fire. Washington had first proposed such a council as a counteroffer to Hanoi's demand for a coalition government in the South. Now, Hanoi accepted it. Luckily for Washington, Kissinger would not have to propose the dismantling of the Thieu regime, which, upon his return from Paris in late September, he had told Nixon represented the only way to achieve a breakthrough in the negotiations and Nixon had then authorized.[4]

This series of concessions showed just how much Hanoi wanted to conclude the negotiations. North Vietnam had always considered the removal of Thieu and the creation of a coalition government to be fundamental aims of the Anti-American Resistance. Now, however, Hanoi abandoned those aims because it had to and because it had come to see that doing so did not destroy but only delayed its revolutionary aims. Concluding the Resistance through compromise rather than military victory meant the postponement of national unity and the revolutionary triumph, not the abandonment of those goals. Tho's proposal also omitted mention of several divisive political issues, leaving them to be resolved after the settlement. The North Vietnamese thus dramatically improved the prospects for a settlement. "There has been some definite progress at today's first session," an elated Kissinger wrote Haldeman of this turn of events; "we can harbor some confidence the outcome will be positive."[5]

The next day, Kissinger submitted a counterdraft, saying no further progress could be made on political issues until Washington had "absolute security on military guarantees." Tho responded that the American side must address the terms of the political settlement he had offered, but he made a "firm promise" to deal positively with military issues at the next meeting if Kissinger would do the same with political matters. "At this juncture," Kissinger reported optimistically, "I believe we have [a] chance to obtain significant progress by maintaining [a] firm position and [I] anticipate progress at tomorrow's session."[6] Kissinger was correct. The two sides began comparing their draft proposals on 10 October, reconciling the differences. When differences on an issue were too great to resolve readily, they left the point for later discussion. Tho and Kissinger also discussed the drafting of unilateral statements and understandings that would be omitted from the official accords to deal with sensitive matters such as the future of American and North Vietnamese troops in Cambodia and Laos, the presence of which the respective governments publicly denied. The accomplishments were positive, and Kissinger extended his stay in Paris to continue the negotiations "in expectation that we may score a major breakthrough," he told Haldeman. Fearing leaks, he told Washington nothing more.[7]

The session on 11 October was a sixteen-hour marathon of the most intense bargaining in the history of the talks. When it was over, the result was a tentative agreement comprising nine chapters and eighteen articles.[8] According to the preamble, which the four parties were to sign, "the Government of the United States of America and the Government of the Republic of Viet-Nam with the concurrence of those other countries allied with them, on the one hand, and the Government of the Democratic Republic of Viet-Nam and the Provisional Revolutionary Government of the Republic of South Viet-Nam, on the other hand," agreed to and undertook to respect and implement the provisions in the accords. If Saigon rejected this signing protocol, Washington and Hanoi would sign a preamble stating that the United States and the DRVN agreed to the provisions of the accords "with the concurrence of" the GVN and the PRG.

Chapter I, "The Vietnamese People's Fundamental National Rights," provided that the United States "shall respect" the sovereignty and territorial integrity of Vietnam, wording that implied that it had not done so in the past. Chapter II dealt with the cessation of hostilities and withdrawal of foreign troops, including the date and conditions for a cease-fire in place, which "shall be durable and without limit of time." On the date of the cease-fire, the United States would cease all military, naval, and air activities against the DRVN and begin deactivating and removing the mines in the waterways and harbors. The chapter created two agencies, a Four-Party Joint Military Commission (FPJMC)[9] to determine the specifics of the troop withdrawal and a Two-Party Joint Military Commission (TPJMC)[10] to specify the areas controlled by the military forces of each party in the South. After the withdrawal of American and other foreign forces, the United States would cease intervening in South Vietnam and dismantle its military bases and facilities; the GVN and the PRG would accept no outside military assistance; and other countries that had aided the Saigon regime would terminate their assistance. The Thieu government remained, but it would have to fend for itself. The text made no references to PAVN troops in the South or to their disposition. Nor did it mention the DRVN as a political entity separate from the RVN. This ran counter to the principle shared by the GVN and Washington, that North Vietnam was a "foreign country" trying to subvert the sovereignty of the RVN. That was the principle behind the whole American effort in Vietnam, and the failure to refer to it gave Hanoi immunity against American retaliation. The failure to recognize the presence of DRVN forces in the South excluded those forces from the jurisdiction of the agreement. If Washington wanted to retaliate against North Vietnam because the activities of its forces violated the agreement, it would have no basis in international law for doing so. Hanoi had finessed this issue of withdrawing its "regular" forces from the South. The result was a major victory for the DRVN side.

Chapter II also specified the date and time and other details of the cease-fire, including the withdrawal of all American forces within sixty days. Chapter III covered the POWs. The two sides agreed to exchange POW lists on the day they signed the cease-fire, to release prisoners simultaneously with the troop withdrawal, and to cooperate on matters relating to missing personnel. Tho and Kissinger failed to agree on the fate of American POWs in Laos and Cambodia or on that of political prisoners in South Vietnam. Hanoi agreed to return "the people of the parties, military as well as civilian, captured and detained in Viet-Nam." Washington, on the other hand, wanted Hanoi to pledge to release "captured military personnel and innocent civilians of the parties" throughout Indochina. As to the question of "Vietnamese civilian personnel" detained in the South, that would "be resolved by the South Vietnamese parties." In the end, Kissinger got no satisfaction concerning prisoners in Laos and Cambodia, only the enmity of Hanoi's negotiators for his refusal to free political detainees in the South.[11]

Chapter IV, "The Exercise of the South Vietnamese People's Right to Self-Determination," dealt with political issues. It declared that the right of the South Vietnamese to self-determination was inalienable and to be respected. "The South Vietnamese people shall decide themselves the political future of South Viet-Nam," the chapter stated, "through genuinely free and democratic general elections under international supervision." To respect this right, the United States renounced its commitments to every political party and personality in the South and agreed to accept the political balance there and make no effort to impose a pro-American government on the South. Washington reserved the right to provide unlimited economic aid to a future South Vietnamese regime, but its commitment to the Thieu regime was effectively compromised. This isolated Thieu and his government and was tantamount to an abandonment of them.

In accepting these terms, Washington signaled that the crusade in Vietnam was over. The draft agreement specified that immediately following the cease-fire, "the two South Vietnamese parties shall hold consultations in a spirit of national reconciliation and concord, mutual respect, and mutual non-elimination to set up an administrative structure [*co cau chinh quyen*] called the 'National Council of National Reconciliation and Concord' [*Hoi dong quoc gia hoa giai va hoa hop*] of three equal segments." The tasks of the council were "promoting [*don doc*] the two South Vietnamese parties' implementation of the signed agreements, maintenance of the cease-fire, preservation of peace, [and] achievement of national reconciliation and concord ensuring democratic liberties." Specifically, the council was responsible for getting the GVN and the PRG to resolve their political differences within three months and for conducting elections to determine the future of the South. Weaker than the coalition government the DRVN and the PRG originally wanted, the NCNRC was nevertheless an agency Hanoi and the PRG could use to consolidate their position in the South. More important, the council put the GVN and the PRG on equal political footings alongside a third neutralist faction. This meant the GVN and the neutralists had to recognize the NLF and grant the PRG political parity with Thieu's government. Such recognition had been a primary aim of revolutionary forces for more than a decade, for it promised the NLF leverage in urban centers, where its influence had been negligible.

Chapter IV also mandated the GVN and the PRG to negotiate reductions of their military forces to prevent a resumption of hostilities. During the cease-fire period, South Vietnam was to pursue a neutralist foreign policy according to the 1954 Geneva Accords, which prohibited military alliances with outside parties and the presence of foreign bases, troops, advisers, or other military resources in South Vietnam. The RVN could, however, have diplomatic and commercial relations with all countries, provided those relations came with no conditions attached to them.

Chapter V, "The Reunification of Viet-Nam and the Relationship Between South and North Viet-Nam," repeated the declaration in the Geneva Accords of 1954 that "the military demarcation line at the seventeenth parallel is only provisional and not a political or territorial boundary." It added that any reunification of the nation was to be accomplished "step by step through peaceful means" and through cooperation between North and South Vietnam free of foreign interference. The chapter set no deadline for reunification, though it specified that North Vietnam should involve itself in no outside military entanglements.

Chapter VI created agencies to supervise the cease-fire. These included the FPJMC and the TPJMC, discussed earlier, as well as an International Commission of Control and Supervision (ICCS) and an International Guarantee Conference (IGC). The ICCS, an impartial body, would be a reconstituted ICSC. It would consist of members from Poland, Hungary, Indonesia, and Canada, with a rotating chairmanship. The draft chapter failed to specify the commission's operating procedures since Tho and Kissinger could not agree whether its decisions must be unanimous or by majority rule. They agreed, however, that it would be responsible for verifying that all parties observed the agreement and for reporting violations to the FPJMC. It would also adjudicate disputes between the signatories, especially the GVN and the PRG. Within thirty days of the signing of the agreement, the IGC would convene to enlist the support of interested foreign nations for the cease-fire and the normalization of Vietnam's relations with the outside world. The conference would consist of representatives from the Soviet Union, China, France, Britain, and the United Nations, as well as the members of the ICCS and the signatories to the agreement. Since the agreement was not a treaty, this was an ingenuous means of securing international recognition of it while minimizing foreign interference in Vietnam. This provision would secure Moscow and Beijing's assent to the terms of the agreement and might encourage the two Communist powers to reduce or end arms shipments to North Vietnam. Should that occur, Hanoi would be more likely to comply with the settlement.

Cambodia and Laos were the subjects of Chapter VII. The four parties pledged to respect the sovereignty and neutrality of these nations in accordance with the Geneva Accords of 1954 and 1962 and to refrain from conducting political and military activities there. They also pledged to respect the right of the "three Indochinese countries" (*ba nuoc Dong Duong*) to settle their problems among themselves. This wording meant that the agreement recognized Vietnam as a single political entity, even before reunification, which flouted the principle that underlay American involvement in South Vietnam, namely, that although the Vietnamese people were one nation, North Vietnam and South Vietnam were separate sovereign political entities. The language also implied that the war in

Vietnam was a civil war and not a confrontation between two states, as Washington and Saigon maintained.

In Chapter VIII, Washington pledged an unspecified sum of money "to healing the wounds of war and to postwar reconstruction" of Indochina, including the DRVN.[12] The phrasing implied that the money was to be considered aid and not reparations or compensation for damages, and thus punishment, as Tho originally wanted. According to the text, the "ending of the war, the restoration of peace in Viet-Nam, and the strict implementation of this agreement will create conditions for establishing a new, equal, and mutually beneficial relationship" between the DRVN and the United States. Chapter IX stipulated that the cease-fire would be effective when the agreement was signed.

As soon as they agreed on this document, Kissinger promised to give Tho Nixon's reaction to it within forty-eight hours. The two men also agreed on a timetable from then until the signing of the agreement. They would meet again on 17 October to tie up loose ends. The next day, Kissinger would fly to Saigon to brief Thieu and on the twenty-first, visit Hanoi. Five days later, the two sides would release the agreement, and on 30 October the four parties would sign it in Paris. To show its appreciation for Tho's cooperation in completing the agreement, the White House announced that Hanoi and its environs would no longer be subject to bombings.[13]

Following the "extremely long session" that concluded this round of negotiations, Kissinger cabled Haldeman that it was "essential I have ample time with the President tomorrow for [a] thorough review of [the] situation since [a] careful game plan is now required."[14] When Kissinger and Haig met Nixon and Haldeman, Kissinger hailed Nixon. "Well, you've got three for three, Mr. President," he said, alluding to Nixon's diplomatic successes in China and the Soviet Union, and now in Vietnam. Kissinger outlined the main provisions of the agreement, without bothering to mention the contentious points just noted. When Kissinger came to the provision concerning aid to the DRVN, Nixon interjected that that was "the most significant thing of all because it's a collapse of Communist principle" and "admits the failure of their system." "An assistance program for Vietnam," Nixon explained later, would serve to "revive United States interests, to create a peace that can last a while. It's not a question of reparations or humanitarian interests; the motivation is the same as after World War II: help our enemies because it's better to do that than to leave them as Communist targets."[15] According to Haldeman, Nixon was "all cranked up" over the settlement and over Haig's approval of it as well, since Haig had always thought that in negotiating with Hanoi "we were screwing Thieu." But Haig voiced no objection to the settlement Kissinger had negotiated, reasoning that Hanoi had settled because it had given up hope of military victory and wanted less hostile relations with Washington.[16] The four men were satisfied; with unexpected swiftness they had settled the administration's biggest problem under terms they felt they could live with. The October session, Kissinger explained later, was "my most thrilling moment in public service" because he and the administration "stood within sight of an exhilarating goal."[17]

The North Vietnamese were also pleased with the draft agreement. They had abandoned none of their goals in agreeing to the settlement. The special politburo committee on the peace talks had worded the draft proposal in a way that guaranteed a favorable balance of forces in South Vietnam. The agreement prohibited the reintroduction of foreign troops after the withdrawal and imposed meaningful restrictions on the activities of antirevolutionary forces. Even if Thieu survived in the short run, there was no fear that the United States would intervene on his behalf. The White House had ostensibly abandoned its commitments to Thieu and relinquished its role as protector of the GVN. Eager to reach what Nixon could call an honorable end to the American engagement in Vietnam, Kissinger turned a blind eye to the fact that he was compromising the future of the Saigon government. That gratified Hanoi. Tho and Thuy cabled Hanoi immediately that the settlement achieved five key objectives: it ended American involvement in Vietnam; recognized the existence of two administrations, two armies, and two zones of control in the South; acknowledged the rights of the South Vietnamese people; obligated the United States to pay for postwar reconstruction; and permitted PAVN forces to remain in the South. Tho and Thuy cautioned that Nixon might reject the agreement. Kissinger's maneuvering in Paris may have been a ploy to improve Nixon's reelection prospects, though Tho and Thuy thought that extremely unlikely.[18]

The claims of many Americans to the contrary notwithstanding, the session that produced the agreement was not one in which North Vietnam accommodated Washington by sacrificing its revolutionary objectives. Rather, Hanoi crafted the proposal of 8 October to give Kissinger and Nixon an agreement they could claim was honorable according to the terms Nixon had outlined in his address on 8 May. Tho repeatedly stressed that point to Kissinger and others after 8 October. The agreement, from Washington's perspective, was thus better rhetorically than it was substantively. Despite some conspicuous concessions, Hanoi protected itself in a welter of inconspicuous details. Put simply, the draft agreement ended the American engagement in the South and with it the commitment to the GVN, compelling Thieu and his government to stand on their own. Sooner or later, the result would be to tip the military and political balance in the South in favor of the Revolution.

After a two-day hiatus, Xuan Thuy and Kissinger's aide Winston Lord met in Paris to discuss details of the draft agreement. Lord brought with him a message that Nixon had read the agreement and was "pleased" with it. "The President accepts the basic draft for an 'agreement on ending the war and restoring the peace in Vietnam,' " Nixon told the negotiators, "except for some technical issues to be discussed between Minister Xuan Thuy and Dr. Kissinger on October 17, and subject to . . . substantive changes without which the U.S. side cannot accept the document."[19]

There were, then, still matters to negotiate. Many of the minor differences involved language and could be resolved in routine negotiations. Some of the substantive differences, however, involved policy decisions. Hanoi, to illustrate, wanted the language describing the release of prisoners to refer to Vietnam, while Washington wanted no location specified so the provisions could be read to apply to all of Indochina. The United States wanted the agreement to permit periodic replacement of the American military equipment of the RVN government, to which Hanoi objected. The DRVN and the PRG both demanded that the POW exchanges include political prisoners in the South, charging that their exclusion was "illegal, unjust, and inhuman." If Washington rejected the latter demand, Hanoi threatened that "the negotiations will meet with very great obstacles."[20] These and other differences led William Sullivan, chief American negotiator of the 1962 Geneva Accords on Laos, to conclude that the tentative agreement was generally "weak."[21]

On 14 October, Nixon reduced the number of bombing sorties against North Vietnam to 200 a day and then to 150 and imposed restrictions on B-52 bombing. But he refused to stop the bombing. "I was not going to be taken in by the mere prospect of an agreement as Johnson had been in 1968," he later explained.[22] On the same day, Nixon informed Tho that the United States could make no promise on political prisoners in South Vietnam without consulting Saigon. He was, however, willing to add a passage to the draft agreement instructing the GVN and the PRG to negotiate a solution to the prisoner issue within three months after the cease-fire. In addition, he was prepared to give verbal assurances that he would pressure the GVN to reach a solution.[23] At this time, Saigon had 36,663 political prisoners and Ambassador Bunker was convinced that Thieu would be reasonable on the release of low-level detainees serving short sentences.[24]

On 17 October, Kissinger and William Sullivan were back in Paris negotiating with Xuan Thuy and Luu Van Loi. The night before, Nixon had told Kissinger to "do what is right for an honorable peace, without regard to the election."[25] During twelve hours of give and take, the two sides agreed on the composition of the IGC and decided to leave the specifics of the elections in South Vietnam to the parties concerned.[26] They still disagreed, however, on the periodic replacement of the GVN's American weaponry and on political prisoners in the South. Thuy proposed to accept the American proposal on the weaponry if Washington would agree to get Saigon to release the political prisoners. Thieu would never agree to that, Kissinger responded, and there was no point agreeing to something he could not deliver. When Kissinger then proposed that the agreement clarify the status of American prisoners in Laos and Cambodia and guarantee their release, it was Thuy's turn to be intransigent. He proposed to make the release of those prisoners conditional on the end of American intervention in Laos, which Kissinger retorted was inconsistent with Tho's earlier statement that Hanoi would agree to the omission of that subject from the agreement. Kissinger also rejected another unilateral statement of Thuy's on Cambodia as inadequate and inconsistent with his earlier assurance that an end to the war in Vietnam would lead promptly to an end to the war in Cambodia.[27]

Prior to these exchanges, the VWP politburo had, on 11 October, expressed a desire to have Kissinger visit Hanoi to symbolize the new relationship between the American and the Vietnamese peoples. Kissinger had responded that the White House would entertain such a request after the two sides had signed the agreement. Nixon and Haldeman had discussed the proposal but rejected it on grounds that to accept it without an agreement might make it appear that "we've given in to Jane Fonda" or that Nixon "is crawling." However, the idea of such a visit at the right time was attractive to them. If the DRVN really wanted such a visit, Nixon could use that not only to bring the Paris negotiations to rapid and successful conclusion but also to encourage Hanoi to live up to the agreement during the crucial first weeks after the cease-fire. Thus, Kissinger told Thuy that if they reached an agreement soon and delayed announcing the visit until after the agreement was signed, the White House would proceed with preparations for it.[28] Thuy accepted that arrangement. Kissinger thought the 17 October meeting had gone well. "We improved the text in many places and resolved every substantive and technical issue but the prisoner issue," he reported to Nixon. "We have made the point that Saigon must be consulted. I will see if Thieu can accept some flexibility on prisoners in exchange for good replacement language. If we need more time, I think Hanoi will agree to [the] schedule slipping a few days—they would be extremely vulnerable to public opinion if they did not." Kissinger would make a recommendation on a schedule to complete the negotiations as soon as he had Thieu's reaction to the draft settlement.[29]

To get this reaction, Kissinger traveled to Saigon with William Sullivan, Philip Habib, now ambassador to South Korea, army chief of staff Creighton Abrams, Pacific forces commander Noel Gaylor, MACV commander Frederick Weyand, Ellsworth Bunker, and Bunker's deputy, Charles Whitehouse. This high-powered panel was in Saigon to brief Thieu on the agreement, perhaps overawe him, and get his endorsement of what Kissinger had done. Nixon told Kissinger to treat the encounter with Thieu as a "poker game" and withhold his "trump card," that is, the chapter in the political provisions, until the final hand. He was to praise the draft as a great achievement because Hanoi got so much less than it wanted. When Kissinger presented the text as Washington's "rock bottom position," Thieu would then be inclined to accept it as the best he could hope for in light of Nixon's determination to end the war.[30]

Accompanied by his own panel of advisers—Hoang Duc Nha; Vice President Tran Van Huong; Prime Minister Tran Thien Khiem; Foreign Minister Tran Van Lam and Lam's deputy, Nguyen Phu Duc; chairman of the RVN Joint General Staff (JGS), General Cao Van Vien; ambassador and chief South Vietnamese negotiator in Paris, Pham Dang Lam; and ambassador to Washington, Tran Kim Phuong—Thieu met Kissinger on 18 October. Kissinger opened the meeting by presenting Thieu a letter from Nixon. "I . . . want you to know that I believe we have no reasonable alternative but to accept this agreement," Nixon wrote. "It represents major movement by the other side, and it is my firm conviction that its implementation will leave you and your people with the ability to defend yourselves and decide the political destiny of South Vietnam." Nixon was certain the agreement was the best they could get and that it met his "absolute" condition that Thieu's government be able to survive. Kissinger then outlined the provisions of the agreement, including those on political matters in South Vietnam after the cease-fire. In doing so, Kissinger emphasized the concessions from Hanoi, which he had thought "impossible." Among these were Thieu's continued stay in office and continued American assistance to his government—though the latter was still being negotiated. Kissinger promised soon to have separate understandings on Cambodia and Laos to end the North Vietnamese presence in those countries. He concluded by insisting that the agreement contained nothing that threatened the GVN.[31]

Thieu, however, had misgivings. He was especially unhappy with the NCNRC, which he felt had too much power and could become a tool of the opposition parties, particularly the PRG. Kissinger told Thieu his fears were misplaced, but if he insisted upon them, he, Kissinger, would press Hanoi to accept a change in the composition of the organization. Noting Thieu's continuing doubts, Kissinger became more insistent. "The tragedy we now face," he told Thieu, "is the fact that if the plan becomes public, Congress will certainly cut off aid. We are already $4 billion and by January we will be $5 billion in the hole because of added costs of the war. We believe that if we present this proposal as a victory we can prevail; if not all we have striven for will be lost."[32] Thieu remained unmoved; and Kissinger later likened his resistance to that of Le Duc Tho during the negotiations.[33] Thieu asked a few questions about the text and the understandings and inquired whether the agreement was necessary for Nixon's reelection. Kissinger responded by giving Thieu a copy of the English-language draft of the agreement but withheld from him the Vietnamese-language version and the schedule he and Tho had worked out for signing the agreement. Although the United States had had the draft settlement for some time, this was the first copy it gave the South Vietnamese. According to a South Vietnamese source, "Thieu undoubtedly was offended at being the last man consulted and then having no real voice because the matter was already decided."[34]

Although this was the first time Thieu was formally presented the text, he was familiar with its content. Two days before, on 17 October, the JGS had brought Thieu a document taken from the bunker of a NLF district commissar in Quang Tri province. Titled "General Instructions for a Cease-Fire," the document included the draft text of an agreement. Although Thieu did not find out until Kissinger handed him an official copy, that draft text was the agreement worked out in Paris between American and North Vietnamese negotiators. That fueled Thieu's anger. "The Americans told me the negotiations were still going on and that nothing was fixed, but the other side already had all the information," he commented later.[35]

When he later read the text more closely, Thieu was incensed at the concessions Kissinger had made to satisfy the DRVN at the expense of the GVN. "I wanted to punch Kissinger in the mouth," Thieu said later. Nha was equally upset. "All of our points and counter-points were washed out," Nha said. "This was tantamount to surrender." Before he met Kissinger again, Thieu had his National Security Council (NSC) analyze the text and give him a list of unacceptable and ambiguous provisions.[36] The council pinpointed five notable problems. The first was the reference to the NCNRC as an "administrative structure." In Vietnamese, the equivalent term, "*co cau hanh chinh*," is similar to a related term, "*co cau chinh quyen*." The latter, however, means "governmental structure" and implies a kind of disguised coalition government, and it was in fact the term used in the Vietnamese version.[37] References to the "three Indochinese countries" (*ba nuoc Dong Duong*) were a second source of concern. For Saigon, the number implied a single Vietnamese polity, suggested that the DRVN government did not recognize the legitimacy of the GVN, and contradicted the principle on which GVN sovereignty rested.[38] Though the RVN constitution of 1967 recognized Vietnam as one nation, the GVN considered North and South Vietnam as two separate states.[39] The GVN rejected the premise that the seventeenth parallel was a provisional, and not a political or territorial, boundary. According to its interpretation of the 1954 Geneva Accords, the notion of "one nation, two countries" had official sanction.[40] Hence, in its view, North Vietnam and South Vietnam, like the United States and the Soviet Union, were two politically distinct sovereign states. "Would you permit Russian troops to stay in the United States," Thieu once asked Haig, "and say that you had reached a peace accord with Russia?"[41] References to the PRG were equally offensive, implying as they did an equivalence to the GVN. For twelve years, Saigon had adamantly refused to acknowledge the existence of the NLF; now, Kissinger was asking Thieu to recognize and deal with its creature as a political equivalent. The terms of the proposed cease-fires in Laos and Cambodia were another source of Thieu's apprehension. Thieu understood that those cease-fires would coincide with the one in South Vietnam, but the United States, evidently, had agreed to drop that provision. The understandings between Washington and Hanoi on this point did not satisfy Saigon. But above all, Thieu and his NSC objected to the fact that North Vietnamese troops could remain in place in South Vietnam after the cease-fire. That, NSC analysts pointed out, posed a direct threat to the RVN and Thieu's government, and thus to the cease-fire agreement itself. Thieu would ask Kissinger for clarifications on these matters and for a Vietnamese-language copy of the settlement.[42]

When the two men met again in the afternoon, Thieu brought up the references to "three" Indochinese countries. Kissinger said that was a typographical error he would correct and moved on to assure Thieu about the NCNRC, which he described as a "miserable little council" that would be consultative and without power. Thieu and Kissinger then joined Cao Van Vien and Creighton Abrams, who were discussing operations Enhance and Enhance Plus. Those operations were the current versions of a plan called the *Consolidated RVNAF Improvement and Modernization Program*, developed by the American military in 1968 to "enhance" the fighting capabilities of the GVN and its military forces. The United States had implemented Enhance in early 1972 to replenish the stockpiles of weapons and equipment South Vietnamese forces had lost during the Spring Offensive. It consisted of accelerated equipment deliveries, and one of its objectives was to improve the combat capabilities of RVN forces before the cease-fire, which would probably preclude future shipments. Enhance Plus, a major augmentation of both ground and air forces of the RVN with the same objective, was to be launched on 20 October, two days after the Kissinger-Thieu talks began, and continue until the peace agreement made further deliveries inadmissible. Under the program, the United States was to deliver more than 300 fighter-bombers, including all of its propeller-driven A-1 aircraft in Southeast Asia, several transport planes, 227 helicopters, 200 armored vehicles and tanks, and 2,000 trucks. Abrams assured Vien that this equipment would be delivered before the cease-fire was signed.[43]

On the day Abrams gave this assurance, Hanoi, in a gesture of serious intent and goodwill, informed Nixon that it accepted Kissinger's earlier proposals concerning the replacement of South Vietnam's military equipment and concerning the POWs as well. The first of these proposals permitted periodic replacement of armaments, munitions, and other war material that had been worn out or damaged on a piece-for-piece basis under joint supervision of the TPJMC and the ICCS. The second accepted the American phrasing on POWs that made no mention of the country in which they were held, thus implying Hanoi's responsibility for returning prisoners in Laos and Cambodia. Hanoi also dropped its demand for the release of political prisoners in the South, acceding to the American proposal that the agreement specify that the release of those prisoners be negotiated by the GVN and the PRG within three months of the cease-fire. With these concessions, Hanoi considered the agreement complete and asked Nixon to propose no further changes in it. Hanoi then repeated for Nixon's benefit the timetable agreed upon on 11 October for completing and signing the agreement, adding, "should the U.S. side continue to seek pretexts to delay the schedule which the two sides have agreed upon, the negotiations would certainly be broken off, the war in Vietnam would drag on and the U.S. side should bear full responsibility for the consequences before the American people, the Vietnamese people and the world's people." In an accompanying verbal message, Hanoi insisted that Nixon accept the agreement by the following day, threatening to release the draft settlement to the press unless he did so.[44]

Despite this message, the settlement was not yet complete. In the verbal message to Nixon, Hanoi rejected a series of unilateral statements Washington wanted to append to the agreement indicating its understanding of private assurances Tho had given to Kissinger during the negotiations. "There is no question that [Hanoi's] work schedule is carefully geared to conditions on the battlefield," Alexander Haig told Kissinger of this message and of Hanoi's rejection of the statements of understanding, "the rigidity of which can hardly be attributed to any other motive."[45] The next day, Nixon nonetheless cabled Prime Minister Pham Van Dong his appreciation of the concessions. With those concessions, he wrote, "the text of the agreement can now be considered complete." However, he demanded modification in the language of one of the accompanying articles and insisted on the statements of understanding. He also asked for written assurances that the DRVN would do what was necessary to secure the release of prisoners in Laos and Cambodia according to the same timetable as those in Vietnam. Washington would never sign an agreement that did not guarantee the return of all American prisoners in Indochina. Nixon accepted the DRVN declaration of 13 October 1972 that committed the two sides to work actively for a cease-fire in Laos within a month after the cease-fire in Vietnam. That declaration bound them to end military activity in Laos, withdraw their forces, and refrain from interfering with the peace process there. Nixon demanded the same kind of assurances on Cambodia. When these ends are tied up, he concluded, "the agreement can be considered complete."[46]

This narrowing of differences between Washington and Hanoi complicated matters for Kissinger in Saigon. The closer the United States and the DRVN came to an agreement, the greater the need to get Thieu's approval of, or acquiescence in, its terms. On 19 October, Kissinger and Bunker told Thieu of Hanoi's latest concessions and smothered him in assurances that the agreement was in his interest. The more Kissinger assured, the greater were Thieu's evident misgivings. Thieu described Hanoi's apparent willingness to end the war as an ambush. He and his staff had concluded that the draft agreement amounted to American capitulation. As a result of this agreement, the United States would not only withdraw from Vietnam but abandon its solemn commitments to Saigon and other "democracies" in Indochina. In the Vietnamese tradition, however, they refused to raise these objections, for to do so would embarrass the Americans; it was better to give them time to discern the objections themselves.

Stubbornly refusing to do that, Kissinger kept trying to reason with Thieu. Saigon had no reason to fear North Vietnamese forces in the South; the ban on the infiltration of more men would make it impossible for Hanoi to topple Saigon by force. The NCNRC posed no challenge to the GVN, which would have veto power over its composition and jurisdiction. Washington would "enforce the settlement" in case of "massive" violation by the other side. This wording, however, may well have increased Thieu's doubts about American intentions after the agreement was signed. Abrams, who was present, added his assurances to Kissinger's. Nixon's commitment to South Vietnam was firm; the military situation in the South was secure. Hanoi had blundered in handling the war; North Vietnamese troops and leadership had been inept. Thieu's doubts remained. At the end of the day, Kissinger told Nixon of Thieu and his advisers, "They undoubtedly feel they need more time, but one senses they will always feel that way. They know what they have to do and it is very painful. They are probably even right." After eight years of depending on the Americans, Kissinger wrote, the South Vietnamese

> simply did not feel ready to confront Hanoi without our direct involvement. Their nightmare was not this or that clause but the fear of being left alone. For Saigon's leaders a cease-fire meant the departure of our remaining forces; they could not believe that Hanoi would abandon its implacable quest for the domination of Indochina. In a real sense they were being left to their own future; deep down, they were panicky at the thought and too proud to admit it. And they were not wrong. We have considered the presence of American forces in Korea essential for the military and psychological balance on that peninsula.[47]

On the morning of 20 October, Kissinger met with Foreign Minister Lam and a team of Lam's NSC advisers. The night before, the Americans had finally given Saigon a copy of the Vietnamese version of the agreement, and the men now confronting Kissinger had studied it closely. Lam went over a list of changes his government wanted, explaining why the changes were necessary. To prevent misunderstanding and remove the possibility of the NCNRC constituting a coalition government, Lam wanted the phrase "administrative structure" deleted from the text. He also wanted references to the DMZ altered to emphasize the seventeenth parallel as a political boundary. That would affirm the sovereignty of the RVN and make attacks across the zone illegal under terms of the agreement. In all, Lam and his advisers recommended twenty-three changes. Dismayed at the degree of dissatisfaction this suggested, Kissinger nonetheless promised to have the changes made. Because Thieu and Nha needed the day to study the agreement further and discuss it with members of the government, Kissinger delayed his next meeting with them until the following morning.[48]

That evening, Nixon received a reply from Pham Van Dong criticizing him for failing to honor the original schedule and delaying the signing of the settlement. He reminded Nixon that the politburo had accepted all of his demands, including his insistence that the two parties pledge themselves to respect the sovereignty of Laos and Cambodia. Hanoi would do its utmost to help its allies resolve their problems with the United States; ending hostilities in Vietnam would facilitate an end to war elsewhere in Indochina. Dong proposed a bilateral statement on Laos that satisfied American requirements and explained that the Pathet Lao had assured the DRVN of its readiness to agree to a cease-fire within a month after a cease-fire in Vietnam. What was more, "The Americans captured in Laos will be promptly released, before December 30, 1972." Once the war in Vietnam was over, the DRVN would work actively to restore peace in Cambodia, a task made easier by the fact that "there is no American captive in Cambodia." Hanoi "decidedly cannot go further than the points agreed upon in the Agreement," Dong added, "and further than its unilateral statements mentioned above."[49]

This was the closest the two sides ever came to ending the war in October 1972. Dong's message met every outstanding American demand. The draft agreement, the unilateral statements and understandings, and the signing schedule were satisfactory to the United States and the DRVN. Pham Van Dong made this explicit, and Haig did the same when he cabled Dong's letter to Kissinger in Saigon. The North Vietnamese, Haig wrote, "appear to have met fully each of our requirements to include acceptance of the delays outlined in your message to them of October 20."[50] The end of the American venture in Vietnam was evidently at hand.

Minutes before he left to meet Thieu on 21 October, Kissinger received Haig's cable, which informed him that in view of the breakthrough with Dong, "we are now at the hard point, and your meeting with Thieu this morning becomes crucial."[51] Thieu refused to follow the script. At the morning session, he and Nha reiterated their objections to the draft agreement and Kissinger repeated his assurances. Kissinger then handed Thieu a letter from Nixon. "Were you to find the agreement to be unacceptable at this point and the other side were to reveal the extraordinary limits to which it has gone in meeting demands upon them," Nixon wrote, "it is my judgment that your decision would have the most serious effects upon my ability to continue to provide support for you and for the Government of South Vietnam."[52] Still, Thieu resisted. He could not, in the name of the people of South Vietnam, embrace an agreement that ended the American alliance and jeopardized the existence of the RVN itself. He asked for an end to the meeting so he could confer with the National Assembly and hear from Lam the American response to the changes proposed in the draft agreement. Kissinger interpreted this as an encouraging sign and cabled Nixon, "I think we finally made a breakthrough."[53]

Kissinger and Thieu met again the following morning. In the forty-five-minute session, they got nowhere. Thieu refused to accept the agreement in its current form, which Kissinger took to mean that Thieu was angling for the best terms he could get; and the two men agreed to meet again later in the day. The latter meeting was decisive. Thieu, whose command of English was excellent, spoke only in Vietnamese, with Nha translating. He told Kissinger what Kissinger dreaded the most: he would not accept the present agreement or any other agreement, and his decision was final. His patience had run out, he said speaking vehemently. Washington had connived with Moscow and Beijing to sell out his government and people, and he would have no part in it.[54] "Ever since the U.S. asked me to resign and bargained with me on the time of my resignation," he told Kissinger, "had I not been a soldier I would have resigned. . . . However great the personal humiliation for me I shall continue to fight. My greatest satisfaction will be when I can sign a peace agreement. I have not told anyone that the Americans asked me to resign, since they would share my humiliation, but have made it appear voluntary on my part." The draft agreement confirmed his worst fears. The time had come for him to cease dancing to the tune of American honor. He would tolerate Nixon's self-serving craftiness no longer. He would instead do what he had to do. "I see that those whom I regard as friends have failed me," he said.[55] "It was the duty of America to fight for its allies, not to be an *avocat du diable*."[56]

At the end of the day, Kissinger wrote Haig: "Thieu has just rejected the entire plan or any modifications of it and refuses to discuss any further negotiations on the basis of it."[57] The collapse of that draft agreement was Washington's worst fear. Haig had explained earlier in a cable to Kissinger that the worst-case scenario concerning the agreement was for Hanoi to accept the last changes proposed by Washington while Thieu remained intransigent and denounced the negotiations publicly, thereby nullifying the prospects for a prompt conclusion to the war. In the end, not only did Hanoi accept the last changes and Saigon refuse to approve the final package, but Thieu would go public in opposition.[58]

On the morning of the twenty-third, Kissinger stopped by to see Thieu on his way to the airport. He pleaded for the agreement one last time, in vain. Thieu reiterated that the agreement failed to establish the DMZ as a secure border, gave too much power to the NCNRC, and left North Vietnamese troops in the South after the cease-fire. The last was "the key issue" that bothered Thieu.[59] Kissinger promised to do what he could to have these provisions amended, and with what he later called a "sense of tragedy," he left Saigon.[60]

In the final analysis, Thieu rejected the agreement because he felt betrayed not only by its provisions on key issues but by the lack of consultation and by the deceit of Kissinger and others in trying to foist the settlement off on him. The agreement had been negotiated "over the head of the GVN," and Thieu resented the fact that he had been kept ignorant of the negotiations. Worse than this personal betrayal was the fact that the agreement permitted PAVN forces to remain in the South after a cease-fire. Saigon estimated those forces to number 250,000 or 300,000, while Washington estimated them at no more than 145,000. Whatever their number, the agreement permitted Hanoi to continue to supply them. Militarily, the agreement gave Hanoi "everything it wanted on a plate" while saddling the GVN with a set of political arrangements that were "unworkable." The NCNRC envisaged in the accord did not reflect the balance of political forces in the South; the "recognized territorial base" the accord gave the PRG enhanced its status to the point that "the PRG would be able to set up a capital" and its foreign minister, Mrs. Binh, "would be able to receive ambassadors." Finally, circumstances in and out of South Vietnam and the United States would bind Saigon. The DRVN and the PRG would be free to continue their clandestine activities, while everything the GVN did would receive the closest scrutiny. When Nixon was reelected, Thieu and his advisers concluded, Washington would negotiate a better deal.[61]

Thieu's rejection of the agreement was a "devastating disappointment" to the White House, which had worked anxiously and patiently to make an agreement against overwhelming odds. "We went through exhaustive negotiations," Kissinger recalled, "sustained by the hope that our effort would reconcile those who gave priority to peace with those who gave priority to their concept of honor, recognizing the anguish of both sides."[62] Thieu had dashed this hope. That was disconcerting when it happened, though the White House had reckoned the possibility of such an eventuality "quite high."[63] In a fit of anger, Kissinger, the administration's strongest supporter of a quadripartite agreement, recommended that Nixon end the bombing and sign a bilateral agreement with Hanoi. Bunker agreed that it would be "difficult" to continue the negotiations since Hanoi had met every American demand, but he objected to both of Kissinger's recommendations without concessions from Hanoi.[64] Nixon and Haig sided with Bunker, since Kissinger's proposals would likely alienate other allies in Southeast Asia and antagonize domestic groups who supported the administration. Given the friction between

Thieu and Kissinger, Haig later decided it had been a mistake to send Kissinger to Saigon. According to Haig, Thieu distrusted Kissinger and Kissinger had little tolerance for Thieu's "incurable habit of pointing out the flaws in the draft agreement."[65]

On 22 October, Nixon restricted the bombing above the twentieth parallel while Haig undertook to "defuse" Kissinger's anger and disappointment by trying to rationalize Thieu's position. "You should not underrate the substantive justification for Thieu's intransigence," he told Kissinger. "He, in effect, is being asked to relinquish sovereignty over a large and indescript portion of South Vietnamese territory. He has never agreed to such a concession and given his paranoia about what has brought us to this point, it is understandable that he would now accept an open break."[66] Kissinger immediately recognized that a bilateral settlement with Hanoi would be detrimental to American interests and was therefore an untenable solution. Haig's reasoning, however, failed to ease Kissinger's resentment toward Thieu, and the relationship between the two men was never restored. Calmer heads later estimated that Thieu's stance had had three bases: genuine objections to basic aspects of the agreement; desires to rally non- and anti-Communist South Vietnamese to meet the challenge of the post-cease-fire period; and hopes to lay groundwork for blaming the United States for the inevitable difficulties the agreement would cause him and the people of South Vietnam.[67]

On the day he learned of Thieu's rejection, Nixon contacted Pham Van Dong. He expressed his appreciation for the DRVN's accommodation of American demands but added that his government had to accommodate Saigon on some matters in the negotiations. "Unfortunately," Nixon wrote, "the difficulties in Saigon have proved somewhat more complex than originally anticipated. Some of them concern matters which the U.S. side is honor-bound to put before the DRV side." He urged Hanoi to do nothing until he sent a more explicit message within twenty-four hours and affirmed his commitment to the substance of the agreement. Citing a *Newsweek* interview in which Dong revealed some of the terms of the agreement, Nixon insisted that that breach of confidence gave Hanoi "major responsibility" for his difficulties with Saigon.[68]

The interview was indeed a source of irritation to Washington. On 21 October, while Kissinger was still in Saigon, the White House and the GVN received transcripts of an interview Pham Van Dong had given Arnaud de Borchgrave of *Newsweek* magazine. De Borchgrave was not responsible for this *coup de maître*; on the contrary, Dong had approached him. Ignoring the long-standing agreement for confidentiality on the talks, Dong detailed aspects of the agreement and what he thought the agreement obligated the parties to do.[69] His remarks were alternately truthful and provocative. He referred to a "three-sided coalition of transition" and to arrangements to "promote democracy and speed national concord in the south," a calculated misrepresentation of the role the NCNRC was to play in the post-cease-fire South. Admitting that Hanoi wanted Thieu and his government out of office, Dong said, "The political situation in the south is such that one must have a government that reflects the realities." As to the Vietnamese people, he said, "Reunification is in our blood, in our hearts. But no one is thinking about practical details." He also reported, falsely, that the agreement provided that "all military and civilian detainees, not only Americans, on both sides must be released at the same time." Finally, on the subject of postwar reparations, he said, quite irresponsibly, that "America is responsible for all material damages inflicted on us" and "it is an imperative obligation for America to contribute to the rebuilding of our devastated economy."[70]

Whatever use Nixon tried to make of this interview in the cable to Dong, what Dong said was not what Nixon wanted said in public at this juncture. Dong's remarks revealed not only some of the provisions of the peace plan but something of Hanoi's intentions and of its interpretations of the plan. They also gave Thieu every reason to believe that his understanding of the agreement was correct. Most disturbing to Thieu was Dong's remark that the NCNRC was the foundation for a coalition government. That justified his worst fears and heightened his mistrust of Washington as well as Hanoi. If the VWP politburo intended the interview to widen the gap between Washington and Saigon, the intention was realized.[71]

These maneuvers paralleled an intensification of military activity in South Vietnam. Because of the impending cease-fire in place, each side undertook to expand the "place" it controlled. On 20 October, Hanoi informed its southern operatives of the provisions of the latest agreement and the schedule for signing it and completing the peace process. The message predicted that the United States and the GVN would announce a unilateral cease-fire on 28 October and proceed to ignore it. Hanoi therefore directed its forces to be ready to attack no later than 30 October, because "the best time for great victories will be between the date the cease-fire agreement is signed and the date it goes into effect." The forces were to put particular emphasis on seizing and interdicting major transportation arteries.[72] Hanoi had evidently planned this "landgrabbing" earlier and more systematically than the Nixon administration imagined.[73] According to a 4 October document titled "Plan of General Uprising When a Political Solution Is Reached" captured by ARVN troops, the plan had three stages. A preparatory stage began with close study of the peace agreement to find loopholes and form propaganda teams of individuals to make sure the masses understood the agreement properly. As part of the effort, cadres were to requisition every available sewing machine and produce as many NLF flags as possible. On the day the cease-fire took effect, the flags were to be hoisted over homes, hamlets, and hills. As that day approached, armed units would hinder the movement of enemy forces while political activists infiltrated every populated hamlet. The purpose of this activity was to convince whatever control agency that showed up that the PRG administered the area. During the second stage, on the three days before the cease-fire, military units would make concentrated assaults to expand existing enclaves while political demonstrations would seek to destabilize the GVN and otherwise undermine its confidence and tarnish its image. When the cease-fire took place, forces loyal to the Revolution would consolidate the gains made in the earlier stages. Since the cease-fire failed to materialize, only isolated units put these plans into effect and did so with no significant results.[74]

In spite of this escalation of activity and the setback with Thieu, optimism remained high in the White House. "If Hanoi was willing to abandon the main outlines of its political plan," Haig figured, "it may be in the final analysis equally susceptible to paying the price to obtain a cessation of U.S. actions against the North."[75] By this time, however, Nixon felt little compulsion to reach an agreement before the election. On 23 October, he told his inner circle that political expediency made an election-eve settlement undesirable. He intended to continue talking "so that there is no decisive action taken before that time and that we can maintain [an] aura of progress through November seventh." Meanwhile, he would not exploit the delay to supply South Vietnamese forces beyond the aid already promised. In fact, a Haig memorandum of 23 October suggests something like the opposite. "We worked all day yesterday on turning off equipment in order to keep from appearance of major knee-jerk bureaucratic reaction," Haig wrote. "We will let about ten percent of the total in, all of which was scheduled for delivery in any event. The rest has been wound down. With respect to the F-5s, we . . . have, of course, backed off."[76]

To quell rumors that the United States was about to abandon his government or that his government was about to come to terms with Hanoi, Thieu addressed a national radio and television audience on 24 October. He assured the South Vietnamese people that Nixon would not let the RVN fall to the Communists, and he, Thieu, would never accede to a peace agreement that imposed a coalition government on the South or permitted North Vietnamese troops to remain in the South after a cease-fire. In what amounted to a repudiation of the Paris negotiations, he proposed that Saigon and Hanoi negotiate a solution to their own problems. He urged his people to stay alert in the event of a cease-fire. "We have planned measures," he said, "to win over people and protect our land, wipe out enemy forces and ensure safety along communications lines . . . [and] in the villages and hamlets." If and when a cease-fire came, it would be on Saigon's terms.[77]

No sooner had Thieu finished his address than Hanoi released the terms of the agreement. Because the entire text would compromise the politburo's public stance on important matters, the portions of the text released were those that gave the impression that the agreement conformed fully to American and South Vietnamese objectives. The release and an accompanying accusation that Washington had reneged on a schedule to sign and implement the peace accord, coming as they did on the heels of Thieu's speech, destroyed the prospects for an immediate settlement.[78] To control the damages, Nixon had Kissinger explain the situation to the American people and defend the administration's position. It was during this explanation that Kissinger said, "We believe peace is at hand." Reporters then and historians since have interpreted that statement to mean that Kissinger expected a settlement within days, but in a secret memorandum dated 27 October, Kissinger suggested, "With continued good will on both sides—and the continued support of the American people—this could be finalized in a matter of weeks."[79] A day later, Kissinger's acolyte William Sullivan confided to Canadian diplomats in Washington that the "earliest date for [a] cease-fire could come two or three weeks hence."[80] Because the media interpreted "peace is at hand" literally, the failure of an agreement to materialize at once fueled another round of criticism of the administration.

Hanoi and Washington finalized an agreement each found palatable in October. However, Kissinger's failure to consult adequately with Saigon in the weeks leading up to the breakthrough delayed the end of the war. Presented with a fait accompli but unwilling to behave as the puppet his critics claimed him to be, Thieu rejected the agreement. His insistence that the agreement be significantly amended was motivated by genuine concern for the future of South Vietnam as well as a desire to assert his autonomy. Hoping to capitalize on the situation and driving a wedge between its enemies, Hanoi turned down offers to reopen the talks. Peace was impending but not yet at hand.

North Vietnamese troops in Hue during the 1968 Tet Offensive.
Courtesy of Revolution Museum, Hanoi.

Le Duc Tho, member of the VWP politburo and DRVN special adviser to the
secret/private Paris negotiations.
Courtesy of Revolution Museum, Hanoi.

Le Duc Tho (left) and Xuan Thuy, head of the DRVN delegation in Paris.
Courtesy of Revolution Museum, Hanoi.

North Vietnamese and American negotiators meeting privately in Paris in 1968.
Le Duc Tho (far left) and Xuan Thuy (to Tho's left) represent the DRVN; Averell
Harriman (far right) heads the American delegation.
Courtesy of Revolution Museum, Hanoi.

North Vietnamese troops in action in South Vietnam in 1969.
Courtesy of Revolution Museum, Hanoi.

PRG and DRVN envoys meet in Paris. PRG foreign minister Nguyen Thi Binh
(fourth from left) heads the PRG delegation; Xuan Thuy (fourth from right)
leads the DRVN team.
Courtesy of Revolution Museum, Hanoi.

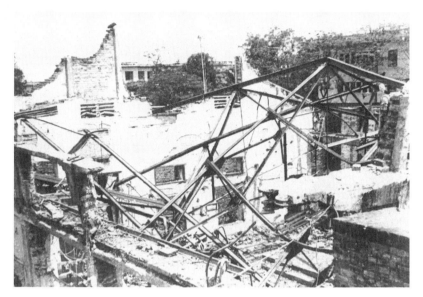

The Bach Mai power station in Hanoi, destroyed by American bombs on
22 December 1972.
Courtesy of Revolution Museum, Hanoi.

The last private meeting between North Vietnamese and American negotiators
at Saint-Nom-la-Bretèche on 13 January 1973.
Courtesy of Revolution Museum, Hanoi.

Henry Kissinger initials the Paris Agreement, 23 January 1973.
Courtesy of Revolution Museum, Hanoi.

Le Duc Tho initials the Paris Agreement, 23 January 1973.
Courtesy of Revolution Museum, Hanoi.

CHAPTER FIVE

Accommodating Thieu

NOVEMBER 1972

Despite the events of late October, which Hanoi took to reveal Wash- ington's duplicity in the negotiations, Nixon won reelection with 60 percent of the vote. That he overwhelmed the peace candidate, McGovern, in one of the most lopsided victories in American history, unnerved Hanoi. In September, the VWP politburo had tried to force Nixon to accept a settlement because of its own assessment that reelection would stiffen Nixon's resolve at the bargaining table and thus set back the Revolution. Now, he had won reelection without an agreement, and in a way that seemed a mandate for his Vietnam policies. This suggested a prolonged status quo, something the DRVN and its forces in the South could not endure. Since 1969, Vietnamization had steadily expanded the Saigon government's support base and the pacification policy had revolutionary units on the defensive. At the same time, the armed forces of the RVN had grown stronger and ever increasing numbers of the South Vietnamese people were developing ties of interest and well-being to Thieu's regime. In September 1972, the politburo estimated that in parts of the South 70 to 80 percent of households had members (*nguoi nha*) working for the enemy.[1]

Accordingly, leaders in Hanoi spent the days following Nixon's reelection evaluating strategy, which had recently emphasized the diplomatic mode of struggle. They decided there was no point in pressing further for a negotiated settlement. Further concessions would set back the Revolution. It was acceptable to step backward to take two steps forward, but the Paris negotiations had stalemated after a step backward. Moreover, Washington would now interpret too evident an interest in settling as a sign of desperation. That would encourage Kissinger to withdraw some of his standing offers and might lead him to make new demands. Furthermore, to accept changes in the agreement at the behest of Saigon would amount to recognizing Thieu and the GVN as independent players in the negotiations. Hanoi thus instructed Le Duc Tho and Xuan Thuy to let Kissinger make the next move. Unless he agreed to return to the October text without meaningful modification, they were to spurn whatever he proposed, refuse to discuss anything of substance already agreed to, and speak only to voice their indignation at Washington's failure to honor the schedule to sign the agreement and implement the cease-fire.[2]

Though it saw no reason to be accommodating, Hanoi still felt a settlement was possible. "If the Americans/puppets [in Saigon] secure an advantage on the battlefield," the politburo decided, "[if] the Americans can take advantage of détente with the Soviet Union and China to create difficulties for us, [and if they] uphold their absurd demands and use the [Saigon] puppets [as an excuse] to prolong the negotiations, then the war will continue. We must do our best to prevent and prepare for those difficulties." Ideally, Tho and Thuy would soon get Kissinger's endorsement of the terms agreed on in October. If that proved impossible, the DRVN must make sure the strategic balance in the South did not deteriorate, for that would undermine Hanoi's bargaining position.[3]

Faced with the possibility of continued deadlock in Paris, the politburo turned again to the military mode of struggle. Less than a month after directing its forces in the South to reduce the number of combat operations and conduct wider propaganda efforts, it ordered the curtailment of political work and the escalation of military activity until "complete victory" was achieved.[4] "The task of our army in this new situation," the order read, "is to build up, reorganize, and develop its forces, continue the implementation of offensive attacks, defeat the enemy's plans and acts of aggression in the South, defeat the war of destruction . . . in the North, execute well the tasks of assisting the front regardless of conditions, [and] overcome incorrect perceptions and thoughts such as illusions of peace, negotiation expectations, and indifference and lack of vigilance."[5]

The purpose once again was to change the balance of forces in the South. Toward that end, PAVN and NLF units went on the offensive in early November around the Thach Han River, at Dong Ha, Ai Tu, the Cua Viet region, and elsewhere. Between 22 and 25 November, forces in Tay Nguyen attacked northern Gia Lai, seizing portions of Duc Co; and in the lower central highlands, other forces "liberated" ninety-five hamlets and over 13,000 people in November and December. Elsewhere, attacks on My Tho, Ben Tre, and Bac Lieu extended the area controlled by revolutionary forces by 1,000 hamlets and 100,000 people. These moderate successes placed the enemy on the defensive and, to a modest degree perhaps, helped the negotiators in Paris.[6]

In early November, Nixon told Thieu that Hanoi's release of portions of the draft agreement would not change American policy. In spite of this and other setbacks, Washington would continue the search for peace on the terms agreed to in October. Nixon reiterated the assurances Kissinger had given Thieu in Saigon regarding the NCNRC and the deletion of the reference to "three" Indochinese states. Thieu's speeches and other public statements were jeopardizing the peace process, Nixon told Thieu, urging him to refrain from further public criticism of the agreement or the negotiations and imploring him to maintain the unity that had always characterized relations between Washington and Saigon. "Disunity," Nixon said, "will strip me of the ability to maintain the essential base of support which your Government and your people must have in the days ahead, and which I am determined to provide." Only cooperation would enable him to secure "the amendments which we are certain to obtain."[7] This was the first of several letters Nixon sent Thieu after Kissinger's failed talks in Saigon. The war could not drag on much longer, and he and Thieu would have to sign a peace agreement with Hanoi and the PRG. He had spent four years getting a decent settlement, and it was time to complete the effort. Despite Saigon's difficulties with the settlement, Nixon would not spend his second term preoccupied with Vietnam. He had to end the involvement, and to do that he had to have Thieu's signature on the negotiated settlement. "Peace with honor" required some semblance of South Vietnamese approval. To make the extrication as painless as possible, Nixon was determined to get Thieu's acquiescence before he signed an agreement.

Neither pleas nor assurances moved Thieu, who adamantly opposed any compromise with Hanoi. The October agreement might appeal to Washington, but it was unacceptable to Saigon. Excluded from the private negotiations, Thieu felt no obligation to endorse the results. In fact, he considered the agreement an affront to his credibility. Accepting it would give credence to Hanoi's claim that he was an American lackey. The North Vietnamese, Thieu later explained, "had always accused us of being America's puppet. Now Kissinger was treating us like one. There was no effort to treat us as an equal."[8] Thieu's rejection of the agreement attested to his stature as an independent leader. Whether the desire to manifest that position was the only reason for his rejection is unclear. Nationalism, anticommunism, and personal pique are equally plausible reasons. Whatever the reason, his independence was a problem for Washington. For Thieu, it was also a gamble. He had no assurance that the White House would not abandon Saigon to make its own deal with Hanoi. But the gamble worked, for the time being at least. Washington accepted Thieu's decision and rejected that option. Thieu's popularity in South Vietnam increased dramatically in late October.[9] In rural as well as urban areas, the ICSC reported, Thieu had the "strongest support ever."[10]

Under these circumstances, Nixon did not force the agreement on Saigon. Thieu had risked his partnership with Nixon, and unless Nixon was prepared to expose the one-sidedness of that partnership, he had little leverage over Thieu. Besides, the White House was not desperate enough to impose an agreement on the RVN at that time. National honor still resonated among Nixon and his advisers, and, as Haldeman put it, the commitment to South Vietnam involved the nation's honor. "They've relied on us," Haldeman reasoned.[11] Moreover, whether Nixon concluded the negotiations before or after the election made no difference by late October. It was obvious by then that that issue would have no serious bearing on the election, and Nixon had no incentive to risk the uncertainties of an open break with a longtime ally. "The President wanted a settlement," wrote Alexander Haig, "but not at any cost."[12]

On 4 November, Hanoi agreed to an American request to resume the private negotiations.[13] When he learned the talks would resume, Thieu convened his NSC to discuss the situation. Among those attending the 6 November meeting were Vice President Huong, Prime Minister Khiem, and General Vien. They discussed the draft agreement, the events of late October, and Nixon's manifest desire to conclude the negotiations as soon as possible. Thieu promised to insist on the amendments he pressed on Kissinger in October; but, he added resignedly, he expected to have to sign a cease-fire agreement in December. Thieu had inferred this timetable from Washington's publicly expressed desire to have American prisoners home before Christmas. To Thieu, this meant that Nixon would increase the pressure on Saigon and that he would have eventually to give in. Saigon police chief Nguyen Khac Binh, who may have been a CIA operative, reported this to the White House, where it kindled hopes that the end of the war was near. Washington knew that at last Thieu would bend, and sign.[14]

A few days later, Haig arrived in Saigon to negotiate a "game plan" for the upcoming round of private talks. He brought with him a letter in which Nixon used the firmest language yet to express his unhappiness with Thieu's response to the October agreement. Saigon had distorted the terms of the agreement; its attacks upon it had been "unfair and self-defeating," serving as they did to accentuate the rift between South Vietnam and the United States. The settlement "reflects major concessions by the other side, protects the independence of South Vietnam, and leaves the political future to the South Vietnamese people themselves." Nixon pledged to press Hanoi for a "de facto unilateral withdrawal of some North Vietnamese divisions," but he reminded Thieu that his only option was to accept the accords and with them Washington's continued support. "If you will give me continued trust," Nixon concluded, "together we shall succeed."[15]

The next day, Thieu told Haig he would insist on the clarifications and other changes he had pressed on Kissinger.[16] He justified this in a letter congratulating Nixon on his reelection and praising him for his support of the South Vietnamese people. But the core of the letter was insistent. Thieu pleaded with Nixon to make the removal of North Vietnamese forces a prerequisite for a cease-fire. "If a settlement allows North Viet Nam to maintain its forces in South Viet Nam," Thieu charged, "then our struggle and the sacrifices we made during so many years would have seemed purposeless. Our allies would then be portrayed as aggressors, the South Vietnamese troops would be placed in the position of mercenaries fighting for an erroneous cause, a cause which we do not even dare to spell out." It was unjust to accuse Thieu of distorting the peace agreement when all he did was call attention to an "important aspect" of it. To ensure the moral and psychological balance in the political struggle sure to follow a cease-fire in the South, Nixon must stand firm on this issue. On other matters, Thieu was less pressing but nonetheless insistent. He wanted the reference to "three Indochinese countries" changed to "the Indochinese States" and the ambiguity concerning the NCNRC removed to make it clear the body had no governing authority. Specifically, he wanted the term "*co cau chinh quyen*" (governmental structure) replaced with "*co cau hanh chinh dac tranh bau cu*" (administrative structure in charge of elections). This would delimit the council's function as organizing and supervising elections. Thieu also asked Nixon to delete the phrase "three *equal* segments" in the provision defining the composition of the NCNRC; to have the DMZ defined as a political boundary; to reconsider the membership of Poland and Hungary on the ICCS; to insist that the conference on international guarantees occur only after cease-fires were in effect in Laos and Cambodia; and to have Laos, Cambodia, and Japan invited to that conference. These changes, Thieu concluded, would permit an "honorable and fair" settlement of the war.[17]

The White House read this letter to mean that Thieu's chief, and perhaps only real, objection to the October agreement was the continued presence of North Vietnamese forces in the South after the cease-fire. The other objections could be worked out, but to ask the DRVN to withdraw its troops at this juncture might jeopardize the agreement itself. At one time in the negotiations Hanoi had been willing to discuss withdrawing its forces provided Washington linked the withdrawal to the release of political prisoners in the South. The GVN had rejected that quid pro quo as "illogical." If Hanoi wanted the release of those prisoners, Saigon had said, it must reciprocate by arranging the release of the South Vietnamese civilians "detained by the Communists throughout Indochina." As to the withdrawal of North Vietnamese forces from the South, that, the GVN insisted, had to be unconditional. Not long thereafter, Washington dropped the issue because of the intransigence on both sides and conceded that PAVN troops could remain in the South. The matter had therefore not been an issue in the October negotiations, and Thieu's objections put the White House in a difficult position. Thieu "will go along only if we at least explore the issue of North Vietnamese troops in the South," Haig cabled Kissinger concerning the issue. "He wanted a reference to timing and some means of verification. Like you, I am very uncertain that Hanoi will accept this. On the other hand . . . without Thieu's acquiescence, I'm not sure I know where we are. If he refuses to accept the cease-fire negotiated by us under conditions that are unacceptable to him, have we really settled anything?"[18]

Nixon did not ignore Thieu's objections, but neither did he accommodate them. He would pursue most of the requested changes "with the utmost firmness," he told Thieu, and keep Saigon informed on the progress of his effort. But Thieu would have to be flexible, especially on substantive matters, the most important of which was North Vietnamese forces in the South after the cease-fire. Tho and Kissinger had discussed that subject at length, and it was clear that the United States had nothing to offer that would entice Hanoi to withdraw the troops. Nixon proposed to deal with the problem by seeking stronger language on the DMZ and adding provisions for the reduction of forces on both sides in the South on a one-to-one basis. Nixon refused to promise that Cambodia and Laos would participate in the IGC. He had no objection to their presence at the conference as observers, but the matter of their participation required the cooperation of Hanoi, and to raise the issue now would complicate the negotiations and delay the cease-fire. Regarding Japan's participation, Nixon asked Kissinger to raise the matter in Paris, but he gave no assurance on it because Hanoi had always resisted Japanese involvement in the peace process and Japan's participation might be conditional upon India's participation. On the composition of the ICCS, Nixon rejected Thieu's objection to Poland and Hungary. "What we both must recognize," he said in a revealing statement, "is that the supervisory mechanism in itself is in no measure as important as our own firm determination to see to it that the agreement works and our vigilance with respect to the prospect of its violation." Nixon remarked in closing that he would not be able to secure everything Thieu wanted. He therefore urged Thieu to be patient and yielding. "You have my absolute assurance," he added, "that if Hanoi fails to abide by the terms of this agreement it is my intention to take swift and severe retaliatory action." If Thieu continued to reject the agreement, Nixon would have to consider "other alternatives."[19]

On 14 November, Saigon raised four new objections to the agreement. One of these concerned the language on civilian prisoners and was a special problem for Kissinger. Saigon wanted to remove the requirement that the two sides resolve the issue within three months after the cease-fire.[20] On 18 November, Nixon wrote Thieu again expressing his growing impatience with this continuing barrage of proposed changes to the agreement. Reiterating his determination to reach a settlement that was as satisfactory as possible, he exhorted Thieu to stop demanding additional revisions and drop his demand for the withdrawal of North Vietnamese forces. "The express references to North Vietnamese troops in the South have the disadvantage of legitimizing any forces that may remain," Nixon pointed out impatiently, and "are clearly unobtainable." In addition, he rejected Thieu's proposal to alter the composition of the ICCS and said with respect to other proposed changes, "I am not prepared to scuttle the agreement or to go along with an accumulation of proposals which will have that practical consequence."[21]

As this tilting continued, Washington studied the merits of a bilateral agreement with Hanoi. John Negroponte, a member of Kissinger's staff, drafted a copy of such an agreement, which he gave to Kissinger on 15 November. Its basic provisions were similar to those in the October agreement, though it included nothing on the military or political situation in the South except a series of innocuous statements urging the Vietnamese parties to cease fire, release their prisoners, seek reconciliation, and establish a process to create a new and mutually satisfactory government. Unless the Vietnamese parties decided otherwise through negotiations, there would be no international supervision after the cease-fire Negroponte envisioned; though in Cambodia and Laos control commissions like those created in 1954 and 1962 would have that role.[22]

The new round of private negotiations began on 20 November. Tho read a five-page statement denouncing Washington for the failure of the October agreement. "We have been deceived by the French, the Japanese, and the Americans," said Tho at one point, "but the deception has never been so flagrant as this time." Kissinger tried to ease the tension by noting his own contribution to Vietnamese reunification—those in the South and the North now agreed with each other in hating him. Tho was unimpressed. Kissinger assured Tho that Washington still wanted a settlement and was prepared to "work within the framework" of the October agreement to that end. Having said that, he submitted a list of sixty-nine modifications as "our side's" new position on that agreement, trying to obscure the fact that the proposed changes originated in Saigon. In fact, only two days before Kissinger submitted the list to Tho, Ellsworth Bunker had received it from Thieu's NSC.[23] Its origins showed. It included objections to almost every major provision of the agreement, its evident purpose being "to impress on Nixon that Kissinger had been careless, duped, or had given in to the North Vietnamese."[24] None of this fooled the North Vietnamese, whose negotiators complained at once that the proposed changes "were aimed at increasing the political and legal strength of the puppet Saigon regime and undermined the prestige of the revolution in the South."[25] Even Kissinger thought what he was asking was unreasonable. The proposed modifications, he later wrote, "went so far beyond all that we had envisaged in both public and private negotiations that it undoubtedly strengthened the already firm position of Hanoi to stick to its positions and to wait until we were in a stranglehold by the deadline fixed by Congress."[26]

Incensed by Kissinger's move, Tho responded the next day by withdrawing concessions his side had already made. He renewed the demand that Thieu resign following the cease-fire and asked for an accelerated withdrawal of American forces. He insisted that the PRG be named throughout the agreement and the naming be in the context of the territory it controlled in South Vietnam. As to Saigon's demand that PAVN forces be withdrawn from the South, Tho reiterated that these troops were volunteers for the NLF and the PRG and Hanoi lacked jurisdiction over them. Kissinger had accepted that argument in agreeing to the October draft, and Tho refused to reopen the issue. In this atmosphere, the two sides could do little more than haggle.[27]

On 22 November, the negotiators met again, this time for six hours. At the insistence of the PRG, Tho retracted the October agreement on civilian prisoners and demanded that all political prisoners in the South be freed in lockstep with the POWs and the withdrawal of foreign troops. Though Hanoi initially objected to the retraction because it could seriously compromise the negotiations, PRG officials were adamant.[28] In return for concessions on this issue and minor changes in the political chapter, Tho told Kissinger that Hanoi would move some PAVN units in northern South Vietnam across the DMZ and end the war in Laos sooner than earlier agreed. Hanoi would specify the number of troops to be removed from the South after Washington agreed to concessions on the political prisoners and several minor issues. Since written commitments on such sensitive matters could be compromising, Hanoi would agree to these arrangements only in verbal understandings not included in a formal agreement. Kissinger rejected that. The release of American prisoners was to be linked to no other issue, including the fate of political prisoners in South Vietnam. With respect to the other changes Saigon wanted, Tho agreed to some modifications in the language concerning the DMZ but refused to discuss substantive political changes, including Kissinger's request that American civilian advisers be allowed to remain in South Vietnam following the cease-fire. Kissinger wanted the advisers to remain because the administration believed RVN military forces would be unable to operate sophisticated American equipment without them. Tho rejected the proposal, demanding that all civilians doing military work be withdrawn with military forces. Those doing "economic work," however, could remain.[29]

Kissinger and Tho spent most of the next meeting, on 23 November, discussing Cambodia, Laos, and the status of the DMZ. Kissinger pressed for simultaneous cease-fires in Cambodia, Laos, and Vietnam. Continued war in the other countries, he said, might force Washington to bomb Vietnamese border areas, which could renew the war in Vietnam. The closer the cease-fires elsewhere were to the one in Vietnam, the better the chance for a lasting peace. Regarding the DMZ, Kissinger proposed to add to the October draft a statement that "North and South Vietnam will respect the DMZ and each other's territory as provided for in Article 24 of the 1954 Geneva Agreement." Tho proposed instead, "Pending the unification of Vietnam, South and North Vietnam will respect the DMZ on either side of the provisional demarcation line." Kissinger accepted that. He then brought up the changes Thieu wanted concerning the NCNRC. At that, Tho pounded his fist on the table. He was willing to modify some aspects of the October text, he exclaimed, but there was a limit to what the VWP politburo would tolerate. The "words we have proposed cannot be changed," he told Kissinger, "three components, councils at various levels, the name of the Council. We'll make no concessions on these points."[30]

On the way to the next session, Haig and Kissinger accosted Tho outside the negotiating venue to warn him of the "grave dangers" Hanoi risked if the talks collapsed. To make sure Tho understood what he meant, Kissinger read him a message from Nixon. Meant to force movement in the Paris talks, the message contained the bluntest language Nixon had ever used concerning the negotiations. Addressed to Kissinger, the cable is worth quoting at length:

> The President is very disappointed in the lack of progress in the negotiations to date. Under the circumstances, unless the other side shows the same willingness to be reasonable that we are showing, I am directing you to discontinue the talks and we shall then have

to resume military activity until the other side is ready to negotiate. They must be disabused of the idea they seem to have that
we have no other choice but to settle on their terms. You should in-
form them directly without equivocation that we do have another
choice and if they were surprised the President would take the
strong action he did prior to the Moscow summit and prior to the
election, they will find now, with the election behind us, he will
take whatever action he considers necessary to protect the United
States' interests.[31]

When the meeting began, Kissinger said that it was essential that the
settlement he obtained show "convincingly" that Washington had tried
to effect the changes Saigon wanted in the October text. Tho again rejected Kissinger's efforts to do that, and the session adjourned after an
hour and a half. However, Kissinger thought the tone of Tho's rejection
was sober and conciliatory; and he cabled Nixon that his note had been
"invaluable." According to Kissinger, Tho had drawn "heavily upon
communist jargon about oppressed people's reacting strongly to threats,
but the manner in which he outlined his position clearly indicated that
the message got through."[32] Another meeting, on 25 November, was
equally unproductive, and at the end of it, Kissinger proposed and Tho
accepted a ten-day recess in the talks.[33]

In Washington, the six days Kissinger, Haig, and Sullivan had just
spent in Paris were torturous. There had been some improvement in the
language of the draft agreement on the DMZ, on Laos and Cambodia,
and in the preamble; and Hanoi had agreed to compress the time for a
cease-fire in Laos and to commit "all countries" to respect the sovereignty and integrity of Vietnam, wording that had the advantage of not
singling out the United States. Despite its curt public rhetoric, Hanoi was,
the White House believed, more conciliatory than Saigon. Notwithstanding its public rejection of further negotiations in October, Hanoi had
negotiated seriously in November. Though the achievements in the latest
negotiations were technical and minor, the VWP politburo had shown
continued willingness to reach a settlement, which could not be said of
the GVN. Haldeman described Hanoi as "tough, but not unmanageable."[34] Still, major differences remained, and the North Vietnamese
negotiators were increasingly unyielding. They refused to concede anything in the political chapter and persisted demanding that civilian advisers in the South withdraw with military forces and that political prisoners in the South be released simultaneously. They were willing to
move the cease-fire in Laos closer to that in Vietnam and to withdraw a

contingent of PAVN forces from the South; but the price they asked for those concessions was too high to pay. For Saigon's sake, the White House had to have changes in the political chapter and the right to leave civilian advisers in the South after the withdrawal; and for its own sake, it had to keep the return of American prisoners separate from the fate of political prisoners in the South. Kissinger, in fact, wanted to leave the fate of political prisoners to Thieu to use to bargain for the removal of North Vietnamese forces from the South.[35]

The inflexibility of Thieu and the GVN was especially distressing to Kissinger, whose task it was to maneuver between the two Vietnamese sides without sacrificing Washington's interests. On 23 November, he wrote Bunker from Paris that a settlement satisfactory to everyone might be impossible. "The real tragedy," he wrote, "is that Thieu's intransigence in October may well have lost us a unique opportunity to arrive at a settlement." Kissinger's contempt for Saigon was growing, and increasingly evident. "We find ourselves," he told Bunker, "held in suspension between two fanatical forces who do not appear to be able to bring themselves to the minimum essential concessions that are necessary."[36] It was Thieu who now prevented an agreement, and thus "peace with honor." He had become, in Kissinger's thinking, no better than the North Vietnamese. Thieu's stubbornness, however, reflected his dedication to the preservation of the South Vietnamese state; he genuinely—and rightfully—believed that the October agreement threatened the future of the RVN. American withdrawal under the terms of that agreement would enable North Vietnam to press harder for the unification of Vietnam by force. The failure of Kissinger to recognize that made him as contemptible to Thieu as Thieu had become to Kissinger.[37]

During November, therefore, the White House found itself pitted against Saigon as well as Hanoi. Taxing as that was, the administration saw no reason to panic; negotiating peace had the support of the American public and Congress. But by the end of the month, administration support in Congress was eroding as the negotiations dragged on without evident progress. On 24 November, a check by the White House of its leading supporters in the Senate found them willing to cut off military and other assistance to Saigon if Thieu continued to block an agreement. Nixon took this finding seriously, estimating that Congress could take such action by 1 February 1973. "The fat is in the fire," he wrote Kissinger of this prospect; "it is time to fish or cut bait."[38] Equally disturbing to Nixon was the fact that some members of his administration were reaching the same conclusion as the senators. Secretary of Defense Melvin Laird, JCS chairman Thomas Moorer, and Deputy Secretary of Defense Kenneth Rush were among those now urging Nixon to reach an agreement with or without Saigon's acquiescence. In light of congressional opinion, they thought, the White House had no other choice. "They just will not understand your reluctance to approve an agreement for the end of the war," Laird told Nixon of Congress and the American people, "when that agreement is so much better than your own May 8 announcement." Laird and Moorer were confident Vietnamization had been successful and that RVN troops could defend themselves and the South. If Hanoi deceived the United States by violating an agreement it signed, Washington had ways of dealing with that.[39]

By late November, the White House had concluded that it must have a settlement or Congress would end aid to Saigon and let the war run its course without further American involvement. To avert that, Nixon estimated that he had to have an agreement signed by 8 December to have things finalized before Congress reconvened in January.[40] Consequently, Nixon stepped up pressure on Thieu as well as Hanoi. "You must tell Thieu that I feel we have now reached the crossroads. Either he trusts me and signs what I have determined is the best agreement we can get or we have to go it alone and end our own involvement in the war on the best terms we can get," he instructed Kissinger in late November. "I do not give him this very tough option by personal desire, but because of the political reality in the United States it is not possible for me, even with the massive mandate I personally received in the election, to get the support from a hostile Congress to continue the war when the North Vietnamese on October 8 offered an agreement which was far better than both the House and the Senate by resolution and directive to the President during this last session indicated they thought we ought to accept."[41]

Nixon had finally concluded that once he had a palatable agreement, Thieu and the RVN would have to accept it or fend for themselves. But Thieu was not easily intimidated. He, too, had hopes and principles and ideas of honor, though he had come to recognize that he needed Nixon more than Nixon needed him. He and his government would have to mute their criticism of the agreement and think in terms of compromise. Kissinger had pressed these points on Nguyen Phu Duc, a Thieu adviser on foreign affairs, and on the rest of the South Vietnamese delegation in Paris. "Imagine the attitude of a Midwesterner who reads every day," he told Duc of press reports from Saigon, that South Vietnamese leaders are accusing the United States of "betrayal" and are saying of Nixon's stance in the negotiations, "We think we are watching a political suicide." What impressed Hanoi, Kissinger continued, was not signed agreements whatever their terms but "whether the B-52s may come again." If Washington and Saigon "convince" Hanoi of their unity of purpose on matters related to peace and of Washington's determination to not let Saigon down, Kissinger added, "the agreement will be kept."[42]

As he increased the pressure on Saigon, Nixon prepared to deal with Hanoi. To "bring the enemy to his knees" and break the deadlock, he instructed the navy to prepare for expanded bombing of Hanoi and Haiphong. The result was a plan to bomb every target of strategic value with the exception of the dikes, which remained off-limits.[43] Nixon also set in motion plans to help the RVN cope with the dwindling revenues and reduced economic activity that resulted from the reduction of American personnel. Toward the latter end, Defense Secretary Laird restructured the Overseas Private Investment Corporation (OPIC), which Washington had set up in the mid-1960s to "enhance the effectiveness of American private capital in friendly developing countries." The agency encouraged private investment in the RVN through incentives, including direct loans, preinvestment services, currency convertibility, and insurance against losses due to war or expropriation. In South Vietnam, the aim was to overcome the shortage of foreign capital and the absence of a solid economic infrastructure.[44] But the effort there was too little and too late. The OPIC never generated levels of investment sufficient to sustain economic growth after the Americans left; and the RVN found itself in a precarious position as it faced the prospects of a cease-fire and the withdrawal of allied troops.[45]

At the conclusion of the November negotiations, Tho and Thuy told Hanoi that the alterations Kissinger was then proposing were unacceptable because they changed the substance of the October agreement. Their assessment was significant for its tone as well as its substance. "The United States changed the content of the Agreement and reversed all important issues, seeking to renegotiate. Each chapter was substantively amended, as well as each protocol. The absurd demands of the Americans," the assessment continued, "concern the withdrawal of northern forces, the reduction and demobilization of soldiers, the elimination of each side's established zones of control in the South after the cease-fire, the administration in South Vietnam (elimination of the three-component [NCNRC] and elimination of its lower ranks), the demilitarized zone, international supervision and control, and the problem of Laos and Cambodia." Cumulatively, the proposed changes "undermine the recognized, fundamental principle that in the South there are two administrations, two armies, two zones [of control], and three political forces." Clearly, Tho and Thuy concluded, the United States "refuses to end its military involvement in the South of Vietnam" and preferred to continue the war rather than settle it. For strategic reasons and the importance attached to leaving South Vietnam with "honor," Washington was seemingly intent on forcing further concessions before agreeing to peace. The best the DRVN could do was "wait out" the White House. That meant intractability at the bargaining table while Congress and public opinion forced Nixon to end the war.[46]

The VWP politburo accepted the essence of this assessment. It believed, however, that the DRVN should continue to press for settlement but only on terms already agreed to. "We should seek to direct the Americans to refrain from changing the Agreement," Hanoi advised Tho and Thuy. "At the same time," it continued, the DRVN should "be prepared to retract some ancillary points advanced recently in order to compel the United States to respect the Agreement [we] had agreed to" and "reach a [new] settlement as soon as possible." By then, many in the VWP believed that the PRG's intransigence, specifically its demand that political prisoners be freed according to the same schedule as POWs, was unnecessarily prolonging the hostilities. "We had come very close to reaching an agreement when southerners sabotaged the entire plan," one official commented.[47] At the risk of alienating the PRG and NLF, the politburo now seriously considered dropping the demand for the release of political prisoners in the South. That would show flexibility without risk to substance and might push Washington to settle. But "we should not be hasty and feel pressured by the time factor," it added.[48]

Fearing the diplomatic situation would deteriorate in the short run, the DRVN readied for a resumption of the bombing on an unprecedented level of brutality. Nixon's recent message might be a bluff, but that was far from certain. On 27 November, the politburo instructed its air defense forces to prepare for B-52 bombings of Hanoi and Haiphong and five days later arranged for "the immediate evacuation of elders, children, and other individuals who were not indispensable to [Hanoi's] production and defense."[49] Following the resumption of bombing back in May, the city had evacuated 340,000 people, but progress in Paris and the bombing halt in October prompted many of them to return. Now, 70,000 people were again evacuated to the countryside, between 2 and 4 December. When the bombing resumed on 18 December, that number had surpassed 200,000 people.[50]

On 26 November, Nixon told Thieu that any further changes he wanted in the agreement would have to be requested through Nixon personally. He asked that Thieu's assistant, Nguyen Phu Duc, come to Washington to act as the medium through whom the two presidents could discuss the agreement and square their differences before Kissinger asked Tho about additional changes. If Duc delayed his arrival, Nixon would proceed without Thieu.[51] Duc arrived three days later, which Nixon considered a positive sign, and on 29 November Nixon met Duc and Ambassador Tran Kim Phuong. Duc handed Nixon a twenty-five-page letter from Thieu denouncing Hanoi for its intransigence and duplicity and the October agreement for its unsavory character and insisting on the withdrawal of North Vietnamese troops from South Vietnam before a cease-fire. Thieu offered to release 10,000 North Vietnamese military prisoners if that would hasten the return of American POWs.[52] This was Thieu's bid to ease Nixon's concerns over the POWs and to buy time before having to confront Nixon or sign an unacceptable settlement. If the POWs were home by Christmas, Thieu reasoned, Nixon might feel less compulsion to complete an agreement before Congress convened on 3 January. Nixon rejected that reasoning. Saigon would have to accommodate Nixon's concerns or go its own way. To Duc and Phuong, Nixon berated the GVN for delaying the agreement and emphasized the dangers of further delay because of pressure in Congress to end the war or cut off aid to Saigon. The cutoff could come as early as 13 January, he warned.[53]

Despite Nixon's two-and-a-half-hour effort, Duc refused to budge. Later, he told Kissinger, Haig, and Lord bluntly that if the chief concern of the United States was a deal on the POWs, it should stop fighting and talk to Hanoi. As far as Saigon was concerned, no circumstances, not even the prospect of unilateral American withdrawal and a cutoff of aid, would lead it to accept a settlement that permitted North Vietnamese troops to remain in the South. When Kissinger said that he could get the North Vietnamese troops just below the DMZ withdrawn if Thieu would release the political prisoners, Duc replied of the North Vietnamese, "It is not a question of *de facto* withdrawals if they can maintain the principle that they can stay." A bilateral agreement between Washington and Hanoi would not be binding on Saigon, Duc pointed out, and would have none of the weight in international law of a multilateral agreement covering the region. "Unilaterally one can say anything," he said, voicing his contempt for Hanoi's promises.[54] This defiance revealed the extent of the GVN's commitment to its own purposes and people. If the Saigon government had been a self-serving dictatorship concerned only with the interests of its leaders, it would have submitted to Washington's demands to ensure the continued flow of American aid. However, it dared Washington to make a separate deal at the risk of the GVN's chances of survival. Although in the end the GVN would renounce that position, the fact that it held firm for as long as it did constitutes further proof that leaders in Saigon were not mere puppets of the American government.

Such manifestations of independence on the part of the GVN had a significant bearing on the course of the negotiations between Hanoi and Washington, and they tormented Nixon.

Nixon's handwritten notes from his encounter with Duc reveal the extent to which he was perturbed at Saigon and at media reports that Kissinger and Haig had exceeded their authority in the negotiations. According to some of the American media, especially since late October, Nixon had detached himself from the Vietnam negotiations and Kissinger and Haig were directing the peace talks. Nixon felt, to the contrary, that he had kept a tight rein on the talks. "K[issinger] + Haig," he scribbled, "have not made one move I have not personally authorized."[55] He was sending Kissinger back to Paris with precise instructions to "bargain harsh." "I have directed," Nixon wrote with Duc's comments and the GVN stance in mind, "that agreement be reached at this [next] meeting." Nixon's situation vis-à-vis Congress dictated that directive. Thieu would survive if he agreed; if he did not, Congress would cut off aid. "My hands [are] tied," he mused; "all will be lost" if Thieu resists. He had to settle. "I have ordered it. I will not change." All Nixon needed now was cooperation from Hanoi.[56]

Before seeing Duc the next morning, Nixon met with Kissinger, Haig, Laird, Kenneth Rush, and the military chiefs of staff. Nixon called the meeting to convey to the military his convictions that the peace agreement was sound, that he would accept it with or without Thieu's assent, and that he would react massively to Hanoi's violations of it.[57] General William Westmoreland had recently told him that a decent peace agreement must include the withdrawal of all North Vietnamese forces from the South and an accommodation of Saigon's political concerns. But the fact was, Nixon said, that the American people did not support those elements. "The U.S. has stayed one step ahead of the sheriff, just missing fund cutoffs," he said of the situation in Congress. Hanoi and the PRG had agreed to the demands he had made on 8 May for a cease-fire, release of the POWs, assistance in accounting for MIAs, and the right of the South Vietnamese people to determine their own future without interference from a government dominated by Communists. "If the American people knew all the details of what has been offered," Nixon confided, "they would never continue to support a prolongation of the war." Kissinger then made a lengthy presentation on the substantive features of the agreement. Concerning the 38,000 political prisoners in South Vietnam, he explained that the October accords provided that their fate be negotiated by the GVN and the PRG, a provision Hanoi had subsequently rejected in favor of a linkage between the release of those prisoners and the American POWs. The significance of the issue, Kissinger explained, derived from the fact that the political prisoners were the only asset Saigon had in negotiating the withdrawal of North Vietnamese troops from the South. Kissinger was confident he could get the original provision restored.[58]

Nixon, Kissinger, and Haig then met Duc and Phuong. After Kissinger summarized Nixon's conversation with the military leaders, Duc stated bluntly, "If North Vietnam in the next round of negotiations remained adamant, then President Thieu would prefer that the United States explore a bilateral termination of its participation in the conflict directly with Hanoi and leave Saigon to continue the struggle." Thieu, Duc said, had told him, in effect, "It would be preferable to die now than to die bit by bit." Duc acknowledged that that course of action would be detrimental to Saigon, but it was better than surrender to Hanoi. Nixon understood this position and made it clear to Duc that once he concluded an agreement, Thieu would receive no more aid unless he signed it. If Thieu refused to sign but then reconsidered, discussions between him and Nixon must be within the framework of the agreement. Once he had an agreement, Nixon would be willing to meet Thieu at Midway, "not to discuss or negotiate the pros and cons of the agreement but . . . to give his personal assurances to President Thieu of continued aid and prompt enforcement."[59] The next day, Duc told Kissinger he "would greatly appreciate the opportunity to talk face to face with the North Vietnamese." Kissinger responded categorically, "At this stage it is impossible to change the course of events."[60]

The threat of a congressional cutoff of funds for South Vietnam, repeatedly stressed by Nixon and Kissinger to South Vietnamese officials, was real. However, Nixon and Kissinger exaggerated it. The administration was always more than "one step ahead of the sheriff" on this as on other matters, and the probability of a cutoff by 13 January was nil. Nixon himself had only recently estimated that a congressional decision to end assistance to Saigon would not come before 1 February. Why the deception? First, Nixon wanted out of Vietnam and was prepared to do whatever was necessary to get Thieu's endorsement of the agreement. Second, Nixon misrepresented the intentions of Congress to avoid having to misrepresent his own intentions. Since faith in Nixon was essential for Saigon to accept and thereafter respect the agreement, Nixon could not suggest that he had simply had enough and intended to end the war immediately. The more Nixon "demonized" Congress, the easier it was to present himself as the friend of South Vietnam and worthy of Thieu's trust. By January 1973, Nixon was so desperate for Thieu's endorsement that he increased the pressure on Thieu by having hawkish Senators Barry Goldwater and John Stennis issue statements that unless Thieu signed the agreement they would support legislation to end aid to Saigon.[61] The politics of deception thus served the Nixon administration well in the negotiations.

Kissinger's consultations with Hanoi and Saigon in November failed to reconcile the Vietnamese parties and produce an agreement. With time becoming increasingly pressing for the Nixon administration, the stage was set for the final showdown.

CHAPTER SIX

Showdown

Before Kissinger left Washington for the next round of negotiations, Nixon gave him precise instructions concerning the changes he wanted in the draft agreement. The most significant of these separated the release of political prisoners in South Vietnam from that of the American POWs. If he could resolve that and the differences over the NCNRC and Laos and Cambodia, Kissinger was to consider the agreement complete and Nixon would permit no more substantive changes. Once Kissinger and Tho had agreed on these matters, Kissinger was to set a timetable for signing the agreement, within ten days or two weeks. Since time was of the essence, Kissinger was to remain in close contact with Nixon during the negotiations. Thus, Nixon would be in a position to offer immediate responses to North Vietnamese proposals, expedite completion of an agreement, and preclude another round of talks. Though Nixon thought Thieu would never sign an agreement Kissinger negotiated, he instructed Kissinger to press Tho for the changes Thieu wanted. "It must be made absolutely clear to the North Vietnamese negotiators that the concerns of both sides must be met," he told Kissinger. "Just as they claim their principles, so do we have principles which we must and will respect. We have an obligation to continue presenting as forcefully as possible the concerns of our allies as well as our own views on what is required to make the agreement as satisfactory as possible. Accordingly, if the North Vietnamese are intransigent across the board, I will be prepared to authorize you to suspend the negotiations." Resolute as he now was to proceed without Thieu, Nixon still wanted to do everything he could to make the settlement as palatable as possible for him. The more Kissinger did to accommodate the GVN, the less Thieu might resist the final agreement.[1]

The twenty-second session of the secret/private talks opened on 4 December in Paris. The meeting was attended by Kissinger, Haig, Sullivan, Tho, Thuy, and interpreter Nguyen Dinh Phuong. Tho stated that the DRVN would not respond to threats; if Washington wanted an agreement it would have to offer serious proposals. Kissinger replied that it had always been Washington's "firm determination" to reach a settlement; its threats were responses to evidence of Hanoi's insincerity in negotiating. On substantive matters, Kissinger offered his "utmost proposal," a return to the October agreement, with six important changes. Washington wanted the preamble altered so the GVN would not have to sign a text that mentioned the PRG and wanted the Vietnamese-language text modified by substituting *co cau hanh chinh* (administrative structure) for *co cau chinh quyen* (governmental structure) in order to clarify the status of the NCNRC as a nongovernmental council. Kissinger also wanted to insert clauses specifying parallel reductions of all armed forces in the South on a one-for-one basis and the return of demobilized soldiers to their "native place" and stating that "the South and the North will respect the DMZ and each other's territory." The first of these clauses would have the effect of reducing PAVN forces in the South, and the second would deny North Vietnamese units the right to intervene in the South by specifying that the South was a separate political entity. In addition, Kissinger wanted the withdrawal of PAVN forces from the South linked to the release of political prisoners there and was willing to agree that the United States would use its influence in Saigon to secure the release of those prisoners if North Vietnam removed some of its troops from the South. Finally, Kissinger wanted the provisions concerning Laos and Cambodia modified to delete the phrase "the armed forces shall remain within their national borders" and replace it with "no use of forces against each other." Kissinger came away from the session believing the North Vietnamese would accept, or at least negotiate, these points.[2]

When the two delegations reconvened, Tho rejected all of Kissinger's points. The English text could describe the NCNRC as an "administrative structure" if Washington desired, he said, but the Vietnamese version had to read *co cau chinh quyen* or, perhaps, *co cau quyen luc* (literally, "structure of authority"). In either case, the name of the PRG had to appear in the preamble, since all parties to the agreement, especially Saigon, had to recognize the reality that there existed in South Vietnam two political entities and two military forces. Tho also wanted the political prisoners released within two months instead of three, which to Kissinger was a step backward. Tho then reiterated demands for the withdrawal of American civilian technicians and for certain lesser changes as well. This response angered Kissinger, who said that taken together, Tho's demands destroyed the substance of the agreement as it then stood. At that, Tho offered to go back to the October agreement. Kissinger promised to respond to that the next day, after consulting Nixon.[3]

"It is not impossible that Tho is playing chicken and is waiting for us to cave tomorrow," Kissinger wrote Nixon assessing this exchange. "But I do not think so. There is almost no doubt that Hanoi is now ready to break the negotiations and go another round. Their own needs for a settlement are now outweighed by the attractive vision they see of our having to choose between a complete split with Saigon or an unmanageable domestic situation." Kissinger dismissed the idea of going back to the October draft; to do so would amount to abandoning Thieu and admitting defeat. To keep the talks going, he thought, Nixon had only two options, neither of them promising. The first, which Tho was unlikely to accept and Thieu sure to reject, was to accept the recent improvements made in the language on Laos and Cambodia, the DMZ, and arms replacements and to ask Hanoi to drop its latest demands. The second, which made more sense but was sure to end the talks, was to accept the recent improvements, narrow American demands to changes in the language concerning the NCNRC and to the insertion of a statement that PAVN forces were in the South illegally, and ask Hanoi to drop its demands concerning political prisoners and civilian advisers in the South. Kissinger supported neither of these options and favored breaking off the talks immediately. Doing that would hurt Nixon in the short run but was necessary for "our national honor" and "principled policy." In a televised address announcing that bold move and making clear that the American involvement in Indochina was nearing its end, Nixon could rally the American people behind the escalated bombing that represented the only way left to make Hanoi see the futility of continued obstruction. A Harris poll in early December gave Nixon approval ratings of 64 percent generally, a record high for the year, and 59 percent for his handling of the Vietnam issue. Similarly, 63 percent thought Nixon was doing all he could to end the war, and a majority believed he should sign no agreement that failed to address the concerns of South Vietnam. The "silent majority" supporting his policies was larger than ever. These numbers suggested that Nixon could survive another round of talking and bombing, something Kissinger highlighted in his report. Nonetheless, Nixon rejected Kissinger's advice, instructing him instead to continue the talks and press Tho for changes in the draft agreement.[4]

Kissinger postponed the meeting scheduled the next day, 5 December, for further consultation with the White House. In a second cable, he asked Nixon again to suspend the talks. That would strengthen the justification for stepped-up bombing without further alienating Hanoi, which at this point seemed disinclined to negotiate responsibly. Since settlement was not imminent, the United States had to take the initiative, Kissinger thought, and its only options were intensified bombing and a public relations effort to influence American and world opinion. In the latter effort, the administration should explain that what it wanted was military disengagement in return for the POWs. To blunt the charge that the White House itself was stalling, Nixon should explain the efforts his administration had made to keep the peace talks alive and focused on an equitable settlement. "This seems to be what Thieu prefers," observed Kissinger, "and the extra time we have bought and will buy would allow for the GVN to survive on its own." But Washington should continue to consult Moscow and Beijing. "The only remaining thing to do" now, after a long string of disappointments, Kissinger wrote, "is to pursue a firm policy until we get our men back and can disengage with honor."[5] Given the precariousness of the situation, Nixon, not Kissinger, should be the first to speak publicly on the subject. Nixon's words carried more weight, and Nixon could appeal to ordinary Americans, as Kissinger could not. But, Kissinger told Nixon, "if it is your judgment that I should go first, I will of course be glad to attempt it." Nixon's advisers believed Nixon was overusing television and recommended that he reject Kissinger's suggestion, which he did.[6] "I realize that you think that if I go on television that I can rally the American people to support an indefinite continuation of the war simply for the purpose of getting our prisoners back," Nixon wrote Kissinger. "I would agree that this is a possibility at this time. But, that can wear very thin within a matter of weeks—particularly as the propaganda organs—not only in North Vietnam, but in this country, begin to hammer away at the fact that we had a much better deal in hand, and then because of Saigon's intransigence, we were unable to complete it." At this point, the White House had to "weigh the option of taking the heat for massively increased bombing for 8 months for the limited purpose of getting our prisoners back. This action carries with it the high possibility that South Vietnam, in that period, will collapse due to the fact that we may well have the Congress, despite all our efforts, cut off military and economic assistance to Saigon as the story unfolds that Saigon's intransigence was really the cause for the break up of the talks."[7] Under these circumstances, Nixon felt it worthwhile to try to salvage the talks. Accordingly, he instructed Kissinger to continue the negotiations, giving him permission to threaten Tho that if it became necessary the administration was prepared to go to Congress for funds to intensify the bombing and build up South Vietnam's military and economic capabilities. If Tho still refused to budge, Nixon would consider Kissinger's approach.[8]

The talks resumed on 6 December at a house in Gif-sur-Yvette.[9] After ritual sparring, Tho offered a symbolic redisposition of PAVN forces in the South in return for accelerated release of political prisoners. Kissinger countered by proposing that the two moves be simultaneous. Tho failed to respond. But in explaining his inflexibility on the issues involved, Tho, intentionally or not, let it slip that the DRVN was having as much difficulty with its allies as the United States was having with Saigon. The PRG had been hounding Hanoi ever since Hanoi accepted Indonesia as a member of the international supervisory commission; and the VWP politburo had had to deal with the indignation of its allies in Cambodia and Laos over its negotiations with Washington about matters involving those countries. Leaders of the Pathet Lao had told Hanoi to make no commitments on their behalf, since "Communists sometimes had acute contradictions" among themselves. "Each side has its own difficulties and now there are two alternatives," Tho observed. "One is that we return to the text of the agreement that was agreed [to] previously. Changes, if any, would only involve details and not substantive questions or principles. Alternatively, both sides will make changes. You propose yours and we ours. If [we do that], we shall have to discuss again a number of issues. Each side has its own principles and positions. The negotiations will drag [on] and be difficult. . . . Of these two alternatives, you choose any you want. We are prepared for that. The choice is yours." Kissinger found this constructive and said he would let Nixon know of the offer. But whatever Nixon's response, Kissinger advised, Tho should be prepared to remove *co cau chinh quyen* from the text, since doing so was for Nixon a "religious principle"; he would accept no wording that suggested a coalition government. Rather than responding to that directly, Tho suggested deleting "both sides will respect each other's territory" along the DMZ, since that alluded to the presence of PAVN troops in the South and suggested that the RVN was politically as legitimate as the DRVN. Before the meeting adjourned, the Americans said they would the next day present on a take-it-or-leave-it basis the minimum conditions necessary for a settlement. Tho indicated a willingness to discuss details but not changes to the substantive terms of the October settlement.[10]

In reporting this to the White House, Kissinger advised Nixon to insist on the changes achieved in the last week but subsequently rescinded. The American side had to have satisfaction on the NCNRC problem, three months for withdrawal and prisoner exchanges, and a preamble that omitted mentions of the PRG. It must also have understandings that North and South Vietnam would refrain from the use of force against each other and would work to make the ICCS functional by the time of the cease-fire; that all signatories would honor prisoner-exchange schedules; and that Hanoi would arrange for the cease-fire in Laos to become effective within fifteen days after the one in Vietnam. Kissinger thought the most difficult of these changes were those concerning the NCNRC, which Tho considered substantive, and omitting mention of the PRG in the agreement. Hanoi was "obviously under tremendous pressure from the Viet Cong on this issue," Kissinger said of the latter. But should he achieve the two most difficult changes, Kissinger would recommend that Nixon back down on the issue concerning civilian advisers in the South after the cease-fire and be satisfied with a sentence in the agreement to the effect that North and South Vietnam would negotiate the details of cross-DMZ movements.[11]

Getting Hanoi to accept these proposals would be difficult, Kissinger realized, but the chief problem was Saigon. "We can be certain," he wrote at this point, "that even this modified agreement will be rejected by Saigon, which has dug itself into the position of demanding what amounts to surrender by the other side." Since the outcome of the negotiations by this time depended on the Vietnamese parties, Kissinger observed, "We must face the reality that this agreement may lack the foundation of minimum trust that may be needed. Thus it could well break down." To get the Vietnamese parties to accept and respect a negotiated settlement, Kissinger warned, will require a "posture of constant readiness and willingness to intervene" to keep Saigon in line and Hanoi and the PRG from "nibbling at the edges."[12]

Nixon directed Kissinger to go ahead with the plan. "Your objective," he said, "should be to . . . put forward a proposal for an agreement that the North Vietnamese can and should be willing to accept, that we can and should live with and that Saigon can and should live with." If Kissinger succeeded with Hanoi but not Saigon, "we will have to go it alone." If he failed with Hanoi, he was to say he had to consult Washington and end this round of negotiations. He was not, however, to present the offer as final. Nixon was willing to extend the negotiations one more round, using the time to increase the bombing and mining. Collapse of the talks as a result of American proposals followed by an increase in the bombing, Nixon feared, "will exacerbate our relations with the Russians," lose the administration "the essential Congressional support for continued assistance to South Vietnam," and leave the country "with the bitter POW issue hanging over our heads." The uncertainties behind these concerns meant Nixon could not rely much longer on bombing. With luck, he might be able to continue the talks and manipulate public opinion to see Hanoi as the culpable party, thereby buying the time necessary to reach an acceptable settlement.[13]

Le Duc Tho began the session on 7 December by asking that the two sides go back to the October agreement. Kissinger said that was not feasible and presented as an alternative the minimum position he had discussed with Nixon. Tho in turn went over the changes he agreed to in November and subsequently withdrew. To Kissinger's astonishment, he now acceded to most of them, with modification. He agreed to the change on Laos and Cambodia, provided Kissinger accept language on the DMZ that neutralized the change Saigon insisted on. He also wanted to restore the original language on the independence of postwar Vietnam. He rejected the proposal to remove the reference to the PRG from the preamble but agreed to reduce the interval between the cease-fires in Vietnam and Laos. More significantly, he announced that the DRVN dropped its demand that the release of political prisoners in the South be part of the final agreement but wanted to reserve the right to revive that demand in the future.[14] Like Washington, Hanoi now seemed prepared to renounce the interests of its ally—and the prospects for a workable and lasting peace—to expedite a settlement.

These accommodations raised the hopes of American negotiators. Kissinger was confident he could narrow the remaining differences the next day. This placed the problem of Saigon in bolder relief. The White House still had no way of ensuring that the GVN would respect any settlement. "The agreement in October was workable," Kissinger wrote summarizing the situation. "The changes we have gotten since then have improved it. The problem we would face if we settle cannot be fixed by specific clauses. They have to do with the attitude of South and North Vietnam. With respect to the South, the agreement would be sound if the GVN accepted it enthusiastically and implemented it positively. It is another matter if they consider it an enormous defeat and are dragged into it." Concerning North Vietnam, "it is now obvious as the result of our additional exploration of Hanoi's intentions that they have not in any way abandoned their objectives or ambitions with respect to South Vietnam. What they have done is decide to modify their strategy by moving from conventional and main force warfare to a political and insurgency strategy within the framework of the draft agreement." According to Kissinger's assessment of the situation, "we can anticipate no lasting peace in the wake of a consummated agreement, but merely a shift in Hanoi's *modus operandi*. We will probably have little chance of maintaining the agreement without evident hair-trigger U.S. readiness, which may in fact be challenged at any time, to enforce its provisions."[15]

If he made no progress the next day, Kissinger advised, the White House would have two options: stalemate the talks and prolong the war, or accept the agreement as presently negotiated and retain the right to react to violations of it. Kissinger could justify a recess in the talks because Hanoi refused to withdraw its forces from the South or to agree to the principle of nonintervention in the future. If Nixon chose the second of Kissinger's options, he must be prepared to retaliate swiftly and decisively to DRVN violations of the agreement. Kissinger based these assessments not on the merits of the draft agreement but on the fact that the current balance of forces could not produce a better one. "No war in history," he reminded Nixon, "has been settled on better terms than the reality of forces on the battlefield could justify."[16] Nixon chose Kissinger's second option. Its drawbacks, he believed, were less than those of breaking off the talks and escalating the bombing. Getting Thieu's approval of the settlement in its present form would be a "monumental problem," but Nixon felt he had no choice. "There must be no turning back and no second guessing," he said. "The decision has been made."[17]

At the 8 December meeting, Kissinger reviewed the differences between the two sides. These included wording in the preamble and concerning the NCNRC, the timetable for demobilizing Vietnamese forces, the status of the DMZ, the withdrawal of civilian advisers from the South, the fate of political prisoners in the South, and the statement that "the United States shall respect" the rights of the people of Vietnam. Concerning the last point, Kissinger insisted that to accept this wording, which singled out the United States, was "tantamount to an American surrender." Tho countered that for him to agree to the wording Kissinger proposed—"the parties shall respect"—was absurd, for it implied that the Vietnamese people agreed to respect their own rights. Concerning the DMZ, Kissinger was prepared to delete "North and South Vietnam will not use force against each other," provided Tho accepted "the two parties will respect the DMZ." In exchange for suitable wording concerning the NCNRC, Kissinger agreed to delete language requiring demobilization of Vietnamese forces in ninety days in return for an understanding that the Vietnamese parties would solve the issue themselves within three months after the cease-fire. Lastly, Kissinger agreed to get Saigon to accept the reference to the PRG in the preamble if Tho accepted either the reference to "the four Indochinese states" (*bon quoc gia Dong Duong*) or Kissinger's wording on the DMZ in the text of the agreement.[18]

Tho responded that an agreement must name the parties that sign it. If Washington accepted his earlier proposal that only the United States and the DRVN sign the agreement, they could do so with the "concurrence," respectively, "of the Government of the Republic of Vietnam" and "of the Provisional Revolutionary Government of South Vietnam." On other matters, Tho was equally accommodating. He finally agreed to remove *co cau chinh quyen* (governmental structure) from the Vietnamese text and to refer to the NCNRC by name without reference to its nature or structure. "To set up an administrative structure called the National Council of National Reconciliation and Concord" would then read "to set up a National Council." He also agreed to delete "three" as the number of Indochinese countries (rejecting the term "states"), leaving the number unspecified, and to a withdrawal schedule of 120 rather than sixty days for the 1,300 military and 5,000 civilian advisers in the South. Kissinger countered with a two-year schedule, which Tho rejected. As to who was to respect the rights of the Vietnamese people, Tho proposed "the United States and other countries," which Kissinger accepted. Finally, on political prisoners, Tho agreed to drop once and for all the demand for their release, provided Kissinger consented to the wording on that issue in the October agreement and withdrew his demand for the demobilization of North Vietnamese soldiers in the South. Kissinger felt that on the whole, Tho's proposals were reasonable. He even confided to Tho that Nixon would probably welcome them and Hanoi and Washington could finalize the agreement. He cautioned, however, that Hanoi might have to go further to meet Nixon's concerns about the DMZ and civilian advisers in the South. The White House could concede no more on those issues, since "that's a question of national honor."[19]

Hanoi's response to these developments was positive. "We must strongly object to the American formula," the VWP politburo instructed Tho on the DMZ, "because it would create many complications" for the Revolution. However, Washington was obviously unwilling to assent to the wording Hanoi wanted. The politburo therefore proposed a rewording to the effect that the North and the South would respect the provisional demarcation and, pending reunification, negotiate "the modalities for movement across the provisional demarcation line." It was important to Hanoi that the agreement say nothing to imply the presence of PAVN soldiers in the South or that the DRVN had failed to respect the DMZ in the past. Concerning the issue of civilian advisers, the politburo instructed Tho to go back to the original arrangement and accept American assurances that their withdrawal would take place within two years after the cease-fire.[20]

At the next day's session there was more progress. Washington had accepted the new wording on respecting the rights of Vietnam, the reference to the PRG in the preamble of a text to be signed by the United States and the DRVN only, and the understanding on demobilization of Vietnamese troops in the South. Tho was glad to see Washington finally being sensible. He told Kissinger Hanoi accepted the continued presence of American civilian advisers in the South, provided the acceptance took the form of an understanding omitted from the written agreement. Tho then brought up the language noted above concerning the DMZ. Kissinger suggested that the wording note that North and South Vietnam will discuss modalities for "civil movement," which would bar civilian movement across the DMZ pending agreement between the two Vietnams and prohibit military movement. Washington would in turn agree to eliminate the statement that "North and South Vietnam will respect each other's territory." Despite Kissinger's insistence, Tho refused to budge. "I have been criticized very harshly" by Hanoi, Tho said, explaining his refusal. "For me to seek such a formula is unreasonable. Last week I exchanged [views] several times with Hanoi. But our government none-theless instructed me to stiffen the formula that I reached with you. The truth is that at the demarcation line, one side is the North, one side is the liberated areas of the [PRG]." The United States and the DRVN, he continued, "do not need to discuss the modalities for movement across the demarcation line, but as we try to settle with you, we propose that [earlier] formula. That is the truth."[21]

On the day of these exchanges, Nixon and Haig reviewed the situation in Southeast Asia and in Paris. Nixon complained that the administration was in a compromising position now because he had pushed too hard for a preelection cease-fire. Haig retorted that even if Hanoi gave in on the DMZ, the agreement would still be unacceptable to Thieu. Like Kissinger, Haig had reservations about the DRVN's willingness to settle during this round and reservations, too, about the sincerity of the other Vietnamese parties. Whatever Hanoi signed, Hanoi would violate when in its interests to do so. When that occurred, the United States had to be pre-pared to act, and as Nixon put it, that meant bombing not on a "tit-for-tat" basis but "all-out, regardless of potential civilian casualties." The two men also discussed the possibility of dispatching Vice President Spiro Agnew to Saigon to tell Thieu again that the United States would cut off support for his government if he rejected the settlement.[22] This was in response to information from Ambassador Bunker, who advised from Saigon that Thieu would remain a problem whatever Washington agreed to. "He has gotten himself into a situation," Bunker said of Thieu, "be-cause of the rigidity of the posture he has assumed and the widespread support for it he has whipped up, that will make it extremely difficult for him to survive should he now acquiesce."[23]

The negotiations took a new turn at the next session, on 11 December. With only the issue of the DMZ apparently left to resolve, Tho reneged on some of his recent concessions. He rejected the preamble and the signing arrangements Washington had accepted the previous day, asked that the PRG be a signatory to the accords, and demanded written as-surances that no civilian technicians would remain in South Vietnam after the military withdrawal, though a provision to the contrary could remain in the public text to avoid political embarrassment. Kissinger asked Tho about VWP politburo instructions concerning the DMZ, but Tho said he had no new ones. The two delegations then agreed to meet the next day. Kissinger concluded that Tho "wanted no agreement, at least on this round. The possibility that we might cave in had obviously occurred to him as well." Kissinger was disconcerted that his recent requests to Moscow and Beijing to help end the war were unanswered.[24]

After the session, Tho and Thuy advised Hanoi to accept the American proposal on the DMZ and on the other matters recently agreed upon. Now, they thought, was an opportune time to settle. Settling would end American involvement in Vietnam and the threat of more air strikes. In a message to Hanoi, Tho estimated that if the DRVN missed this opportunity and the United States refused to yield, the negotiations "may be suspended for some time, and the war will continue; although [the Americans] do not really have the capacity to prolong [the war]," he argued, "they might attack fiercely and intensely and after some time demand a resumption of the talks. If we do not convene [for negotiations], then the war will continue and the Americans will put the blame on us. If we reveal that the only substantive issue left [to negotiate] is that of the demilitarized zone, then we will have difficulty explaining; public opinion may infer that we do not respect the demilitarized zone [and] that we want to continue the infiltration of troops [into the South]."[25]

The best course, then, was to settle in this round. "We are not under pressure," Tho and Thuy deduced, "but we must recognize this opportune moment. Currently, the United States needs a settlement, [but] if we press too much, we will lose this opportunity." Thereafter, the Americans might intensify the war and "we may suffer losses in the North which would partially affect the situation in the South." The politburo was unyielding: Hanoi would reject the American phrasing on the DMZ, whatever the consequences. It would, however, accept alternative phrasing to the effect that North and South Vietnam would respect the "provisional" military demarcation line and begin negotiations aimed at normalizing relations. Tho could add to that phrasing a sentence saying, "Among the questions to be discussed, there are the modalities for movement across the provisional military demarcation line"; but the reference to "civil movement" in the American proposal was unacceptable.[26]

On 12 December, Tho proposed this wording, adding that there could be no reference to civilian movement. Kissinger interpreted the addendum to mean that it left open the possibility of military movement, and he rejected it. The status of the DMZ was thus the last substantive issue to be resolved; but the wording of the preamble and the method of signing the final agreement now emerged as major procedural problems. Tho reiterated his demand that the PRG be named in the preamble and a signatory to the final settlement. This led Kissinger to suspect that Tho wanted to antagonize Saigon, which was the last thing Washington needed at this juncture. Faced with an impasse, the two men moved on to the understandings and to a series of "protocols" Kissinger proposed on 20 November to elaborate on certain provisions of the agreement. Here, they made progress, confirming three understandings, and Tho gave Kissinger the DRVN versions of the protocols on implementing the cease-fire and on the responsibilities and operations of the ICCS. William Sullivan and Nguyen Co Thach, with their respective teams of experts, met later to verify the compatibility of the English and Vietnamese drafts of the agreement and to review the protocols.[27]

Tho had to return to Hanoi for consultations on 14 December, which meant that the next day's meeting would be the last of the current round. That evening, Kissinger told Nixon, "Hanoi has decided to play for time. . . . Their consistent pattern is to give us just enough each day to keep us going but nothing decisive which could conclude an agreement. On the other hand, they wish to insure that we have no solid pretext for taking tough actions."[28] Throughout this tedious progression, Nixon's instructions had remained the same: "consummate an agreement if one can be realistically achieved." Only if Tho took "an absolutely unacceptably negative stance" was Kissinger to recess, and even then not break off, the talks.[29] To get Thieu to acquiesce in the agreement, Nixon asked Kissinger what he thought of sending Vice President Agnew to Saigon. Kissinger's response was positive.[30]

The session of 13 December was the one "that finally exploded the negotiations." At nine o'clock in the morning the two teams of translators and technical experts gathered to compare texts. On the DRVN side, Luu Van Loi raised half a dozen questions about language and presented demands Tho had earlier dropped.[31] Among other points, Loi reintroduced the demands for the release of political prisoners (within two months of agreement) and references to the PRG. He also asked for the elimination of nine references to the GVN and retention of the verb *don doc* (to supervise) in the section defining the responsibilities of the NCNRC, which Kissinger had asked to remove because Thieu felt it gave the council jurisdiction over the GVN, and to which Tho had agreed. The Americans were furious at this but accepted some of the changes Loi wanted. Since Tho had to leave Paris the next day, he proposed suspending the negotiations, but the two sides agreed to continue them for the time being through diplomatic notes.[32]

After this session, Kissinger told Nixon, "Hanoi is almost disdainful of us because we have no effective leverage left, while Saigon in its short-sighted devices to sabotage the agreement knocks out from under us our few remaining props." Again, he thought Nixon had two options: to increase pressure on Hanoi by intensifying the bombing and on Thieu by threatening to withhold aid or to continue the present course by agreeing to another round of talks in January. The options boiled down to whether the White House would give Hanoi a last chance to repent or force it through the purgatory of another round of intensified air strikes.[33] The White House was divided over how to proceed. Haig, who distrusted Hanoi, wanted the air strikes resumed and intensified, as did others on Kissinger's staff, among them Jon Howe, John Holdridge, and Richard Kennedy. Nixon, on the other hand, hesitated. "The President . . . went through a long exposition of the fact of how difficult this [new bombing] would be," Haig wrote Kissinger. "The American people would not understand and the realities were that it was the U.S. and not Hanoi that was backing away from the agreement because we had, in effect, placed additional demands on them." Nixon added, Haig told Kissinger, "that the other culpable party was Saigon and not Hanoi and that we can expect a massive push from the left charging us with being tools of Thieu. When you combine this logic with an equally adamant refusal to attempt to rally the American people to do what is right, it is obvious we are faced with some very difficult obstacles here." If the talks led nowhere and he had to intensify the bombing, Nixon would go all the way on that option. He understood that he and his allies in Saigon shared the blame for dragging out the war. He thus rejected the idea of going on television to plead for support. He would instead keep quiet, do what he had to do when he had to do it, and take responsibility for what he did.[34]

When the teams of experts met on 14 December, the DRVN representatives submitted a Vietnamese-language text of the protocol on prisoners. The text incorporated several points Hanoi had failed to obtain in the negotiations. Among these were an exchange of the names of civilian detainees, release of all political prisoners within sixty days, and supervision of prisoner releases by the TPJMC, and thus by the NCNRC.[35] Colonel George Guay, who had succeeded Vernon Walters as American military attaché in Paris, called the Vietnamese text a "horror."[36] At a subsequent meeting of experts, on 16 December, the Vietnamese "stonewalled from beginning to end." That day, the talks broke indefinitely as the North Vietnamese refused to set a date for future negotiations.[37]

While the United States and the DRVN thus sparred and haggled, Thieu worked to sabotage their efforts. On 4 December, he discussed with his cabinet alternatives to the accords being negotiated in Paris. The resulting proposal called for a one-month truce through the holiday season; withdrawal of foreign troops from the South, including those from the North; termination of all bombing and mining; exchange of American and North Vietnamese POWs; negotiations between Saigon and Hanoi to "lay a basis for promoting serious and productive negotiations to advance toward a solution for ending the war and restoring the peace"; and UN-supervised elections in the South open to all parties, including the NLF, to establish a new government. To encourage the release of American prisoners, Saigon would unilaterally release 10,000 of the POWs it held. Provided the current balance of forces continued, the one-month truce would begin on 15 December. During the month, Thieu, Vice President Huong, and Prime Minister Khiem would resign from office in favor of a temporary "Government of Conciliation" headed by ARVN general Tran Van Don and composed of Buddhists and other non-Communist opposition elements. This interim government would conduct the elections and oversee the creation of the new permanent government based on the election results. Thieu thought this arrangement would enhance his credibility in the United States. The sooner he stepped down, the sooner Congress and the American people would absolve him of obstructing peace and release of the POWs. Thieu had apparently concluded that Nixon held him personally responsible for hindering the negotiations. This proposal, he hoped, would convince Nixon that he was wrong. In fact, there were two problems with Thieu's plan, either one of which would cause the PRG/NLF and Hanoi to reject it and refuse to participate in it. The first, as Tran Van Don himself pointed out, was that the arrangement ensured Thieu's election as head of the new government. The second, as RVN foreign minister Tran Van Lam revealed, was that under the Nixon doctrine, the RVN would still be eligible for American financial and material aid should Thieu's plan be implemented and the United States withdraw from Vietnam under its terms.[38]

Thieu made his plan public on 12 December while Kissinger and Tho were negotiating in Paris. In an address to the South Vietnamese National Assembly, he discussed the state of affairs in Indochina and offered his proposals for resolving them. Hanoi and the NLF, he argued, had arrogated to themselves the role of tyrants "who can talk with the United States and force the latter to sign an agreement while the RVN is only a puppet, bound to implement the agreement." The root of the problem was Hanoi's refusal to recognize the South as a sovereign political entity that would never accept an agreement injurious to the South Vietnamese people or to their partnership with Washington. "The United States must continue to provide economic and military assistance to the small and underdeveloped countries in the area so they may fight to defend their own independence and freedom," Thieu insisted. As leader of the free world, the United States could not abandon its responsibility to a small nation that had proven itself worthy of assistance. "The proof" of this worthiness "is that in only 3 years, almost one-half million American troops have withdrawn," Thieu said. "This is unprecedented in the history of war, because 28 years after peace was restored in Europe the United States continues to maintain more than 300,000 troops there, and 18 years after peace was restored in Korea scores of thousands of American troops are still there." In detailing his peace proposal, Thieu offered to release not 10,000 POWs but 1,015 disabled North Vietnamese prisoners plus an unspecified number of others on the first day of the truce. He concluded by calling for national unity and cooperation from all political and religious factions in meeting the challenges facing the country.[39]

Bunker told the White House that Thieu's proposal amounted to a repudiation of the settlement Kissinger was negotiating in Paris. In Bunker's view, the offers of a Christmas truce and release of prisoners were amateurish ploys designed to sway American and world opinion by showing an ostensible commitment to peace and to the return of the POWs.[40] Haig thought Thieu was positioning himself to reject any agreement Kissinger negotiated. "Thieu seems to have begun to realize both that we will sign the agreement and that he must continue to have U.S. support," Haig said. "However, he has not yet drawn the conclusion that he too should sign the agreement, much less approach the settlement with confidence. He may be considering pushing publicly for a more limited, essentially U.S.-DRV bilateral, arrangement adding up to release our prisoners for our withdrawals and a bombing halt with perhaps a limited cease-fire." That approach "would leave out the political matters entirely, reserving that for GVN-NLF negotiations." Thieu's purpose in doing this, Haig believed, was "to scuttle the present agreement while still looking reasonable to the American public by being willing to pay a price to help us get our prisoners back."[41] Signing an agreement would thus produce a confrontation with Thieu and "possibly his overthrow." The upcoming mission of Vice President Agnew, now set for 17 December, would either get Thieu's acceptance of the Paris settlement or strengthen Washington's position for a confrontation. "Certainly, after Thieu's speech," Haig wrote, "regard on our side for Thieu's sensitivities should no longer be a factor."[42]

The next day, Thieu rallied support for his proposal by meeting for three hours with 100 southern political leaders. He explained his rejection of the draft settlement, arguing that it failed to protect the interests of the South Vietnamese people. It would inevitably lead to a Communist takeover in the South, which was "too high a price to pay for the release of 600 US POWs." Thieu noted the possibility of the cutoff of American aid, which could come within two months if his government pursued its independent course. Whatever happened, he predicted, the RVN was bound to suffer. The dilemma was easy to comprehend but impossible to solve. If he signed the agreement, the domestic situation would deteriorate, making a Communist victory likely. If he refused to sign it, Washington would cut off aid, and a Communist takeover was equally likely. Thieu was not convinced that Washington would react to even flagrant violations of a peace settlement.[43]

In the end, the negotiations in Paris in early December produced no agreement. The two sides came within one substantive change of a settlement, but the VWP politburo was obviously not eager enough for agreement to make one more concession. At the risk of provoking another round of intensified bombing, it opted to defer the settlement against the advice of its negotiators. Just why the politburo made that decision is unclear. Possibly, the PRG reacted so strongly to the concession Hanoi made in December—particularly on the issue of civilian prisoners—that ultimately the politburo decided to rescind those concessions. One author, in fact, albeit equivocally, suggests that was the case.[44] A more convincing explanation seems to be that VWP leaders concluded that time was on their side, that they stood to lose little by deferring agreement until January and might gain a great deal. The new Congress might compel Nixon to end the war by refusing to fund it, in which case the White House would have to accept a settlement placing few restraints on the activities of revolutionary forces in the South. In that case, Hanoi would secure the total disengagement of foreign troops in return for a pledge to release the American POWs, an exchange Hanoi would gladly accept. Should the new Congress fail to force Nixon's hand, the politburo could agree to a settlement after one more round of talks. As to the possibility of renewed bombing, the leaders of the DRVN were prepared to run that risk. After all, success in the Anti-American Resistance and in the Revolution had rarely come easily. "The enemy may send 50,000 soldiers, 1 million soldiers or even more to strengthen its war of aggression in the South," Ho Chi Minh had said expressing this spirit back in 1966. "He can deploy thousands of aircraft and intensify its war of destruction against the North. But our people's resistance is fierce and resolute. The will of the enemy is weak and dwindling. The war may last another 5 years, 10 years, 20 years or perhaps longer. Hanoi, Haiphong, as well as other cities and bases may be destroyed. But the Vietnamese people are not afraid. Nothing is more precious than independence and freedom."[45] The Vietnamese had been sacrificing since 1945. The progress of the Revolution was all they had to show for the sacrifice. The DRVN wanted to preserve this progress, even at the risk of more suffering, more death, and more destruction.

After the December negotiations, the atmosphere in Washington was solemn. When Kissinger had left for Paris on 4 December, the White House had hopes of completing a settlement. A dozen days later, the hopes had collapsed. The prospects for peace and for the release of the prisoners before Christmas had evaporated. To make matters worse, Thieu was more recalcitrant than ever. On the morning of 14 December, Nixon met with Kissinger and Haig in the Oval Office to plan the next move. "We were agreed that if we did nothing we would wind up paralyzed," Kissinger said, "in effect prisoners of whatever maneuver Hanoi might choose to inflict on us." They could not return to the October draft; to do so would be to admit defeat, to collapse American resolve, to concede the inability to enforce whatever agreement they finally got.[46]

Its back to the wall, the administration had to take action, and the only option it felt it had was intensified bombing. Kissinger spoke in favor of an air campaign much like the previous ones. "We could overcome the dilemma," he thought, "only by an immediate showdown with both Hanoi and Saigon."[47] Haig, on the other hand, wanted a much more massive bombing campaign that included intense raids against targets above the twentieth parallel. Nixon sided with Haig and decided that within a few days he would step up the bombing and mining for about two weeks. To maximize the effects, he would authorize strikes against targets in the immediate vicinity of central Hanoi and Haiphong. The United States had heretofore spared the two cities but would now assault them with waves of B-52 bombers. The losses, Nixon knew, would be considerable, but he would continue the assault until Hanoi agreed to consider his minimum conditions for a cease-fire and release of the prisoners. This was "the most difficult decision I made during the entire war," Nixon later recalled, but also the most "clear cut."[48] Kissinger later explained that the VWP leadership committed a "cardinal error" when it cornered Nixon in December. "Nixon was never more dangerous than when he seemed to have run out of options. He was determined not to have his second term tormented like the first by our national trauma—especially when a settlement had seemed so near."[49]

The decision owed much to Alexander Haig. As Watergate began to overtake members of Nixon's inner circle, including Haldeman, and Kissinger spent more time abroad, Haig became Nixon's most trusted adviser on Vietnam.[50] More than anyone else, he convinced Nixon of the necessity of the massive bombing. A conservative, seasoned warrior, a disciple of General Curtis Lemay (who once suggested that the United States press for victory in Vietnam by bombing the North "back to the stone age") on the value of airpower, Haig had supported the negotiations; but as agreement proved elusive, he concluded that massive bombing was the only action that would bring Hanoi around. The failure of the

December talks affirmed that conclusion.[51] "If we were going to strike the enemy," he figured, "then we should strike hard at its heart and keep on striking until the enemy's will was broken. No matter what the level of bombing, the level of denunciation in Congress and the press would be the same, but the political consequences of a limited effort that did not succeed would be worse than those for an all-out effort that did." Regardless of the intensity of the bombing, "questions would be raised about the morality of this action. The reality was that any operation that sacrificed lives and did not do the job was morally indefensible."[52] The B-52 was the weapon of choice for this campaign. It was an all-weather aircraft, and the weather over the North would probably be bad throughout the operation. Also, it maximized the shock effect, for a single B-52 carried up to thirty tons of 500- and 750-pound bombs. Though used in Vietnam since 1965, B-52s had never in large numbers bombed targets proximate to the heavily defended urban core of Hanoi and Haiphong.[53]

On 15 December, the White House learned that Le Duc Tho had refused to answer a journalist's questions on the status of the talks. That kindled Kissinger's hopes, and he asked Nixon to delay the bombing twenty-four hours thinking the VWP politburo might make an encouraging move. Besides, to begin the attacks on 17 December as originally planned would send the wrong signal, he argued, since Tho would be in Beijing that day and Beijing as well as Tho might construe that as an affront. Nixon accepted Kissinger's argument, but as he waited, his patience ran out. Late on 15 December, he instructed George Guay, the American military attaché in Paris, to give Hanoi an ultimatum to accept the text of the settlement as it stood on 23 November, with some changes, and agree to resume the Paris talks after 26 December.[54] Unless Hanoi responded within seventy-two hours, it would bear the consequences of intensified bombing. When it did not respond, Nixon on 18 December dispatched the first wave of B-52s against Hanoi and Haiphong. The Vietnamese later claimed they received the ultimatum only after the first bombers were in the air.[55]

On 15 and 16 December, Nixon collected his thoughts before this final act of the American engagement in Vietnam. He was distraught at the inconclusiveness of the negotiations. He had gone to the limits of reasonableness; to go further to accommodate Hanoi would endanger Saigon. That would "bring peace now, but plant seeds for war later." He wanted "peace with honor," by which he meant "a peace that will last." He refused to accept an agreement that in the guise of bringing peace left conditions that encouraged war. "We have talked for 4 years . . . we have been patient and we insist on changes because after a long war we don't want a short peace," he mused. "We won't allow peace talks as cover for build up for more war." The bombing would be an "all out effort to resolve differences at the conference table" and end the hostilities. Contrary to popular belief, on the eve of the bombing, Nixon was more concerned about Hanoi than Saigon. That the bombing might impress on Thieu the strength of the American commitment and thus encourage him to sign the agreement is not even suggested in Nixon's personal notes. On the contrary, forcing the VWP politburo to flinch was his pressing imperative; a bilateral deal was better than no deal at all.[56]

On 16 December, Kissinger discussed the stalemated negotiations with the press. Without mentioning the upcoming bombing, he reviewed the history of the negotiations, explained administration behavior over the previous month, and reiterated Nixon's commitment to a negotiated settlement. He spoke of the difficulties in reconciling the Vietnamese and English versions of the agreement and the protocols. The two sides had come close to settling in late November and again in December, only to see agreement slip away. Thieu was not the obstacle. "If an agreement is reached that meets the stated conditions of the President, if an agreement is reached that we consider just," Kissinger said, "no other party will have a veto over our actions." "We want to move from hostility to normalization and from normalization to cooperation," he said to Hanoi, but the United States would never accept a settlement that amounted to a "disguised form of victory for the other side." "We will not be blackmailed into an agreement." "We will not be stampeded into an agreement and if I may say so, we will not be charmed into an agreement, until its conditions are right."[57]

On 17 December, American planes dropped additional mines to paralyze water transport in the North. Late in the afternoon of 18 December, the new bombing campaign, code-named Linebacker II, commenced. On that day, 129 B-52s, in three waves, hit military targets, factories, and the rail system around Hanoi.[58] Preceding this attack, smaller, faster, and more versatile fighter-bombers struck airfields, SAM sites, and other defensive installations along the flight path of the B-52s. Altogether, the attacks lasted five hours, during which 94 percent of the planes released their ordnance on assigned targets.[59] In Washington, Kissinger commended Nixon. He had selected the most efficacious course, that of "brutal unpredictability."[60]

The DRVN was not caught off guard by the attack itself but was taken aback by its magnitude. It had been preparing for strikes since late November. The Army Party Committee had predicted that the United States "may well move to rashly use B-52s to strike at targets in Hanoi and Haiphong"; and Truong Chinh had warned that "the intention of the enemy may well be to strike massively and forcefully." Since 4 December, defense units had been on continuous alert.⁶¹ When the bombers appeared, air defense units fired more than 200 missiles at them, shooting down three of the B-52s. Cruising at 30,000 feet, the big bombers were in the optimum effective range of the missiles.⁶² Considering the damage inflicted by the Americans on that day, however, that was a bitter victory.

The White House judged these losses acceptable and ordered that the bombing be continued. The morning after the first strikes, Nixon pressed upon JCS chairman Thomas Moorer the importance of the bombing. "This is your chance to use military power effectively to win this war," he told Moorer, "and if you don't, I'll consider you personally responsible."⁶³ In his diary that day, Nixon wrote, "I remember Churchill's admonition in his book on World War I, that one can have a policy of audacity or one of caution, but it is disastrous to try to follow a policy of audacity and of caution at the same time. It must be one or the other. We have now gone down the audacious line and we must continue until we get some sort of break."⁶⁴

The next day, Xuan Thuy responded publicly to the charges Kissinger made in his 16 December press conference and commented on the bombing. He emphasized the American refusal to adhere to the 20 October draft, including the insistence on substantive changes to that draft that violated the rights of the Vietnamese people and ignored "the realities—which have been previously recognized by the United States—that in South Vietnam there are two governments, two armies, three political forces." He warned of the dangers of a settlement that left Vietnam divided and denounced the Americans for insisting on substantive language changes after both sides had agreed on the Vietnamese version. Thuy's summary of the diplomatic situation reflected the tone as well as the substance of Hanoi's concerns and is worth quoting at length:

> The deliberate distortion by the U.S. side of facts related to the private meetings since 20 November, 1972, is aimed at deceiving U.S. and world public opinion, in an attempt to lay blame on the D.R.V.N. side and concealing the Vietnamization policy in South Viet Nam, using military force in order to force the Vietnamese people to accept the terms imposed by the United States. This scheme is evidenced by the massive introduction into South Viet Nam of armaments, war material and military personnel disguised as civilians since October 1972, the frenzied intensification of the aggressive war in the two zones of Viet Nam, in Laos and Cambodia, the U.S. condoning of the Saigon Administration's arrogant demands and

preparations for the sabotage of the Agreement even before its signing. What is called a "massive communist effort" to launch an attack throughout South Viet Nam before the cease-fire is nothing but a brazen fabrication to conceal the dark designs of the White House.[65]

Within hours, the B-52s returned. Like the first raids, those on 19 and 20 December were intense, and antiaircraft units again had some success. The SAMs hit no B-52s on the nineteenth, but on the following night 220 missiles shot down six of the bombers. That was enough to impress Washington; but the effort was costly to the DRVN.[66] Hanoi assumed the bombing would last only three days and thus directed antiaircraft forces to expend as many missiles as necessary to have an effect. The massive firings depleted inventories, though the downing of so many bombers added to Nixon's anxiety, partly because it increased the number of POWs and MIAs.[67] Meeting with Haldeman and Kissinger on the twentieth, Nixon alluded repeatedly to "the B-52 loss problem," observing that if the losses continued to average three aircraft a day, "it's going to be very tough to take."[68] But he did not consider halting the campaign. On the contrary, he said publicly that it would continue. "If the enemy detected any reticence in our actions, they would discount the whole exercise."[69]

As the bombing began, Haig arrived in Saigon. Because the situation was precarious, Nixon sent Haig instead of Vice President Agnew to consult with Thieu, since Haig was better informed about the Paris negotiations. When Haig met Thieu on 19 December, he brought with him a letter from Nixon, the crux of which was that Haig's mission was Nixon's "final effort to point out to you the necessity for joint action and to convey my irrevocable intention to proceed [to an agreement], preferably with your cooperation but, if necessary, alone." Nixon wanted Thieu to understand that Washington was on the verge of an agreement, that Hanoi's stalling was temporary, and that as soon as Hanoi met Nixon's minimum requirements, he would sign an agreement. "These actions are meant to convey to the enemy my determination to bring the conflict to a rapid end," Nixon said of the intensified bombing and mining, "as well as to show what I am prepared to do in case of violation of the agreement." At the same time, he warned Thieu, "I do not want you to be left, under any circumstances, with the mistaken impression that these actions signal a willingness or intent to continue U.S. military involvement if Hanoi meets the requirements for a settlement which I have set forth." Thieu's continued recalcitrance would be detrimental to the South's relations with the United States. "I am convinced that your refusal to join us would be an invitation to disaster—the loss of all that we together have fought for over the past decade. It would be inexcusable above all because we will have lost a just and honorable alternative." Haig thus carried with him Nixon's "absolutely final offer" to Thieu to cooperate. Haig was in Saigon not to negotiate but to communicate Washington's intention to reach an agreement immediately. "The time has come for us to present a united front in negotiating with our enemies," Nixon concluded, "and you must decide now whether you desire to continue to work together or whether you want me to seek a settlement with the enemy which serves U.S. interests alone."[70]

After Thieu finished reading the letter, Haig said, "Under no circumstance will President Nixon accept a veto from Saigon in regard to a peace agreement." Shocked by the bluntness of these warnings, Thieu remained silent for a moment and then asked a series of questions about North Vietnamese troop withdrawals from Laos and Cambodia as well as South Vietnam. Haig replied that bans in the agreement on infiltration and the demobilization principle made inevitable the demise of North Vietnamese units below the seventeenth parallel if Hanoi abided by the settlement. "It is obvious that there will be no peace as a result of this agreement," Thieu told Haig. "After the cease-fire, the enemy will spread out his troops, join the Viet Cong, and use kidnaping and murder with knives and bayonets." He added, "Given the realities of the situation, what I am being asked to sign is not a treaty for peace but a treaty for continued U.S. support." Haig nodded in agreement.[71]

The next day, the twentieth, Thieu confessed privately that he felt the weight of pressure to accept the settlement, especially with the bombing in progress. He thought he understood why Nixon wanted his assent; but assent was not Thieu's choice. He felt certain Nixon would never retaliate against the North for violating the accords because "the US would not risk having new POWs." Thieu could not understand why a nation as powerful as the United States was "paralyzed" by a few POWs and willing to sacrifice a nation of seventeen million people to get them released. That marked the "end of power," he thought. The agreement would result in a Communist government in South Vietnam within six months.[72]

Later on the twentieth, Thieu and Nha met with Haig and Bunker. Thieu, who showed up five hours after the meeting had been scheduled, gave Haig a letter to Nixon. In it, he acknowledged Nixon's ultimatum and attempted to "waffle" by urging Nixon to insist on the withdrawal of North Vietnamese troops from the South and to refuse to recognize the PRG as a legitimate governmental unit. "Thieu has again performed in identical fashion," a disappointed Haig reported to Kissinger, "after suggesting to both Bunker and myself yesterday that he would, in effect, go along in the pragmatic recognition that this was the only way to obtain continued U.S. assistance." Haig thought Nixon's options were now clear. He could either sign an unsatisfactory agreement or recognize the failure to reach an agreement and withdraw American forces in return for the release of the POWs. Pending the release, the bombing and mining could continue. Although it never eventuated, what Haig believed was Nixon's second option is significant since it suggests that in late December the Nixon administration entertained the possibility of unilaterally disengaging from Vietnam if the bombing was unsuccessful. This is remarkable; for the first time in the decade-old commitment to South Vietnam, an American administration considered admitting defeat and withdrawing without "honor." This is only one of the reasons the stakes were so high in the "Christmas bombing."[73]

After hearing what happened in Saigon—including the fact that Thieu had kept Haig waiting for five hours before their final meeting and then insisted that the withdrawal of North Vietnamese troops from the South was the price of his assent to an agreement—Nixon said to Haldeman, "Haig has now joined the club, he got kicked in the teeth by Thieu." Banter aside, Nixon's course of action was still unclear; he was still weighing his options. Thieu was unwilling to sign an agreement; the bombings might not achieve their purpose. Nixon decided to have Kissinger try to get a bilateral agreement after New Year's day, a task Kissinger did not relish. The problem was to find a way to do that without "sinking" South Vietnam. Hanoi would in all probability accept a separate settlement, but the price would be a cutoff of aid to Saigon. "If we go bilaterally," Nixon said, "there will be no cease-fire, but we would argue that South Vietnam is now in a position where they can stand on their own feet." Opposing a separate accord, Kissinger suggested that Thieu might be stalling to make a record for himself and intended to give in at the end. By the end of the meeting, Kissinger had convinced Nixon to forego the separate accord and to ask instead for a new round of talks to begin on 3 January, during which Washington would negotiate without regard to Thieu. "We would now treat Thieu with total silence," Haldeman later wrote, "not give him another chance." As gloomy as the prospects were, Nixon hoped "something may still happen."[74] On 22 December, Nixon asked Hanoi for a meeting on 3 January in Paris, offering to suspend the bombing north of the twentieth parallel on 31 December if Hanoi agreed and to halt it altogether during the session itself.[75]

To reduce the losses, Washington decided to deploy only thirty B-52s on 21 December. Most of the day's targets were in or around Hanoi and thus in well-defended areas. The SAMs struck four of the bombers.[76] Such losses created dissension among the flight crews. Many pilots believed the flight patterns increased their vulnerability. Large aircraft flying in close formation eased the task of SAM operators. "We had a formation approximately 70 miles long of one aircraft behind the other lumbering toward North Vietnam all using the same route, altitude and heading," one pilot said, summarizing the problem from the crew's standpoint. "If 36 aircraft turned at a certain point to a certain heading, it does not require much of an educated guess to decide where to aim at number 37."[77] The airmen's plea attracted public attention after one of them wrote Maryland senator Charles Mathias Jr. criticizing the air force and the flight patterns.[78] Nixon "raise[d] holy hell" because of the complaints as well as the losses and directed the Pentagon to rectify the problem at once. Beginning on 22 December, the planes flew at different times along different routes and the number of B-52 sorties was limited to thirty a day. At the same time, the air force sent fighter-bombers armed with sophisticated weapons to attack missile storage facilities and radar sites and otherwise reduce the danger from the SAMs. It also prohibited strikes in the immediate vicinity of Hanoi, the most heavily defended area, and ordered bomb-release intervals compressed.[79] As a result of these measures, no planes were lost on 22, 23, and 24 December. At six o'clock in the evening Hanoi time on the twenty-fourth, Nixon ordered a thirty-six-hour Christmas truce, hoping unsuccessfully that the VWP politburo would use the interval to signal a willingness to resume negotiations.[80]

On 26 December, the largest, most concentrated B-52 raid in history signaled a resumption of the bombing. On Nixon's personal order, 120 aircraft raided ten target complexes in Hanoi, Haiphong, and Thai Nguyen. Within one fifteen-minute period, the planes dropped 4,000 tons of bombs, leveling among other sites, accidentally or deliberately, Kham Thien Street in a densely populated area of Hanoi. The damage, extending eighteen blocks, included 215 people killed and 257 injured, 534 homes destroyed and 1,200 damaged, and hundreds of shops, cafés, restaurants, markets, schools, temples, and other structures damaged or destroyed.[81] The SAM-suppression measures limited American losses to two bombers, including one that crashed while attempting to land in Thailand.

That afternoon, Hanoi notified the White House of its willingness to resume the Paris talks. To impress upon Nixon that the bombing was not the reason for this decision, the VWP politburo told Nixon that halting the bombing was not a precondition for further talks. Hanoi proposed that the talks resume on 8 January to give Tho time to recover his health; at that time it hoped to "settle the remaining questions with the U.S. side."[82] Sensing the significance of this opening, Nixon worked personally with Kissinger on a reply, which he dispatched on the twenty-seventh. If the talks had to be postponed until 8 January, Nixon hoped the technical discussions could resume on 2 January, which was the day before the new Congress convened. Nixon also warned that substantive matters not specified in the agreement must not be raised in discussions of the wordings of the protocols. He would cease bombing above the twentieth parallel within thirty-six hours after the two sides publicly agreed on these arrangements.[83] Hanoi confirmed its acceptance of the arrangements on the following day.[84]

On the previous day, 27 December, sixty B-52s struck near Hanoi and the Chinese border, and though two of the bombers were lost, 120 additional sorties bombed in and around Hanoi on the twenty-eight and twenty-ninth with no loss of planes. At seventeen minutes before midnight on the twenty-ninth, the Americans dropped the last bomb of the Linebacker II campaign. By then, North Vietnam had depleted its SAM stockpiles and Hanoi's aerial defenses were exhausted. Aware of this, Nixon still halted the bombing above the twentieth parallel, although "light" bombing continued below that parallel. He told Hanoi that he would "make one final major effort to see whether a settlement within the October framework can be worked out."[85] He warned that Kissinger would spend no more than four days in Paris on this round and that "a repetition of the procedures followed in December could lead to a collapse of the talks" and a resumption of the bombing.[86] The next day, Nixon announced publicly that a new round of negotiations would begin on 8 January.[87]

By this time, Thieu knew an agreement was imminent and he would have to sign it. With that in mind, he moved to position himself and his party for the elections that an agreement would entail. On 27 December he decreed that to avoid dissolution, political parties must establish branches and enroll at least 5 percent of the registered voters in every city of South Vietnam and at least 25 percent of the voters in twenty-two of the forty-four provinces; offer candidates for every seat in every election for the National Assembly; and get at least 25 percent of the vote if they ran a candidate for the presidency.[88] Tran Van Huyen, leader of the Vietnamese Nationalist Party (Viet Nam Quoc Dan Dang), said of the decree that of the twenty-four parties in the South, only Thieu's recently formed Democratic Party could meet the criteria; and the decree would thus drive people "into the arms of the Communists."[89]

Between 18 and 29 December, 200 B-52s flew 729 sorties from Guam and Thailand and other aircraft flew 1,216 sorties.[90] Together, they dropped 20,370 tons of bombs, the vast majority of them in or around Hanoi, and severely battered North Vietnamese military capabilities. According to American assessments, the bombing damaged or destroyed 1,600 military complexes, 372 trucks and railway cars, 25 percent of the DRVN's petroleum stockpiles, 80 percent of its electrical power plants, and countless factories and other assets. There was also extensive damage to railways and airfields. Against this onslaught, North Vietnamese air defense units fired an estimated 884 SAMs, which left them with few of those vital weapons.[91] The cost to the United States was high: fifteen B-52s and eleven other aircraft were lost.[92] Of the downed B-52 crewmen, thirty-three were captured, fourteen killed, and fourteen missing.[93]

Hanoi publicly hailed the results as a great victory, "America's Dien Bien Phu of the skies."[94] In Vietnamese reckoning, Nixon ended the bombing because the United States could no longer take the losses. The American effort thus faltered and failed. Moreover, Washington hid the extent of its losses, which according to the PAVN included thirty-four B-52s and forty-seven other aircraft shot down.[95] According to Hanoi mayor Tran Duy Hung, the success against the B-52s was due to the fact that the downed pilots captured on the first night of the raids had in their possession technical data on the planes they were flying. "It was very precious documentation for us because these were the latest B-52 D's and B-52 G's with no less than 17 electronic jamming devices to fool our radar warning system and escape conventional missile guidance systems." This knowledge allegedly permitted technicians to neutralize the jamming systems, which improved the effectiveness of the missiles.[96]

In the United States, criticism of the Christmas bombing was widespread and intense. Congressman Daniel Flood of the House Defense Appropriations Committee denounced the Pentagon for its ineffectiveness, expressing his disbelief to JCS chairman Moorer that the military was "handcuffed by some little country called North Vietnam and completely knocked off balance," that "this little backward country, these gooks . . . are knocking down your B-52s like clay pigeons, with all the sophisticated hardware which was beyond our own ken, being run by 'gooks.'"[97] In a poll of senators during the bombing, *Congressional Quarterly* found forty-five opposed the bombing, nineteen supported it, and nine withheld their opinion.[98] "We cannot read about the heavy bombing without a deep and despairing sense that peace is not at hand," said Senator Edward Kennedy of Massachusetts. "Congress must and will act on the people's mandate for peace."[99] Former ambassador to Saigon Maxwell Taylor was more perplexed. "If we cannot expect to achieve a supervised cease-fire, general elections, a negotiated coalition or a prompt return of our prisoners in a finite time," he said, "it is hard to see how we can expect to attain our present objective of a negotiated peace assuring a fair deal for South Vietnam. May it not be time to reconsider the possibility and even desirability of terminating our American commitment without resort to a formal agreement involving Hanoi and the Vietcong?"[100]

The media were even more critical of Nixon and the bombing. Anthony Lewis of the *New York Times* accused Nixon of acting like "a maddened tyrant," and Lewis's colleague James Reston charged him with waging "war by tantrum."[101] The *Times* itself charged that the bombs falling on Hanoi "have dimmed the prospects not only for peace in Indochina but for the wider détente for which all mankind has prayed."[102] The *Washington Post* thought Nixon had "conducted a bombing policy . . . so ruthless and so difficult to fathom politically as to cause millions of Americans to cringe in shame and to wonder at their President's very sanity."[103] Columnist Joseph Kraft called the bombing "senseless terror which stains the good name of America."[104] "Over and over again Mr. Nixon has tried to bomb Hanoi into submission," added the *St. Louis Post Dispatch*. "It has not worked before and it will not work today."[105]

The reactions of other governments were equally hostile. Canada and Australia, two of Washington's close allies, were openly critical. "We found it very difficult to understand the reasons for that bombing," Canadian secretary of state for External Affairs Mitchell Sharp said publicly, "or the purpose which it was intended to serve. We deplore that action."[106] At the Vatican, Pope Paul, who rarely spoke on American activities in Indochina, condemned the "sudden resumption of harsh and massive war actions."[107] In China, the first anti-American rally in more than a year protested the bombings and the Foreign Ministry denounced them threateningly. "Should the American government not cease subverting the peace enjoyed by the people of Viet Nam," the ministry said in identical messages to Washington and Hanoi, "and pursue its campaign of aggression, the Chinese people are determined to take whatever action necessary to support the resistance against the Americans and ensure the complete victory of the people of Viet Nam."[108] It is no wonder that Kissinger remembered December as "the most painful and difficult period, especially since we had thought we were so close to peace."[109]

Though the physical destruction was massive, the bombing caused surprisingly few civilian casualties. Despite Hanoi's claims, there never was "an escalation of genocide to an all-time high."[110] Even if that had been Nixon's intent, it could not have occurred because Hanoi and Haiphong had been evacuated. The bombing had nothing in common with that of Hamburg, Dresden, or Tokyo during World War II, for instance.[111] Though the tonnage expended over the two Vietnamese cities approximated that in each of those earlier, infamous efforts, there was little or no deliberate bombing of residential areas. Most of the damage to residential areas was caused by errant bombs.[112] In early January 1973, the Central Committee of the VWP confirmed the deaths of 1,318 civilians in Hanoi and 305 in Haiphong and injuries to an additional 1,261 civilians from the bombing between 18 and 29 December.[113]

The December raids constituted a desperate attempt on the part of the Nixon administration to bring about a final breakthrough in the talks and end America's involvement in the war on honorable terms. As it turned out, the conduct and intensity of the campaign created impressions favorable to Washington in both Saigon and Hanoi. In the United States, however, the Christmas bombing exacerbated public and congressional disillusionment with the war. In the last days of 1972, signing an agreement thus became an end in itself for both Washington and Hanoi.

CHAPTER SEVEN

Final Round

JANUARY 1973

Before Kissinger flew back to Paris for the last round of talks, he and Nixon held a continuing series of discussions. From 2 January until Kissinger left Washington five days later, the two men met at least three hours each day, either alone or with other members of the administration, to review strategies and establish contingencies in the event of North Vietnamese intransigence. At Camp David on 6 January, Nixon suggested that at that point almost any settlement would be tolerable. "I put it to Henry quite directly," he wrote in his diary, "that even if we could go back to the October 8 agreement we should take it, having in mind the fact that there will be a lot of details that will have been ironed out so that we can claim some improvements over that agreement."[1] Kissinger resisted that stance, thinking it hurt Thieu's chances of survival, but Nixon's case was convincing under the circumstances, and he came to accept it. Kissinger later explained that he accepted Nixon's case partly because "I was sure it would not come to that."[2]

Nixon informed Thieu of his position. In a letter dated 5 January, he told Thieu the conditions under which he would settle. If the North Vietnamese met his concerns on the DMZ, the signing protocol, and the machinery to supervise the cease-fire, he said, "We will proceed to conclude the settlement." Referring to recent congressional initiatives to end the war, he pleaded for Thieu's cooperation, reiterating that the best guarantee for the survival of South Vietnam "is the unity of our two countries which would be gravely jeopardized if you persist in your present course." He pledged to continue American assistance after the settlement and to "respond with full force should the settlement be violated by North Vietnam."[3]

Nixon could hold out no longer. A settlement was the only way he could regain the trust of the electorate lost during the Christmas bombing. The bombing had polarized American society as never before, scandalizing even longtime supporters of the war.[4] Most pressing of all was Nixon's need to placate his critics in Congress. On 2 January, the House Democratic caucus voted 154 to 75 to cut off funds for military activity in

Indochina once American troops were withdrawn and the prisoners released.[5] Two days later, the Senate Democratic caucus endorsed a similar policy by a vote of thirty-six to twelve.[6] The message was clear: Nixon must secure an agreement or be humiliated by a cutoff of funds. The war and the negotiations had both dragged on so long that probably most Americans had lost faith in the administration's willingness or ability to settle through negotiation. More than ever before, members of Congress openly questioned Nixon's willingness to end the war, charging that he was not negotiating seriously and intended to prolong the involvement in Indochina. He had reneged on an agreement back in October to get the prisoners released in exchange for the troop withdrawal. In the face of this growing criticism, nothing preoccupied Nixon more than ending the involvement in Vietnam. He even put off preparation for his upcoming inaugural address. "I think until he gets Vietnam settled," Haldeman wrote in his diary, "everything else is going to pretty much stay in the background, and there won't be much concentration on anything."[7]

In Hanoi, the mood was equally tense. The December bombing reconfirmed Nixon's will to pressure DRVN leaders to settle, even if it meant devastating the North Vietnamese economy. The bombings had destroyed the state's industrial capacity and transport system, nullifying the progress painstakingly made between 1969 and 1971.[8] Every area of economic activity had suffered notably, including the production of electricity, coal, fertilizer, machine tools, and textiles. The diversion of monies from the economy into the war compounded these losses, as did the diversion of human resources. In 1972, Hanoi spent 32 percent of its budget for economic development on rebuilding transport and communication lines. That was nearly three times the amount allocated for that purpose in 1961–64 and equal to that allocated in 1965–68, when bombing had been continuous. Compared to 1964, 11 percent more of the labor force was diverted into war-related work.[9] The North could endure this dislocation and loss only because the economy was subsistence-based. But the dislocation and losses threatened the revolutionary struggle by inhibiting the efforts to build socialism in the North and to resist the Americans in the South.[10]

The latter was of special concern. The bombing seriously impeded the activities of Resistance forces in the South. General Tran Van Tra, whose command was in the southern region of the South, later recalled the situation. "Our cadres and men were fatigued, we had not had time to make up for our losses, all units were in disarray, there was a lack of manpower, and there were shortages of food and ammunition," he said. "The troops were no longer capable of fighting."[11] The situation was so bad in western South Vietnam that the commander there recommended a cessation of hostilities to permit a reorganization of forces. Under these conditions, dissension developed among the cadres. Many now believed that prolonging the hostilities was futile, and they lost interest in fighting. Some even defected and exposed revolutionary cells, aggravating the problem. The shortage of qualified men and women made it impossible to deal effectively with the resulting dislocations. Too many southern cadres, though loyal, were too young or too old or lacked the qualities of effective leadership. This was due in part to the relocation of military cadres to the North to boost economic development or meet pressing military needs there. These difficulties increased as a result of the December bombing.[12] The failure of China and the Soviet Union to pressure Washington diplomatically exacerbated the difficulties. A French external affairs adviser who traveled frequently to North Vietnam and had diplomatic contacts there deduced at the end of 1972 that it would be difficult for the VWP leadership to continue its war of resistance because of "the almost complete state of destruction in the North" and China's desire to prevent Hanoi from controlling all of Indochina.[13]

For these reasons the VWP politburo again turned to the diplomatic mode of struggle and agreed to a new round of negotiations. "Our requirement at that point," wrote historian Hoang Van Thai, "was to secure a partial victory to create conditions conducive to complete victory."[14] Though a negotiated accord would impede the Revolution, Hanoi and the NLF needed time to regroup, recuperate, and consolidate. After the December bombing, Truong Chinh wrote, "we needed time to build up the country as well as our forces."[15] Beijing also urged the politburo to settle at that point. "The U.S. effort to exert pressure through bombing has failed," Zhou Enlai told Le Duc Tho on 3 January. "Nixon was facing many international and domestic problems. It seems that he intends to retreat from Vietnam and Indochina. During the negotiations," he continued, "you should both adhere to principles and show necessary flexibility. Let the Americans leave as quickly as possible. In half a year or one year the situation will change."[16] The instructions Tho and Thuy received from the politburo were thus the same as those Kissinger had from Nixon: go to Paris and finalize an agreement. The agreement should be as similar as possible to the draft accords of 20 October, but that was not to be insisted upon.[17] A compromise with the enemy to secure the future of the Revolution was the same strategy the nationalists had adopted in 1954 after eight years of fighting the French.[18]

On 2 January, the technical teams resumed work on the text of the protocols. William Sullivan, who headed the American team, later reported that the Vietnamese team no longer acted "like a victorious outfit." "It was a measure of the extremity in which Hanoi found itself," Kissinger observed later, "that it felt it could not wait for the almost certain aid cutoff and proceed with the negotiations." However, if the North Vietnamese no longer behaved like a "victorious outfit," neither did the Americans. The teams thus resolved a number of important issues over the next few days, leaving problematic matters to Tho and Kissinger.[19]

On 8 January, again at Gif-sur-Yvette, Tho and Kissinger began the twenty-third private session of the talks. Tho opened with a prepared statement denouncing the recent bombing, and Kissinger replied that Hanoi's intransigence in the negotiations had necessitated the display of force. That inflamed Tho, who responded by castigating Washington in an improvised speech. Kissinger interrupted him, "I have heard many adjectives [in those comments]; I propose you do not use such words." When tempers subsided, Kissinger tested the effects of the bombing by proposing that the agreement of 23 November be the "basis for discussion" in this round. That agreement contained strong language on the obligation of the parties to respect the DMZ and permitted American civilian advisers to remain in the South after the cease-fire. Kissinger also wanted the phrase "administrative structure" omitted from the section on the NCNRC, as he and Tho had previously agreed, and the signing arrangement agreed upon in December retained. Tho argued instead that the basis for discussion be the 11 December draft, in which only the DMZ issue was unresolved, and that they work out new wording in the preamble and a new method of signing. Kissinger accepted this, and thus the agenda was set. The negotiators would settle on the DMZ, the preamble, and the signing procedures, then the understandings, and finally the protocols of implementation.[20]

The next day, the ninth, what Kissinger described as a "breakthrough" occurred.[21] At a private residence in Saint-Nom-la-Bretèche, near Versailles, he and Tho deliberated for six hours in the most productive session since 11 October. They agreed that the crucial section on the DMZ would read, "Among the questions to be discussed, there is the modalities for civilian movement across the provisional military demarcation line." That was what Kissinger had asked for on 8 and 9 December and Tho had rejected on instruction from the politburo. Concerning the preamble and method of signing, Tho proposed that the United States and the DRVN initial the agreement and the four parties sign it later. Kissinger objected that Saigon would never sign an agreement that named the PRG in the preamble. Since they could not resolve the matter, the two men moved on to less substantial issues. There, they made progress, as

Kissinger told Nixon, "with some give on both sides but in a completely satisfactory way that protects our position."[22]

The negotiators then turned to the understandings. In addition to the text and the protocols, the Paris Agreement included eight secret understandings. These covered American spying in the DRVN; the return of prisoners; and the withdrawal of American civilians from South Vietnam, Laos, and Cambodia and of American warships from the Gulf of Tonkin. Discussion of the remaining differences on these points was constructive, and Kissinger and Tho expected to resolve them the next day. Tho conceded that the release of political prisoners in South Vietnam would not be linked to the release of American prisoners, a position the PRG now accepted, he told Kissinger, as a result of "a long and perseverant persuasion of mine over [PRG foreign minister] Madame Binh." "The United States signs the agreement," the understanding now read, "with the explicit understanding that the return of all U.S. military and civilian prisoners throughout Indochina is guaranteed unconditionally and is not linked in any way with the settlement by the South Vietnamese parties of the question of civilian detainees in South Vietnam." Because Tho agreed to prepare special statements on the release of American prisoners in Laos and Cambodia, Kissinger agreed to language in the accord itself that mentioned the release of POWs in Vietnam only. Once the negotiators cleared up other details and technicalities, that would leave only the differences in the protocols, being worked out by Sullivan and Thach and the technical teams. Tho and Kissinger agreed that as soon as other obstacles were out the way, they would see personally to finalizing the protocols. In the course of the meeting, according to Kissinger, Tho confided that what had brought the politburo to settle was the Christmas bombing and the belief that congressional pressure would have little effect on Nixon in the immediate future.[23]

In a dispatch to Washington, Kissinger told Nixon of the progress. However, he warned against complacency and stressed the need for secrecy. "There must not be the slightest hint of the present status to the bureaucracy, Cabinet members, the Congress, or anyone else," Kissinger warned. "If a wave of euphoria begins in Washington, the North Vietnamese are apt to revert to their natural beastliness, and the South Vietnamese will do their best to sabotage our progress." He also noted that since much work remained on the protocols, the administration could ill-afford to raise expectations, especially in light of past reversals at the last minute. Convinced by Tho's actions that the bombing had had a positive influence, Kissinger urged Nixon to maintain his fierce posture. "The slightest hint of eagerness could prove suicidal," he wrote. Kissinger was thus optimistic, despite the task he and Nixon still faced of getting Saigon's acquiescence.[24] After reading Kissinger's message, Nixon told Haldeman and Kennedy that Kissinger was probably once more over-estimating the willingness of Hanoi to settle. He expected Le Duc Tho cynically to "back down the hill" the next day and noted that Saigon was still a "massive problem." Despite these reservations, Nixon was buoyed by Kissinger's message, replying that it was the best birthday present he had received in sixty years.[25]

Tho and Kissinger met again for four hours on 10 January, and the momentum and candid constructiveness of the previous day continued. After reviewing the unilateral statements and understandings already agreed upon, the American side proposed that the initialing of the agreement by Kissinger and Tho, scheduled for Hanoi, take place instead in Paris on 23 January and that Kissinger visit Hanoi after the signing. That way, the agreement could be announced before Nixon's upcoming inauguration and the period between the end of the talks and the announcement of their success would be compressed. Tho took the proposal under advisement but said that should he accept it, Kissinger would have to visit Hanoi within a week after the signing. Kissinger agreed to that schedule because it placed his visit in the context of postwar relations rather than ending-the-war obligations. The delegations then recessed, to meet again the next day.[26]

Assuming no change by the VWP politburo, Kissinger expected to complete the negotiations on 12 January and return to Washington the following day. Within twenty-four hours of that, he would dispatch Haig to Saigon and Nixon could end the bombing by 16 January, in order to sustain the positive atmosphere in Paris. Haig would spend no more than sixty hours in Saigon, lest Thieu interpret a longer stay to signal American hesitancy over abandoning him, thereby encouraging his inflexibility. Also, Kissinger needed Haig's help in resolving technical details before the signing ceremony. On 19 January, the White House would announce that Kissinger would return to Paris on the twenty-second to conclude the negotiations and perhaps initial the agreement. As soon as Tho and Kissinger initialed the agreement, Nixon would address the nation and the world and report the successful conclusion of the negotiations. On the twenty-sixth, the quadripartite signing ceremony would ensue, in Paris. Finally, around 1 February, Pham Van Dong would host Kissinger in Hanoi to arrange the implementation of the agreement.[27] Nixon approved this schedule, except he would announce the settlement before the initialing. He told Kissinger that evening that the new agreement was "infinitely preferable" to previous versions and said he would make every effort to ensure that the VWP politburo accepted it.[28]

The meeting on 11 January was extraordinarily productive. While the technical teams worked on the protocols, Tho and Kissinger spent six hours ironing out remaining differences. They resolved the question of the preamble and signing procedures in a way that not only satisfied Washington and the DRVN but would, they both hoped, mollify Saigon and the PRG. At the beginning of the meeting, Tho suggested that rather than naming the signatories the preamble refer to "the Parties participating in the Paris Conference." Kissinger then proposed two separate signings, one with the United States and the DRVN, another with the four parties. Tho accepted that arrangement, provided the text signed by Hanoi and Washington name the four parties in the preamble. As for the text signed by the four parties, Tho thought it unnecessary to name the parties. Kissinger accepted this formula, provided each of the four parties sign the text on a different page. Tho thought it preferable to have everyone sign on the same page. They settled on two pages, one for the DRVN and the PRG, the other for the United States and the GVN. The protracted haggling over symbols rather than substance prompted Kissinger to write, "The negotiations had begun in 1968 with a haggle over the shape of the table; they ended in 1973 with a haggle . . . over the same problem."[29]

On the same day, Tho and Kissinger completed the secret understandings. In them, Hanoi agreed to help shorten the interval between the cease-fires in Vietnam and Laos from thirty to fifteen days and gave "ironclad guarantees" on the return of American prisoners in Laos and Cambodia. Hanoi could not, however, promise a prompt end to hostilities in Cambodia. KCP/Khmer Rouge dependence on Hanoi had diminished, and a rift had developed between the two Communist camps. "When discussing with our allies in Cambodia," Tho told Kissinger, "it is not as easy as when we discuss with our allies in Laos."[30] Washington, in turn, pledged to use its influence to secure the release of political prisoners in the South within ninety days. Kissinger got no understanding on the withdrawal of the 300,000 PAVN troops in the South, but he let Tho know that the efficacy of American influence regarding the political prisoners would be contingent upon progress in the withdrawal of PAVN forces. This understanding was oral rather than written, but it provided the GVN with leverage in dealing with the issue. That was bound to trouble the NLF and the PRG, since most of the political prisoners were members of or sympathizers with those organizations. Even if the understanding had no concrete effect, it had the potential of pitting the PRG against Hanoi. The fate of the political prisoners now rested in the hands of Hanoi, and failure to secure their release might widen the "credibility gap" between northern and southern leaders of the Revolution. Those matters resolved, Tho announced the politburo's assent to the proposal that the agreement be initialed in Paris, provided Washington agreed that the initialing occur on 23 January and Kissinger visit Hanoi within ten days of the signing. Public announcement of the settlement could be made on 18 January. In agreeing to this, Kissinger made no mention of Nixon's desire to make the public announcement, lest Tho deduce that Nixon was anxious for a settlement before the inauguration.[31]

At four o'clock in the afternoon on 11 January 1973, the agreement, the secret understandings, the unilateral statements, and the arrangement for signing were complete. All that remained was to reconcile the Vietnamese and English texts and complete the protocols—and, for the Americans, to get Thieu's acquiescence. "The only way to bring Thieu around will be to tell him flatly that you will proceed, with or without him," Kissinger told Nixon on the last point. "If he balks and we then initial, there will still be 3 to 4 days between the initialing and signing for the pressures to build up." He had alerted Tho to the fact that it might be necessary to reopen the discussions if Saigon refused to sign the agreement; but Kissinger advised Nixon not to postpone the initialing, as that might compromise the agreement itself.[32] Washington had achieved "100 percent on substance," Kissinger told Nixon, and Thieu could not be allowed to compromise the settlement.[33]

To expedite agreement on the protocols, Tho and Kissinger joined the technical discussions the next day. During six hours of negotiations, they cleared away most of the differences. They compromised on the size of ICCS forces to supervise the cease-fire, and at Tho's insistence agreed that the commission could inspect South Vietnamese detention centers. They also agreed on the size of the TPJMC but had problems with areas of control and modalities for the stationing of troops in the South after the cease-fire. Unable to agree on specifics for implementing the cease-fire in place, Tho and Kissinger agreed instead on the general principle that "the Two-Party Joint Military Commission . . . will determine the zones controlled by each Party and the modalities for the stationing of troops." That arrangement reflected the eagerness of both delegations to complete the negotiations regardless of the peace they produced. Still suspicious of the verbal pledge of American assistance to Hanoi after the war, Tho asked that the pledge be written into the protocols. The White House feared the reaction in and out of Congress to such a pledge, so Kissinger proposed instead that the matter be settled in an exchange of notes between the two governments. Since the negotiations had not resolved the issue of American prisoners in Laos to Washington's satisfaction, Kissinger said that the White House would give Hanoi a note pledging $3 billion in postwar aid to Vietnam in exchange for an accounting of

Americans held in Laos. William Sullivan warned Kissinger of the danger of that arrangement. "If you agree with this scenario," he said, "greatest caution should be against any inference that we are paying ransom to get prisoners out."[34]

On 13 January, a final session completed the settlement. The two sides confirmed the texts of the agreement and the associated understandings, unilateral statements, and protocols. While the technical experts finished reconciling the English and Vietnamese texts, Tho and Kissinger agreed on timetables for signing and implementing the agreement. The bombing and mining would cease on 15 January, and four days later Washington would announce the end of military operations in Vietnam. On 23 January, Tho and Kissinger would initial the agreement in Paris and the following day announce the initialing and release the agreement and the protocols to the press. Three days later, on 27 January, the four parties would sign the agreement in Paris and the cease-fire in place would begin. On the twenty-ninth, the Vietnamese parties would begin talks in Saigon and the ICCS would commence its oversight duties. The next day, Nixon was to send Hanoi the note regarding postwar assistance and a day later announce Kissinger's visit to Hanoi. Finally, the IGC on Vietnam would convene in Paris on 26 February. Tho and Kissinger thereafter exchanged views on Kissinger's talks in Hanoi. At Tho's insistence, they agreed that the talks would focus on American assistance and diplomatic relations between the United States and the DRVN.[35]

To celebrate completion of the talks, the two delegations attended a luncheon, the first social event in the history of the negotiations. Tho made what Kissinger termed "very warm and solemn remarks" about the intention of the DRVN to adhere to the agreement. He also spoke of his and Hanoi's desire for better relations with Washington and reiterated the commitment to peace in Indochina. Kissinger toasted a lasting peace. Before returning to Washington, he issued a statement cleared by Tho that the two men had completed "very extensive and very useful talks."[36]

Over the next few days, the technical experts completed the language of the protocols. They agreed that each party would contribute four and a half million French francs to the ICCS and that the two South Vietnamese parties would exchange lists of civilian prisoners and locations where the prisoners were held. The DRVN also finally agreed that within fifteen days of the signing the parties holding POWs would designate Red Cross societies to inspect their prisons. On 19 January, the protocols were complete.[37]

When he returned to the negotiating table on 8 January, Kissinger noted for the first time since mid-October that the North Vietnamese negotiators were "very polite."[38] The December bombings were responsible for the change and for the settlement that followed. Nixon had been correct when he told Haldeman, "Only by the strong action we took in December were we able to convince the enemy that the enemy should settle and not take the risk of waiting for the Congress to give them even more than they were willing to settle for with us."[39] On the other hand, the White House was also pressured by the outcry over the brutal display of force. It had to be equally cooperative in the January talks, since the price for the bombing was the loss of congressional support for continuing the war. This mutual necessity to settle forced the Americans and the North Vietnamese to accommodate each other on important issues and ignore issues they could not agree on, such as the presence of North Vietnamese troops and American advisers in the South after the cease-fire.

Some historians have contended that the "breakthrough" in January was due to the fact that Washington had to have a settlement, whatever the terms. Hanoi was not in need of a settlement, according to this view, and agreed to settle only because to do so was an effortless way to get the United States out of Vietnam once and for all. Gareth Porter has written, for example, that the "failure" of the December bombing forced the White House to accept terms it had earlier rejected, making the Paris Agreement possible. The failure of the bombing thus showed that "apparent strength could be transformed into diplomatic failure." Paralleling the failed bombing was the congressional threat to cut off funding for the war, which reinforced the necessity for Nixon to settle at any cost. Accordingly, the administration capitulated on substantive issues and otherwise bent over backward to accommodate new demands by the North Vietnamese. Hanoi's objective, in this interpretation, was an agreement on the terms of the October draft, which is what Hanoi got. "By its political and military failure," Porter writes in a study based largely on American press accounts, "the bombing of Hanoi and Haiphong made the Paris Agreement possible"; "it forced Nixon and Kissinger to accept the very terms which they had rejected in October, November, and December."[40]

One problem with this interpretation is that it fails to explain why Hanoi agreed to return to the negotiating table before the new Congress met and acted to end the war. Had the bombing been the failure Hanoi publicly said it was, the Vietnamese leadership would never have agreed to Nixon's request to resume the talks. When Hanoi stalemated and indefinitely suspended the talks in December, it suggested an unwillingness to resume them in the near future. Only a change of circumstances serious enough to threaten its ability to sustain the Resistance and the Revolution could cause such an about-face. The VWP politburo agreed to the White House request on 26 December to resume the talks because the bombing had crippled the DRVN's vital organs and thereby jeopardized the Revolution. The January negotiations were clearly a two-sided affair in which both sides made substantive concessions. For example, the DRVN accepted language that recognized the DMZ as an informal boundary while the two halves of Vietnam remained politically divided (although the agreement also stipulated that the DMZ was "only provisional and not a political or territorial boundary"). In the ICCS protocol, the size of the supervisory force agreed upon, 1,160 members, far exceeded the 250 members originally proposed by Hanoi. On another consequential matter, the signing protocol, the North Vietnamese accepted the American formula, namely, an arrangement Thieu could accept. Finally, the DRVN accepted the presence of American advisers in the RVN after the cease-fire, and agreed to link the release of political prisoners to the demobilization of PAVN units in the South. As noted above, that was important because it gave Washington and Saigon leverage, however small, that neither had anticipated. Although the United States conceded less than the DRVN and the PRG during the January meetings, its earlier concessions included in the October draft remained in the January settlement.

That the January talks finalized the agreement makes those talks notable; it likewise makes the importance of the December bombing conclusive. Washington and Hanoi signed the Paris Agreement less than thirty days after the White House ended Linebacker II. The bombing broke the pattern of negotiation in which the DRVN backed away from settlement at the last moment by reopening one or more issues already settled, sometimes with no more evident justification than an unwillingness to settle. The issue most frequently used for that purpose was demanding that the release of POWs be linked to the release of political prisoners in the South, which Hanoi knew the White House would never accept. On the other side, the political fallout over the bombing forced Nixon to complete an agreement before the new Congress had time to act against the war. That meant the White House could impose no additional demands on Hanoi. The bombing was thus the most significant reason for the completion of the agreement in January 1973.[41]

In retrospect, it is fair to say that the December bombing was a "cruel necessity."[42] The agreement it produced dramatically reduced the violence in Vietnam. Stephen Ambrose has written that the bombing was "too little, too late," that Nixon had "taken the heat for an all-out offensive without delivering one."[43] Mark Clodfelter has shown, more aptly, that Nixon could have made such a massive show of force only in 1972. Linebacker II was "the *proper* instrument to apply," Clodfelter has written, "given Nixon's specific *goals* and the political and military situation that *then* existed."[44] The White House was not out to destroy Hanoi or wipe the DRVN off the map; it wanted to negotiate a disengagement that enabled the United States to withdraw from Vietnam under conditions that were not too harmful to American credibility and provided the GVN some hope of surviving. The success of this strategy depended in the final analysis on the bombing and its effectiveness, which Nixon had laid the basis for through détente with the Soviets and rapprochement with China. Those initiatives gave Nixon a free hand in Vietnam to achieve limited objectives without concern about "widening" the war. The conditions in late 1972 were thus unprecedented, and under those conditions, the December bombing proved effective in allowing for the completion of an agreement and ending the American intervention in Vietnam on terms satisfactory to the Nixon administration.

The White House felt little elation as it completed the agreement. It still faced the daunting task of getting Thieu to sign it. If Thieu refused, Nixon would have no choice but to withdraw assistance from his government, and that, Nixon and Kissinger believed, would damage American credibility in foreign affairs. Thailand was already showing signs of anxiety over American willingness to honor its commitment in Southeast Asia. To reassure Bangkok, the White House had invited Thai officials to Washington, where Kissinger provided "assurances" of Nixon's resolve to protect American friends and interests in the region.[45] The Thais were "skittish," Kissinger reported, particularly in view of Chinese initiatives in the region and "the growing internal insurgency supported by Peking and Hanoi."[46] The Thai episode bothered the White House; the cornerstone of its foreign policy was protection of American interests and national honor. Haldeman confided to himself in mid-January that the concern in Vietnam was still "the honor of this country," because "a country without honor has no authority." Opponents of the war were making the preservation of that goal difficult. Nixon's critics resented every success he had and for that reason erected endless obstacles to the administration's efforts to end the war honorably. This frustration was so deep, Haldeman thought, that their ulterior ambition may be to "kill [the administration's] foreign policy based on patriotism, national honor, etc."[47]

The demands of "honor" made it imperative that Thieu sign the agreement. His or his representative's presence at the signing ceremony would vindicate Nixon's decision to defer to Thieu's objections to the October agreement, just as it would raise the nation's stature in world affairs. Since so much was at stake, the White House spared no effort to secure Thieu's assent. "Brutality is nothing," Nixon confided in Kissinger, "you have never seen it if this son-of-a-bitch doesn't go along, believe me." The first step in securing Thieu's assent was sending a special envoy to Saigon. Because of Thieu and Nha's distrust of Kissinger, Nixon gave this sensitive assignment to Haig, against whom the ruling circle in Saigon had no apparent animosity. With Kissinger and Haldeman present, Nixon instructed Haig not to discuss the settlement with Thieu but to present himself as a messenger from Nixon, who "has been totally in charge" of the Paris negotiations and "will go ahead" with the accords "regardless" of what Thieu did or thought. Haig was to maintain this hard line throughout his discussions with Thieu. "The only diplomacy you exercise is to trick him," Nixon instructed, to prevent him from "shooting [his] mouth off" before Nixon's upcoming inauguration. Should Thieu criticize Kissinger or the agreement, Haig was to tell him that in doing so, "he takes on the P[resident] personally." Secrecy and guile were thus Washington's strategies in dealing with Thieu. In a recent game of five-card-stud poker, Nixon told Haig analogously, he had an ace in the hole and drew the matching king, queen, jack, and ten. Another player had a possible full house showing. To keep the others in the game and build up the pot, Nixon played as if he had nothing. The moral, Nixon explained, is to bluff when you have nothing and keep quiet when you have a royal flush. "We're sitting on a royal flush now," Nixon said, "but we won't get a big pot unless we're mum."[48]

Haig carried to Saigon a letter from Nixon, which he immediately delivered to Thieu. Nixon notified Thieu that he and Hanoi had reached an agreement. To get Thieu's assent to it, he listed the improvements over the October draft it represented. If the United States had to sign the agreement alone on behalf of the anti-Communist side, Nixon warned dramatically, "I shall have to explain publicly that your Government obstructs peace." The result of that would be "an inevitable and immediate termination of U.S. economic and military assistance which cannot be forestalled by a change of personnel in your government."[49] That did little to move Thieu, who was still unnerved and mystified by Washington's insistence on settling. The settlement now agreed upon lacked balance and included provisions Thieu could never condone. He told Haig he was confident his army could contain the enemy forces now in the South, but the North Vietnamese troops posed a psychological as well as military challenge to the South Vietnamese people and Thieu was not sure he could get his people to resist them indefinitely. Despite this resistance, Haig remained optimistic; but at the end of the day he still had no definite answer on Thieu's willingness to sign the agreement. Nixon thought Thieu's delay was a "pretty cheap shot."[50]

In his reply to Nixon's letter, Thieu noted that the agreement left unresolved such basic issues as the disposition of North Vietnamese units in the South at the time of the cease-fire and accepted the conceit of the Communists that they had a government parallel to his own in the South. Moreover, the protocols recognized Communist "areas of control" and "police forces" in the South, thus attributing to the Communists the functions of government. "Since this is a matter of life and death for the RVN," Thieu wrote Nixon, "I must point out to you that the draft Agreement, in its present form, does not materialize any substantial progress. On the contrary, it contains many serious setbacks in comparison with previous texts." Specifically, Thieu continued, the present agreement accepts the North's thesis that the DMZ is not a political and territorial boundary between two Vietnams, and it says nothing about the obligations of the Vietnamese parties to "respect each other's territory in accordance with Article 24 of the Geneva Agreement," to demobilize military forces in the South on a "one to one basis," or to return those forces "to their native places." It fails to specify the composition of the NCNRC, and it uses the term *don doc* (to supervise) in discussing the functions of the council, thereby suggesting that the council has jurisdiction over the GVN. Thieu was equally unhappy that the text of the agreement failed to mention the GVN by name while it specified that relations between the South Vietnamese parties were to be governed by the principle of "equality." Thieu also did not understand how the DRVN could participate in the FPJMC when it refused to acknowledge the presence of its troops and its involvement in the war below the seventeenth parallel. He also wanted to know in what capacity and under what name the PRG would participate in the IGC, since the GVN would involve itself in no activity that implied recognition of a parallel political entity in the South. Finally, Thieu wondered why the ICCS would have no presence in North Vietnam to oversee compliance with the settlement there.[51]

Conceivably, Thieu refused to accept the agreement because he doubted the RVN's capacity to stand on its own after the American disengagement and as long as North Vietnamese troops remained in the South. Over the years, Saigon had developed a wartime dependence on the Americans that became so overwhelming that it reduced South Vietnam and its people to the role of collaborators. The war came to be waged by Americans using American strategies, weaponry, and soldiers. The resulting dependency eventually became so complete that even the faults of the American system saturated South Vietnam. The American war machine, to illustrate, was greased by wastage, by unlimited supplies of practically everything. Adapting to that meant, as Nguyen Cao Ky later noted, unlearning the lessons of scarcity the French had taught their South Viet-

namese allies during their fight against the Viet Minh.[52] This robbed the
ARVN of the self-reliant resourcefulness that circumstances forced their
North Vietnamese counterparts to cultivate and intensified the feelings of
dependency. The American takeover of most aspects of the war in the
South gradually undermined the ability of the South Vietnamese to defend themselves. Vietnamization, ostensibly aimed to counterbalance this
effect, had had too little time to accomplish its purpose before the Americans withdrew. This is what made the withdrawal of American forces so
disturbing for Thieu and his government. They had become too dependent to stand suddenly on their own.[53] What made matters worse was that
the Americans never encouraged the RVN to provide or do for itself. The
GVN and the United States never collaborated to develop the infrastructure, whether economic, political, or military, necessary to make the RVN
self-sustaining. Vietnamizing the war thus meant little more than Vietnamizing the body count, which became less and less American and more
and more Vietnamese. When the results became evident, by 1972–73, the
South Vietnamese had lost their integrity as an independent people. That
the agreement allowed periodic replacements of arms was significant; but
since it also allowed thousands of North Vietnamese troops to remain in
the South, those replacements would probably never be sufficient and
sooner or later would end. Thieu knew there was little support in Congress for continued American involvement in Vietnam. If he refused to
sign the agreement, assistance from Washington would end soon. If he
signed, he might thereby not only provide Nixon, Kissinger, and others
the "decent interval" they wanted between the American withdrawal
and Saigon's collapse but encourage Congress to continue financial assistance to his government during the interval. Either way, American assistance was coming to an end. The second alternative was less unappealing
than the first only because it bought a little time. Thieu and his government might use the continued aid to restructure the armed forces, reconsider tactics, and retrain soldiers. By thus benefiting from the delay, the
GVN might survive longer.

Despite his objections to the agreement and the harsh rhetoric he used
in conveying them to Nixon, Thieu hinted that he might sign the agreement if he was satisfied that the North would withdraw its troops from
the South as the political provisions were implemented there; that the
two Vietnams pledged to respect "each other's territory in accordance
with Article 24 of the 1954 Geneva Agreement"; that Hanoi agreed to the
insertion of "permanent" before "political and territorial boundary" in
the article on the DMZ; that the references to "areas of control" and
"police forces" were omitted from passages concerning the PRG in the
protocols; and that the passage be deleted from the bilateral text stating

that the United States and the DRVN were signing the agreement "with the concurrence of" the GVN and the PRG. Without promising to sign if these conditions were met, Thieu suggested that favorable action on these points would effect a "united front of our two Governments towards peace and freedom."[54]

Thieu's letter triggered the most consequential exchange between Saigon and Washington in the history of the American involvement in Vietnam. Nixon responded immediately that he had "decided irrevocably on [his] present course" and that the alternative to Thieu's signing the agreement was an immediate cutoff of American assistance to the RVN. "We only have one decision before us," Nixon said, "whether or not to continue in peacetime the close partnership that has served us so well in war." There was nothing he could do about Thieu's concerns; for two and a half months he had asked the GVN, futilely, to participate in drafting the agreement and the protocols. It was too late to change them now. To restate Washington's commitment to Saigon, Nixon was willing to send Vice President Agnew to Saigon on 28 January, the day after the agreement was to be signed. Nixon was also prepared to affirm publicly that the United States recognized the GVN as the sole government of South Vietnam, repudiated the right of foreign troops to remain in South Vietnam after the cease-fire, and intended to react violently to violations of the agreement by Hanoi or the NLF.[55]

Thieu repeated his misgivings in another letter to Nixon on 20 January. He blamed the lateness of his criticism of the protocols on the fact that he received copies of them, in English, only on 11 January and had not yet received copies in Vietnamese. Down to his "barest minimum" position, Thieu again objected to North Vietnamese troops in the South after the cease-fire and told Nixon that some of the wording in the protocols would hamper the ability of the GVN police to maintain law and order. He especially wanted the police to be armed with rifles as well as revolvers. "This is a very reasonable demand," he told Nixon on the latter point, "the more so that it relates to an innovation made by the Communists in the latest draft." In a gesture that suggested he was reconciling himself to the accords, Thieu proposed that if Hanoi rejected the changes he wanted, Washington and Hanoi incorporate them into an understanding apart from the agreement. He also asked Nixon for an understanding that North Vietnamese forces in the South following the cease-fire would either regroup and withdraw once the NCNRC was in place; remain in place, regroup once the council was in place, and withdraw before the general elections; or withdraw according to a schedule negotiated by the GVN and the PRG before the elections in the South. Thieu's chief concern was still that the presence of North Vietnamese forces threatened the right of the South Vietnamese people to determine their own future. "These proposals are most reasonable," he told Nixon, "and are the very strict minimum indispensable to give the RVN a chance for survival, and therefore they deserve a last supreme effort vis-à-vis the Communist side." Toward that end, Thieu would dispatch Foreign Minister Lam to Paris the next day to work with Kissinger on the issues he raised.[56]

The modifications Thieu sought were minimal. As much as anything, they were an effort to save face, to let Nixon know that he was still a head of state with room to maneuver. Thieu understood Nixon's predicament. Nixon, too, had his back to the wall because of congressional pressure to end the war. On the eve of his second inaugural, he had yet to keep promises he made four years earlier. There was nothing he wanted more than to tell the American people at his inaugural that the American involvement in Vietnam had finally and honorably ended. As long as Thieu held out, he could not do that.

Nixon answered Thieu's letter immediately. There was no reason to review the agreement, he said, especially in light of recent statements by Senators John Stennis and Barry Goldwater that the aid to Saigon would cease unless the GVN signed the agreement.[57] Nevertheless, he promised to see what, if anything, Kissinger could do about the changes Thieu sought. If Kissinger could do nothing, Thieu could circumvent the prohibition against his police force carrying rifles by citing the presence of North Vietnamese in the South as one of the "unusual circumstances" under which the agreement permitted the police to be so armed. That Nixon could make such a suggestion was a measure of the vagueness of the agreement. Concerning North Vietnamese forces in the South, Nixon listed provisions in the agreement and protocols that, he said, rendered their presence illegal and ineffective. Thieu thus had no reason to be alarmed. Bluntly, Nixon added that he had to know whether Thieu would sign the agreement. If he did not know by noon of the following day, he would act without him. Having dispatched this ultimatum, Nixon went off to his inaugural ceremony.[58]

Nixon's assurances concerning North Vietnamese soldiers were not altogether baseless, provided Hanoi abided by the agreement. The agreement specified that reunification would be peaceful and by mutual consent, and thus without coercion. The use or even threat of force was thus illegitimate, as was the introduction of new troops or war matériel except as replacement. The United States and the DRVN pledged not to interfere in the exercise of the right of the South Vietnamese people to self-determination, and the agreement several times affirmed the independence and sovereignty of the RVN. The Vietnamese parties were to undertake negotiations as soon as possible to arrange, among other things, the demobilization of belligerent forces in the South. They also pledged to respect the DMZ and refrain from using Laos and Cambodia as sanctuaries and bases for waging war in South Vietnam. Lastly, though the agreement itself did not compel Hanoi to withdraw its forces from the South after the cease-fire, Kissinger had made it clear to North Vietnamese negotiators that Hanoi could not expect compliance with the provisions concerning the release of political prisoners unless PAVN troops were demobilized. To further reassure Thieu, Nixon offered to send Saigon a note summarizing his understanding of the issue of North Vietnamese troops in the South after the cease-fire.[59]

After reading Nixon's letter of 20 January, Thieu decided to sign the agreement and informed Nixon of his decision before the ultimatum expired. In return, he asked Nixon for statements that the United States recognized the GVN as the legal government of South Vietnam and that Hanoi had no right to station troops in its territory.[60] "I have done my best," Thieu said as he handed Ambassador Ellsworth Bunker the letter to Nixon. "I have done all that I can do for my country."[61] Thieu later said he agreed to sign the agreement "primarily to help the U.S. secure the release of its prisoners of war" and to appease Congress. He would "try" to abide by the accords, but after the American disengagement and the return of the POWs, "the provisions of the agreement would no longer matter." If American aid continued, the GVN would be "free to cope with the Communists."[62]

The statements Thieu asked for were consistent with American policy, and Nixon gave them. In his response, Nixon extolled Thieu's "tenacity and courage" in defending the interests of the South Vietnamese people and in preserving their "freedom and independence." Though he had the assent he needed, Nixon promised to ask for the changes Thieu wanted in the agreement. He had already instructed Sullivan to raise them in the technical talks and Kissinger to pursue them with Le Duc Tho and consult about them with RVN foreign minister Lam. Whatever the outcome of these efforts, the agreement and the protocols would be initialed on 23 January and signed four days later. To assuage Thieu's worries about the protocols, Nixon told him, "We do not agree that these documents are more legally binding in their obligations than the Agreement itself." In concluding, Nixon repeated his plea for cooperation. "With your strong leadership and with continuing strong bonds between our countries," he wrote, "we will succeed in securing our mutual objectives."[63] On 21 January, William Sullivan and Xuan Thuy discussed Thieu's request that his civilian police and security personnel be permitted to carry rifles as well as revolvers, but they made no progress. The next day, when Thuy refused to budge, Sullivan announced that Washington and Saigon would consider the forces in question to be paramilitary groups and exempt from restrictions on weaponry. Thuy did not object, which eliminated the last hurdle to agreement.[64]

The struggle to get Thieu's assent to the agreement thus ended successfully for Washington. That said no more about Saigon's willingness to honor the agreement, however, than did the willingness of the DRVN, the PRG, or the United Stated to sign it. In fact, Thieu's reaction to news of the initialing of the agreement was that the South had entered "a new phase of resistance."[65] Nonetheless, Nixon was optimistic. Though he knew there would be violations of the cease-fire, he believed it was in Thieu's interest to endeavor to comply with the agreement, at least in the short run. After all, what would be the point of an agreement for Nixon that was not at least partially or temporarily implemented and could not be enforced? Without conviction on that point, what would become of "peace with honor"?

Nixon's conviction that Thieu would comply with the agreement rested primarily on the fact that American air units would remain in Southeast Asia to enforce the agreement and deter DRVN aggression.[66] Nixon believed that Thieu, like himself, recognized that airpower was the key to the future of the Saigon regime and thus of South Vietnam itself. "What really counts is not the agreement," Nixon once told Kissinger about the prospects of peace in Vietnam, "but my determination to take massive action against North Vietnam in the event they break the agreement."[67] Nixon and his advisers understood that no document by itself would stand between Hanoi and its determination to topple the Saigon regime and reunify the two Vietnams. Kissinger had even shared that position with Thieu, telling Thieu in late 1972, "Your protection is our unity. You won't be able to wave a document at [the North Vietnamese], whatever is in it."[68] Because in the end Thieu accommodated the United States and assented to the agreement, Nixon intended to protect South Vietnam and punish the North for any flagrant violation of the truce. Assured of such support from the United States, Thieu, Nixon felt, had no reason not to abide by the agreement.

In this reasoning, Nixon was partially encouraged by the Korean precedent. Two decades after a cease-fire there, the two Koreas remained. In fact, South Korea not only survived; it was fast becoming a "tiger state" of East Asia. Although the Korean context was different and American troops remained there to protect the DMZ, Nixon considered the continued presence of American air units in and around South Vietnam to constitute a similar deterrent there. In November 1972, Kissinger and

William Sullivan had explained that parallel to Thieu's advisers. "In 1953, Syngman Rhee did not like the agreement and did not trust us," Kissinger and Sullivan noted. "But we have kept every commitment to South Korea, and today South Korea is in the strongest position and North Korea has come to them and done things they have always said were contrary to their principles."[69] As long as the United States remained thus committed to South Vietnam, this reasoning ran, Hanoi would comply with the terms of a cease-fire. Nixon was convinced that American determination in the form of airpower in the region would deter Hanoi as well as reassure Saigon. "I feel confident," Nixon told Ambassador Bunker in Saigon, "that if we do all we can to deter Hanoi from again seeking a military solution while at the same time encouraging the GVN to negotiate with the other side in a spirit of compromise and reconciliation, peace will finally come to Viet-Nam."[70] Nixon also believed that prospects of American material assistance to North Vietnam would help the cause of Saigon. In fact, he once told Kissinger that aid to the North was "the most effective way to avoid hostilities from breaking out again."[71] If it honored the terms of the agreement, Hanoi would receive substantial amounts of badly needed economic assistance; if it did not, it would receive no assistance and would instead face the B-52s again. The Christmas bombing had shown the VWP politburo how far Nixon was willing to go for the sake of "peace with honor." Threats to repeat that demonstration would therefore not be taken lightly. Because the North stood to lose so much, Nixon calculated, Hanoi would in the end abide by the terms of the agreement.[72]

Tho and Kissinger initialed the "Agreement on Ending the War and Restoring Peace in Viet-Nam" and the accompanying protocols on 23 January 1973. Before the initialing, the two men and their retinues met for four hours to go over last-minute details. The atmosphere at the meeting was affable. To symbolize the new era in Vietnamese-American relations, Xuan Thuy wore a red and blue tie Kissinger had given him earlier in the negotiations, and Kissinger remarked that he had changed some of the pages in the Vietnamese text but Tho would not realize it until the agreement was signed and he was back in Hanoi. More seriously, Tho stated that Hanoi would honor the American request that the POWs be picked up in Hanoi by American planes. Those held in the southern regions of the South, however, would be returned via Saigon. In exchange for the schedule of prisoner releases, Kissinger promised to give Tho a schedule of the withdrawal of American forces. Despite the congenial atmosphere, the two sides continued to dispute the question of postwar American assistance to Vietnam, which consumed three of the four hours of the meeting. Tho wanted written guarantees of the $3 billion Washington had pledged. Kissinger offered written promises of food and other supplies but for the first time raised Washington's need to follow "constitutional processes" in authorizing and appropriating funds for the aid. Since he and Tho got nowhere on the matter, Kissinger proposed that it be the chief topic of his upcoming discussions in Hanoi. When Tho agreed to that, the meeting adjourned and the initialing ceremony ensued. Four years of secret and private negotiations in Paris had come to an end.[73]

In retrospect, the completion of a quadripartite agreement covering military and political issues and including Saigon as a signatory owes more to the obstinacy of Kissinger than to the efforts of any other party. Hanoi had always preferred a bilateral agreement with the United States, provided that agreement included political provisions. In fact, the VWP politburo had been prepared to sign such an agreement back in October. Saigon, on the other hand, had never wanted to be part of any agreement with the North that, among other provisions, would allow the latter to retain troops in the South after a cease-fire. Thieu had been less adamant, however, about a bilateral deal between Washington and Hanoi, if a deal was what Washington insisted on. Within the Nixon administration, most policymakers, including Nixon himself, were prepared in late 1972 to accept a bilateral agreement. In September, when Kissinger conceded to Tho that the United States would accept an agreement covering military as well as political issues, Nixon had demanded that such an agreement be multilateral. An overall agreement signed by the four parties, he reasoned, stood a better chance of producing a favorable peace than one signed by the United Stated and the DRVN on behalf of the GVN and the PRG. Saigon's intransigence, however, caused Nixon to change his mind. The October deal, he felt, had been a good one since it satisfied Washington's principal demands and protected the integrity of South Vietnam. In rejecting it, Thieu had been unreasonable. Accordingly, Nixon decided at first that a bilateral overall agreement with Hanoi was acceptable and, then, that it was preferable. The documentary record on this point is clear. In November and December 1972, and again in January 1973, Nixon instructed Kissinger to finalize a bilateral agreement with Tho. In mid-November, Nixon told Kissinger "to just go ahead and get the best deal we can and then let Thieu paddle his own canoe."[74] A month later, he told aides to treat Thieu "with total silence" and give him no further chance to come between the White House and agreement

with Hanoi.[75] Apparently, Nixon had lost hope that Kissinger would ever
be able to reach an agreement acceptable to Saigon as well as to Washington and Hanoi and decided to jettison the Saigon regime.

Kissinger, however, demurred. Contemptuous as he was of Thieu and
the GVN, he nevertheless worked assiduously to accommodate their
demands in negotiations with Tho. Clearly, Kissinger believed a multilateral agreement was necessary for "peace with honor." Whenever
Nixon insisted on a bilateral agreement with Hanoi, Kissinger rarely
failed to object. In late November, after Nixon reiterated his decision to
make a bilateral deal, Haldeman noted that that was "hard for Henry to
swallow" because Kissinger wanted "to work out the negotiations" and
make Saigon a signatory to any agreement with Hanoi.[76] Eventually,
Kissinger got what he wanted. His insistence on accommodating Saigon
made possible Thieu's eventual assent to a quadripartite agreement, and
with it Nixon's proclamation of "peace with honor."

On the day of the initialing, Nixon announced the outcome on television. The settlement, he said, met the essential conditions he set forth on
25 January and 8 May 1972. Those conditions were an internationally
supervised cease-fire; return of American POWs and an accounting of
the MIAs; withdrawal of American forces from Vietnam; and recognition of the right of the South Vietnamese people to determine their own
future without outside interference. The agreement recognized the GVN
as the legitimate government of South Vietnam and the right of the
United States to continue to assist that government. It therefore had the
support of Thieu and other allied leaders. The United States had achieved
"peace with honor." The settlement was a historic accomplishment, and
"all parties must see to it that this is a peace that lasts, a peace that heals—
and a peace that not only ends the war in Southeast Asia, but contributes
to the prospects of peace in the world." Nixon implored the Vietnamese
people and their leaders on both sides to "scrupulously adhere" to the
agreement; and he extolled his own nation's commitment to its principles and obligations throughout the Vietnamese engagement. Lyndon
Johnson, who died only the day before, would, Nixon was sure, have
welcomed the agreement.[77]

The media, only recently full of criticism of Nixon and the Christmas
bombing, now sang the praises of Nixon and Kissinger. "If it does not
guarantee peace," said the *New York Times*, "this historic pact at least
provides the framework and opportunity for a new era of compromise
and conciliation in Vietnam and elsewhere."[78] Henry Taylor of the *Wall
Street Journal* thought Nixon had shown "great political courage and as-

tounding personal steadfastness" in resisting pressures to agree to "peace at any price."[79] The *Los Angeles Times* thought the agreement much better than the October draft and praised Nixon for his perseverance in the negotiations.[80] The *Washington Post* headlined "Vietnam: A Time for Giving Thanks" and hailed Nixon for his success.[81] The *Washington Evening Star* denounced Nixon's critics and praised the president as a leader who, "despite an uncooperative Congress and the street tactics of a group which seemed more interested in securing the humiliation of the United States than the end of the war, stuck to his guns until what he termed a 'peace with honor' was achieved."[82]

On 27 January 1973, a host of diplomats gathered in Paris to witness the signing of the agreement. As specified in the agreement itself, the four parties signed in the morning and the United States and the DRVN signed a meaningfully different document in the afternoon. After the signing, the signatories celebrated the "end" of hostilities. Canadian ambassador to Washington Léo Cadieux, who was at the celebration, described the atmosphere as initially cold but then surprisingly cordial. *"Toutes les délégations,"* he noted, *"fraternisaient avec pudeur et une réserve qui se dissipa peu à peu après le premier vers de champagne* [All the delegations fraternized with modesty and an inhibition that gradually dissipated after the first glass of champagne]."[83] Nguyen Thi Binh and Tran Van Lam, foreign ministers of the PRG and the GVN, respectively, spoke at length, with no apparent hostility. Binh even referred to Lam as "brother" (*anh*), to the surprise of North Vietnamese delegates standing nearby. For a brief moment the prospect for peace in Vietnam seemed bright. The only glitch occurred when the Polish ambassador undiplomatically congratulated DRVN foreign minister Nguyen Duy Trinh on a *"bonne victoire"* in front of the assembled diplomats.[84]

DRVN authorities hailed the Paris Agreement as a great victory. On 28 January, the Central Committee of the VWP declared that the signing marked the successful end of the Anti-American Resistance and portended the end of the struggle in the South for reunification, that is, of the Revolution. "Our people in the North and in the South," the Central Committee proclaimed, "should be extremely proud and elated by this great victory of the Fatherland." For the North, peace meant a new opportunity to build socialism. The state could rebuild the economy without the prospect of American bombers destroying what was rebuilt. The people had every reason to be relieved, the committee continued, but they must remain vigilant. "The Vietnamese revolution has achieved several important gains, but the struggle of our people must continue to consolidate those victories and achieve still bigger new ones, [and] build a peaceful, unified, independent, democratic and strong Vietnam."[85]

In Saigon, the mood was more sober. Few South Vietnamese believed that the agreement presaged the advent of permanent peace. For Thieu and his supporters, signing an agreement simply meant that the South had entered a "new phase of warfare."[86] Once the Americans completed the withdrawal of forces and the prisoner exchange with Hanoi, hostilities would resume, albeit on a subdued scale. The situation in the South would likely revert to what it had been before Americanization in 1965, which meant an increase in terrorism and other subversive activities below the seventeenth parallel. After more than twenty-five years of war and negotiations, no supporter of the Thieu regime believed the Paris accords would compel Hanoi to cease its efforts in the South. Signing an agreement was merely a ploy by Hanoi to get the Americans out of the war and pave the way for renewed aggression in the South on terms more favorable to the North. Only the specter of American retaliation would prevent Hanoi from achieving its goal after 1973.[87]

Western scholars and diplomats have argued that the agreement of January 1973 would have been completed four months earlier had the White House accepted the October draft. A key member on Kissinger's staff, John Negroponte, for example, has argued that the delay served no useful purpose, that in fact "we bombed them into accepting our concessions."[88] Such assertions assume erroneously that Washington controlled the negotiations as well as events in Vietnam and could dictate war or peace as it wished and on terms acceptable to all parties. They therefore discount the aspirations and role of the Vietnamese parties in the peace process, particularly those of Thieu and the GVN, making those parties passive rather than active agents in Vietnamese-American diplomacy. Such formulations reflect the America-centered conception of American diplomatic history, the idea that Washington acts and other nations and peoples react. That was not the case in Vietnam, either in fighting the war or in negotiating the agreement.

The Paris Agreement did not materialize in October 1972 because circumstances beyond Washington's control prevented that. First was the mood in Saigon, which favored rejection of a negotiated settlement generally and the October draft specifically. Thieu had never truly approved of Washington's negotiations with Hanoi. Particularly abhorrent to him had been the political provisions concerning the future of South Vietnam. Not only did those provisions compromise the future of South Vietnam and his regime, but they had been negotiated behind his back and presented to him as faits accomplis. Accordingly, Thieu could not accede to the October agreement without discrediting himself as well as his position, his government, and the South Vietnamese people.

The second circumstance was the refusal of Hanoi—and the PRG—to indulge Saigon and Washington by making those final concessions—specifically, on language on the DMZ—that could have successfully concluded the negotiations. Though Hanoi negotiated resolutely in the fall of 1972, it was not desperate enough to go the distance after Kissinger met with Thieu in Saigon. For the VWP politburo, a negotiated settlement was not an end in itself; it became an end only when it became the best available way of furthering the Revolution. That was not the case in October, when Hanoi made public the terms of the draft settlement knowing that that changed the politics of the negotiations and would delay completion of an agreement and a cease-fire.

A third circumstance that delayed the signing of the agreement was Kissinger's insistence on accommodating Saigon at the bargaining table in order to get Thieu's assent to a final, quadripartite settlement. "The viability of any agreement depends on the willing cooperation of the parties," Kissinger wrote later. "Once Thieu balked, we were doomed to what actually followed. We could not in all conscience end a war on behalf of the independence of South Vietnam by imposing an unacceptable peace on our ally." Moreover, had the Nixon administration attempted to force an agreement on Thieu days before the presidential election, "we would have been justly accused of playing politics with the destiny of millions."[89] As previously discussed, the White House may have accepted a bilateral settlement in late October or early November had it not been for Kissinger. Eager as he was for a settlement, Nixon deferred to Kissinger and accepted his interpretation of "peace with honor."

An agreement and cease-fire thus failed to materialize in the fall of 1972 because the political, military, and diplomatic climates were unpropitious for each of the four parties involved. Each had reason to put off settlement at that time. The battlefield situation was nonthreatening; and although difficult, conditions in the United States and North Vietnam were tolerable for the time being. No one in power considered time to be of the essence; no one needed an agreement just then. Every party thus contributed to delay the signing.

In January 1973, however, the situation was different. Both the United States and the DRVN were desperate for an agreement, and the result was the "spirit of accommodation" previously missing from the negotiations. The White House now needed a settlement for several reasons. The last American and allied forces would soon leave South Vietnam, and with them would go the leverage their presence gave Washington. By January 1973, only 23,516 American and 35,516 foreign allied servicemen were in the South.[90] Congress and American opinion demanded a settlement, and Nixon could resist the demand no longer without risking future assistance to Saigon. Hanoi had equally compelling reasons for finalizing an agreement. The bombing and mining campaigns had wrought economic as well as military havoc in North Vietnam, and Vietnamization and pacification had caused political and military setbacks in the South. Le Duan himself later admitted that the bombing "completely obliterated our economic foundation."[91] That was particularly unsettling to the VWP politburo because since 1965, the population of the DRVN had increased by four million while the GNP was now the same as it had been in the early 1960s. Unless rectified, that situation would soon cause further economic and social dislocation. Potential reductions in aid from the Soviet Union and China compounded the problems faced by the Resistance.[92]

It was this combination of domestic constraints and military difficulties that caused the White House and the VWP politburo to accept a negotiated settlement in January 1973 and to do so against the misgivings of the GVN and the PRG. Nixon had to placate his critics on Capitol Hill, and the DRVN had to lick its wounds with reduced assistance from Beijing and Moscow. As DRVN prime minister Dong told the National Assembly in early 1973, it was time to "rely mainly on our own forces" and solidify the economic base of the country.[93] To achieve those objectives, a cease-fire was necessary. Hanoi, therefore, accepted "the solution advanced by the United States at the Paris Conference" to conclude the "Anti-American Resistance for National Salvation."[94]

Beyond the Paris Agreement

1973–1975

On 1 February, the United States and the DRVN executed the secret quid
pro quo Kissinger and Tho agreed to in mid-January. In exchange for a
pledge by Nixon of aid to Vietnam "in [the] range of $3.25 billion" over
five years, Hanoi provided Washington a list of American military and
civilian prisoners in Laos.[1] Since the list contained only ten names—eight
servicemen and two civilians—Nixon had the DRVN representative in
Paris told the next day that the White House had records of 317 Americans unaccounted for in Laos and it was "inconceivable that only ten of
these men would be held prisoner in Laos." The United States had made
clear its "extreme concern" with the prisoner issue, Nixon pointed out,
and "there can be no doubt therefore that the implementation of any
American undertaking is related to the satisfactory resolution of this
problem."[2] Five days later, Hanoi responded that to the best of its knowledge the list handed over on 1 February was "a complete, full list" but
"the different parties will assist one another in obtaining information
about the missing and the dead."[3] After that exchange, the White House
put the matter to rest.

On 10 February, four days after the latter exchange, Kissinger arrived
in Hanoi for a three-day visit. There, he and DRVN prime minister Dong
discussed American aid, agreeing to set up a Joint Economic Commission
(JEC) to work out the specifics of America's aid program for Indochina.
"It is understood that the recommendations of the [JEC]," Kissinger told
Dong, "will be implemented by each member in accordance with its own
constitutional processes." Dong rejected the restriction. For four years
the Nixon administration had been able to fund the war, he told Kissinger, and it could now do the same for the reconstruction program without bothering Hanoi about congressional involvement. After Kissinger
promised that the White House would do what it could to honor Nixon's
pledge, the two men discussed the normalization of relations. The dialogue was constructive. Assuming the adherence of both sides to the
terms of the Paris Agreement, Kissinger and Dong expected their coun-

tries to be able to exchange ambassadors within months. The outlook for normal relations, and with it the prospects for peace in Vietnam, seemed promising.[4]

On 26 February, the IGC convened in Paris. All of the invited countries sent delegates, who endorsed the Paris Agreement and pledged to promote its implementation. The two Vietnamese sides, however, engaged in raucous exchanges, accusing each other repeatedly of violating the letter and spirit of the accords. PRG foreign minister Nguyen Thi Binh denounced the GVN and the United States for interfering with the implementation of the agreement and sabotaging the peace. "Thousands" of sweeps by their forces in "liberated" areas demonstrated that "the United States and the Saigon administration have not yet renounced to work against the peace and national concord."[5] DRVN representatives corroborated these allegations and made others of their own to the same effect.[6] Tran Van Lam denied the allegations on behalf of the RVN and charged the PRG with 4,595 violations of the cease-fire since 28 January. Despite what Binh said, Lam insisted, the GVN was the only "elected, constitutional, and legal" government in South Vietnam.[7]

This behavior evidenced the fact that neither of the South Vietnamese parties was primarily concerned about peace. Considering that the GVN and the PRG had been reluctant to accept the Paris Agreement since both felt betrayed by it, that was comprehensible. Hence, the fighting in the South did not cease. Within less than a month after the cease-fire, areas of South Vietnam were engulfed in "extremely heavy fighting."[8] Under the circumstances, it was not long before PAVN forces joined the fighting. "While we have no indication that American forces are involved in the continuing hostilities," a Canadian representative on the ICCS reported in mid-March, "it seems clear from the information we have received that the three Vietnamese parties are still engaged in hostile activities designed to enlarge their areas of control." "It is incontestable," he continued, "that the cease-fire [has] not . . . been effective throughout Viet-Nam."[9] ICCS records show clearly that all of the Vietnamese parties violated the cease-fire. In a typical incident, the ICCS investigated a PRG complaint that the VNAF had bombed its airfield at Duc Co. The commission unanimously found that "on 19 February 1973 bombs were dropped from straight-wing, propeller-driven RVN aircraft known as AD6 type at Duc Co, killing and wounding [PRG] personnel and damaging houses and material."[10] The commission received repeated complaints from the GVN of the DRVN infiltrating men and supplies into the South after the cease-fire. Investigating one such complaint, ICCS representatives found that "the DRVN, without being deterred one scintilla by the Paris Agreement, has been infiltrating massive armed NVA troop units into Cambodia and South Viet-Nam." The investigators concluded that "there never was the slightest indication during the 4 ½ months following the Cease-fire, that the DRVN has modified its infiltration policy. This policy of unrelenting infiltration down the Ho Chi Minh Trail is graphically illustrated by the piling up of 7, 12, or even 20 infiltration units of approximately 500 men each in a Cambodian rest station when the infiltration pipeline was blocked for 15 days during the month of April."[11] Such breaches of the agreement, which occurred daily, showed conclusively that none of the Vietnamese parties wanted the kind of peace promised by the agreement.

Despite the resumption of hostilities, Nixon felt there was still hope for the Paris Agreement to work. Originally, Nixon had calculated that Saigon and Hanoi would respect the accords, at least in the short run. In light of the early violations by both sides, he reformulated his calculation. The peace had obviously not succeeded in the short run, but, he now believed, it might succeed in time. "What we may be seeing," he wrote Ambassador Bunker in Saigon on 5 May 1973, "is the slow working out of a balance of forces which, once achieved, could lead to a stable cease-fire." After reading reports that the level of fighting was declining, he told Bunker, "We can hope that this decline will continue until each side accepts the balance of forces as the best of a bad bargain. If events do take this course, there will also be hope that the two sides will commence to negotiate a political settlement in earnest."[12]

Nixon's thinking was wishful. The fighting did in fact abate in the spring of 1973 but soon intensified. Nixon's hope that the agreement would work, though seemingly genuine, did not prevent Washington from contributing indirectly to the reintensification of hostilities. For only a limited time the White House encouraged Saigon to honor the accords. Kissinger cabled Bunker on 28 February that it was "particularly urgent that President Thieu shows restraint as long as there are any U.S. prisoners remaining under Communist control."[13] "While it is clear that the other side has and is violating the cease-fire," Bunker had already told Thieu, "we cannot afford to have the agreement threatened, especially the release of American prisoners, by actions which are under our control."[14] Clearly, Washington was more concerned about the return of the prisoners than ending the conflict in Vietnam or enforcing the peace agreement. With fading prospects for peace, it became imperative that a semblance of peace last long enough to extricate American forces and get the prisoners released, thereby attesting to the viability of the accords. A "decent interval" was necessary for the claim of "peace with honor."

That the hostilities did not cease completely surprised few people. In a cabinet meeting before he initialed the agreement, Kissinger had spoken of "inevitable violations" of the cease-fire.[15] "There was not a single senior member of the Nixon Administration," Kissinger later affirmed, "who did not have doubts about the precariousness of the agreement."[16] Besides the unwillingness of both sides to abide by it, the Paris Agreement was vulnerable because of its own vagueness. The convoluted language of a number of key provisions invited conflicting readings and thus renewed warfare. Though they completed and signed a settlement, the Paris negotiators agreed on little that was concrete enough to guarantee mutual assent in the long run. Kissinger aide Winston Lord confessed later that some of the key provisions were left vague because that was "the only way" the two sides could agree on language and complete an agreement in January.[17] Kissinger even joked about that during the negotiations. "My successor eight years from now," he told Tho, "will have to meet with the Special Advisor [Tho] and try to understand what we agree to here. . . . I pity my successor."[18]

The ambiguities were such that the United States and the DRVN opened a special forum to assess the meaning of certain provisions of the agreement. Between May and June 1973, the forum convened on twelve occasions.[19] Predictably, the discussions were fruitless. A main area of disagreement concerned the cease-fire in place. Because of the nature of the war, a cease-fire in place—a "leopard spot" cease-fire—created a crazy-quilt of areas controlled by one side or another with varying degrees of effectiveness. This encouraged each side to try to consolidate and enlarge its areas of control. Had the parties opted for a "zebra stripe" cease-fire instead, one in which jurisdiction over individual spaces was assigned by an oversight commission, the fighting might have been more successfully curtailed. Under such an arrangement, violations might have been less frequent since the provocations might have been more clearly identifiable. Though considered by the negotiators, that arrangement was rejected because unanimous agreement on who held what areas and with what degree of certainty was too difficult to specify. Insisting on it would have significantly delayed the conclusion of the negotiations and the signing of the agreement, which neither Hanoi nor Washington could afford in January 1973. That the negotiators had weakened the oversight body, the ICCS, by limiting its functions and jurisdiction did not help this situation. As a result of the weakening, the ICCS could act only with the unanimous consent of its members, which immediately paralyzed it. Individual commissioners could and did investigate and denounce violations of the agreement by all sides, but they had no means of acting upon their findings or punishing violators. In the final analysis, the commission did little more than count violations of the cease-fire.[20]

Further undermining the Paris Agreement was the fact that the English and Vietnamese versions differed on fundamentals in order to accommodate the interests of each side. The English version made the existence of two Vietnamese states—as Washington and Saigon insisted—more explicit than the Vietnamese text, which referred to *"mien Nam Viet Nam"* and *"mien Bac Viet Nam"* (the southern region of Vietnam and the northern region of Vietnam). The equivalents of the English phrasing—*"[nuoc] Nam Viet Nam"* and *"[nuoc] Bac Viet Nam"* ("South Vietnam [country]" and "North Vietnam [country]")—were missing from the Vietnamese text. While the agreement stated that the partition at the seventeenth parallel was not a political or territorial boundary, the manner of referring to the two halves of Vietnam in the Vietnamese text reinforced the conception of Vietnam as one nation and one country. The war in Vietnam, the Vietnamese text made explicit, was a civil war; it was never a war of aggression waged by one sovereign country against another, as Washington and Saigon had claimed at the outset.[21] Hence, the language that each side considered definitive differed on what was at the heart of the war—and the peace. That reflected the fact that the cease-fire was the product of parties more concerned with their own imperatives than with peace itself. The Paris Agreement was therefore not a peace treaty but a diplomatic arrangement each of the four parties needed or had to accept at the moment. When that moment passed, each felt free to act as its interests dictated without regard to the agreement.

As a consequence, the accords were never implemented. In March 1973, the United States pulled its remaining military personnel from Vietnam and the four parties completed the release of military prisoners. That was all the Paris Agreement really achieved. Washington gave no postwar aid to Vietnam, Hanoi continued to infiltrate soldiers and supplies into the South, the NLF sustained the guerrilla campaign there, and Saigon refused to arrange the elections to create a new government below the seventeenth parallel.

At its Twenty-first Plenum in July 1973, the Central Committee of the VWP recommended the gradual escalation of political and military activity in the South in response to Saigon's flagrant and continued violations of the cease-fire.[22] Despite the objections of the PRG/NLF and some PAVN field commanders who urged the resumption of all-out warfare, the politburo ultimately heeded the advice of the Central Committee.[23] According to one American scholar, Hanoi believed that victory could be achieved through a struggle that remained essentially political and legal. Moreover, abiding by the spirit of the agreement would increase the legitimacy of Communists in the South, protect areas controlled by revolutionary forces, and avert the reintroduction of American forces.[24] Considering the devastating effects of the December 1972 bombings, that was the most sensible decision. In November 1973, Le Duan himself acknowledged that military units in the South were not ready for war as they still faced significant "difficulties and hardships."[25]

Through the rest of 1973 and most of 1974, North Vietnamese political and military authorities, the PRG/NLF, as well as revolutionary commanders in the South debated whether to continue the struggle on current terms or to resume full-scale war.[26] In November 1974, the VWP politburo finally decided that reconciliation and reunification were incompatible with the Paris accords and approved an ACC proposal to launch an all-out effort to conquer the South. The decision was prompted by two circumstances. First was the realization that Thieu would not relent power unless he was forcibly removed. Second, and more important, was the certainty that the American people and Congress would tolerate no new involvement and the White House no new POWs. Following Nixon's resignation on 9 August 1974, Saigon had no ally in Washington powerful and resolute enough to cause a resumption of the bombing.[27] Hanoi thus proceeded with preparations for the offensive, which included mobilizing PAVN troops and upgrading the Ho Chi Minh Trail to "ensure an uninterrupted traffic flow" of men and supplies to the South "all year round."[28]

The PAVN high command estimated that it would take at least two years to accomplish the conquest of South Vietnam. Progress would be slow because the armed forces had to move carefully. After the signing of the Paris Agreement, the Soviets had ended military assistance to the North according to the wishes of Washington.[29] Similarly, China had substantially reduced its aid to North Vietnam in 1974.[30] Moscow and Beijing having thus sacrificed the Vietnamese Revolution for the sake of a new rapport with the United States, PAVN forces had to use stockpiled weapons, of which there were limited supplies.[31] South Vietnamese forces would further hinder the progress of revolutionary units. While their morale may not have been high, they possessed an impressive arsenal, compliments of Washington's Vietnamization policy and operations Enhance and Enhance Plus. With more than half a million men under arms, Saigon's army would surely prove a formidable foe.

As it turned out, success came swiftly. In mid-December, revolutionary forces attacked Phuoc Long province, along the Cambodian border.

The campaign, intended as a trial run, was a dramatic success. Hoping to capitalize on the resulting élan, Hanoi ordered preparations for the second phase of the offensive, an attack on the central highlands to isolate northern and southern South Vietnam. Resupplied with weapons, munitions, armored vehicles, and other matériel seized from fleeing ARVN forces, North Vietnamese units went into action in mid-March 1975. Within two weeks, PAVN forces were poised for an attack against Saigon and the rest of the South. On 2 April, Hanoi approved the assault, which it dubbed the "Ho Chi Minh Campaign." Facing imminent defeat, Thieu resigned and fled the country on 21 April. Nine days later, Saigon fell.[32] The Revolution ended victoriously.

The triumph of revolutionary forces was predictable after 1973. After all, they had held the initiative for much of the duration of the war. Only the effectiveness of American firepower had contained them. Remarkable, however, was the short time those forces needed to take Saigon and bring the Revolution to a successful culmination. When Tho and Kissinger signed the agreement in Paris, North Vietnam was exhausted economically and militarily. Similarly, revolutionary forces in the South were in a weakened state, having experienced acute shortages of food and ammunition, among other difficulties. One factor that accounts for the quick turnaround was the cessation of the bombing. Peace in the North allowed Hanoi to resume the building of socialism, which in turn bolstered the economy and permitted a strengthening of the armed forces. However, the precipitate fall of Saigon owes more to the shortcomings of South Vietnamese troops and leaders than to the strength of revolutionary forces. The morale of ARVN troops, fragile after the withdrawal of American forces, collapsed following the beginning of the invasion. South Vietnamese troops lacked the confidence and determination of their North Vietnamese counterparts. They had rarely had the opportunity to prove themselves in combat since the Americanization of the war in 1965. When the opportunity arose, during the invasion of Laos in 1971, for example, the results had been mixed. In that context, setbacks suffered in late 1974 and early 1975 rapidly broke the ARVN forces' spirit and will to fight. Poor strategic decisions by Thieu and the ARVN high command aggravated the situation. The premature withdrawal of forces from the central highlands in 1975 was especially detrimental.[33] Such blunders undermined not only the anti-Communist cause in the South but the position of Thieu himself. Domestic opposition to Thieu had increased drastically after 1973. His evident reluctance to honor the Paris Agreement and allow the war to abate antagonized South Vietnamese liberals and moderates, as well as Buddhists and Catholics.[34] The rapid erosion of popular support in late 1974 and early 1975 left Saigon with few assets to counter enemy forces.

Though Nixon had promised retaliatory actions against cease-fire violations and threats to the Saigon regime, no such actions occurred. Until his death, Nixon blamed this on congressional opposition to renewed American military activity. The Paris Agreement was far from perfect, Nixon acknowledged, but it was workable. "I think that the biggest flaw of the Paris Peace Accords of 1973 was that the cease-fire provisions allowed North Vietnamese forces to stay in some South Vietnamese territory captured in the '72 invasion," Nixon declared later. "But at least we backed up the goddamn treaty with power" until Congress intervened and made effective retaliation virtually impossible. Thus, Congress had caused the United States and South Vietnam to "lose the peace."[35] To this assessment, Kissinger later added that the refusal of Congress to allow at least token numbers of American forces to remain in South Vietnam after the cease-fire—as had been done at the conclusion of earlier wars in Europe and Korea—was a key factor in the rapid collapse of South Vietnam. "American troops have been in Europe for two generations," Kissinger wrote; "the armistice in Korea has been protected by American forces for over forty years. Only in Vietnam did the United States, driven by internal dissent, agree to leave no residual forces; in the process, it deprived itself of any margin of safety when it came to protecting the agreement that was eventually reached."[36]

In the end, promises of aid to and threats of retaliatory action against the North—the linchpins of the agreement—did not hold. Nixon and Kissinger too readily blamed Congress for that failure. In planning for the aftermath of the Paris Agreement, the Nixon administration never took account of the certain opposition of Congress—and of the American people—to any resumption of American involvement in the hostilities in Vietnam, whatever the provocation. In effect, Nixon and Kissinger negotiated an agreement that was conditional upon the cooperation not only of Saigon, Hanoi, and the PRG/NLF but of Congress and the American people as well. It was not entirely up to Nixon and his administration to enforce the agreement Kissinger and Tho negotiated. To enforce its provisions Nixon needed congressional and popular support, something he knew he never had and that he never solicited. Moreover, the agreement provided some incentives for Saigon, Hanoi, and the PRG to honor its terms, but there were no incentives in or out of the agreement for Congress and the American population to support a resumption of American involvement in the hostilities under any circumstance. The only incentive Nixon could offer for such a resumption was the preservation of American credibility in the Cold War. The failure to realistically consider the attitudes of Congress and the people toward a resumption of hostilities or the continued commitment of American forces to South Vietnam in the event of cease-fire violations makes Nixon and Kissinger as much responsible as Congress for the collapse of the agreement, if blame for the collapse is to be assessed in such personal terms.

Initially, the VWP politburo expected to defeat the Americans using military activity as the primary mode of struggle. In pursuing "peace with honor," however, the Nixon administration implemented policies that threatened the revolutionary cause in North and South Vietnam. Unable to neutralize the effects of those policies militarily, Hanoi turned to diplomacy to end the Anti-American Resistance. The contents of the Paris Agreement reflected the inability of the military and political struggles to drive the United States out of Vietnam. Ideological and diplomatic forces combined with contradictions within the United States to enable the DRVN to overcome the American intervention through negotiations, and thereby save the Revolution. The fall of Saigon in the spring of 1975 took place in the propitious context created by the Paris accords. In the end, diplomacy proved to be the linchpin of the Resistance and a determinant element in the Vietnamese Revolution.

For the United States, diplomacy ended the long and futile commitment to South Vietnam on terms short of capitulation. After 1968, there was never any doubt that Washington would fail to eradicate the "Communist" presence in South Vietnam. In the Cold War context, however, Nixon felt that capitulation—unconditional withdrawal of American forces—would be detrimental to American strategic interests elsewhere. In the end, he secured an agreement that softened the blow of defeat and thereby avoided the most obvious consequences of capitulation to American credibility.

The professed purpose of both sides in the Paris negotiations, and of everyone who hoped for their success, had been peace—to "give peace a chance," in the words of the American antiwar movement. Peace, however, was a term defined variously and nebulously by the negotiators as well as others involved in the war and interested in its termination. Was the essence of peace the absence of hostilities? Or was it the end of foreign intervention in the South? Was it bound inextricably to "honor"? Or was peace the right of the people of Vietnam collectively, or of the North and the South separately, to determine their political future free of force or coercion? Or, finally, was it the triumph of socialism and the Vietnamese Revolution? The incompatibility of these definitions, essences, or interpretations meant that "to give peace a chance" was a phrase of wildly unstable signification. It also meant that Hanoi, Washington, Saigon, and the PRG wanted a peace that conformed to their respective but quite different aspirations. Thus, peace—a peace that would satisfy all interested parties, a peace that grew out of the protracted, convoluted negotiations in Paris, a peace unimposed by one side on the other or by one party on another, a peace that was not bitter—never had a chance in Vietnam.

"AGREEMENT ON ENDING THE WAR AND RESTORING PEACE IN VIET-NAM"

(draft settlement of 20 October 1972, re-created by author)

The Government of the United States of America and the Government of 191
the Republic of Viet-Nam with the concurrence of those other countries
allied with them on the one hand, and the Government of the Democratic Republic of Viet-Nam and the Provisional Revolutionary Government of the Republic of South Viet-Nam, on the other hand;

With a view to ending the war and restoring peace in Viet-Nam on the
basis of respect for the Vietnamese people's fundamental national rights
and the South Vietnamese people's right to self-determination, and to
contributing to the consolidation of peace in Asia and the world;

Have agreed on the following provisions and undertake to respect and
to implement them:

Chapter I

THE VIETNAMESE PEOPLE'S FUNDAMENTAL NATIONAL RIGHTS

Article 1

The United States respects the independence, sovereignty, unity, and
territorial integrity of Viet-Nam as recognized by the 1954 Geneva
Agreements on Viet-Nam.

Chapter II

CESSATION OF HOSTILITIES—WITHDRAWAL OF TROOPS

Article 2

A cease-fire shall be observed throughout South Viet-Nam as of _____
hours (Indochina time), on _____, 1972, i.e., _____ hours G.M.T., on
_____, 1972.

At the same hour, the United States will stop all its military activities
against the territory of the Democratic Republic of Viet-Nam by ground,
air and naval forces, wherever they may be based, and end the mining
of the territorial waters, ports, harbors, and waterways of the Democratic
Republic of Viet-Nam. The United States will remove, permanently

deactivate or destroy all the mines in the territorial waters, ports, harbors, and waterways of North Viet-Nam as soon as this Agreement goes into effect.

The complete cessation of hostilities mentioned in this Article shall be durable and without limit of time.

Article 3

The parties undertake to maintain the cease-fire and to ensure a lasting and stable peace.

As soon as the cease-fire goes into effect:

(a) The United States forces and those of the other foreign countries allied with the United States and with the Republic of Viet-Nam shall remain in-place pending the implementation of the plan of troop withdrawal. The Four-Party Joint Military Commission described in Article 11 shall determine the modalities.

(b) The armed forces of the two South Vietnamese parties shall remain in-place. The Two-Party Joint Military Commission described in Article 12 shall determine the areas controlled by each party and the modalities of stationing.

(c) The regular forces of all services and arms and the irregular forces of the parties in South Viet-Nam shall stop all offensive activities against each other and shall strictly abide by the following stipulations:

—All acts of force on the ground, in the air, and on the sea shall be prohibited;

—All hostile acts, terrorism and reprisals by both sides will be banned.

Article 4

The United States will not continue its military involvement or intervene in the internal affairs of South Viet-Nam.

Article 5

Within sixty days of the signing of this Agreement, there will be a total withdrawal from South Viet-Nam of troops, military advisers, and military personnel, including technical military personnel and military personnel associated with the pacification program, armaments, munitions, and war material of the United States and those of the other foreign countries mentioned allied with the United States and with the Republic of Viet-Nam. Advisers from the above-mentioned countries to all paramilitary organizations and the police force will also be withdrawn within the same period of time.

Article 6

The dismantlement of all military bases in South Viet-Nam of the United States and of the other foreign countries allied with the United States and with the Republic of Viet-Nam shall be completed within sixty days of the signing of this Agreement.

Article 7

From the enforcement of the cease-fire to the formation of the government provided for in Article 9 (b) and 9 (i) of this Agreement, the two South Vietnamese parties shall not accept the introduction of troops, military advisers, and military personnel including technical military personnel, armaments, munitions, and war material into South Viet-Nam.

The two South Vietnamese parties shall be permitted to make periodical replacement of armaments, munitions and war material which have been worn out or damaged after the cease-fire, on the basis of piece-for-piece, of the same characteristics and properties, under the supervision of the Joint Military Commission of the two South Vietnamese parties and of the International Commission of Control and Supervision.

Chapter III

THE RETURN OF CAPTURED MILITARY PERSONNEL
AND FOREIGN CIVILIANS OF THE PARTIES

Article 8

(a) The return of captured military personnel and foreign civilians of the parties shall be carried out simultaneously with and completed on the same day as the troop withdrawal mentioned in Article 5. The parties shall exchange complete lists of the above-mentioned captured military personnel and foreign civilians on the day of the signing of this Agreement.

(b) The parties shall help each other to get information about those military personnel and foreign civilians of the parties missing in action, to determine the location and take care of the graves of the dead so as to facilitate the exhumation and repatriation of the remains, and to take any such other measures as may be required to get information about those still considered missing in action.

(c) The question of the return of Vietnamese civilian personnel detained in South Viet-Nam and not covered by 8 (a) above will be resolved by the South Vietnamese parties on the basis of the principles of Article 21 (b) of the Agreement on the Cessation of Hostilities in Viet-Nam of July 20, 1954. The two South Vietnamese parties will do so in a spirit of national reconciliation and concord, with a view to ending hatred and enmity, in order to ease suffering and reunite families. The two South Vietnamese parties will do their utmost to resolve this question within three months after the cease-fire comes into effect.

Chapter IV

THE EXERCISE OF THE SOUTH VIETNAMESE PEOPLE'S
RIGHT TO SELF-DETERMINATION

Article 9

The Government of the United States of America and the Government of the Democratic Republic of Viet-Nam undertake to respect the following principles for the exercise of the South Vietnamese people's right to self-determination.

(a) The South Vietnamese people's right to self-determination is sacred, inalienable, and shall be respected by all countries.

(b) The South Vietnamese people shall decide themselves the political future of South Viet-Nam through genuinely free and democratic general elections under international supervision.

(c) The two South Vietnamese parties undertake to respect the cease-fire and maintain peace in South Viet-Nam, settle all matters of contention through negotiations, and avoid all armed conflict.

(d) The United States declares that it respects the South Vietnamese people's right to self-determination; it is not committed to any political tendency or to any personality in South Viet-Nam; and it does not seek to impose a pro-American government in Saigon.

(e) Immediately after the cease-fire, the two South Vietnamese parties will:

—achieve national reconciliation and concord; end hatred and enmity; prohibit all acts of reprisal and discrimination against individuals or organizations that have collaborated with one side or the other;

—ensure the democratic liberties of the people: personal freedom, freedom of speech, freedom of the press, freedom of meeting, freedom of organization, freedom of political activities, freedom of belief, freedom of movement, freedom of residence, freedom of work, right to property ownership, and right to free enterprise.

(f) Immediately after the cease-fire, the two South Vietnamese parties shall hold consultations in a spirit of national reconciliation and concord, mutual respect, and mutual non-elimination to set up an administrative structure called the National Council of National Reconciliation and Concord of three equal segments. The Council shall operate on the principle of unanimity. After the National Council of National Reconciliation and Concord has assumed its functions, the two South Vietnamese parties will consult about the formation of councils at lower levels. The two South Vietnamese parties shall sign an agreement on the internal matters of South Viet-Nam as soon as possible and do their utmost to accomplish this within three months after the cease-fire comes into effect, in keeping with the South Vietnamese people's aspirations for peace, independence and democracy.

(g) The National Council of National Reconciliation and Concord shall have the task of promoting the two South Vietnamese parties' implementation of the signed agreements, maintenance of the cease-fire, preservation of peace, achievement of national reconciliation and concord and ensurance of democratic liberties. The National Council of National Reconciliation and Concord will organize the free and democratic general elections provided for in Article 9 (b) and decide the procedures and modalities of these general elections. The institutions for which the general elections are to be held will be agreed upon through consultations between the two South Vietnamese parties. The National Council of National Reconciliation and Concord will also decide the procedures and modalities of such local elections as the two South Vietnamese parties agree upon.

(h) The question of Vietnamese armed forces in South Viet-Nam shall be settled by the two South Vietnamese parties in a spirit of national reconciliation and concord, equality and mutual respect, without foreign interference, in accordance with the postwar situation. Among the questions to be discussed by the two South Vietnamese parties are steps to reduce the military numbers on both sides and to demobilize the troops being reduced.

(i) South Viet-Nam will pursue a foreign policy of peace and independence. It will respect the military provisions of the 1954 Geneva Agreements on Viet-Nam which prohibit the joining of any military alliance or military bloc or the maintenance by foreign powers of military bases, troops, military advisers, and military personnel on its territory. It will maintain relations with all countries irrespective of their political and social systems and accept economic and technical aid from any country with no political conditions attached. The acceptance of military aid by South Viet-Nam in the future shall come under the authority of the government set up after the general elections in South Viet-Nam.

Chapter V

THE REUNIFICATION OF VIET-NAM AND THE RELATIONSHIP
BETWEEN SOUTH AND NORTH VIET-NAM

Article 10

As stipulated in the 1954 Geneva Agreements on Viet-Nam, the military demarcation line at the 17th parallel is only provisional and not a political or territorial boundary.

The reunification of Viet-Nam shall be carried out step by step through peaceful means on the basis of discussions and agreements between North and South Viet-Nam, without coercion or annexation by either party, and without foreign interference. The time for reunification will be agreed upon by North and South Viet-Nam.

Pending reunification, South and North Viet-Nam shall promptly start negotiations toward the reestablishment of normal relations in various fields.

Pending reunification, South and North Viet-Nam shall not join any military alliance or military bloc and shall not allow foreign powers to maintain military bases, troops, military advisers, and military personnel on their respective territories, as stipulated in the 1954 Geneva Agreements on Viet-Nam.

Chapter VI

THE JOINT MILITARY COMMISSIONS, THE INTERNATIONAL COMMISSION OF CONTROL AND SUPERVISION, THE INTERNATIONAL CONFERENCE

Article 11

(a) The Government of the United States of America, the Government of the Republic of Viet-Nam, the Government of the Democratic Republic of Viet-Nam and the Provisional Revolutionary Government of the Republic of South Viet-Nam shall immediately designate representatives to form a Four-Party Joint Military Commission with the task of ensuring joint action by the parties in implementing the following provisions of this Agreement:

—The first paragraph of Article 2; regarding the enforcement of the cease-fire throughout South Viet-Nam;

—Article 3 (a), regarding the cease-fire by U.S. forces and those of the other foreign countries allied to the United States and the Republic of Viet-Nam;

—Article 3 (c), regarding the cease-fire between all parties in South Viet-Nam;

—Article 5, regarding the withdrawal from South Viet-Nam of U.S. troops and those of the other foreign countries allied with the United States and with the Republic of Viet-Nam;

—Article 6, regarding the dismantlement of military bases in South

Viet-Nam of the United States and those of the other foreign countries allied with the United States and with the Republic of Viet-Nam;

—Article 8, regarding the return of captured military personnel and foreign civilians of the parties.

(b) The Four-Party Joint Military Commission shall operate in accordance with the principle of consultations and unanimous agreement. Disagreements shall be referred to the International Commission of Control and Supervision.

(c) The Four-Party Joint Military Commission shall begin operating immediately after the signing of this Agreement and end its activities after the implementation of the first paragraph of Article 2, Article 3 (a) and 3 (c), and Articles 5, 6 and 8 of this Agreement.

(d) The four parties shall agree immediately on the organization, the working procedure, means of activity, and expenditures of the Four-Party Joint Military Commission.

Article 12

(a) The Government of the Republic of Viet-Nam and the Provisional Revolutionary Government of the Republic of South Viet-Nam shall immediately designate representatives to form a Two-Party Joint Military Commission composed of the two South Vietnamese parties with the task of ensuring joint action by the two South Vietnamese parties in implementing the following provisions of this Agreement concerning the two parties:

—The first paragraph of Article 2, regarding the enforcement of the cease-fire throughout South Viet-Nam, when the Four-Party Joint Military Commission has ended its activities;

—Article 3 (b), regarding the cease-fire between the two South Vietnamese parties;

—Article 3 (c), regarding the cease-fire between all parties in South Viet-Nam, when the Four-Party Joint Military Commission has ended its activities;

—Article 7, regarding the introduction of troops into South Viet-Nam and all other provisions;

—Article 9 (h), regarding the question of Vietnamese armed forces in South Viet-Nam.

Disagreements shall be referred to the International Commission of Control and Supervision. After the signing of this Agreement, the Two-Party Joint Military Commission shall agree immediately on the measures and organization aimed at enforcing the cease-fire and preserving peace in South Viet-Nam.

Article 13

(a) After the signing of this Agreement, an International Commission of Control and Supervision shall be established immediately.

(b) Until the International Conference makes definitive arrangements, the International Commission of Control and Supervision will report to the four parties on matters concerning the control and supervision of the implementation of the following provisions of this Agreement:

—The first paragraph of Article 2, regarding the enforcement of the cease-fire in South Viet-Nam;

—Article 3 (a), regarding the cease-fire by U.S. forces and those of the other foreign countries allied to the United States;

—Article 3 (c), regarding the cease-fire between all the parties in South Viet-Nam;

—Article 5, regarding the withdrawal from South Viet-Nam of U.S. troops and those of the other foreign countries allied with the United States and with the Republic of Viet-Nam;

—Article 6, regarding the dismantlement of military bases in South Viet-Nam of the United States and those of the other foreign countries allied with the United States and with the Republic of Viet-Nam;

—Article 8, regarding the return of captured military personnel and foreign civilians of the parties.

The International Commission of Control and Supervision shall form control teams for carrying out its tasks. The four parties shall agree immediately on the location and operation of these teams. The parties will facilitate their operation.

(c) Until the International Conference makes definitive arrangements, the International Commission of Control and Supervision will report to the two South Vietnamese parties for the control and supervision of the implementation of the following provisions of this Agreement:

—The first paragraph of Article 2, regarding the enforcement of the cease-fire throughout South Viet-Nam;

—Article 3 (b), regarding the cease-fire between the South Vietnamese parties;

—Article 3 (c), regarding the cease-fire between all parties in South Viet-Nam, when the Four-Party Joint Military Commission has ended its activities;

—Article 7, regarding the introduction of troops into South Viet-Nam and all other provisions;

—Article 9 (b), regarding the free and democratic general elections in South Viet-Nam;

—Article 9 (h), regarding any agreements reached between the two South Vietnamese parties on the reduction of the military numbers of the Vietnamese armed forces in South Viet-Nam and the demobilization of the troops being reduced.

The International Commission of Control and Supervision shall form international control teams for carrying out these tasks. The two South Vietnamese parties shall agree immediately on the location and operation of these teams. The parties will facilitate their operation.

(d) The International Commission of Control and Supervision shall be composed of representatives of four countries: Canada, Hungary, Indonesia and Poland. The chairmanship of this Commission will rotate among the members for specific periods to be determined by the Commission.

(e) The International Commission of Control and Supervision shall carry out its tasks in accordance with the principle of respect for sovereignty.

(f) The International Commission of Control and Supervision shall operate in accordance with the principle of consultations and unanimity.

(g) The International Commission of Control and Supervision shall begin operating when a cease-fire comes into force in Viet-Nam. As regards the provisions in Article 13 (b) concerning the four parties, the International Commission of Control and Supervision shall end its activities when the Commission's tasks of control and supervision regarding these provisions have been fulfilled. As regards the provisions in Article 13 (c) concerning the two South Vietnamese parties, the International Commission of Control and Supervision shall end its activities on the request of the government formed after the general elections provided for in Article 9 (b).

(h) The four parties shall agree immediately on the organization, means of action, and expenditures of the International Commission of Control and Supervision. The relationship between the International Commission and the International Conference will be agreed upon by the International Commission and the International Conference.

Article 14

The parties agree on the convening of an International Conference within thirty days of the signing of this Agreement to acknowledge the signed agreements; to guarantee the ending of the war, the maintenance of peace in Viet-Nam, the respect of the Vietnamese people's fundamental national rights, and the South Vietnamese people's right to self-determination; and to contribute to and guarantee peace in Indochina.

The United States and the Democratic Republic of Viet-Nam will propose to the following parties that they participate in this International Conference: the Union of Soviet Socialist Republics, the People's Republic of China, France, the United Kingdom, the four countries of the International Commission of Control and Supervision, and the Secretary General of the United Nations, together with the parties participating in the Paris Conference on Viet-Nam.

Chapter VII

REGARDING CAMBODIA AND LAOS

Article 15

(a) The Government of the United States of America, the Government of the Republic of Viet-Nam, the Government of the Democratic Republic of Viet-Nam, and the Provisional Revolutionary Government of the Republic of South Viet-Nam shall strictly respect the Cambodian and Lao peoples' fundamental national rights as recognized by the 1954 Geneva Agreements on Indochina and the 1962 Geneva Agreements on Laos, i.e., the independence, sovereignty, unity, and territorial integrity of these countries. They shall respect the neutrality of Cambodia and Laos.

The Government of the United States of America, the Government of the Republic of Viet-Nam, the Government of the Democratic Republic of Viet-Nam, and the Provisional Revolutionary Government of the Republic of South Viet-Nam undertake to refrain from using the territory of Cambodia and the territory of Laos to encroach on the sovereignty and security of other countries.

(b) Foreign countries shall put an end to all military activities in Cambodia and Laos, totally withdraw from and refrain from reintroducing into these two countries troops, military advisers and military personnel, armaments, munitions and war material.

(c) The internal affairs of Cambodia and Laos shall be settled by the people of each of these countries without foreign interference.

(d) The problems existing between the three Indochinese countries shall be settled by the Indochinese parties on the basis of respect for each other's independence, sovereignty, and territorial integrity, and non-interference in each other's internal affairs.

Chapter VIII

THE RELATIONSHIP BETWEEN THE UNITED STATES OF AMERICA
AND THE DEMOCRATIC REPUBLIC OF VIET-NAM

Article 16

The United States expects that this Agreement will usher in an era of reconciliation with the Democratic Republic of Viet-Nam as with all the peoples of Indochina. In pursuance of its traditional policy, the United States will contribute to healing the wounds of war and to postwar reconstruction of the Democratic Republic of Viet-Nam and throughout Indochina.

Article 17

The ending of the war, the restoration of peace in Viet-Nam, and the strict implementation of this Agreement will create conditions for establishing a new, equal and mutually beneficial relationship between the Democratic Republic of Viet-Nam and the United States on the basis of respect for each other's independence and sovereignty, and non-interference in each other's internal affairs. At the same time this will ensure stable peace in Viet-Nam and contribute to the preservation of lasting peace in Indochina and Southeast Asia.

Chapter IX

OTHER PROVISIONS

Article 18

This Agreement shall come into force as of its signing. It will be strictly implemented by all the parties concerned.

Done in _____ on _____, 1972, in Vietnamese and English. The Vietnamese and English texts are official and equally authentic. Subsequently, a French text will be prepared for reference.

For the Government of the United States of America	For the Government of the Republic of Viet-Nam
_____	_____
William P. Rogers Secretary of State	Tran Van Lam Minister for Foreign Affairs
For the Government of the Democratic Republic of Viet-Nam	For the Provisional Revolutionary Government of the Republic of South Viet-Nam
_____	_____
Nguyen Duy Trinh Minister for Foreign Affairs	Nguyen Thi Binh Minister for Foreign Affairs

"AGREEMENT ON ENDING THE WAR AND RESTORING PEACE IN VIET-NAM"

(signed in Paris on 27 January 1973 by the four parties)

The Parties participating in the Paris Conference on Viet-Nam, 203

With a view to ending the war and restoring peace in Viet-Nam on the basis of respect for the Vietnamese people's fundamental national rights and the South Vietnamese people's right to self-determination, and to contributing to the consolidation of peace in Asia and the world,

Have agreed on the following provisions and undertake to respect and to implement them:

Chapter I

THE VIETNAMESE PEOPLE'S FUNDAMENTAL NATIONAL RIGHTS

Article 1

The United States and all other countries respect the independence, sovereignty, unity, and territorial integrity of Viet-Nam as recognized by the 1954 Geneva Agreements on Viet-Nam.

Chapter II

CESSATION OF HOSTILITIES—WITHDRAWAL OF TROOPS

Article 2

A cease-fire shall be observed throughout South Viet-Nam as of 2400 hours G.M.T., on January 27, 1973.

At the same hour, the United States will stop all its military activities against the territory of the Democratic Republic of Viet-Nam by ground, air and naval forces, wherever they may be based, and end the mining of the territorial waters, ports, harbors, and waterways of the Democratic Republic of Viet-Nam. The United States will remove, permanently deactivate or destroy all the mines in the territorial waters, ports, harbors, and waterways of North Viet-Nam as soon as this Agreement goes into effect.

The complete cessation of hostilities mentioned in this Article shall be durable and without limit of time.

Article 3

The parties undertake to maintain the cease-fire and to ensure a lasting and stable peace.

As soon as the cease-fire goes into effect:

(a) The United States forces and those of the other foreign countries allied with the United States and the Republic of Viet-Nam shall remain in-place pending the implementation of the plan of troop withdrawal. The Four-Party Joint Military Commission described in Article 16 shall determine the modalities.

(b) The armed forces of the two South Vietnamese parties shall remain in-place. The Two-Party Joint Military Commission described in Article 17 shall determine the areas controlled by each party and the modalities of stationing.

(c) The regular forces of all services and arms and the irregular forces of the parties in South Viet-Nam shall stop all offensive activities against each other and shall strictly abide by the following stipulations:

—All acts of force on the ground, in the air, and on the sea shall be prohibited;

—All hostile acts, terrorism and reprisals by both sides will be banned.

Article 4

The United States will not continue its military involvement or intervene in the internal affairs of South Viet-Nam.

Article 5

Within sixty days of the signing of this Agreement, there will be a total withdrawal from South Viet-Nam of troops, military advisers, and military personnel, including technical military personnel and military personnel associated with the pacification program, armaments, munitions, and war material of the United States and those of the other foreign countries mentioned in Article 3 (a). Advisers from the above-mentioned countries to all paramilitary organizations and the police force will also be withdrawn within the same period of time.

Article 6

The dismantlement of all military bases in South Viet-Nam of the United States and of the other foreign countries mentioned in Article 3 (a) shall be completed within sixty days of the signing of this Agreement.

Article 7

From the enforcement of the cease-fire to the formation of the government provided for in Articles 9 (b) and 14 of this Agreement, the two South Vietnamese parties shall not accept the introduction of troops, military advisers, and military personnel including technical military personnel, armaments, munitions, and war material into South Viet-Nam.

The two South Vietnamese parties shall be permitted to make periodic replacement of armaments, munitions and war material which have been destroyed, damaged, worn out or used up after the cease-fire, on the basis of piece-for-piece, of the same characteristics and properties, under the supervision of the Joint Military Commission of the two South Vietnamese parties and of the International Commission of Control and Supervision.

Chapter III

THE RETURN OF CAPTURED MILITARY PERSONNEL AND FOREIGN CIVILIANS, AND CAPTURED AND DETAINED VIETNAMESE CIVILIAN PERSONNEL

Article 8

(a) The return of captured military personnel and foreign civilians of the parties shall be carried out simultaneously with and completed not later than the same day as the troop withdrawal mentioned in Article 5. The parties shall exchange complete lists of the above-mentioned captured military personnel and foreign civilians on the day of the signing of this Agreement.

(b) The parties shall help each other to get information about those military personnel and foreign civilians of the parties missing in action, to determine the location and take care of the graves of the dead so as to facilitate the exhumation and repatriation of the remains, and to take any such other measures as may be required to get information about those still considered missing in action.

(c) The question of the return of Vietnamese civilian personnel captured and detained in South Viet-Nam will be resolved by the two South Vietnamese parties on the basis of the principles of Article 21 (b) of the Agreement on the Cessation of Hostilities in Viet-Nam of July 20, 1954. The two South Vietnamese parties will do so in a spirit of national reconciliation and concord, with a view to ending hatred and enmity, in order to ease suffering and reunite families. The two South Vietnamese parties will do their utmost to resolve this question within ninety days after the cease-fire comes into effect.

Chapter IV

THE EXERCISE OF THE SOUTH VIETNAMESE PEOPLE'S
RIGHT TO SELF-DETERMINATION

Article 9

The Government of the United States of America and the Government of
the Democratic Republic of Viet-Nam undertake to respect the following
principles for the exercise of the South Vietnamese people's right to self-
determination:

(a) The South Vietnamese people's right to self-determination is sacred, inalienable, and shall be respected by all countries.

(b) The South Vietnamese people shall decide themselves the political
future of South Viet-Nam through genuinely free and democratic general elections under international supervision.

(c) Foreign countries shall not impose any political tendency or personality on the South Vietnamese people.

Article 10

The two South Vietnamese parties undertake to respect the cease-fire
and maintain peace in South Viet-Nam, settle all matters of contention
through negotiations, and avoid all armed conflict.

Article 11

Immediately after the cease-fire, the two South Vietnamese parties will:

—achieve national reconciliation and concord, end hatred and enmity, prohibit all acts of reprisal and discrimination against individuals or
organizations that have collaborated with one side or the other;

—ensure the democratic liberties of the people: personal freedom,
freedom of speech, freedom of the press, freedom of meeting, freedom of
organization, freedom of political activities, freedom of belief, freedom of
movement, freedom of residence, freedom of work, right to property
ownership, and right to free enterprise.

Article 12

(a) Immediately after the cease-fire, the two South Vietnamese parties
shall hold consultations in a spirit of national reconciliation and concord,
mutual respect, and mutual non-elimination to set up a National Council
of National Reconciliation and Concord of three equal segments. The
Council shall operate on the principle of unanimity. After the National
Council of National Reconciliation and Concord has assumed its functions, the two South Vietnamese parties will consult about the formation

of councils at lower levels. The two South Vietnamese parties shall sign an agreement on the internal matters of South Viet-Nam as soon as possible and do their utmost to accomplish this within ninety days after the cease-fire comes into effect, in keeping with the South Vietnamese people's aspirations for peace, independence and democracy.

(b) The National Council of National Reconciliation and Concord shall have the task of promoting the two South Vietnamese parties' implementation of this Agreement, achievement of national reconciliation and concord and ensurance of democratic liberties. The National Council of National Reconciliation and Concord will organize the free and democratic general elections provided for in Article 9(b) and decide the procedures and modalities of these general elections. The institutions for which the general elections are to be held will be agreed upon through consultations between the two South Vietnamese parties. The National Council of National Reconciliation and Concord will also decide the procedures and modalities of such local elections as the two South Vietnamese parties agree upon.

Article 13

The question of Vietnamese armed forces in South Viet-Nam shall be settled by the two South Vietnamese parties in a spirit of national reconciliation and concord, equality and mutual respect, without foreign interference, in accordance with the postwar situation. Among the questions to be discussed by the two South Vietnamese parties are steps to reduce their military effectives and to demobilize the troops being reduced. The two South Vietnamese parties will accomplish this as soon as possible.

Article 14

South Viet-Nam will pursue a foreign policy of peace and independence. It will be prepared to establish relations with all countries irrespective of their political and social systems on the basis of mutual respect for independence and sovereignty and accept economic and technical aid from any country with no political conditions attached. The acceptance of military aid by South Viet-Nam in the future shall come under the authority of the government set up after the general elections in South Viet-Nam provided for in Article 9 (b).

Chapter V

THE REUNIFICATION OF VIET-NAM AND THE RELATIONSHIP
BETWEEN NORTH AND SOUTH VIET-NAM

Article 15

The reunification of Viet-Nam shall be carried out step by step through peaceful means on the basis of discussions and agreements between North and South Viet-Nam, without coercion or annexation by either party, and without foreign interference. The time for reunification will be agreed upon by North and South Viet-Nam.

Pending reunification:

(a) The military demarcation line between the two zones at the 17th parallel is only provisional and not a political or territorial boundary, as provided for in paragraph 6 of the Final Declaration of the 1954 Geneva Conference.

(b) North and South Viet-Nam shall respect the Demilitarized Zone on either side of the Provisional Military Demarcation Line.

(c) North and South Viet-Nam shall promptly start negotiations with a view to reestablishing normal relations in various fields. Among the questions to be negotiated are the modalities of civilian movement across the Provisional Military Demarcation Line.

(d) North and South Viet-Nam shall not join any military alliance or military bloc and shall not allow foreign powers to maintain military bases, troops, military advisers, and military personnel on their respective territories, as stipulated in the 1954 Geneva Agreements on Viet-Nam.

Chapter VI

THE JOINT MILITARY COMMISSIONS, THE INTERNATIONAL COMMISSION OF CONTROL AND SUPERVISION, THE INTERNATIONAL CONFERENCE

Article 16

(a) The parties participating in the Paris Conference on Viet-Nam shall immediately designate representatives to form a Four-Party Joint Military Commission with the task of ensuring joint action by the parties in implementing the following provisions of this Agreement:

—The first paragraph of Article 2, regarding the enforcement of the cease-fire throughout South Viet-Nam;

—Article 3 (a), regarding the cease-fire by U.S. forces and those of the other foreign countries referred to in that Article;

—Article 3 (c), regarding the cease-fire between all parties in South Viet-Nam;

—Article 5, regarding the withdrawal from South Viet-Nam of U.S. troops and those of the other foreign countries mentioned in Article 3 (a);

—Article 6, regarding the dismantlement of military bases in South Viet-Nam of the United States and those of the other foreign countries mentioned in Article 3 (a);

—Article 8 (a), regarding the return of captured military personnel and foreign civilians of the parties;

—Article 8 (b), regarding the mutual assistance of the parties in getting information about those military personnel and foreign civilians of the parties missing in action.

(b) The Four-Party Joint Military Commission shall operate in accordance with the principle of consultations and unanimity. Disagreements shall be referred to the International Commission of Control and Supervision.

(c) The Four-Party Joint Military Commission shall begin operating immediately after the signing of this Agreement and end its activities in sixty days, after the completion of the withdrawal of U.S. troops and those of the other foreign countries mentioned in Article 3 (a) and the completion of the return of captured military personnel and foreign civilians of the parties.

(d) The four parties shall agree immediately on the organization, the working procedure, means of activity, and expenditures of the Four-Party Joint Military Commission.

Article 17

(a) The two South Vietnamese parties shall immediately designate representatives to form a Two-Party Joint Military Commission with the task of ensuring joint action by the two South Vietnamese parties in implementing the following provisions of this Agreement:

—The first paragraph of Article 2, regarding the enforcement of the cease-fire throughout South Viet-Nam, when the Four-Party Joint Military Commission has ended its activities;

—Article 3 (b), regarding the cease-fire between the two South Vietnamese parties;

—Article 3 (c), regarding the cease-fire between all parties in South Viet-Nam, when the Four-Party Joint Military Commission has ended its activities;

—Article 7, regarding the prohibition of the introduction of troops into South Viet-Nam and all other provisions of this Article;

—Article 8 (c), regarding the question of the return of Vietnamese civilian personnel captured and detained in South Viet-Nam;

—Article 13, regarding the reduction of the military effectives of the two South Vietnamese parties and the demobilization of the troops being reduced.

(b) Disagreements shall be referred to the International Commission of Control and Supervision.

(c) After the signing of this Agreement, the Two-Party Joint Military Commission shall agree immediately on the measures and organization aimed at enforcing the cease-fire and preserving peace in South Viet-Nam.

Article 18

(a) After the signing of this Agreement, an International Commission of Control and Supervision shall be established immediately.

(b) Until the International Conference provided for in Article 19 makes definitive arrangements, the International Commission of Control and Supervision will report to the four parties on matters concerning the control and supervision of the implementation of the following provisions of this Agreement:

—The first paragraph of Article 2, regarding the enforcement of the cease-fire throughout South Viet-Nam;

—Article 3 (a), regarding the cease-fire by U.S. forces and those of the other foreign countries referred to in that Article;

—Article 3 (c), regarding the cease-fire between all the parties in South Viet-Nam;

—Article 5, regarding the withdrawal from South Viet-Nam of U.S. troops and those of the other foreign countries mentioned in Article 3 (a);

—Article 6, regarding the dismantlement of military bases in South Viet-Nam of the United States and those of the other foreign countries mentioned in Article 3 (a);

—Article 8 (a), regarding the return of captured military personnel and foreign civilians of the parties.

The International Commission of Control and Supervision shall form control teams for carrying out its tasks. The four parties shall agree immediately on the location and operation of these teams. The parties will facilitate their operation.

(c) Until the International Conference makes definitive arrangements, the International Commission of Control and Supervision will report to the two South Vietnamese parties on matters concerning the control and supervision of the implementation of the following provisions of this Agreement:

—The first paragraph of Article 2, regarding the enforcement of the cease-fire throughout South Viet-Nam, when the Four-Party Joint Military Commission has ended its activities;

—Article 3 (b), regarding the cease-fire between the two South Viet-namese parties;

—Article 3 (c), regarding the cease-fire between all parties in South Viet-Nam, when the Four-Party Joint Military Commission has ended its activities;

—Article 7, regarding the prohibition of the introduction of troops into South Viet-Nam and all other provisions of this Article;

—Article 8 (c), regarding the question of the return of Vietnamese civilian personnel captured and detained in South Viet-Nam;

—Article 9 (b), regarding the free and democratic general elections in South Viet-Nam;

—Article 13, regarding the reduction of the military effectives of the two South Vietnamese parties and the demobilization of the troops being reduced.

The International Commission of Control and Supervision shall form control teams for carrying out its tasks. The two South Vietnamese parties shall agree immediately on the location and operation of these teams. The two South Vietnamese parties will facilitate their operation.

(d) The International Commission of Control and Supervision shall be composed of representatives of four countries: Canada, Hungary, Indonesia and Poland. The chairmanship of this Commission will rotate among the members for specific periods to be determined by the Commission.

(e) The International Commission of Control and Supervision shall carry out its tasks in accordance with the principle of respect for the sovereignty of South Viet-Nam.

(f) The International Commission of Control and Supervision shall operate in accordance with the principle of consultations and unanimity.

(g) The International Commission of Control and Supervision shall begin operating when a cease-fire comes into force in Viet-Nam. As regards the provisions in Article 18 (b) concerning the four parties, the International Commission of Control and Supervision shall end its activities when the Commission's tasks of control and supervision regarding these provisions have been fulfilled. As regards the provisions in Article 18 (c) concerning the two South Vietnamese parties, the International Commission of Control and Supervision shall end its activities on the request of the government formed after the general elections in South Viet-Nam provided for in Article 9 (b).

(h) The four parties shall agree immediately on the organization, means of activity, and expenditures of the International Commission of Control and Supervision. The relationship between the International

Commission and the International Conference will be agreed upon by the International Commission and the International Conference.

Article 19

The parties agree on the convening of an International Conference within thirty days of the signing of this Agreement to acknowledge the signed agreements; to guarantee the ending of the war, the maintenance of peace in Viet-Nam, the respect of the Vietnamese people's fundamental national rights, and the South Vietnamese people's right to self-determination; and to contribute to and guarantee peace in Indochina.

The United States and the Democratic Republic of Viet-Nam, on behalf of the parties participating in the Paris Conference on Viet-Nam, will propose to the following parties that they participate in this International Conference: the People's Republic of China, the Republic of France, the Union of Soviet Socialist Republics, the United Kingdom, the four countries of the International Commission of Control and Supervision, and the Secretary General of the United Nations, together with the parties participating in the Paris Conference on Viet-Nam.

Chapter VII

REGARDING CAMBODIA AND LAOS

Article 20

(a) The parties participating in the Paris Conference on Viet-Nam shall strictly respect the 1954 Geneva Agreements on Cambodia and the 1962 Geneva Agreements on Laos, which recognized the Cambodian and the Lao peoples' fundamental national rights, i.e., the independence, sovereignty, unity, and territorial integrity of these countries. The parties shall respect the neutrality of Cambodia and Laos.

The parties participating in the Paris Conference on Viet-Nam undertake to refrain from using the territory of Cambodia and the territory of Laos to encroach on the sovereignty and security of one another and of other countries.

(b) Foreign countries shall put an end to all military activities in Cambodia and Laos, totally withdraw from and refrain from reintroducing into these two countries troops, military advisers and military personnel, armaments, munitions and war material.

(c) The internal affairs of Cambodia and Laos shall be settled by the people of each of these countries without foreign interference.

(d) The problems existing between the Indochinese countries shall be settled by the Indochinese parties on the basis of respect for each other's independence, sovereignty, and territorial integrity, and non-interference in each other's internal affairs.

Chapter VIII

THE RELATIONSHIP BETWEEN THE UNITED STATES
AND THE DEMOCRATIC REPUBLIC OF VIET-NAM

Article 21

The United States anticipates that this Agreement will usher in an era of reconciliation with the Democratic Republic of Viet-Nam as with all the peoples of Indochina. In pursuance of its traditional policy, the United States will contribute to healing the wounds of war and to postwar reconstruction of the Democratic Republic of Viet-Nam and throughout Indochina.

Article 22

The ending of the war, the restoration of peace in Viet-Nam, and the strict implementation of this Agreement will create conditions for establishing a new, equal and mutually beneficial relationship between the United States and the Democratic Republic of Viet-Nam on the basis of respect for each other's independence and sovereignty, and non-interference in each other's internal affairs. At the same time this will ensure stable peace in Viet-Nam and contribute to the preservation of lasting peace in Indochina and Southeast Asia.

Chapter IX

OTHER PROVISIONS

Article 23

This Agreement shall enter into force upon signature by plenipotentiary representatives of the parties participating in the Paris Conference on Viet-Nam. All the parties concerned shall strictly implement this Agreement and its Protocols.

Done in Paris this twenty-seventh day of January, One Thousand Nine Hundred and Seventy-Three, in English and Vietnamese. The English and Vietnamese texts are official and equally authentic.

[separate numbered page]

For the Government of the United States of America	For the Government of the Republic of Viet-Nam
_____	_____
William P. Rogers	Tran Van Lam
Secretary of State	Minister for Foreign Affairs

[separate numbered page]

For the Government of the Democratic Republic of Viet-Nam	For the Provisional Revolutionary Government of the Republic of South Viet-Nam
_____	_____
Nguyen Duy Trinh	Nguyen Thi Binh
Minister for Foreign Affairs	Minister for Foreign Affairs

"AGREEMENT ON ENDING THE WAR AND RESTORING PEACE IN VIET-NAM"

(signed in Paris on 27 January 1973 by the
United States and North Vietnam)

The Government of the United States of America, with the concurrence   215
of the Government of the Republic of Viet-Nam,

The Government of the Democratic Republic of Viet-Nam, with the concurrence of the Provisional Revolutionary Government of the Republic of South Viet-Nam,

With a view to ending the war and restoring peace in Viet-Nam on the basis of respect for the Vietnamese people's fundamental national rights and the South Vietnamese people's right to self-determination, and to contributing to the consolidation of peace in Asia and the world,

Have agreed on the following provisions and undertake to respect and to implement them:

[Text of Agreement, Chapters I–VIII, is the same as in Appendix B.]

Chapter IX

OTHER PROVISIONS

Article 23

The Paris Agreement on Ending the War and Restoring Peace in Viet-Nam shall enter into force upon signature of this document by the Secretary of State of the Government of the United States of America and the Minister for Foreign Affairs of the Government of the Democratic Republic of Viet-Nam, and upon the signature of a document in the same terms by the Secretary of State of the Government of the United States of America, the Minister for Foreign Affairs of the Government of the Republic of Viet-Nam, the Minister for Foreign Affairs of the Democratic Republic of Viet-Nam, and the Minister for Foreign Affairs of the Provisional Revolutionary Government of the Republic of South Viet-Nam. The Agreement and the protocols to it shall be strictly implemented by all the parties concerned.

Done in Paris this twenty-seventh day of January, One Thousand Nine Hundred and Seventy-Three, in English and Vietnamese. The English and Vietnamese texts are official and equally authentic.

For the Government of
the United States of
America

For the Government of
the Democratic Republic
of Viet-Nam

_____

_____

William P. Rogers
Secretary of State

Nguyen Duy Trinh
Minister for Foreign Affairs

Notes

CDFAITHS Canadian Department of Foreign Affairs and International Trade Historical Section, Ottawa, Canada
CF Central Files
CNA Canadian National Archives, Ottawa, Canada
DFAITF Department of Foreign Affairs and International Trade Files
GPE East Asia Division
HNLDC Hanoi National Library Document Collection, Hanoi, Vietnam
HPAMDC Hanoi People's Army Museum Document Collection, Hanoi, Vietnam
NPMP Nixon Presidential Materials Project, College Park, Maryland
POW/MIA Documents Relating to POW/MIA Matters among the Nixon White House Files of the National Security Council
RG Record Group
SF Special Files
SMOF Staff Member and Office Files
VSA3 State Archives Center 3, Government of the Socialist Republic of Vietnam, Hanoi, Vietnam
WHCF White House Central Files
WHSF White House Special Files

Preface

1. From Kissinger's news conference of 24 January 1973, reproduced in Department of State, *Bulletin*, 12 February 1973, 155–89.

Chapter One

1. The early stage of the American military commitment to South Vietnam is discussed in Spector, *Advice and Support*; Kahin, *Intervention*; and Fitzgerald, *Fire in the Lake*.
2. Department of State, *Threat to the Peace*, 15, 53.
3. Department of State, *Aggression from the North*, iii, 29.
4. Gelb and Betts, *Irony of Vietnam*, 139.
5. On Rolling Thunder see John T. Smith, *Rolling Thunder*, and Drew, *Rolling Thunder*.
6. Officially called the Dang Lao Dong Viet Nam, the VWP was the forerunner to the Vietnamese Communist Party (Dan Cong San Viet Nam), created in 1976. The VWP had been preceded by the Indochinese Communist Party (Dang Cong San Dong Duong), founded in Hong Kong by Ho Chi Minh in 1930. For a survey of the rise of communism in Vietnam see Van der Kroef, *Communism*, 36–57. For further elaboration see Duiker, *Communist Road to Power*; Huynh Kim Khanh, *Vietnamese Communism*; and *History of the Communist Party of Vietnam*.

7. On the 1959 decision see Le Mau Han, *Dang cong san Viet Nam*, 80–81; Brigham, *Guerrilla Diplomacy*, 9–10; and Le Duan, *Ve chien tranh*, 413–14. See also Le Duan, *Thu vao Nam*, which constitutes the best history of the North's involvement in the war in the South. On the significance of Le Duan's *Thu vao Nam* see Tran Minh Truong, "*Thu vao Nam*."

8. Quoted in Brigham, *Guerrilla Diplomacy*, 10.

9. The pejorative "Viet Cong" to designate NLF members and sympathizers comes from the Vietnamese phrase *Viet Nam cong san*, or "Vietnamese Communist." On the NLF see Truong Nhu Tang, *Viet Cong Memoir*; Pike, *Viet Cong*; Brigham, *Guerrilla Diplomacy*; and Tran Van Tra, *Nhung chang duong lich su*, 231–42, which describes Hanoi's position regarding the NLF.

10. Le Duan, *Tiep tuc nghien cuu xay dung*, 4.

11. Nguyen Thanh Le, *Cuoc dam phan Pari*, 21.

12. Le Duan and a clique including VWP theoretician Truong Chinh dominated North Vietnamese / Vietnamese politics from the early 1960s until Le Duan's death in 1986. Ho Chi Minh's deteriorating health caused him to lose much of his leverage within the VWP after 1961. By 1965, he had been sidelined, along with other senior revolutionaries—including the architect of the victory over the French at Dien Bien Phu, General Vo Nguyen Giap—who questioned the merits of armed struggle against the United States and its allies in Saigon. See Bui Tin, *Following Ho Chi Minh*.

13. "Hanoi's refusal to accept a political settlement," Douglas Pike wrote, "was not the result of rigid unreasonable stubbornness in the Vietnamese character or some fanatic intransigence. It was simply a product of Hanoi's objective—unification. Some goals in warfare are given to negotiated compromise. Conflict over political power and control of territory are, at least in theory, negotiable, as they can be shared and divided. But unification by its very nature was an indivisible objective." See Pike, *Vietnam and the Soviet Union*, 93. According to another theory, Hanoi refused to consider compromise because it considered the Anti-American Resistance a "sacred war." See Gurtov, *Hanoi on War and Peace*.

14. Several veterans of the Franco-Vietnamese war felt betrayed by the actions of the DRVN government to the point that they quit the Viet Minh after the signing of the Geneva Accords (Sen Gupta, "Soviet Union and Vietnam," 560).

15. See "Four-Point Position of the DRVN Government (Presented by Premier Pham Van Dong to the DRVN National Assembly on April 8, 1965)" in *Bases for a Settlement*, 26–27, and Pham Van Dong, *Bao cao chinh tri cua Chinh phu*, 33.

16. Chen Jian, *Mao's China*, 221–29; Gaiduk, *Soviet Union and the Vietnam War*, 36–37.

17. See Logevall, *Choosing War*. Logevall draws on the documentary records of Canada, France, England, and Sweden—in addition to the United States—to study the origins of the American military commitment to South Vietnam in an international context.

18. Gardner, "Lyndon Johnson and Vietnam," 213.

19. The proposal is summarized in Harriman, *America and Russia*, 119 n. 8.

20. On pre-1968 Vietnamese-American diplomacy see Luu Van Loi and Nguyen Anh Vu, *Tiep xuc bi mat*; Kraslow and Loory, *Secret Search*; Thies, *When Governments Collide*; Herring, ed., *Secret Diplomacy*; and Brigham, "Vietnamese-American Peace Negotiations."

21. Quoted in Trung tam khoa hoc xa hoi, *Thang loi khang chien chong My*, 130. The primacy of military activity during this period is also evoked in Nguyen Dinh Uoc, "Dau tranh ngoai giao," 16.

22. *Mot so van kien*, 38–39.

23. See Department of State, *Aggression from the North*.

24. Herring, ed., *Secret Diplomacy*, xxv.

25. Tran Van Tra, "Tet"; Van Tien Dung, *Buoc ngoat lon*, 183–234.

26. On Tet and its aftermath in the United States see Oberdorfer, *Tet!*; Hoopes, *Limits of Intervention*; and Lorell et al., *Casualties*, 71–79.

27. Cohen, *America in the Age of Soviet Power*, 172.

28. Berman, *Lyndon Johnson's War*, 200–201.

29. *Nhan dan*, 4 April 1968.

30. Le Duc Tho, *Mot so van de*, 4.

31. Johnson, *Vantage Point*, 505; Luu Van Loi and Nguyen Anh Vu, *Cac cuoc thuong luong*, 12.

32. Harriman, *America and Russia*, 126–27; Johnson, *Vantage Point*, 507.

33. Luu Van Loi and Nguyen Anh Vu, *Cac cuoc thuong luong*, 14–15.

34. Ibid., 15–16; Harriman, *America and Russia*, 127–28.

35. For Thieu's position on the quadripartite talks see Nguyen Tien Hung and Schecter, *Palace File*, 22–23, and Bui Diem, *Jaws of History*, 239.

36. Johnson, *Vantage Point*, 514; Luu Van Loi and Nguyen Anh Vu, *Cac cuoc thuong luong*, 21–34.

37. Luu Van Loi and Nguyen Anh Vu, *Cac cuoc thuong luong*, 36.

38. Allan Goodman is less specific in his estimation of Hanoi's intentions. He writes that in sitting with the Americans while avoiding serious bargaining and sustaining the armed struggle in South Vietnam, or "fighting while talking," North Vietnam strove to "buy time to strengthen its military capabilities in South Vietnam and weaken the will of those [forces] on the side of Saigon." See Goodman, *Search for a Negotiated Settlement*, ix.

39. Johnson, *Vantage Point*, 518, 525.

40. Luu Van Loi and Nguyen Anh Vu, *Cac cuoc thuong luong*, 39.

41. Brigham, *Guerrilla Diplomacy*, 78.

42. Bui Diem, *Jaws of History*, 239; Nguyen Tien Hung and Schecter, *Palace File*, 22–23.

43. Xuan Thuy is quoted in Luu Van Loi, *50 nam ngoai giao*, 277–78.

44. See, for example, the excellent Vien nghien cuu chu nghia Mac-Lenin, *Lich su Dang*, 414–15.

45. Quoted in Kissinger, *White House Years*, 237.

46. Quoted in *Nhung su kien lich su*, 448.

47. Former secretary of defense Clark Clifford quoted in Summers, *Arrogance of Power*, 298.

48. Bundy, *Tangled Web*, 47.

49. Bo Truong Bo cong nghiep nang, "Bien Ban: Hop Bo ngay 8 va 9-4-1969 ve viec khoi phuc," 15 April 1969, Ho so: Khoi phuc nam 1969, VV, #1359, Phong: Bo cong nghiep nang vu ke hoach, V S A 3.

50. Burchett, *Vietnam North*, 66.

51. Vu Quoc Tuan and Nguyen Xuan Lai, "Politique économique," 220.

52. Nguyen Tien Hung, *Economic Development*, 140–41.

53. Van Dyke, *North Vietnam's Strategy*, 193.

54. *Face aux bombes*.

55. Cao Van Luong, "Thang loi cua cuoc khang chien chong My," 2; Van Tao, "Mien Bac xa hoi chu nghia," 12–14.

56. Truong Chinh, "Cung co mien Bac," 31.

57. Cao Van Luong, "Doc lap dan toc," 8.

58. Pham Van Dong, *Bao cao chinh tri cua Chinh phu*, 45.

59. Nguyen Duy Trinh, *Mien Bac xa hoi chu nghia*, 18.

60. Ho Chi Minh, *Tuyen tap*, 772.

61. Le Duan, *Cach mang xa hoi chu nghia*, 17.

62. See Chesneaux, "Les fondements historiques," and Huynh Kim Khanh, *Vietnamese Communism*, 212–22.

63. Hy Van Luong, *Revolution in the Village*, 201.

64. Quoted in *History of the Communist Party of Vietnam*, 195.
65. Hai Thu, *Nord Viêtnam*, 54.
66. Nguyen Thi Thap, *Lich su phong trao phu nu*, 109.
67. Maclear, *Vietnam*, 329.
68. Le Thi Nham Tuyet, *Phu nu Vietnam*, 296.
69. For a detailed account of Rolling Thunder and its shortcomings see John T. Smith, *Rolling Thunder*.
70. Nixon, *Memoirs*, 349.
71. The idea of disengagement from war in Southeast Asia on "honorable" terms had a historical precedent. In his memoirs, former French army chief of staff Paul Ély explained that the aim sought by Paris in Indochina in 1953, when the war appeared to have been lost, was *"de créer des conditions militaires permettant au gouvernement de trouver une solution politique satisfaisante, honorable, à l'affaire d'Indochine. Il s'agissait, en définitive, de démontrer au Viêt-minh qu'il n'avait aucune chance de nous vaincre par les armes et qu'il devait par conséquent accepter de transiger* [to bring about military conditions that allowed the (French) government to find a satisfactory, honorable political solution to the Indochinese issue. That essentially implied demonstrating to the Viet Minh that it had no chance to defeat us by force of arms and that it therefore had to agree to bargaining]." See Ély, *L'Indochine*, 25.
72. From Nixon's acceptance speech of 8 August 1968 in Misc. Material 1970, Haldeman Notes, Box 48, SMOF: H. R. Haldeman, WHCF, NPMP.
73. Nixon, *Memoirs*, 298.
74. Rodman, *More Precious Than Peace*, 124.
75. Ibid., 129; Kissinger, *White House Years*, 228. On the de Gaulle–Nixon parallel see also Kissinger, *Diplomacy*, 674–75.
76. Kissinger Memorandum for Nixon, 1 March 1969, Paris Talks—Misc. through Mar. 1969, Paris Talks/Meetings, Box 3, POW/MIA, NPMP.
77. Kissinger Memorandum for Nixon, 18 September 1971, Encore—Sept. 1971–Feb. 15, 1972: Speech of President, Jan. 25, 1972, For the President's Files—Winston Lord, Vietnam Negotiations, Box 4, POW/MIA, NPMP. See also Donelly, "Settlement of Sorts," 58–59.
78. Kissinger, *White House Years*, 237.
79. Inscribed on Kissinger Memorandum for Nixon, 27 November 1969, President's Daily Briefs—Nov. 1969, President's Daily Briefings, Box 1, POW/MIA, NPMP.
80. Kissinger Memorandum for Nixon, 27 February 1970, President's Daily Briefs—Feb. 2–28, 1970, President's Daily Briefings, Box 1, POW/MIA, NPMP.
81. Kissinger Memorandum for Nixon, 28 January 1969, President's Daily Briefs—Jan. 28–31, 1969, President's Daily Briefings, Box 1, POW/MIA, NPMP. Ambassadors Philip Habib and Henry Cabot Lodge had both previously participated in the plenary discussions.
82. Nguyen Huu Hop, "Tim hieu mat tran dau tranh ngoai giao," 36.
83. Luu Van Loi and Nguyen Anh Vu, *Cac cuoc thuong luong*, 66–75.
84. Kissinger, "Viet Nam Negotiations."
85. From the Thieu address reproduced in Republic of Viet-Nam, *On Peace and Manpower Requirements*, 5.
86. Bui Diem, *Jaws of History*, 228.
87. See statement by RVN foreign minister Tran Chanh Thanh in Republic of Viet-Nam, *Peace and Beyond*, 6–7.
88. Republic of Viet-Nam, *Inaugural Address by President Nguyen Van Thieu*, 3.
89. The NLF's Ten Points program is reproduced in *Bases for a Settlement*, 29–33. The content of Nixon's 14 May proposal appears in Kissinger, *White House Years*, 270–71.
90. Kissinger Memorandum for Nixon, 24 June 1969, and Rogers Cable for Bunker/Lodge, 10 March 1969, CF: FO-6-1 Paris Talks [1969–70], 1969–74, Box 33, SF: Confidential Files, WHSF, NPMP.

91. Bui Diem, *Jaws of History*, 262.
92. Ibid., 260–61; République du Viêt-Nam, *Les négociations de paix*, 12–13.
93. On the creation of the PRG see Truong Nhu Tang, *Viet Cong Memoir*, 145–55, and Brigham, *Guerrilla Diplomacy*, 87–89.
94. Viet Nam Cong Hoa, *Tuyen bo cua tong thong Viet Nam Cong Hoa*.
95. Bui Diem, *Jaws of History*, 262–63.
96. Karnow, *Vietnam*, 496–97.
97. Luu Van Loi and Nguyen Anh Vu, *Cac cuoc thuong luong*, 84–85.
98. Bundy, *Tangled Web*, 79; Luu Van Loi and Nguyen Anh Vu, *Cac cuoc thuong luong*, 86; Nixon, *Memoirs*, 394. The White House addressed the letter to Ho Chi Minh because it erroneously assumed he was still head of the VWP.
99. Luu Van Loi and Nguyen Anh Vu, *Cac cuoc thuong luong*, 91–92.
100. Walters, *Silent Missions*, 509–10; Mai Van Bo, *Tan cong ngoai giao*, 165–68.
101. Luu Van Loi and Nguyen Anh Vu, *Cac cuoc thuong luong*, 100.
102. See Kissinger, *White House Years*, 226–77.
103. For an incisive exposé of the Nixon doctrine by its architect see Laird, *Nixon Doctrine*, 3–23. In his memoirs, Nixon wrote that an optimistic public report by British counterinsurgency expert Robert Thompson on the prospects of Vietnamization was a powerful incentive for the White House to endorse that policy. See Nixon, *Memoirs*, 405.
104. As of the time Nixon announced the gradual withdrawal of American forces, more than 31,000 Americans had died in Indochina and three times that number had been wounded. See Kahin and Lewis, *United States in Vietnam*, 402.
105. Kissinger, *Diplomacy*, 681.
106. William S. Turley, *Second Indochina War*, 130.
107. Ban chi dao tong ket chien tranh, *Tong ket cuoc khang chien chong My*, 76.
108. Nguyen Duy Trinh, *Mat tran ngoai giao*, 90.
109. *Giai phap chinh tri bay diem va hai diem them chot noi ro them cua Chinh phu cach mang lam thoi cong hoa mien Nam Viet Nam*, 1972, HNLDC. "Pacification" consisted of joint American–South Vietnamese programs to "win the hearts and minds" of the rural population in South Vietnam and deny support to enemy forces.
110. Ho Khang, "Thu giai trinh 'My hoa,'" 16–19.
111. Cao Van Luong, "Thang loi cua cuoc khang chien chong My," 6; Trung tam khoa hoc, *Thang loi khang chien chong My*, 117.
112. Van Tien Dung, *Cuoc khang chien chong My*, 102–3.
113. Vien nghien cuu chu nghia Mac-Lenin, *Lich su Dang*, 480–81.
114. On the adverse effects of America's military involvement in Cambodia see Shawcross, *Sideshow*; Kiernan, *How Pol Pot Came to Power*; and Kiernan, *Pol Pot Regime*, 16–25.
115. *Washington Post*, 10 July 1970; Michael Clodfelter, *Vietnam in Military Statistics*, 178–79.
116. Rodman, *More Precious Than Peace*, 128.
117. Johnson and McAlister, *Right Hand of Power*, 532.
118. Van Tien Dung, *Cuoc khang chien chong My*, 47–48.
119. These figures are from Vien nghien cuu chu nghia Mac-Lenin, *Lich su Dang*, 442–44. This evidence is corroborated by Robert Komer, former head of the pacification program in South Vietnam, who observed that "the enemy's cumulative losses during his Tet and follow-up offensives were a major factor in forcing him to revert to a protracted war strategy in 1969–71." See Komer, *Bureaucracy at War*, 147, and Hunt, *Pacification*, 144–279.
120. Vien lich su, *Lich su cuoc khang chien chong My*, 40; Ngo Vinh Long, "Tet Offensive," 25–40.
121. The Ho Chi Minh School was a VWP theoretical school that trained cadres.
122. Ban chap hanh Trung uong Dang lao dong Viet Nam, *Van ban huong dan thi hanh cac*

Nghi quyet, 3–7; Vien nghien cuu chu nghia Mac-Lenin, *Lich su Dang*, 442, 461–63; Komer, *Bureaucracy at War*, 147.

123. Le Mau Han, *Dang cong san Viet Nam*, 92.

124. Quoted in Cao Van Luong, "Thang loi cua cuoc khang chien chong My," 6.

125. Luu Van Loi and Nguyen Anh Vu, *Cac cuoc thuong luong*, 104–13.

126. By 1972, "new" proposals or programs had been presented by the Washington/Saigon side on 7 October 1970, 31 May 1971, and 11 October 1971, and by the Hanoi/PRG side on 17 September 1970, 26 June 1971, and 1 July 1971.

127. Memorandum of Conversation—Secret Paris Talks, 26 July 1971, Camp David—Sensitive Vol. X, For the President's Files—Winston Lord, Vietnam Negotiations, Box 4, POW/MIA, NPMP.

128. Memorandum of Conversation—Secret Paris Talks, 31 May 1971, Camp David—Sensitive Vol. XI, For the President's Files—Winston Lord, Vietnam Negotiations, Box 4, POW/MIA, NPMP.

129. Kissinger Memorandum for Nixon, 7 January 1971, President's Daily Briefs—Jan. 3–31, 1972, President's Daily Briefings, Box 1, POW/MIA, NPMP.

130. Kissinger Memorandum for Nixon, 28 September 1970, Camp David—Sensitive Vol. VI, For the President's Files—Winston Lord, Vietnam Negotiations, Box 4, POW/MIA, NPMP.

131. Kissinger Memorandum for Nixon, 22 September 1970, Paris Talks, July–Sept. 1970, Paris Talks/Meetings, Box 3, POW/MIA, NPMP.

132. Nguyen Ngoc Hung, Conversation, 18 July 1996, Hanoi, Vietnam.

133. On the Laotian operation see Nguyen Duy Hinh, *Lam Son 719*, and Nolan, *Into Laos*, 103–55.

134. Kissinger Memorandum for Nixon, 28 May 1971, Camp David—Sensitive Vol. VII, For the President's Files—Winston Lord, Vietnam Negotiations, Box 4, POW/MIA, NPMP; Nguyen Thanh Le, *Cuoc dam phan Pari*, 66.

135. Nguyen Tien Hung and Schecter, *Palace File*, 16–17.

136. Kissinger Memorandum for Nixon, 28 May 1971, Camp David—Sensitive Vol. VII, For the President's Files—Winston Lord, Vietnam Negotiations, Box 4, POW/MIA, NPMP.

137. Memorandum of Conversation—Secret Paris Talks, 26 June 1971, and Kissinger Memorandum for Nixon, 27 June 1971, in Camp David—Sensitive Vol. VIII, For the President's Files—Winston Lord, Vietnam Negotiations, Box 4, POW/MIA, NPMP.

138. Haldeman, *Diaries*, 298, 313, 315.

139. Marr, "National Liberation Front," 528.

140. Kissinger Memorandum for Nixon, 26 July 1971, Camp David—Sensitive Vol. X, For the President's Files—Winston Lord, Vietnam Negotiations, Box 4, POW/MIA, NPMP.

141. Kissinger Memorandum for Nixon, 16 August 1971, Camp David—Sensitive Vol. XI, For the President's Files—Winston Lord, Vietnam Negotiations, Box 4, POW/MIA, NPMP.

142. Nguyen Thanh Le, *Cuoc dam phan Pari*, 71.

143. Michael Clodfelter, *Vietnam in Military Statistics*, 223. A "sortie" is an individual flight by an individual aircraft.

144. U.S. Congress, *Statement of Information*, 90–103. A congressional investigation later revealed that some strikes of late 1971 were the result of falsified reports of attacks on American reconnaissance aircraft prompted by General John Lavelle. See U.S. Congress, *Unauthorized Bombing of Military Targets in North Vietnam: Hearings* and *Unauthorized Bombing of Military Targets in North Vietnam: Report*.

145. Kissinger Memorandum for Nixon, 18 September 1971, Encore—Sept. 1971–Feb. 15, 1972: Speech of President, Jan. 25, 1972, For the President's Files—Winston Lord, Vietnam Negotiations, Box 4, POW/MIA, NPMP.

146. U.S. Congress, *Congressional Quarterly Almanac*, 305.

147. The speech is reproduced in National Archives and Records Administration, *Richard Nixon, 1972*, 901–9.

148. Poll results are cited in Bundy, *Tangled Web*, 82.

149. Nixon later claimed that the "silent majority" speech was "my greatest speaking triumph, apart from the fund speech, which saved my political career." Nixon is quoted in Crowley, *Nixon in Winter*, 252.

Chapter Two

1. Dang lao dong Viet Nam, *Nghi quyet Hoi nghi Trung uong lan thu 20*, 3.

2. Tran Vu, "1971," 4.

3. The Fatherland Front was created in 1955. During the Anti-American Resistance, the organization's official mandate was to rally the country's unions, political parties, and religious groups behind the Revolution.

4. Truong Chinh, *Ve cong tac Mat tran hien nay*, 48–49.

5. Dang lao dong Viet Nam, *Tai lieu nghien cuu ve "Nghi quyet Hoi nghi Trung uong lan thu 20": tai lieu nghien cuu cua cac chi bo Ban tuyen huan Trung uong (1972)*, 1972, HNLDC.

6. Pham Van Dong, *Kien tri ra day manh su nghiep chong My*, 23–24.

7. *Cuoc khang chien chong My*, 154.

8. From the summary of the Twentieth Plenum of the VWP Central Committee, in Ban nghien cuu lich su Dang Trung uong, *50 nam hoat dong*, 216.

9. Ban chap hanh Trung uong Dang cong san Viet Nam, *Chi thi ve viec dong vien cong nhan vien*, 5.

10. Haldeman, *Diaries*, 475.

11. Kissinger Memorandum for Nixon, 6 October 1971, Encore—Sept. 1971–Feb. 15, 1972: Speech of the President, Jan. 25, 1972, For the President's Files—Winston Lord, Vietnam Negotiations, Box 4, POW/MIA, NPMP; the political report in VN–Oct. 7 Peace Initiative 2–30, Numerical Subject Files, Foreign Affairs and Defense, Box 26, SMOF: Ronald Ziegler, WHCF, NPMP.

12. Nixon had suggested the existence of secret negotiations earlier. During a 3 November 1969 address to the nation, Nixon declared that "we have taken other significant initiatives which must remain secret to keep open some channels of communication which may still prove productive." During a 20 July 1970 news conference, he asserted that he had given latitude to American delegates in France "to discuss the proposals that we have made both in public and in private sessions to the North Vietnamese and the VC."

13. Nixon, *Memoirs*, 585. Nixon made the announcement also because he feared that the existence of secret talks would eventually be leaked to the press. According to Nixon, two individuals who had access to Kissinger's negotiating files were in a position to do just that. The first was a navy yeoman suspected of having previously been the source of a leak during the Indo-Pakistan conflict. The second was a former member of Kissinger's staff who resigned over the administration's policy in Cambodia and was now foreign policy adviser for Edmund Muskie's presidential campaign. See ibid., 586.

14. A copy of the proposal may be found in File #3, RN 8-Point Peace Plan (Contains Top Secret/Sensitive) I [2–18] [1 of 3], Numerical Subject Files, Foreign Affairs and Defense, Box 28, SMOF: Ronald Ziegler, WHCF, NPMP.

15. Ibid.

16. The details of that arrangement were worked out during a visit to Saigon by Kissinger deputy Alexander Haig in September 1971. See Nguyen Tien Hung and Schecter, *Palace File*, 45–49.

17. *Nhan dan*, 29 January 1972; Kissinger Memorandum for Nixon, 28 January 1972,

President's Daily Briefs—Jan. 3–31, 1972, President's Daily Briefings, Box 1, POW/MIA, NPMP.

18.   *Nhan dan*, 29 January 1972. The documents were the DRVN Nine Points proposal of 26 June 1971; the PRG Seven Points proposal of 1 July 1971; the American Eight Points proposal of 11 October 1971; the American Eight Points proposal of 25 January 1972; American messages dated 11 October, 3 and 19 November 1971; and two DRVN messages dated 25 October and 17 November 1971. The authenticity of the documents was confirmed by the Nixon White House. See Holdridge Memorandum for Kissinger, 31 January 1972, #2 Paris Talks #3 2–18 RN 8-Point Peace Plan Speech 1/25/72 [2 of 2], Numerical Subject Files, Foreign Affairs and Defense, Box 24, SMOF: Ronald Ziegler, WHCF, NPMP.

19.   *Nhan dan*, 3 February 1972.

20.   Ibid.

21.   The idea of détente with the Soviets had been fermenting since April 1969. See Kissinger, *White House Years*, 141–44, and Nixon, *Memoirs*, 391.

22.   Garthoff, *Détente and Confrontation*, 248–61; Wich, *Sino-Soviet Crisis Politics*. Kissinger first became aware of the seriousness of the Sino-Soviet rift during a meeting with Foreign Service officer and China expert Allen Whiting in 1969. See Whiting, "Sino-American Détente," 336.

23.   Nixon had earlier in his career endorsed the position that China was the primary agent responsible for the insurgency in Vietnam. In a 1964 speech before the American Society of Newspaper Editors, he remarked that Vietnam was "the right place to take effective action against Chinese aggression." See *Washington Post*, 19 May 1964. As president, however, Nixon repudiated that position.

24.   Reichley, *Conservatives in an Age of Change*, 107; Kissinger, *White House Years*, 168.

25.   On the "ping-pong diplomacy" and Kissinger's secret visit to Beijing see Chen Jian, *Mao's China*, 257–68. In February and March 2002, the *New York Times* ran a series of articles about the Nixon administration based on newly declassified documents and the release of more hours of "Nixon tapes." Among the articles were two pieces by Elaine Sciolino alleging that Kissinger was so eager to "bring the Vietnam War to an end" that he told the Chinese during his secret visit to China in July 1971 that the United States was prepared to withdraw from Vietnam "[w]ith or without negotiations" and "unilaterally." Sciolino quotes historian Stanley Karnow as saying, "Unilaterally is the key thing. This is new to me," to make the point that this is indeed a major revelation (*New York Times*, 28 February and 3 March 2002). The Nixon administration never seriously considered that contingency, as this study demonstrates.

26.   Excerpts from the letter are quoted in Nixon, *Memoirs*, 586.

27.   Nixon, *No More Vietnams*, 105–6.

28.   For further details on the events of 1964 see Moïse, *Tonkin Gulf*, 48–49.

29.   On Chinese and Soviet assistance to the Vietnamese revolutionary cause see, respectively, Qiang Zhai, *China and the Vietnam Wars*, and Gaiduk, *Soviet Union and the Vietnam War*.

30.   Cadieux Cable to GPE, 26 October 1972, File 31-13-Viet-ICSC-12, Vol. 4, DFAITF, CDFAITHS; Cadieux Cable to GPE, 27 November 1972, 1, File 21-13-Viet-ICSC-12, Vol. 5, DFAITF, CDFAITHS.

31.   Cadieux Cable to GPE, 27 November 1972, File 21-13-Viet-ICSC-12, Vol. 5, DFAITF, CDFAITHS.

32.   Haldeman, *Diaries*, 488.

33.   Ibid., 498–99; Nixon, *Memoirs*, 588–89.

34.   For the text of the communiqué see *Peking Review*, 3 March 1972.

35.   On Sino-Vietnamese relations during this period see Qiang Zhai, *China and the Vietnam Wars*, 193–202, and Gilks, *Breakdown of the Sino-Vietnamese Alliance*. The Viet-

namese position is detailed in Smyser, *Independent Vietnamese*, and Buu Kinh, "Nord-Viêtnam."

36. On the Nixon visit to China, consult, in addition to the memoirs of Nixon and Kissinger, Haldeman, *Diaries*, 499–514.

37. Van Tien Dung, *Cuoc khang chien chong My*, 102.

38. Qiang Zhai, *China and the Vietnam Wars*, 136, 195–96. The table on page 136 details the amount of Chinese assistance to North Vietnam between 1964 and 1975.

39. On Chinese opposition to negotiations between the United States and North Vietnam during the early stages of the war see Qiang Zhai, "Opposing Negotiations."

40. The Vietnamese claim that the most noticeable increases were not in weapons shipments but in edible commodities.

41. Dang cong san Viet Nam, *Su that ve quan he Viet Nam–Trung Quoc*, 50, 59, 62.

42. Nguyen Co Thach, *Vi hoa binh va an ninh*, 10.

43. Quoted in *Nhung su kien lich su Dang*, 584.

44. As part of the planning process, Hanoi sent envoys to Moscow and Beijing to secure additional material assistance as well as pledges of support for the attack. See Gaiduk, *Soviet Union and the Vietnam War*, 231–32.

45. Quoted in *Nhung su kien lich su Dang*, 585.

46. The assault on the central highlands was dubbed the Nguyen Hue battle. Western historians, particularly American authors, erroneously allude to the entire campaign as the Nguyen Hue offensive.

47. Quoted in Hoc vien Quan su cao cap, *Cuoc khang chien chong My*, 239.

48. Van Tien Dung, "Hai thang loi," 4.

49. Van Tien Dung, *Cuoc khang chien chong My*, 104. See also Tran Van Tra's comments quoted in Isaacs, *Without Honor*, 18. Tra observed that the aim of the offensive was to score a decisive victory and force Washington to sign an agreement reflecting capitulation.

50. Van Tien Dung, *Cuoc khang chien chong My*, 105–6 n. 1.

51. Nguyen Phung Minh et al., *Nam Trung Bo khang chien*, 445.

52. Haldeman, *Diaries*, 528.

53. Kissinger, *White House Years*, 1099.

54. The two best histories of the offensive in English are Ngo Quang Truong, *Easter Offensive*, and G. H. Turley, *Easter Offensive*.

55. Luu Van Loi and Nguyen Anh Vu, *Cac cuoc thuong luong*, 204.

56. Nixon Memorandum for Kissinger, 20 April 1972, April 1972, Kissinger, Trip to Moscow, President's Speech File, 1969–74, Box 74, SF: President's Personal Files, WHCF, NPMP. Emphasis is Nixon's. See also Nixon, *Memoirs*, 587–88.

57. Kissinger Cable for Haig, 21 April 1972, April 1972, Kissinger, Trip to Moscow, President's Speech File, 1969–74, Box 74, SF: President's Personal Files, WHCF, NPMP.

58. Kissinger Cable for Nixon, 22 April 1972, April 1972, Kissinger, Trip to Moscow, President's Speech File, 1969–74, Box 74, SF: President's Personal Files, WHCF, NPMP.

59. Ibid.

60. Nixon Cable for Kissinger, 23 April 1972, April 1972, Kissinger, Trip to Moscow, President's Speech File, 1969–74, Box 74, SF: President's Personal Files, WHCF, NPMP.

61. Ibid.

62. Kissinger Cable for Nixon, 24 April 1972, April 1972, Kissinger, Trip to Moscow, President's Speech File, 1969–74, Box 74, SF: President's Personal Files, WHCF, NPMP.

63. Kissinger Cable for Haig, 24 April 1972, April 1972, Kissinger, Trip to Moscow, President's Speech File, 1969–74, Box 74, SF: President's Personal Files, WHCF, NPMP.

64. Nixon, *Memoirs*, 592.
65. Kissinger Cable for Haig, 24 April 1972, April 1972, Kissinger, Trip to Moscow, President's Speech File, 1969–74, Box 74, SF: President's Personal Files, WHCF, NPMP.
66. Bo Quoc phong, *Lich su nghe thuat chien dich*, 421.
67. Nixon Flash Cable for Andrews, 26 April 1972, Wednesday, April 26, 1972—Vietnam Report, President's Speech File, 1969–74, Box 74, SF: President's Personal Files, WHCF, NPMP.
68. Haig Memorandum for Nixon, 24 April 1972, April 1972, Kissinger, Trip to Moscow, President's Speech File, 1969–74, Box 74, SF: President's Personal Files, WHCF, NPMP.
69. The mining of Haiphong harbor was first suggested to Nixon by Alexander Haig. However, that contingency had been contemplated by American military planners since 1964 and presented to Lyndon Johnson by Walt Rostow in a 6 May 1967 memorandum. See Prados, *Hidden History*, 264–65.
70. Haldeman, *Diaries*, 532.
71. Quoted in Nixon, *Memoirs*, 593–94.
72. Abrams Report, 3 May 1972, Haig Speech File (Vol. 7) March 72–June 72 [2 of 3], Speech Files, Box 48, SMOF: Gen. Alexander Haig, WHCF, NPMP.
73. Kissinger Memorandum for Nixon, 2 May 1972, Camp David—Sensitive Vol. XII, For the President's Files—Winston Lord, Vietnam Negotiations, Box 4, POW/MIA, NPMP.
74. Ibid.
75. Luu Van Loi and Nguyen Anh Vu, *Cac cuoc thuong luong*, 215.
76. Haldeman, *Diaries*, 536; Nixon, *Memoirs*, 595. Nixon was also beginning to feel intense congressional pressure. On 17 April, after hearing Secretary of State William Rogers's defense of the administration's bombing policy in Indochina, the Senate Foreign Relations Committee voted to terminate funding for American combat operations in Indochina after 31 December. See Knappman, ed., *South Vietnam*, 54–61.
77. Nixon, *Memoirs*, 535, 602.
78. Ibid., 600–601. In his memoirs, Kissinger is less forthright about his position. See Kissinger, *White House Years*, 1174.
79. Haldeman, *Diaries*, 550.
80. Haig and McCarry, *Inner Circles*, 286.
81. Ibid., 204–5.
82. Since 6 April, Haig had been preparing a contingency for the bombing of all military targets in northern Vietnam and for the mining of ports should the ARVN prove unable to hold the PAVN. See ibid., 282.
83. On the 4 May meeting see Haldeman, *Diaries*, 551–54; Nixon, *Memoirs*, 601–2; and Kissinger, *White House Years*, 1179–80.
84. Haldeman, *Diaries*, 556. Nixon had used the "Rubicon" analogy on at least two occasions at this juncture. On 13 May 1972, Nixon told Kissinger after he decided to sacrifice the summit for Vietnam, "In effect, we have crossed the Rubicon and now we must win" (Nixon, *Memoirs*, 594).
85. Kissinger, *White House Years*, 1179.
86. See Colson Memorandum for Nixon, 6 January 1972, and Hallett Memorandum for Colson, 3 January 1972, in H. Miscellaneous Materials 1972, Haldeman Notes, Box 48, SMOF: H. R. Haldeman, WHCF, NPMP.
87. Kahn's article appeared in the 18 November 1972 edition of the *Saturday Review*. Nixon's copy of the article was found in Briefing, undated, Vietnam—Kahn, Name/Subject File, 1969–74, Box 16, SF: President's Personal Files, WHCF, NPMP.
88. U.S. Congress, *United States–Vietnam Relations*, 21.

89. Briefing, undated, Vietnam—Rostow, Name/Subject File, 1969–74, Box 16, SF: President's Personal Files, WHCF, NPMP.
90. Nixon's address of 8 May 1972 is reproduced in U.S. President, *Weekly Compilation*, 11 May 1972, 23–36.
91. The term "Linebacker" was chosen by Nixon himself and reflected the president's passion for football. That infatuation went even further, as the American president liked being addressed as "Quarterback" in flash messages sent to him from Paris or Saigon by Kissinger.
92. CIA Intelligence Memorandum ("The Overall Impact of the US Bombing and Mining Program on North Vietnam"), August 1972, I, Follow Up Analysis of Rather/Szulc Stories Assessing Mining and Bombing of North Vietnam, Haldeman Confidential Files, Box 46, SMOF: H. R. Haldeman, WHCF, NPMP.
93. Gaiduk, *Soviet Union and the Vietnam War*, 237–38.
94. Dobrynin, *In Confidence*, 202.
95. Haldeman, *Diaries*, 559.
96. From the memorandum quoted in Nixon, *Memoirs*, 607. Emphasis is Nixon's.
97. Quoted in Mark A. Clodfelter, *Limits of Air Power*, 164.
98. Regular self-defense combatants were to spend five to seven days a year in training; cadres, fifteen days, except for those serving in "strategic provinces" (that is, regions most susceptible to being heavily attacked in the event of a renewal of air raids), who had to spend fifteen to twenty days; and higher ranking cadres, twenty days, except for those in war zones who had to spend twenty-five days.
99. Dang lao dong Viet Nam, *Nhung van kien co ban*.
100. Brezhnev quoted in Safire, *Before the Fall*, 448.
101. Qiang Zhai, *China and the Vietnam Wars*, 203.
102. Nixon, *No More Vietnams*, 141; Herring, *America's Longest War*, 242. The Moscow visit was diplomatically more productive than the series of meetings with Mao and Zhou Enlai. The latter were significant more for their symbolic value than for their substance. While Nixon devoted a lot of his time in the USSR to discussing important issues, he spent the majority of his time in China sightseeing, attending semi-official functions, and going to state dinners. According to Haldeman, Nixon himself believed that "the Russian trip goes to the heart of what people are worried about" and, consequently, "creates a greater reaction than China's more superficial effect." See Haldeman, *Diaries*, 571.
103. Situation Room Memorandum for Kissinger, 21 April 1972, April 1972, Kissinger, Trip to Moscow, President's Speech File, Box 74, SF: President's Personal Files, WHCF, NPMP.
104. Vietnamese sources published during and after the Sino-Vietnamese border war of 1979 reveal that Hanoi was deeply offended by China's attitude toward the war after 1971. The response to Moscow's behavior, which Hanoi considered equally damaging, was never made public because of Hanoi's dependence on Soviet assistance, which continued until 1990. Today, Vietnamese sources rarely mention Moscow and Beijing's dealings with the United States during the war. For details on the DRVN's public response to Chinese overtures to the United States during the Resistance see Lawson, *Sino-Vietnamese Conflict*, 242–47. On North Vietnamese anxiety over Soviet behavior see Pike, *Vietnam and the Soviet Union*, 91–93.
105. On the mining see Ethell and Price, *One Day*, 14–15, and Van Tien Dung, *Cuoc khang chien chong My*, 124–25. The types of mines used by the United States were the MK36, weighing 500 pounds, the MK52, weighing 1,000 pounds, and the MK55, weighing 2,000 pounds. Once dropped, they sank to the ocean floor and monitored underwater signals emanating from a ship's magnetic field, propeller wash, engine noise, and decreased pressure from its wake. The right combination of those elements sparked an explosion. See Tilford, *Setup*, 233, and Marolda, ed., *Operation End Sweep*.

106. Twelve of the ships were Soviet, five Chinese (PRC), three U.K./Hong Kong, two Cuban, one East German, three Polish, and five Somalian.

107. CIA Intelligence Memorandum ("The Overall Impact of the US Bombing and Mining Program on North Vietnam"), August 1972; Nguyen Tu Duong, *Duong mon tren bien*, 123–27; Tong cuc hau can Bo quoc phong, *Lich su bo doi Truong Son*, 280.

108. CIA Intelligence Memorandum ("The Overall Impact of the US Bombing and Mining Program on North Vietnam"), August 1972.

109. Ibid.

110. Turner, "Pave Strike," 62, 65; Glines, *Compact History*, 340.

111. On the Thanh Hoa and other bridges see Lavalle et al., *Tale of Two Bridges*.

112. Uy ban dieu tra toi ac chien tranh cua de quoc My o Viet Nam, "Toi ac chinh quyen Nixon trong buoc leo thang chien tranh tu thang 4/1972 den nay," 14 June 1972, Ho so: Toi ac cua My trong viec dung khong quan tien hanh chien tranh xam luoc Viet Nam, VV, #100, Phong: Uy ban dieu tra toi ac chien tranh cua de quoc My o Viet Nam, VSA3.

113. Hoang Van Khang, *Dang thang B-52*, 106.

114. On the effectiveness of B-52 strikes during the offensive see Sheehan, *Bright Shining Lie*, 780–83, and Morzek, *Air Power*, 144–45. The success of the bombing in deterring the invasion was even acknowledged in a *Nhan dan* editorial that stated: "We would have accomplished our goal in April of this year had Nixon not re-Americanized the war with his navy and air force. Because the war was re-Americanized, we were unable to drive ahead" (*Nhan dan*, 25 September 1972).

115. O'Ballance, *Wars in Vietnam*, 169–70.

116. Nguyen Thanh Le, *Cuoc dam phan Pari*, 77–78.

117. Quoted in Van Tien Dung, *Cuoc khang chien chong My*, 124–25.

118. Ibid., 130–31.

Chapter Three

1. Uy ban dieu tra toi ac chien tranh cua de quoc My o Viet Nam, "Toi ac huy diet cua chinh quyen Nixon doi voi cac khu dong dan o mien Bac Viet Nam trong buoc leo thang chien tranh tu 4/1972 den nay," September 1972, Ho so: Tai lieu cua Uy ban dieu tra toi ac cua de quoc My o Viet Nam ve toi ac cua My o Viet Nam, VV, #101, Phong: Uy ban dieu tra toi ac cua de quoc My o Viet Nam, VSA3.

2. Khac Huynh, "Dam phan Pari," 24; Nguyen Thanh Le, *Cuoc dam phan Pari*, 78–79.

3. Le Duan, *Thu vao Nam*, 302–3; Le Duan, *Ve chien tranh*, 425–26.

4. Le Duan, *Ve chien tranh*, 426.

5. *Nhan dan*, 14 August 1972.

6. Ibid., 2 March 1972.

7. From Truong Chinh's speech at the Third Congress of the Vietnam Fatherland Front, reproduced in Truong Chinh, *Selected Writings*, 689.

8. *Doan ket*, 12 August 1972.

9. *Nhan dan*, 12 August 1972; Tran Nham, *Nghe thuat biet thang*, 37.

10. Haig and McCarry, *Inner Circles*, 296.

11. From a Nguyen Duy Trinh letter for Pham Van Dong, quoted in Luu Van Loi and Nguyen Anh Vu, *Cac cuoc thuong luong*, 222. See also Le Duan, *Thu vao Nam*, 298.

12. Le Duan and Pham Van Dong, *Ve to chuc lai san xuat*, 7–9.

13. Luu Van Loi and Nguyen Anh Vu, *Cac cuoc thuong luong*, 226; Memorandum of Conversation—Secret Paris Talks, 19 July 1972, Camp David—Sensitive Vol. XIV, For the President's Files—Winston Lord, Vietnam Negotiations, Box 4, POW/MIA, NPMP.

14. Memorandum of Conversation—Secret Paris Talks, 19 July 1972, Camp David—Sensitive Vol. XIV, For the President's Files—Winston Lord, Vietnam Negotiations, Box 4, POW/MIA, NPMP. Kissinger later modified the prisoner proposal to state

that the prisoner release could take place after the cessation of acts of force and mining against the DRVN, simultaneous to the withdrawal of foreign troops.

15. Ibid.

16. Ibid.

17. Kissinger Memorandum for Nixon, 20 July 1972, Camp David—Sensitive Vol. XVI, For the President's Files—Winston Lord, Vietnam Negotiations, Box 4, POW/MIA, NPMP.

18. Luu Van Loi and Nguyen Anh Vu, *Cac cuoc thuong luong*, 234–35.

19. From the excerpt of the transcript of a news conference held by President Nixon at the White House on 29 June 1972, reproduced in Department of State, *Bulletin*, 17 July 1972, 83.

20. Kissinger, *White House Years*, 1307–8.

21. See Hai Thu, *Nord Viêtnam*; Momyer, *Air Power*, 33.

22. This approach was commonly called the "San Antonio Formula." On 29 September 1967, in an address before the National Legislative Conference in San Antonio, Texas, Johnson stated: "The United States is willing to stop all aerial and naval bombardments of North Vietnam when this will lead promptly to productive discussions. We, of course, assume that while discussions proceed, North Vietnam would not take advantage of the bombing cessation or limitation" (Johnson, *Vantage Point*, 267). This formula was first suggested by Canadian prime minister Lester B. Pearson during an address at Temple University in 1965. See Herring, ed., *Secret Diplomacy*, 106.

23. Quoted in Roger Morris, *Uncertain Greatness*, 164.

24. *Ha Noi moi*, 29 June 1972.

25. *New York Times*, 28 July 1972.

26. NSC Memorandum for Ron Ziegler, 2 August 1972, Paris Talks, File #3, RN 8-Point Peace Plan (Contains Top Secret/Sensitive) I [2–18] [1 of 3], Numerical Subject Files, Foreign Affairs and Defense, Box 24, SMOF: Ronald Ziegler, WHCF, NPMP.

27. Bunker Cable for Kissinger, 25 July 1972, Backchannel Messages—To: Amb. Bunker—Saigon—1972, Backchannel, Box 3, POW/MIA, NPMP; Memorandum of Conversation—Secret Paris Talks, 1 August 1972, and Kissinger Memorandum for Nixon, 3 August 1972, C[amp] D[avid] 1972, May 2–Oct. 7, 1972 [2 of 4], Files for the President—Vietnam Negotiations, Box 4, POW/MIA, NPMP.

28. Luu Van Loi and Nguyen Anh Vu, *Cac cuoc thuong luong*, 241–44.

29. Stephen J. Morris, *Why Vietnam Invaded Cambodia*, 56.

30. For more details on the deterioration of the Hanoi-KCP relationship see ibid., 48–58.

31. Kissinger, *White House Years*, 1315–16; Kissinger Memorandum for Nixon, 26 August 1972, Camp David—Sensitive Vol. XVII, For the President's Files—Winston Lord, Vietnam Negotiations, Box 4, POW/MIA, NPMP.

32. Luu Van Loi and Nguyen Anh Vu, *Cac cuoc thuong luong*, 247–51; Kissinger, *White House Years*, 1318–19.

33. See the two memoranda of conversation between Nguyen Van Thieu and Kissinger dated 17 and 18 August 1972 in John Negroponte Negotiations Files, 1972–73, Vol. II, Jon Howe Subject Files, Box 7, POW/MIA, NPMP.

34. Memorandum of Conversation—Thieu-Kissinger Meeting, 18 August 1972, John Negroponte Negotiations Files, 1972–73, Vol. II, Jon Howe Subject Files, Box 7, POW/MIA, NPMP.

35. Nguyen Tien Hung and Schecter, *Palace File*, 67.

36. From the 31 August 1972 letter reproduced in ibid., 375.

37. Luu Van Loi and Nguyen Anh Vu, *Cac cuoc thuong luong*, 251.

38. Ibid., 255.

39. Ibid., 257.

40. That the failure of the Spring Offensive set the stage for the Paris Peace Agreement is discussed in Thompson, *Peace Is Not at Hand*, 120–21, and Lomperis, *War Everyone Lost*, 88–90.

41. Ulsamer, "Airpower Halts Invasion," 60; Michael Clodfelter, *Vietnam in Military Statistics*, 201.

42. "North Vietnamese Diplomats Comment on DRV's Situation, Relations with Allies," in Kissinger Memorandum for Nixon, 28 June 1972, H[enry] A. K[issinger]/President Memos (NVN), Situation in Vietnam, May–Aug. 1972, Vietnam Subject Files, Box 2, POW/MIA, NPMP.

43. See Nguyen Khac Vien's comments in Marr and Werner, *Tradition and Revolution*, 149.

44. Portes, *Les Américains*, 238–39. Two comprehensive accounts of the program are Andradé, *Ashes to Ashes*, and Valentine, *Phoenix Program*.

45. In January 1966, the ARVN was comprised of 569,000 soldiers (Michael Clodfelter, *Vietnam in Military Statistics*, 196).

46. That the behavior of the PRC and the Soviet Union had a significant impact on Hanoi's attitude toward negotiations is discussed in Hyland, *Mortal Rivals*, 5. Hyland was an aide on Kissinger's staff.

47. "North Vietnamese Diplomats Comment on DRV's Situation."

48. *Nhan dan*, 19 August 1972.

49. Uy ban dieu tra toi ac chien tranh cua de quoc My o Viet Nam, "De an ve dot len an My nem bom huy diet cac thanh pho va cac khu dong dan," 29 September 1972, Ho so: Len an chinh quyen Nixon nem bom huy diet cac thanh pho va cac khu dong dan o hai mien nuoc ta, VV, #94, Phong: Uy ban dieu tra toi ac chien tranh cua de quoc My o Viet Nam, VSA3.

50. "North Vietnamese Diplomats Comment on DRV's Situation."

51. "Phuong huong va nhiem vu ke hoach nam 1974–1975 va cong tac lap ke hoach nhap khau vat tu thiet bi nam 1974," 10 March 1973, Ho so: Chi thi cua Bo cong nghiep nang ve lap ke hoach nhap khau ve vien tro nam 1974, VV, #1275, Phong: Bo cong nghiep nang vu ke hoach, VSA3.

52. Le Duan, *Thu vao Nam*, 316–18. The average "letter to the South" was 1,000 words in length; this letter was three times that length.

53. Ibid., 326, 330.

54. Luu Van Loi and Nguyen Anh Vu, *Cac cuoc thuong luong*, 258.

55. On McGovern's involvement in the North Vietnamese–American diplomatic process see Berman, *No Peace*, 82–102.

56. *Nhan dan*, 11 September 1972; *New York Times*, 12 September 1972.

57. The ICSC was established in 1954 by the Geneva Accords. Its mandate was to supervise and arbitrate the implementation of the agreements.

58. Negroponte Memorandum for Kissinger, 18 September 1972, John Negroponte Negotiations Files, 1972–73, Vol. II, Jon Howe Vietnam Subject Files, Box 5, POW/MIA, NPMP.

59. "Major Differences between New U.S. Proposal and DRV September 15 Plan (minus political provisions)," Camp David—Sensitive Vol. XVIII, For the President's Files—Winston Lord, Vietnam Negotiations, Box 4, POW/MIA, NPMP.

60. Luu Van Loi and Nguyen Anh Vu, *Cac cuoc thuong luong*, 260–63.

61. Ibid., 264–65.

62. Memorandum of Conversation—Secret Paris Talks, 15 September 1972, C[amp] D[avid]—1972, May 2–Oct. 7, 1972 [2 of 4], Files for the President—Vietnam Negotiations, Box 4, POW/MIA, NPMP. Allan Goodman contends that this "foundation for a conceptual breakthrough" took place during the May 1972 summit in Moscow, at which point Kissinger indicated to Soviet foreign minister Gromyko that Washington was prepared to sign an agreement incorporating political as well as a military provisions. The document cited above, however, negates that conten-

tion and proves the "conceptual breakthrough" occurred in mid-September. See Goodman, *Lost Peace*, 123–33.

63.   *Nhan dan*, 15 August 1972.

64.   Haig Memorandum for Nixon, 15 September 1972, President's Daily Briefs—Sept. 1972, President's Daily Briefings, Box 1, POW/MIA, NPMP.

65.   Haldeman, *Diaries*, 614; Kissinger, *White House Years*, 1333.

66.   Luu Van Loi and Nguyen Anh Vu, *Cac cuoc thuong luong*, 265–66.

67.   The congruity of American and Vietnamese sources is discussed further in the bibliographical section.

68.   Haig Memorandum for Nixon, 15 September 1972, President's Daily Briefs—Sept. 1972, President's Daily Briefings, Box 1, POW/MIA, NPMP.

69.   For a critical assessment of the "madman" theory see Kimball, *Nixon's Vietnam War*, 76–86.

70.   Truong Nhu Tang, *Viet Cong Memoir*, 214.

71.   On congressional votes on Vietnam see Niehaus and Shuey, *Legislation Restricting Involvement*, and Kissinger, *White House Years*, 1307.

72.   Lehman, *Executive*, 215.

73.   Haldeman, *Diaries*, 613.

74.   See the chart in Lewy, *America in Vietnam*, 147.

75.   From the cable quoted in Kissinger, *White House Years*, 1335.

76.   Kissinger Memorandum for Nixon, 28 September 1972, Camp David—1972, May 2–Oct. 7, 1972, [1 of 4], Files for the President—Vietnam Negotiations, Box 4, POW/MIA, NPMP.

77.   Luu Van Loi and Nguyen Anh Vu, *Cac cuoc thuong luong*, 270; Memorandum of Conversation—Secret Paris Talks, 27 September 1972, Camp David—1972, May 2–Oct. 7, 1972 [1 of 4], Files for the President—Vietnam Negotiations, Box 4, POW/MIA, NPMP.

78.   Haig and McCarry, *Inner Circles*, 294–96. In his memoirs Kissinger is less forthright about the presence of this provision in the proposal but suggests its existence. "I recommended that we put a number of options before Thieu as political proposals for the next meeting," he wrote. "We might agree to elections for a Constituent Assembly instead of presidential elections" (Kissinger, *White House Years*, 1338).

79.   Haldeman, *Diaries*, 620–21.

80.   Ibid. The account in Haldeman's diaries disproves the conventional belief that Kissinger exceeded his authority when he tried to strike a deal before the election. It clearly shows that Nixon was behind Kissinger when the latter returned to Paris in early October.

81.   Kissinger Cable to Bunker, 27 September 1972, Backchannel Messages—To: Amb. Bunker—Saigon—Sept. 1972 [Part 2], Backchannel, Box 3, POW/MIA, NPMP.

82.   Haig and McCarry, *Inner Circles*, 294–96; Nguyen Tien Hung and Schecter, *Palace File*, 72–73.

83.   Haldeman, *Diaries*, 623–24.

84.   Luu Van Loi and Nguyen Anh Vu, *Cac cuoc thuong luong*, 273–75.

85.   Author interview with Luu Van Loi, 12 June 1996, Hanoi, Vietnam; Luu Van Loi, *50 nam ngoai giao*, 338.

Chapter Four

1.   Hoang Van Thai, *Tran danh ba muoi nam*, 467–68.

2.   Luu Van Loi and Nguyen Anh Vu, *Cac cuoc thuong luong*, 278–79; Nguyen Thanh Le, *Cuoc dam phan Paris*, 99–100.

3.   Luu Van Loi and Nguyen Anh Vu, *Cac cuoc thuong luong*, 282–83.

4.   Kissinger, *White House Years*, 1343–44; Haig and McCarry, *Inner Circles*, 299.

5.   Kissinger Cable for Haldeman, 8 October 1972, Haldeman Miscellaneous Materials, 1972, Haldeman Notes, Box 48, SMOF: H. R. Haldeman, WHCF, NPMP.

6. Ibid.

7. Haldeman, *Diaries*, 625; Kissinger Cable for Haldeman, 11 October 1972, Haldeman Miscellaneous Materials, 1972, Haldeman Notes, Box 48, SMOF: H. R. Haldeman, WHCF, NPMP.

8. Since there are no copies of the 11 October draft settlement available for public scrutiny, I used a copy of the settlement dated 27 October 1972 and, looking at the modifications brought to the text during the interval, re-created the first version. Without quoting the text in its entirety, I have in the paragraphs that follow described the provisions included in that draft. The 27 October copy of the "Agreement on Ending the War and Restoring Peace in Viet-Nam" can be found in General Speech Material [2 of 5], Speech Files, Box 44, SMOF: Alexander M. Haig, Jr., WHCF, NPMP.

9. The four parties were the United States, the GVN, the DRVN, and the PRG.

10. That included the two South Vietnamese parties, the GVN and the PRG.

11. See copies of the DRVN draft of Chapter III and the American copy of the same chapter attached to Memorandum of Conversation—Secret Paris Talks, 13 October 1972, October C[amp] D[avid] Originals—HAK[issinger], [Folder 2 of 4], For the President's Files—Winston Lord, Vietnam Negotiations, Box 4, POW/MIA, NPMP.

12. Kissinger proposed American aid in the amount of $1.5 billion, $600 million of which would go to the DRVN.

13. Memorandum of Conversation—Secret Paris Talks, 13 October 1972, October C[amp] D[avid] Originals—HAK[issinger], [Folder 2 of 4], For the President's Files—Winston Lord, Vietnam Negotiations, Box 4, POW/MIA, NPMP; Nixon, *Memoirs*, 691.

14. Kissinger Cable for Haldeman, 12 October 1972, Haldeman Miscellaneous Materials, 1972, Haldeman Notes, Box 48, SMOF: H. R. Haldeman, WHCF, NPMP.

15. Haldeman, *Diaries*, 703.

16. Nixon, *Memoirs*, 691–92; Kissinger, *White House Years*, 1360–61; Haldeman, *Diaries*, 627–29.

17. Kissinger, *White House Years*, 1345–47.

18. Luu Van Loi and Nguyen Anh Vu, *Cac cuoc thuong luong*, 308.

19. Nixon's message is quoted in Memorandum of Conversation—Secret Paris Talks, 13 October 1972, Camp David—Sensitive Vol. XX, For the President's Files—Winston Lord, Vietnam Negotiations, Box 4, POW/MIA, NPMP.

20. Guay Cable for Haig—Message from DRV, 14 October 1972, Camp David—Sensitive Vol. XX, For the President's Files—Winston Lord, Vietnam Negotiations, Box 4, POW/MIA, NPMP.

21. *Le Monde*, 1 November 1972.

22. Nixon, *Memoirs*, 693–94.

23. Haig Cable for Guay—Message from Nixon, 14 October 1972, Backchannel Messages—Paris 26 Patch—1972, Backchannel Messages, Box 3, POW/MIA, NPMP.

24. Bunker Cable for Kissinger, 15 October 1972, Backchannel Messages—From Amb. Bunker—Saigon—Sept. 1972, Backchannel Messages, Box 3, POW/MIA, NPMP.

25. Nixon, *Memoirs*, 694.

26. Memorandum of Conversation—Secret Paris Talks, 17 October 1972, C[amp] D[avid] Documents—Dr. Kissinger TS, Henry A. Kissinger Office Files—Country Files–Far East–Vietnam, Box 6, POW/MIA, NPMP.

27. Haig Cable for Guay, 18 October 1972, Sensitive—Camp David Cable—Oct. 1972, For the President's Files—Winston Lord, Vietnam Negotiations, Box 4, POW/MIA, NPMP.

28. Haldeman Notes, 15 October 1972, H Notes Oct.–Nov.–Dec. 1972 [1 Oct. to 17 Nov. 1972] Part I, Haldeman Notes, Box 46, SMOF: H. R. Haldeman, WHCF, NPMP.

29. Haig Memorandum for Nixon (from Kissinger), 17 October 1972, HAK Paris/Saigon Trip HAKTO Oct. 16–23, 1973, Henry A. Kissinger Office Files—HAK Trip Files, Box 5, POW/MIA, NPMP.

30. Kissinger, *White House Years*, 1365.

31. Nixon's letter and the meeting are discussed in ibid., 1368–70.

32. Bunker Cable for Haig, 22 October 1972, Backchannel Messages—From Amb. Bunker—Saigon—Sept. 1972, Backchannel Messages, Box 3, POW/MIA, NPMP.

33. Kissinger, *White House Years*, 1370.

34. Tran Van Don, *Endless War*, 202.

35. Nguyen Tien Hung and Schecter, *Palace File*, 83.

36. Ibid., 88.

37. Kissinger alleges that his staff noticed the ambiguity on 12 October and that he intended to effect the change during his next session with Tho. See Kissinger, *White House Years*, 1364.

38. Nguyen Tien Hung and Schecter, *Palace File*, 88. Saigon's concerns were tenable. In his memoirs, Kissinger confirms that Hanoi did not recognize the Saigon regime as legitimate. In the negotiations, Kissinger writes, Le Duc Tho "did not regard South Vietnam as a foreign country" and refused to refer to the four states of Indochina because that represented "a total surrender." See Kissinger, *White House Years*, 1354.

39. Nguyen Tien Hung and Schecter, *Palace File*, 88.

40. Ibid., 89.

41. Ibid., 123.

42. Kissinger Memorandum for Nixon, 23 October 1972, Camp David—Sensitive Vol. XXI (1), For the President's Files—Winston Lord, Vietnam Negotiations, Box 4, POW/MIA, NPMP; Nguyen Tien Hung and Schecter, *Palace File*, 88; Tran Van Don, *Endless War*, 202–3.

43. On the two Enhance projects see Le Gro, *Vietnam*, 17–18. On Enhance Plus specifically, consult Dillard, *Sixty Days*, 115.

44. Guay Cable for Haig (DRV Message), 19 October 1972, White House File—Oct. 1972, Col. Guay's File: Paris, Henry A. Kissinger Office Files—HAK Trip Files, POW/MIA, NPMP.

45. Situation Room for Lord (Haig for Kissinger), 19 October 1972, HAK Paris/Saigon Trip TOHAK [2 of 2] Oct. 16–23, 1972, Henry A. Kissinger Office Files—Country Files—Far East–Vietnam, Box 5, POW/MIA, NPMP.

46. Kissinger Cable for Haig, 20 October 1972, US-DRVN Exchanges, Oct. 1972–Jan. 1973, Henry A. Kissinger Office Files—Country Files—Far East–Vietnam, Box 6, POW/MIA, NPMP.

47. Kissinger, *White House Years*, 1375–76.

48. Nguyen Tien Hung and Schecter, *Palace File*, 98–99.

49. The text of this message dated 21 October 1972 is in Camp David—Sensitive Vol. XX, For the President's Files—Winston Lord, Vietnam Negotiations, Box 4, POW/MIA, NPMP.

50. Haig Cable for Kissinger, 21 October 1972, HAK Paris/Saigon Trip TOHAK [1 of 2] Oct. 16–23, 1972, Henry A. Kissinger Office Files—HAK Trip Files, Box 5, POW/MIA, NPMP. The text of the draft agreement as of 20 October 1972—when both Hanoi and Washington considered it satisfactory and complete—is reproduced in Appendix A.

51. Ibid.

52. The cable is quoted in Nixon, *Memoirs*, 700.

53. Quoted in Kissinger, *White House Years*, 1383.

54. Nguyen Tien Hung and Schecter, *Palace File*, 103–5.

55. Thieu is quoted in Kissinger, *White House Years*, 1385.

56. Nguyen Tien Hung and Schecter, *Palace File*, 104.

57. From the cable quoted in Kissinger, *White House Years*, 1386.

58. Haig Cable for Kissinger, 22 October 1972, HAK Paris/Saigon Trip TOHAK [1 of 2] Oct. 16–23, 1972, Henry A. Kissinger Office Files—HAK Trip Files, Box 5, POW/MIA, NPMP.

59. From Haig's testimony in U.S. Senate, *Hearings on the Paris Peace Accords*, 166.

60. The preceding discussion of the Kissinger-Thieu encounter contradicts the claim by revisionist historians Gareth Porter and Gabriel Kolko, journalist Seymor Hersh, and Joseph Amter that Nixon sabotaged the agreement finalized on 20 October. See Porter, *Peace Denied*, 128; Kolko, *Anatomy of a War*, 438; Hersh, *Price of Power*, 589–609; and Amter, *Vietnam Verdict*, 279. That Thieu obstructed the finalization of a settlement in late October is also advanced by Stephen Ambrose in his well-documented *Triumph*, 631–33.

61. GPE Memorandum for Under Secretary of State for External Affairs, "Peace Settlement in Viet-Nam—South Vietnamese Position," 6 November 1972, File 21-13-Viet-ICSC-12, Vol. 4, DFAITF, CDFAITHS.

62. U.S. Senate, *Hearings on the Paris Peace Accords*, 258.

63. Haig Cable for Kissinger, 22 October 1972, HAK Paris/Saigon Trip TOHAK [1 of 2] Oct. 16–23, 1972, Henry A. Kissinger Office Files—HAK Trip Files, Box 5, POW/MIA, NPMP.

64. Bunker Cable for Kissinger, 22 October 1972, HAK Paris/Saigon Trip TOHAK [1 of 2] Oct. 16–23, 1972, Henry A. Kissinger Office Files—HAK Trip Files, Box 5, POW/MIA, NPMP.

65. Haig and McCarry, *Inner Circles*, 300.

66. Haig Cable for Kissinger, 22 October 1972, HAK Paris/Saigon Trip TOHAK [1 of 2] Oct. 16–23, 1972, Henry A. Kissinger Office Files—HAK Trip Files, Box 5, POW/MIA, NPMP.

67. GPE Memorandum for Bureau of Asian and Pacific Affairs, "Viet-Nam Peace Settlement—British Report," 17 November 1972, File 21-13-Viet-ICSC-12, Vol. 4, DFAITF, CDFAITHS.

68. Haig Cable for Guay (Nixon to Pham Van Dong), 22 October 1972, HAK Saigon Trip Memcons, Oct. 19–23, 1972, & Haig Trip Memcons, Nov. 10–12, 1972, For the President's Files—Winston Lord, Vietnam Negotiations, Box 7, POW/MIA, NPMP.

69. Le Duc Tho even scolded Henry Kissinger during one of their private sessions in August because Nixon addressed certain issues that would be covered by the cease-fire agreement during a 27 July press conference (Memorandum of Conversation—Secret Paris Talks, 1 August 1972, C[amp] D[avid]—1972, May 2–Oct. 7, 1972 [3 of 4], For the President's Files—Winston Lord, Vietnam Negotiations, Box 4, POW/MIA, NPMP).

70. The official text of the interview is reproduced in de Borchgrave, "Exclusive from Hanoi."

71. Thieu's reaction to the interview is detailed in Nguyen Tien Hung and Schecter, *Palace File*, 100–101, 115–16.

72. "Hanoi Directive to Southern Cadres on the Agreement" in Nixon Memorandum for Kissinger, 30 October 1972, President's Daily Briefs—Oct. 2–31, 1972, President's Daily Briefings, Box 1, POW/MIA, NPMP.

73. The following discussion is based on the document called "Communist Plan for 'General Uprising,'" dated 4 October 1972, reproduced in Porter, ed., *Vietnam: Definitive Documentation*, 571, and the account in Nguyen Duy Hinh, *Vietnamization*, 126–28.

74. William Le Gro (*Vietnam*, 21) contends that the success of ARVN counterattacks, which nullified nearly all DRVN/NLF gains in the South in late October, was the root cause for the ensuing breakdown in the talks.

75. Haig Cable for Kissinger, 22 October 1972, HAK Paris/Saigon Trip TOHAK [1 of 2] Oct. 16–23, 1972, Henry A. Kissinger Office Files—HAK Trip Files, Box 5, POW/MIA, NPMP.

76. Situation Room Cable for Lord (Haig to Kissinger), 23 October 1972, HAK Paris/Saigon Trip TOHAK [1 of 2] Oct. 16–23, 1972, Henry A. Kissinger Office Files—HAK Trip Files, Box 4, POW/MIA, NPMP. An F-5 is a fighter-bomber. By 1972, it was considered archaic by the Department of Defense and no longer used by American forces in Southeast Asia.

77. *Chinh luan*, 25 October 1972.

78. *Nhan dan*, 26 October 1972.

79. Kissinger Memorandum for Agnew, 27 October 1972, General Speech Material [2 of 5], Speech Files, 1970–74, Box 44, SMOF: Alexander M. Haig, Jr., WHCF, NPMP.

80. Cadieux Cable for Bureau of European Affairs, 28 October 1972, File 21-13-Viet-ICSC-12, Vol. 12, DFAITF, CDFAITHS.

Chapter Five

1. Le Duan, *Thu vao Nam*, 311–12.

2. Luu Van Loi and Nguyen Anh Vu, *Cac cuoc thuong luong*, 326.

3. Ibid., 327.

4. Dang lao dong Viet Nam, *Nhiet liet*.

5. Vien lich su quan su Viet Nam, *Lich su Quan doi*, 425.

6. Ibid., 446–47; Nguyen Hung Phong et al., *Lich su doan 308*, 260–61.

7. From the letter reproduced in Nguyen Tien Hung and Schecter, *Palace File*, 113–15.

8. Thieu quoted in Isaacson, *Kissinger*, 443. For a complete listing of Thieu's grievances see Nguyen Tien Hung and Schecter, *Palace File*, 81–106.

9. *Chinh luan*, 8 November 1972.

10. Jackson Cable for GPE, 22 November 1972, File 21-13-Viet-ICSC-12, Vol. 4, DFAITF, CDFAITHS.

11. Haldeman Notes, 29 October 1972, Haldeman Notes Oct.–Nov.–Dec. 1972 [1 Oct. to 17 Nov. 1972] Part I, Haldeman Notes, Box 46, SMOF: H. R. Haldeman, WHCF, NPMP.

12. Haig and McCarry, *Inner Circles*, 298.

13. Haldeman, *Diaries*, 645.

14. From Police Commissioner Nguyen Khac Binh's report quoted in Bunker Cable for Kissinger, 8 November 1972, Camp David—Sensitive Vol. XXI (1), For the President's Files—Winston Lord, Vietnam Negotiations, Box 4, POW/MIA, NPMP. See also Nixon, *Memoirs*, 718.

15. From the letter quoted in Nguyen Tien Hung and Schecter, *Palace File*, 121–22.

16. Minutes of Haig Meeting with Thieu, 11 November 1972, Camp David—Sensitive Vol. XXI (1), For the President's Files—Winston Lord, Vietnam Negotiations, Box 4, POW/MIA, NPMP.

17. Thieu Letter to Nixon, 11 November 1972, Thieu, Nguyen Van, Name/Subject File, 1969–74, Box 16, SF: President's Personal Files, WHSF, NPMP.

18. Haig and McCarry, *Inner Circles*, 304–5.

19. Nixon Letter to Thieu, 14 November 1972, Thieu, Nguyen Van, Name/Subject File, 1969–74, Box 16, SF: President's Personal Files, WHSF, NPMP.

20. Memorandum, November (undated), Camp David—Sensitive Vol. XXI (2), For the President's Files—Winston Lord, Vietnam Negotiations, Box 4, POW/MIA, NPMP.

21. Nixon Letter to Thieu, 18 November 1972, Thieu, Nguyen Van, Name/Subject File, 1969–74, Box 16, SF: President's Personal Files, WHSF, NPMP.

22. Negroponte Memorandum for Kissinger ("Alternate Proposal for Bilateral U.S.-DRV Agreement"), 15 November 1972, John Negroponte Negotiations Files, 1972–73, Vol. I, Jon Howe Vietnam Subject Files, Box 5, POW/MIA, NPMP.

23. Haig and McCarry, *Inner Circles*, 305.

24. Nguyen Tien Hung and Schecter, *Palace File*, 126.

25. Luu Van Loi and Nguyen Anh Vu, *Cac cuoc thuong luong*, 332.

26. Kissinger, *White House Years*, 1459.

27. Kissinger Memorandum for Nixon, 22 November 1972, Camp David—Sensitive Vol. XXI (2), For the President's Files—Winston Lord, Vietnam Negotiations, Box 4, POW/MIA, NPMP.

28. Brigham, *Guerrilla Diplomacy*, 110.

29. Kissinger, *White House Years*, 1436; Kissinger Memorandum for Nixon, 23 November 1972, Camp David—Sensitive Vol. XXI (2), For the President's Files—Winston Lord, Vietnam Negotiations, Box 4, POW/MIA, NPMP.

30. Kissinger Memorandum for Nixon, 24 November 1972, Camp David—Sensitive Vol. XXI (2), For the President's Files—Winston Lord, Vietnam Negotiations, Box 4, POW/MIA, NPMP.

31. Haldeman Cable for Kissinger, 22 November 1972, Camp David File [Nov.–Dec. 1972], H. R. Haldeman Personal File: Correspondence, Box 14, SMOF: H. R. Haldeman, WHCF, NPMP.

32. Kissinger Cable to Kennedy (for Nixon), 24 November 1972, Camp David—Sensitive Vol. XXI (2), For the President's Files—Winston Lord, Vietnam Negotiations, Box 4, POW/MIA, NPMP.

33. Ibid., 25 November 1972.

34. Haldeman, *Diaries*, 657.

35. Kissinger Memorandum for Nixon, 25 November 1972, Camp David—Sensitive Vol. XXI (2), For the President's Files—Winston Lord, Vietnam Negotiations, Box 4, POW/MIA, NPMP.

36. Kissinger Cable to Bunker, 23 November 1972, Backchannel Messages—To: Amb. Bunker—Saigon—Sept. 1972 [Part 2], Backchannel Messages, Box 3, POW/MIA, NPMP.

37. Thieu's hostility toward Kissinger and the reasons for it are detailed in Nguyen Tien Hung and Schecter, *Palace File*.

38. Kennedy Cable to Guay (Nixon for Kissinger), 24 November 1972, Sensitive— Camp David Cables—Nov. 1972, For the President's Files—Winston Lord, Vietnam Negotiations, Box 4, POW/MIA, NPMP.

39. Laird Memorandum for Nixon, undated, Cease-fire, 1972, Vietnam Subject Files, Box 7, POW/MIA, NPMP.

40. Nixon, *Memoirs*, 719.

41. Nixon Backchannel Message to Kissinger, 24 November 1972, Memos—November 1972, Memoranda for the President, 1969–74, Box 4, SF: President's Personal Files, WHSF, NPMP.

42. Memorandum of Conversation—Meeting with the South Vietnamese, 24 November 1972, GVN Memcons—Nov. 20, 1972–Apr. 3, 1973 [TS 3 of 3], Henry A. Kissinger Office Files—Country Files–Far East–Vietnam, Box 6, POW/MIA, NPMP.

43. Author telephone conversation with U.S. Navy captain John Nicholson, 12 November 1995. See also Nicholson's testimony in Levinson, *Alpha Strike*, 333–35.

44. Laird Memorandum for Nixon, 22 November 1972, Ex FG 13 7/1/72–12/29/72, Executive Files, Box 3, SF: FG (Dept. of Defense), WHSF, NPMP.

45. On this topic see Serong, "Vietnam's Menacing Cease-Fire."

46. Luu Van Loi and Nguyen Anh Vu, *Cac cuoc thuong luong*, 353.

47. Brigham, *Guerrilla Diplomacy*, 110–11.

48. Luu Van Loi and Nguyen Anh Vu, *Cac cuoc thuong luong*, 355.

49. Van Tien Dung, "Hai thang loi," 9.

50. Dang cong san Viet Nam, Ban chap hanh dang bo thanh pho Ha Noi, *Lich su dang bo thanh pho Ha Noi*, 220–21.

51. Kissinger Cable for Bunker, 26 November 1972, Backchannel Messages—To: Amb.

Bunker—Saigon—Sept. 1972 [Part 2], Backchannel Messages, Box 3, POW/MIA, NPMP.

52. Thieu Letter to Nixon, 26 November 1972, Camp David—Sensitive Vol. XXII (1), For the President's Files—Winston Lord, Vietnam Negotiations, Box 4, POW/MIA, NPMP; Kissinger Cable to Bunker, 30 November 1972, Backchannel Messages—To: Amb. Bunker—Saigon—Sept. 1972 [Part 2], Backchannel Messages, Box 3, POW/MIA, NPMP.

53. Memorandum of Conversation—Nixon Meeting with the South Vietnamese, 29 November 1972, Camp David—Meetings with GVN Advisor Duc—Washington, Nov. 29–Dec. 1, 1972—Vol. XXII, Box 4, POW/MIA, NPMP.

54. Haldeman, *Diaries*, 664; Memorandum of Conversation—Meeting with the South Vietnamese, 29 November 1972, GVN Memcons Nov. 20, 1972–Apr. 3, 1973 [TS 3 of 3], Henry A. Kissinger Office Files—Country Files–Far East–Vietnam, Box 6, POW/MIA, NPMP.

55. The documentary record indicates that Kissinger sometimes acted independently in the negotiations and, on a few occasions, even ignored Nixon's instructions. That was especially true in late 1972, when Kissinger pressed the North Vietnamese to accept certain of Saigon's demands in order to finalize an agreement that Saigon would sign. At the Hofstra Presidential Conference in 1987, Kissinger denied this, claiming that he was always subordinate to Nixon in the conduct of foreign affairs. See Friedman and Levantrosser, *Cold War Patriot*, 9.

56. Nixon Notes, 29 November 1972, November 29, 1972—Vietnam Negotiations, President's Speech File, 1969–74, Box 82, SF: President's Personal Files, WHSF, NPMP. Nixon does not mention these notes in his memoirs.

57. Kissinger Memorandum for Nixon, 30 November 1972, Tab A, John Negroponte Negotiations Files, 1972–73, Vol. I, Jon Howe Vietnam Subject Files, Box 5, POW/MIA, NPMP.

58. Haig Memorandum for Nixon's Files ("The President's Meeting with the JCS"), 30 November 1972, Camp David—Sensitive Vol. XXII (1), For the President's Files—Winston Lord, Vietnam Negotiations, Box 4, POW/MIA, NPMP.

59. Haig Memorandum for Nixon's Files ("The President's Meeting with Nguyen Phu Duc"), 30 November 1972, GVN Memcons—Nov. 20, 1972–Apr. 3, 1973 [TS 2 of 3], Henry A. Kissinger Office Files—Country Files–Far East–Vietnam, Box 6, POW/MIA, NPMP.

60. Memorandum of Conversation—Meeting with the South Vietnamese, 1 December 1972, Camp David—Meetings with GVN Advisor Duc, Washington, Nov. 29–Dec. 1, 1972—Vol. XXII, For the President's Files—Winston Lord, Vietnam Negotiations, Box 4, POW/MIA, NPMP.

61. Kissinger states in his memoirs that the White House solicited the public statements of Stennis and Goldwater to make Thieu believe that he was on very thin ice. See Kissinger, *White House Years*, 1470.

Chapter Six

1. Nixon Memorandum for Kissinger, 1 December 1972, HAK Paris Trip—HAKTO and Memos to the President, Etc., Dec. 3–13, 1972 [1 of 2], Henry A. Kissinger Office Files—HAK Trip Files, Box 5, POW/MIA, NPMP.

2. Kissinger Memorandum for Nixon, 4 December 1972, Miscellaneous 1972, Haldeman Notes, Box 48, SMOF: H. R. Haldeman, WHCF, NPMP.

3. Ibid.

4. Ibid. Poll results are from Camp David File [Nov.–Dec. 1972], H. R. Haldeman Personal File: Correspondence, Box 14, SMOF: H. R. Haldeman, WHCF, NPMP.

5. Kissinger Memorandum for Nixon, 5 December 1972, Miscellaneous 1972, Haldeman Notes, Box 48, SMOF: H. R. Haldeman, WHCF, NPMP; Kissinger Cable for

Nixon, 5 December 1972, HAK Paris Trip—Dec. 3–13, 1972—HAKTO and Memos to the President, Etc. [2 of 2], Box 5, Henry A. Kissinger Office Files—Country Files–Far East–Vietnam, POW/MIA, NPMP.

6. Haldeman, *Diaries*, 667.

7. Nixon Cable for Kissinger, 6 December 1972, Camp David—Sensitive Vol. XXII (1), For the President's Files—Winston Lord, Vietnam Negotiations, Box 4, POW/MIA, NPMP.

8. Haldeman, *Diaries*, 667–68; Haig Cable for Kennedy (Kissinger for Nixon), 5 December 1972, Miscellaneous 1972, Haldeman Notes, Box 48, SMOF: H. R. Haldeman, WHCF, NPMP.

9. The meetings of early December alternated between the DRVN site at the Léger House in Gif-sur-Yvette and a townhouse in the Neuilly property of an American businessman.

10. Nguyen Thanh Le, *Cuoc dam phan Pari*, 155–57; Luu Van Loi and Nguyen Anh Vu, *Cac cuoc thuong luong*, 361–64; Kissinger Cable for Kennedy (for Nixon), 6 December 1972, HAK Paris Trip—Dec. 3–13, 1972—HAKTO and Memos to the President, Etc. [2 of 2], Henry A. Kissinger Office Files—Country Files–Far East–Vietnam, Box 5, POW/MIA, NPMP.

11. Haldeman Memorandum for Nixon, 6 December 1972, Miscellaneous 1972, Haldeman Notes, Box 48, SMOF: H. R. Haldeman, WHCF, NPMP.

12. Ibid.

13. Nixon Memorandum for Kissinger, 6 December 1972, Miscellaneous 1972, Haldeman Notes, Box 48, SMOF: H. R. Haldeman, WHCF, NPMP.

14. Kennedy Cable for Haldeman (Kissinger for Nixon), 7 December 1972, Miscellaneous 1972, Haldeman Notes, Box 48, SMOF: H. R. Haldeman, WHCF, NPMP.

15. Ibid.

16. Ibid.

17. Haldeman Cable to Kennedy (Nixon for Kissinger), 8 December 1972, Miscellaneous 1972, Haldeman Notes, Box 48, SMOF: H. R. Haldeman, WHCF, NPMP.

18. Nguyen Thanh Le, *Cuoc dam phan Pari*, 159–61.

19. Kennedy Cable for Haldeman (Kissinger for Nixon), 8 December 1972, Miscellaneous 1972, Haldeman Notes, Box 48, SMOF: H. R. Haldeman, WHCF, NPMP.

20. Luu Van Loi and Nguyen Anh Vu, *Cac cuoc thuong luong*, 375–76.

21. Ibid., 370–71.

22. Haldeman, *Diaries*, 673.

23. Bunker Cable for Kissinger, 7 December 1972, Backchannel Messages—From Amb. Bunker—Saigon—Sept. 1972, Backchannel Messages, Box 3, POW/MIA, NPMP.

24. Kissinger, *White House Years*, 1439.

25. Luu Van Loi and Nguyen Anh Vu, *Cac cuoc thuong luong*, 375.

26. Ibid., 376.

27. Kissinger, *White House Years*, 1439.

28. Ibid., 1441–42.

29. Haig Memorandum for Nixon (from Kissinger), 12 December 1972, Camp David—Sensitive Vol. XXII (2), For the President's Files—Winston Lord, Vietnam Negotiations, Box 4, POW/MIA, NPMP.

30. Haig Cable for Kissinger (from Nixon), 12 December 1972, Camp David—Sensitive Vol. XXII (2), For the President's Files—Winston Lord, Vietnam Negotiations, Box 4, POW/MIA, NPMP.

31. In his memoirs, Kissinger alludes to seventeen changes. The documentary record, however, indicates there were six. See Kissinger, *White House Years*, 1443–44, and Kissinger Cable for Haig, 13 December 1972, Camp David—Sensitive Vol. XVIII, Box 4, POW/MIA, NPMP.

32. Author interview with Luu Van Loi, 12 June 1996, Hanoi, Vietnam; Kissinger Message, 13 December 1972, HAK Paris Trip—HAKTO and Memos to the President, Etc., Dec. 3–13, 1972 [1 of 2], Henry A. Kissinger Office Files—Country Files–Far East–Vietnam, Box 5, POW/MIA, NPMP.

33. Kissinger Message, 13 December 1972, HAK Paris Trip—HAKTO and Memos to the President, Etc., Dec. 3–13, 1972 [1 of 2], Henry A. Kissinger Office Files—Country Files–Far East–Vietnam, Box 5, POW/MIA, NPMP.

34. Haig Cable for Kissinger, 13 December 1972, HAK Paris Trip Dec. 3–13, 1972—TOHAK 100–192 [1 of 2], Henry A. Kissinger Office Files—Country Files–Far East–Vietnam, Box 5, POW/MIA, NPMP.

35. A copy of the English translation of the DRVN protocol on prisoners may be found in Camp David—Sensitive Vol. XXII (2), For the President's Files—Winston Lord, Vietnam Negotiations, Box 4, POW/MIA, NPMP.

36. Guay Cable for Haig, 14 December 1972, John Negroponte Negotiations Files, 1972–73, Vol. I, Jon Howe Vietnam Subject Files, Box 7, POW/MIA, NPMP.

37. From the report quoted in Kissinger, *White House Years*, 1450.

38. The main points of the proposal are presented in Bunker Cable for Kissinger, 4 December 1972, Sensitive—Camp David Cables Dec. 1972, For the President's Files—Winston Lord, Vietnam Negotiations, Box 4, POW/MIA, NPMP.

39. Thieu is quoted in Kissinger Memorandum for Nixon, 13 December 1972, HAK Paris Trip—Dec. 3–13, 1972 TOHAK 100–192 [1 of 2], Henry A. Kissinger Office Files—HAK Trip Files, POW/MIA, NPMP.

40. Ibid.

41. Haig Memorandum for Nixon, 12 December 1972, HAK Paris Trip—HAKTO, and Memos to the President, Etc. Dec. 3–13, 1972 [1 of 2], Henry A. Kissinger Office Files, HAK Trip Files, POW/MIA, NPMP.

42. Haig Memorandum for Nixon, 12 December 1972, Camp David—Sensitive Vol. XXII (2), For the President's Files—Winston Lord, Vietnam Negotiations, Box 4, POW/MIA, NPMP.

43. Kissinger Memorandum for Nixon, 15 December 1972, President's Daily Briefs—Dec. 1–16, 1972, President's Daily Briefings, Box 1, POW/MIA, NPMP.

44. See Brigham, *Guerrilla Diplomacy*, 110–11.

45. From Ho Chi Minh's "Loi keu goi dong bao va chien si ca nuoc" in his *Vi doc lap tu do*, 282.

46. Kissinger, *White House Years*, 1447–48.

47. Ibid., 1446. Nixon maintains that Kissinger advocated intensified bombings south of the twentieth parallel and in southern Laos but was opposed to strikes against North Vietnamese cities above the twentieth parallel. Kissinger, on the other hand, claims that he proposed a resumption of bombings all over North Vietnam, with fighter-bombers—and not B-52s—used to attack targets in or near populated areas. See Nixon, *Memoirs*, 733, and Kissinger, *White House Years*, 1448.

48. Haldeman, *Diaries*, 675; Nixon, *Memoirs*, 734.

49. Kissinger, *White House Years*, 1447.

50. Palmer, *Twenty-Five-Year War*, 124.

51. Kissinger, *White House Years*, 1447.

52. Haig and McCarry, *Inner Circles*, 309.

53. *New York Times*, 31 December 1972.

54. Kissinger, *White House Years*, 1457; Haldeman, *Diaries*, 677.

55. Porter, *Peace Denied*, 365.

56. Nixon Notes, 15 and 16 December 1972, December 15, 1972—Vietnam Notes, President's Speech File, 1969–74, Box 82, SF: President's Personal Files, WHSF, NPMP.

57. Kissinger's press conference is reproduced in Department of State, *Bulletin*, 8 January 1973, 33–41. Marvin and Bernard Kalb and Walter Isaacson claim that the con-

tent of the press conference revealed the existence of a rift between Nixon and Kissinger. They write that Kissinger mentioned Nixon's name fourteen times during the conference "not to pass along Nixon's self-description of his great attributes" but to suggest that Nixon was responsible for the collapse of the talks. See Kalb and Kalb, *Kissinger*, 413, and Isaacson, *Kissinger*, 469. That claim is contradicted by a declassified document dated 15 December 1972 in which Nixon explicitly instructs Kissinger to make repeated references to him, Nixon, in explaining the state of the negotiations. See Nixon Memorandum for Kissinger, 15 December 1972, Camp David—Sensitive Vol. XXII (2), Box 4, POW/MIA, NPMP.

58. McCarthy and Allison, *Linebacker II*, 41. This book is the best account of Linebacker II, specifically the experiences of those who implemented the campaign. For the North Vietnamese perspective see Ho Si Huu et al., *Lich su quan chung phong khong*, 2.

59. McCarthy and Allison, *Linebacker II*, 65. Washington achieved that level of accuracy throughout the campaign.

60. Haldeman, *Diaries*, 679.

61. Dang cong san Viet Nam, Ban chap hanh dang bo thanh pho Ha Noi, *Lich su dang bo thanh pho Ha Noi*, 219.

62. The SA-2 missile typically used by the DRVN against American aircraft was originally designed by the Soviets specifically as an anti-B-52 weapon. In the event of war against the Soviet Union, the United States would have used B-52s to deliver nuclear ordnance. Moscow had thus commissioned the production of a missile effective at that aircraft's average flying altitude.

63. Nixon, *Memoirs*, 732.

64. Ibid., 736.

65. The speech is reproduced in part in Porter, ed., *Vietnam: Definitive Documentation*, 590–91.

66. Ho Si Huu et al., *Lich su quan trung phong khong*, 256–58; McCarthy and Allison, *Linebacker II*, 77, 83, 89.

67. McCarthy and Allison, *Linebacker II*, 83.

68. Haldeman, *Diaries*, 680.

69. Nixon, *Memoirs*, 734.

70. Nixon Letter for Thieu, 17 December 1972, Thieu, Nguyen Van, Name/Subject File, 1969–74, Box 16, SF: President's Personal Files, WHSF, NPMP.

71. Haig and McCarry, *Inner Circles*, 310–11.

72. Kennedy Memorandum for Kissinger (from Haig), 20 December 1972, H[enry] A. K[issinger]/President Memos (NVN), Situation in Vietnam—Sept.–Oct. 1972, Vietnam Subject Files, Box 2, POW/MIA, NPMP.

73. Haig Cable for Kissinger, 20 December 1972, Camp David—Sensitive Vol. XXIII, For the President's Files—Winston Lord, Vietnam Negotiations, Box 4, POW/MIA, NPMP.

74. Haldeman, *Diaries*, 679–80.

75. From the cable quoted in Kissinger, *White House Years*, 1457. See also Nixon, *Memoirs*, 738.

76. Yenne, *SAC*, 110.

77. Kohloff, "BUFs Go Downtown,"50.

78. "B-52 Pilot," 18.

79. McCarthy and Allison, *Linebacker II*, 97.

80. Sharp, *Strategy for Defeat*, 252.

81. Uy ban dieu tra toi ac chien tranh cua de quoc My o Viet Nam, "Tu lieu tong hop ve cuoc leo thang chien tranh pha hoai cua chinh quyen Nixon o mien Bac Viet-nam bang mot luc luong lon khong quan tu 18/12/1972 den 29/12/72," 2 January 1973, Ho so: Toi ac cua My trong viec dung khong quan tien hanh chien tranh xam luoc Viet Nam, VV, #100, Phong: Uy ban dieu tra toi ac chien tranh cua de quoc My o Viet Nam, VSA3; *Kham Thien*, 7.

82. Excerpts from the cable are quoted in Kissinger, *White House Years*, 1457.

83. Nixon, *Memoirs*, 741.

84. Luu Van Loi and Nguyen Anh Vu, *Cac cuoc thuong luong*, 385.

85. Haig was the only influential member of the White House to urge Nixon to continue the bombing. See Haig and McCarry, *Inner Circles*, 313.

86. Nixon's 29 December 1972 message is quoted in Kissinger, *White House Years*, 1459.

87. "Nixon's Blitz Leads Back to the Table."

88. *Tin song*, 28 December 1972.

89. *New York Times*, 29 December 1972.

90. *Washington Star-News*, 20 December 1972; Mark A. Clodfelter, *Limits of Air Power*, 194.

91. These figures are from McCarthy and Allison, *Linebacker II*, 171.

92. U.S. Congress, *Department of Defense Appropriations*, 18.

93. Losses in men were high because a crew of six manned each B-52.

94. Ha Van Lau quoted in Maclear, *Vietnam*, 423.

95. *Quan doi nhan dan Viet Nam, 1972*, 59. In addition to thirty-four B-52s, the DRVN claimed to have shot down five F-111s, twenty-seven U.S. Air Force and eleven U.S. Navy fighter-bombers, three reconnaissance aircraft, and one helicopter.

96. Burchett, *Grasshoppers and Elephants*, 162. The strategy most frequently used by the DRVN was sending out MiG aircraft to determine the altitude, speed, and course direction of three-plane cells of B-52s on bombing runs and firing SAMs in salvos along their flight paths. That allowed for minimal usage of radars, which the Americans could easily incapacitate.

97. U.S. Congress, *Department of Defense Appropriations*, 30.

98. See "The Vietnam Bombing: Senate Opposition Grows" in U.S. Congress, *Congressional Quarterly Weekly Report*, 23 December 1972, 3171.

99. *New York Times*, 27 December 1972.

100. Ibid., 29 December 1972.

101. Ibid., 30 and 28 December, respectively.

102. Ibid., 30 December 1972.

103. *Washington Post*, 7 January 1973.

104. Ibid., 24 December 1972.

105. *St. Louis Post Dispatch*, 19 December 1972.

106. "Canadian Views Vietnam Peace Prospects: A Statement by the Secretary for External Affairs, the Honourable Mitchell Sharp, in the House of Commons," 5 January 1973, File 21-13-Viet-ICCS-73, Vol. I, DFAITF, CDFAITHS.

107. *Washington Post*, 21 December 1972.

108. See "Tuyen bo cua Bo ngoai giao Trung Quoc" in *12 ngay ruc ro chien cong*, 14.

109. U.S. Senate, *Hearings on the Paris Peace Accords*, 379.

110. Democratic Republic of Viet Nam Commission for Investigation of the U.S. Imperialists' War Crimes in Viet Nam, *Late December 1972 US Blitz*, 7.

111. *New York Times*, 22 December 1972; *Washington Post*, 28 December 1972. The bombing of Dresden in February 1945 caused 35,000 civilian deaths; the bombing of Tokyo on 9 and 10 March 1945 caused 83,793. See Mark A. Clodfelter, "Culmination Dresden," 136, and Welden E. Smith, "Strategic Bombing Debate," 183. Some members of the American media accepted North Vietnamese claims that the Nixon administration was "carpet-bombing" its way "across downtown Hanoi." See *Washington Post*, 28 December 1972. The duplicity in such reporting is the subject of Hertz and Rider, *Prestige Press*.

112. An average of 6 percent of bombs dropped by B-52s missed their targets because of bent or damaged fins. See Boyne, *Boeing B-52*, 99.

113. Uy ban hanh chinh thanh pho Ha Noi, "Thong bao dac biet ve view chinh quyen Nixon nem bom bang may bay B.52 huy diet cac trung tam dan cu o thu do Ha Noi tu ngay 18/12/72 den ngay 29/12/72," 30 December 1972, Ho so: Thong bao dac

biet cua Ban diem tra Ha Noi, Nam Ha ve toi ac cua de quoc My gay ra o Ha Noi, Nam Ha nam 1972, VV, #108, Phong: Uy ban dieu tra toi ac chien tranh cua de quoc My o Viet Nam, V S A 3; *Muoi hai ngay dem*, 76; Michael Clodfelter, *Vietnam in Military Statistics*, 224.

Chapter Seven

1. Nixon, *Memoirs*, 743.
2. Kissinger, *White House Years*, 1462.
3. Nixon's letter to Thieu of 5 January 1973, released by former R V N minister of planning Nguyen Tien Hung at a press conference in Washington on 30 April 1975, is reproduced in Porter, ed., *Vietnam: History in Documents*, 424. The letter is also in Thieu, Nguyen Van, Name / Subject File, 1969–74, Box 16, S F : President's Personal Files, W H C F, N P M P. Tad Szulc claims that the possession of two Nixon letters stating the United States would take strong action in the event of enemy violations of the cease-fire convinced Thieu to consent to the January agreement. See Szulc, *Illusion of Peace*, 667. In fact, Nixon incorporated such pledges into several of his dispatches to Thieu.
4. On popular opposition to presidential policy in late 1972 and early 1973 see De-Benedetti and Chatfield, *American Ordeal*, 342–47.
5. *New York Times*, 3 January 1973.
6. Ibid., 5 January 1973.
7. Haldeman, *Diaries*, 684.
8. Ban dieu tra toi ac chien tranh cua de quoc My o Hai Phong, "Bao cao tong ket cong tac dieu tra to cao toi ac chien tranh cua de quoc My o thanh pho Hai-phong," 5 May 1973, Ho so: Bao cao cua Ban dieu tra Hai Phong, VV, #112, Phong: Uy ban dieu tra toi ac chien tranh cua de quoc My o Viet Nam, V S A 3.
9. Vu Quoc Tuan and Nguyen Xuan Lai, "Politique économique," 199–203.
10. By the mid-1960s, the industrial sector contributed only 12 percent to North Vietnam's G N P (amounting to $1.6 billion) and employed fewer than 10 percent of the population, then estimated at 18 million. See the systems analysis paper in *Pentagon Papers*, 227–28.
11. Tran Van Tra, *Ket thuc cuoc chien tranh*, 6.
12. Ban To chuc Trung uong, *May van de*, 5; Uy ban kiem tra cua Ban chap hanh Trung uong Dang lao dong Viet Nam, *De cuong bao cao truoc dang vien*, 5–6.
13. Cable for G P E, 27 November 1972, File 21-13-Viet-I C S C -12, Vol. 5, D F A I T F, C D F A I T H S.
14. Hoang Van Thai, *Tran danh ba muoi nam*, 467.
15. Truong Chinh, *Viet Nam*, 9.
16. Zhou Enlai is quoted in Qiang Zhai, *China and the Vietnam Wars*, 206.
17. Hoang Van Thai, *Tran danh ba muoi nam*, 475.
18. Author interview with Hoan Xuan Tuy, 22 July 1972, Ho Chi Minh City, Vietnam. Tuy was an aide to P A V N general Vo Nguyen Giap during the Dien Bien Phu campaign of 1954.
19. From the cable quoted in Kissinger, *White House Years*, 1461.
20. Luu Van Loi and Nguyen Anh Vu, *Cac cuoc thuong luong*, 387, 392.
21. Kissinger, *White House Years*, 1463.
22. Memorandum of Conversation—Secret Paris Talks, 9 January 1973, Camp David—Sensitive Vol. XXIII, For the President's Files—Winston Lord, Vietnam Negotiations, Box 4, P O W / M I A, N P M P; Kissinger Cable for Nixon, 9 January 1973, Kissinger Messages R E Vietnam Peace Negotiations—January 1973, President's Speech File, 1969–74, Box 82, S F : President's Personal Files, W H S F, N P M P.
23. Memorandum of Conversation—Secret Paris Talks, 9 January 1973; Kissinger Cable for Nixon, 9 January 1973.
24. Kissinger Cable for Nixon, 9 January 1973.

25. Haldeman, *Diaries*, 687.

26. Memorandum of Conversation—Secret Paris Talks, 10 January 1973, Camp David—Sensitive Vol. XXIII, For the President's Files—Winston Lord, Vietnam Negotiations, Box 4, POW/MIA, NPMP; Kissinger Cable for Nixon, 10 January 1973, Kissinger Messages RE Vietnam Peace Negotiations—January 1973, President's Speech File, 1969–74, Box 82, SF: President's Personal Files, WHSF, NPMP.

27. Kissinger Cable for Nixon, 10 January 1973, Kissinger Messages RE Vietnam Peace Negotiations—January 1973, President's Speech File, 1969–74, Box 82, SF: President's Personal Files, WHSF, NPMP.

28. Haldeman, *Diaries*, 688.

29. Kissinger, *White House Years*, 1465.

30. From the memorandum quoted in ibid.

31. Memorandum of Conversation—Secret Paris Talks, 11 January 1973, Camp David—Sensitive Vol. XXIII, For the President's Files—Winston Lord, Vietnam Negotiations, Box 4, POW/MIA, NPMP; Kissinger Cable for Bunker, 11 January 1973, HAK Paris Trip—Jan. 7–14, 1973—HAKTO 1–48, Henry A. Kissinger Office Files—HAK Trip Files, Box 5, POW/MIA, NPMP; Kissinger Cable for Nixon, 11 January 1973, Kissinger Messages RE Vietnam Peace Negotiations—January 1973, President's Speech File, 1969–74, Box 82, SF: President's Personal Files, WHSF, NPMP. The issue of political prisoners ultimately did drive a wedge between Hanoi and the PRG. Northerners, Robert Brigham writes, "would not forget southern objections to the Kissinger-Tho draft and the price that Hanoi had to pay for the delay." Conversely, southern revolutionaries "remembered how casually northerners had dealt with civilian prisoners." See Brigham, *Guerrilla Diplomacy*, 112.

32. Kissinger Cable for Nixon, 11 January 1973, Kissinger Messages RE Vietnam Peace Negotiations—January 1973, President's Speech File, 1969–74, Box 82, SF: President's Personal Files, WHSF, NPMP.

33. Haldeman, *Diaries*, 689.

34. Sullivan Cable for Kissinger, 17 January 1973, Backchannel Messages—26 Patch 1973—Vol. I, Backchannels, Box 7, POW/MIA, NPMP.

35. Luu Van Loi and Nguyen Anh Vu, *Cac cuoc thuong luong*, 407–8; Memorandum of Conversation—Secret Paris Talks, 12 January 1973, Camp David—Sensitive Vol. XXIII, For the President's Files—Winston Lord, Vietnam Negotiations, Box 4, POW/MIA, NPMP; Kissinger Cable for Nixon and Kissinger Cable for Kennedy, 12 January 1973, Kissinger Messages RE Vietnam Peace Negotiations—January 1973, President's Speech File, 1969–74, Box 82, SF: President's Personal Files, WHSF, NPMP.

36. Kennedy Cable for Haldeman (Kissinger for Nixon), 13 January 1973, H Notes Jan.–Feb.–March 1973 [1 January to 6 February 1973] Part I, Haldeman Notes, Box 47, SMOF: H. R. Haldeman, WHSF, NPMP.

37. Kissinger Cable for Bunker, 18 January 1973, Camp David—Sensitive Vol. XXIV, For the President's Files—Winston Lord, Vietnam Negotiations, Box 4, POW/MIA, NPMP; Sullivan Cable for Kissinger, 18 January 1973, Backchannel Messages—26 Patch 1973—Vol. I, Backchannels, Box 3, POW/MIA, NPMP.

38. Kissinger, *White House Years*, 1458.

39. Nixon Memorandum for Haldeman, 25 January 1973, Memos—January 1973, Memoranda for the President, 1969–74, Box 4, SF: President's Personal Files, WHSF, NPMP.

40. Porter, *Peace Denied*, 165.

41. Alan Dawson claims that had Nixon extended Linebacker II, Hanoi would ultimately have accepted a demand for surrender. See Dawson, *55 Days*, 123. Destructive as the bombing was, that is an exaggeration. Vietnamese revolutionaries had been fighting for the independence and unity of their nation for decades. It is

doubtful that, short of a nuclear strike, any bombing effort could have compelled the DRVN and the PRG/NLF to permanently abandon their objectives.

42. Aitken, *Nixon*, 460.

43. Ambrose, *Ruin and Recovery*, 45.

44. Mark A. Clodfelter, *Limits of Air Power*, ix, 177–202. Emphasis is Clodfelter's.

45. The delegate sent by the Thai government was Pote Sarasin, assistant chairman of the Thai National Executive Council and acting foreign minister. After the November 1971 coup in Bangkok, this council acted as the Thai cabinet.

46. Dwight L. Chapin Memorandum for Kissinger, 3 October 1972, David Parker October 1972, Alpha Name Files, Box 105, SMOF: H. R. Haldeman, WHCF, NPMP.

47. Haldeman Notes, 14 January 1973; H Notes Jan.–Feb.–March 1973 [1 January to 6 February 1973] Part I, Haldeman Notes, Box 47, SMOF: H. R. Haldeman, WHCF, NPMP.

48. Ibid.; Kissinger, *White House Years*, 1469; Haldeman, *Diaries*, 693.

49. Nixon's letter is summarized and partly reproduced in Kissinger, *White House Years*, 1469.

50. Haldeman, *Diaries*, 695.

51. Thieu Letter for Nixon, 17 January 1973, Thieu, Nguyen Van, Name/Subject File, 1969–74, Box 16, SF: President's Personal Files, WHSF, NPMP.

52. Nguyen Cao Ky, *How We Lost*, 198–99.

53. On South Vietnam's dependence see the testimonies by former GVN and ARVN members in Hosmer, Keller, and Jenkins, *Fall of Saigon*, 9–15, 38–42.

54. Thieu Letter for Nixon, 17 January 1973, Thieu, Nguyen Van, Name/Subject File, 1969–74, Box 16, SF: President's Personal Files, WHSF, NPMP.

55. Nixon letter for Thieu, 18 January 1973, Thieu, Nguyen Van, Name/Subject File, 1969–74, Box 16, SF: President's Personal Files, WHSF, NPMP.

56. Thieu Letter for Nixon, 20 January 1973, Thieu, Nguyen Van, Name/Subject File, 1969–74, Box 16, SF: President's Personal Files, WHSF, NPMP.

57. The statements were issued at the request of the White House. See Chapter 5.

58. Nixon Letter for Thieu, 20 January 1973, Thieu, Nguyen Van, Name/Subject File, 1969–74, Box 16, SF: President's Personal Files, WHSF, NPMP.

59. Ibid.

60. This letter is not in the NPMP archives. An outline of its content, however, is in Kissinger, *White House Years*, 1470.

61. Thieu is quoted in Nixon, *Memoirs*, 751.

62. Thieu's declarations were reported in Kissinger Memorandum for Nixon, 5 February 1973, President's Daily Briefs—Feb. 1973, President's Daily Briefings, Box 1, POW/MIA, NPMP.

63. Nixon Letter for Thieu, 22 January 1973, Thieu, Nguyen Van, Name/Subject File, 1969–74, Box 16, SF: President's Personal Files, WHSF, NPMP.

64. Kissinger, *White House Years*, 1472.

65. Thieu is quoted in Kissinger Memorandum for Nixon, 24 January 1973, Daily Briefs for the President, Jon Howe Vietnam Subject Files, Box 5, POW/MIA, NPMP.

66. Nixon, *Memoirs*, 433, 435.

67. Kennedy Cable to Guay (Nixon for Kissinger), 24 November 1972, Sensitive—Camp David Cables—Nov. 1972, For the President's Files—Winston Lord, Vietnam Negotiations, Box 4, POW/MIA, NPMP.

68. Memorandum of Conversation—Meeting with the South Vietnamese, 24 November 1972, GVN Memcons—Nov. 20, 1972–Apr. 3, 1973 [TS 3 of 3], Henry A. Kissinger Office Files—Country Files–Far East–Vietnam, Box 6, POW/MIA, NPMP.

69. Ibid.

70. From a Nixon message to Bunker dated 5 May 1973, reproduced in Pike, ed., *Bunker Papers*, 862.

71. Quoted in Ambrose, *Ruin and Recovery*, 57.

72. Nixon, *Memoirs*, 435; Kissinger, *Diplomacy*, 695–96. See also Kissinger, *White House Years*, 1470.

73. Memorandum of Conversation—Secret Paris Talks, 23 January 1973, Camp David—Sensitive Vol. XXIV, For the President's Files—Winston Lord, Vietnam Negotiations, Box 4, POW/MIA, NPMP.

74. Haldeman, *Diaries*, 655.

75. Ibid., 680.

76. Ibid., 663.

77. The speech is reproduced in U.S. President, *Weekly Compilation*, 29 January 1973, 39–45.

78. *New York Times*, 24 January 1973.

79. *Wall Street Journal*, 31 January 1973.

80. *Los Angeles Times*, 25 January 1973.

81. *Washington Post*, 24 January 1973.

82. *Washington Evening Star*, 24 January 1973.

83. Cadieux Cable for Indochina Task Force, 27 January 1973, Part I, File 21-13-Viet-ICSC-12, Vol. 5, DFAITF, CDFAITHS.

84. Ibid., Part II.

85. Dang lao dong Viet Nam, *Loi goi cua Ban chap hanh Trung uong*, 10, 12, 14; *Nhan dan*, 28 January 1973; Bo ngoai giao nuoc Viet Nam Dan chu Cong hoa, *Hiep dinh ve cham dut chien tranh*, 5.

86. Nguyen Tien Hung and Schecter, *Palace File*, 156.

87. Bui Diem, *Jaws of History*, 320.

88. Negroponte is quoted in Ambrose, *Ruin and Recovery*, 50.

89. Kissinger, *White House Years*, 1467.

90. Letter from Headquarters of U.S. Delegation to FPJMC, San Francisco, to ICCS chairman Michel Gauvin, 17 February 1973, File ICCS Meetings 1–30, Vol. 1, Acc 92–93/001, Saigon Files: Misc., Box 55, RG 25, CNA.

91. Dang cong san Viet Nam, *Van kien*, 316.

92. Ban chap hanh Trung uong Dang lao dong Viet Nam, *Nghi quyet cua Hoi nghi lan thu 22 cua Trung uong Dang ve nhiem vu, phuong huong khoi phuc va phat trien kinh te mien Bac trong hai nam 1974–1975 (Nghi quyet 229NQ/TW, 22-1-74)*, tai lieu noi bo—phat hanh den chi bo, HNLDC.

93. Gauvin Cable for GPE, 26 January 1973, File 21-13-Viet-ICSC-12, Vol. 7, DFAITF, CDFAITHS.

94. Tong cuc hau can Bo quoc phong, *Lich su bo doi Truong Son*, 278.

Epilogue

1. Guay Cable for Scowcroft, 1 February 1973, Backchannel Messages—26 Patch 1973—Vol. I, Backchannels, Box 7, POW/MIA, NPMP; Kissinger, *Years of Upheaval*, 40.

2. Scowcroft Cable for Guay (Nixon for Pham Van Dong), 1 February 1973, Backchannel Messages—26 Patch 1973—Vol. I, Backchannels, Box 7, POW/MIA, NPMP.

3. Guay Cable for Scowcroft, 6 February 1973, Backchannel Messages—26 Patch 1973—Vol. I, Backchannels, Box 3, POW/MIA, NPMP.

4. On Kissinger's visit to Hanoi see Kissinger, *Years of Upheaval*, 23–43.

5. "Déclaration de Madame Nguyen Thi Binh, Ministre des affaires étrangères, Chef de la délégation du Gouvernement Révolutionnaire Provisoire de la République du Sud Viêt Nam à la Conférence sur le Viêt Nam," 25 February 1973, File 31, Vol. 3072, Box 57, RG 25, CNA.

6. "Déclaration du Gouvernement de la République Démocratique du Viêt Nam sur

les violations très graves de l'Accord de Paris par les États-Unis et l'administration de Saïgon," 26 February 1973, File 30, Vol. 3072, Box 57, RG 25, CNA.

7. "Discours de Son Exc. Monsieur Tran Van Lam, Ministre des affaires étrangères, Chef de la délégation de la République du Viêt Nam, à la séance inaugurale de la Conférence Internationale sur le Viêt Nam," 26 February 1973, File 36, Vol. 3072, Box 57, RG 25, CNA.

8. Canadian Military Commission (Saigon) Cable for National Defence Headquarters (Ottawa), 1 February 1973, File 21-13-Viet-ICCS, Vol. 2, DFAITF, CDFAITHS.

9. Maj. Gen. McAlpine Report for CanDel Saigon, 15 March 1973, File 3350–1, Vol. 3, Acc 84–85/166, Box 42, RG 24, CNA.

10. ICCS Region HQ III Report, 18 March 1973, File ICCS Meetings 30+ Vol. 2, Acc 92–93/001, Saigon Files: Misc., Box 55, RG 25, CNA.

11. The report dated 19 July 1973 is from File 4, Vol. 3072, Box 57, RG 25, CNA.

12. Nixon message to Bunker, 5 May 1973, in Pike, ed., *Bunker Papers*, 852.

13. Kissinger Cable for Bunker, 28 February 1973, Backchannel Messages—1973—Vol. I [Part I] To: Amb. Bunker—Saigon Through Apr. 1973, Backchannels, Box 3, POW/MIA, NPMP.

14. Bunker Cable for Kissinger, 28 February 1973, Backchannel Messages—1973—Vol. I [Part 2] From: Amb. Bunker—Saigon Through Apr. 1973, Backchannels, Box 3, POW/MIA, NPMP.

15. Haldeman Notes, 23 January 1973, H Notes Jan.–Feb.–March 1973 [1 January to 6 February 1973] Part I, Haldeman Notes, Box 47, SMOF: H. R. Haldeman, WHCF, NPMP.

16. Kissinger, *Diplomacy*, 695.

17. U.S. Senate, *Hearings on the Paris Peace Accords*, 99, 356.

18. Memorandum of Conversation—Secret Paris Talks, 1 January 1973, Camp David—Memcons, Jan. 8–13, 1973—Sensitive—Vol. XXIII, For the President's Files—Winston Lord, Vietnam Negotiations, Box 4, POW/MIA, NPMP.

19. U.S. Senate, *Hearings on the Paris Peace Accords*, 263.

20. Ottawa's own version of the ICCS protocol contained seventy-three articles and was far more comprehensive than that eventually accepted by American and North Vietnamese negotiators. See "Canadian Draft Proposal for a Protocol Governing an International Commission for Viet-Nam," 30 November 1972, File 29—1972/2, Vol. 3161, Box 57, RG 25, CNA.

21. Department of State, *Aggression from the North*, 29. See also Chapter 1.

22. Ban Chap hanh Trung uong Dang, *Nghi quyet Hoi nghi lan thu 21 Ban Chap hanh Trung uong Dang*, HPAMDC.

23. Brigham, *Guerrilla Diplomacy*, 118–19.

24. Duiker, *Communist Road to Power*, 330.

25. Le Duan, *Thu vao Nam*, 354–55; Duiker, *Communist Road to Power*, 333.

26. Duiker, *Communist Road to Power*, 331–35.

27. Bui Tin, *Following Ho Chi Minh*, 79.

28. Hoang Van Thai, *South Vietnam*, 138. A detailed description of North Vietnamese military planning may be found in Bo Quoc phong, *Lich su nghe thuat chien dich*, 467–540.

29. Papp, *Vietnam*, 189.

30. Qiang Zhai, *China and the Vietnam Wars*, 136.

31. Hoang Van Thai, *South Vietnam*, 142.

32. Ibid., 142–43.

33. Duiker, *Communist Road to Power*, 342–43.

34. Chen Min, "Myth and Reality," 529.

35. Nixon is quoted in Crowley, *Nixon in Winter*, 256.

36. Kissinger, *Diplomacy*, 691.

Bibliography

Note on Sources   247

I have found sources from the American and the Vietnamese sides equally useful in compiling this study. Vietnamese and American sources by participants in the secret and private talks are generally compatible. For example, Loi and Vu's work on the Paris negotiations and Kissinger's memoirs rarely contradict one another on the content of the negotiations. Such compatibility facilitates gathering details about the negotiating sessions, reconstructing the history of the talks when documentation is lacking, and, most important, confirming the veracity of the information contained in other published sources. Substantial differences exist in Vietnamese and American sources, but those have to do with interpretive, not factual, matters. While the interpretation in Vietnamese sources is colored by ideological considerations, American sources are similarly colored by personal considerations. Vietnamese interpretations extoll the stoic disposition of the VWP/DRVN and PRG/NLF leaderships specifically and of the Vietnamese people generally. American interpretations, on the other hand, focus on how the primary players on the American side did or did not successfully maintain their own as well as Washington's credibility in negotiating with the Vietnamese parties.

This study is based on documents from the Nixon Presidential Materials Project (NPMP) in College Park, Maryland, compiled by the National Archives and Records Administration (NARA). As a result of the Presidential Recordings and Materials Preservation Act of 1974, Nixon's presidential materials are in the custody of the NARA. At the NPMP, I have drawn extensively from the White House Central Files and White House Special Files collections, but a large portion of the documentation pertaining to the secret and private Paris talks is from the Documents Relating to POW/MIA Matters among the Nixon White House Files of the National Security Council collection. These materials are available as a result of Executive Order 12816 on 22 July 1992, which directed government agencies to declassify documents pertaining to American POWs and MIAs. Although some documents were significantly sanitized before their release, the information that remains is valuable.

Other sources that proved useful for reconstructing the story of the American side were the memoirs of Richard Nixon, Henry Kissinger, H. R. Haldeman, and Alexander Haig. Though sometimes overly partisan, these accounts are congruent with the documentary record. As for secondary sources, some are very useful but even the most insightful are somehow flawed. The histories of the negotiations by Gareth Porter and Allan Goodman are insightful but rely too much on newspaper accounts and lack a foundation in primary sources. Larry Berman's *No Peace, No Honor* and Jeffrey Kimball's *Nixon's Vietnam War* are more recent publications that offer fascinating new perspectives on the Nixon administration's conduct of the war and the negotiations using an impressive array of primary sources. Both Berman and Kimball, however, are at times too vehement in their criticisms of Nixon.

If Western scholarship on Vietnam has a major weakness, it is neglect of the Vietnamese perspectives. Most histories of the war portray the Vietnamese parties—mainly the VWP and DRVN leaderships in Hanoi, the Thieu regime in Saigon, and the PRG/NLF—as passive, without initiative, and only reacting to American actions. This depiction is, of course, inaccurate. The documentary record as well as several excellent secondary sources demonstrate clearly that the Vietnamese parties were active agents in the war and the negotiations and exercised a degree of initiative comparable to that of the Americans.

To comprehend North Vietnam's Anti-American Resistance, the resolutions of VWP Central Committee plenary sessions are remarkably useful. These are now available for public scrutiny. Equally useful are published works and speeches by key VWP and government members, among them Le Duan, Truong Chinh, Pham Van Dong, Nguyen Duy Trinh, and Nguyen Co Thach. Unfortunately, Kissinger's counterparts in the Paris negotiations, Xuan Thuy and Le Duc Tho, published little on their roles in the negotiations. Recent Vietnamese histories of the war, even those sanctioned by the current Vietnamese Communist Party, are also valuable. Since the middle of the 1980s, the time of "renovation," or *doi moi*, there has been a strong tendency among Vietnamese authors to write about the war in a less partisan and more objective way than before. They now discuss the difficulties of the Revolution—in the North as well as in the South— more openly and provide fascinating data that enhance the persuasiveness of their arguments. Though still far from objective, this body of recent works has been of great value to this book.

A few weeks after I arrived in Vietnam in 1996, Luu Van Loi, former assistant to DRVN foreign minister Nguyen Duy Trinh, and Nguyen Anh Vu, also a retired diplomat, published an account of the secret and private Paris negotiations titled *Cac cuoc thuong luong Le Duc Tho–Kissinger tai Paris* (The Le Duc Tho– Kissinger Negotiations in Paris). Loi and Vu had access to the archives of the Vietnamese Foreign Ministry, which are still closed not only to foreign but also to Vietnamese scholars. The quality and importance of the information they offer is exceptional. Although the book has since been published in English under the title *Le Duc Tho–Kissinger Negotiations in Paris*, I used the original text because the language of the negotiations and the wording of the draft and final agreements are more accurate in the Vietnamese version. I am also grateful to Mr. Loi for answering my questions about the Paris negotiations and his role therein. Another, more recent addition to the Vietnamese record on the talks is Nguyen Thanh Le's *Cuoc dam phan Pari ve Viet Nam* (The Paris Negotiations on Vietnam). Le, a former deputy editor in chief of the daily *Nhan dan* and press spokesman for the DRVN delegation in Paris during the talks, offers a revealing look at North Vietnam's diplomatic strategy during the war against the United States.

The Vietnamese State Archives Center 3, the repository for all post-1945 (North) Vietnamese government documents, includes several files on the Paris talks. These, however, are of little help, for the important documents remain in the custody of the Foreign Ministry. The Vietnamese archives, however, contain many documents detailing Hanoi's efforts to develop the industrial base and otherwise promote socialism in the North and describing conditions above the seventeenth parallel during the Resistance.

The story of the South Vietnamese parties—that is, of the PRG/NLF and the Thieu regime—remains largely untold. However, Robert Brigham's well-documented *Guerrilla Diplomacy* is an excellent account of the diplomacy of the

PRG /NLF and Truong Nhu Tang's *A Viet Cong Memoir* offers interesting insights into the activities of southern revolutionaries. The best account of Thieu and the GVN is Nguyen Tien Hung and Jerrold Schecter's *Palace File*. Some documents seized from the Thieu regime are housed at the Vietnamese State Archives Center 2 in Ho Chi Minh City. No records of Saigon's conduct or its understanding of its relationship with Washington, however, are available. No doubt the South Vietnamese government destroyed many of them before its fall. In any case, that piece of the puzzle is missing. For the purpose of more clearly presenting the Saigon government's side of the story, I have relied on American documents. Washington seemingly had several informants close to Thieu, and I came across several of their reports describing Thieu's attitude toward the negotiations and the settlement.

Lastly, I have made use of Canadian archival materials. Between 1954 and 1973, Canada served on two international supervisory commissions for Indochina. As a "third party," Canada produced files that abound with insightful information on the situation in Vietnam. The reports of the second commission, located in the Canadian National Archives and in the files of the Department of Foreign Affairs and International Trade, are especially useful in determining who violated the accords and contributed to the resumption of war after January 1973.

Primary Sources
Document Collections and Repositories

College Park, Maryland
    National Archives and Records Administration
        Nixon Presidential Materials Project
Hanoi, Vietnam
    Government of the Socialist Republic of Vietnam
        State Archives Center 3
    Hanoi National Library Document Collection
    Hanoi People's Army Museum Document Collection
    Hanoi Revolution Museum Photograph Collection
Ottawa, Canada
    Canadian National Archives
    Department of Foreign Affairs and International Trade Historical Section

Interviews and Conversations

Gauvin, Michel. Interview by author. Ottawa, Canada, 5 December 1996.
Hoan Xuan Tuy. Interview by author. Ho Chi Minh City, Vietnam, 22 July 1990.
Luu Van Loi. Interview by author. Hanoi, Vietnam, 12 June 1996.
Nguyen Ngoc Hung. Conversation with author. Hanoi, Vietnam, 18 July 1996.
Nicholson, John. Telephone conversation with author, 12 November 1996.

Government Documents and Documentary Histories
Sources in Vietnamese

Ban chap hanh Trung uong Dang lao dong Viet Nam. *Chi thi ve viec dong vien cong nhan vien chuc day manh san xuat san sang chien dau nhan dip Dai hoi cong doan Viet Nam lan thu III, so 194 CT/TW, ngay 15-1-72* (Instruction on the Mobilization of Workers and Civil Servants to Increase Production and Prepare for War on the Occasion of the 3rd Congress of Trade Unions, Number 194 CT/TW, 15 January 1972). Ha Noi: Nha xuat ban Su that, 1972.
———. *Van ban huong dan thi hanh cac Nghi quyet va Chi thi cua Ban chap hanh Trung*

uong Dang ve cuoc van dong nang cao chat luong dang vien va ket nap dang vien lop Ho Chi Minh (Guiding Act on the Execution of the Resolutions and Instructions of the Party Central Committee on Improving the Quality of Party Members and Admitting Party Members from the Ho Chi Minh School). Ha Noi: Nha xuat ban Su that, 1973.

Ban To chuc Trung uong. *May van de ve nang cao chat luong sinh hoat chi bo* (Problems Concerning the Improvement of the Quality of the Activities of Party Cells). Ha Noi: Nha xuat ban Su that, 1973.

Bo ngoai giao nuoc Viet Nam Dan chu Cong hoa. *Hiep dinh ve cham dut chien tranh lap lai hoa binh o Viet Nam* (Agreement on Ending the War and Restoring Peace in Vietnam). Ha Noi: Vu thuong tin bao chi, 1973.

Dang cong san Viet Nam. *Su that ve quan he Viet Nam–Trung Quoc trong 30 nam qua* (The Truth about Vietnamese-Chinese Relations in the Past Thirty Years). Ha Noi: Nha xuat ban Su that, 1981.

———. *Van kien ve cong tac van dong cong nhan*. Tap III (Documents on the Task of Propagandizing the Workers. Vol. 3). Ha Noi: Nha xuat ban Lao dong, 1982.

Dang lao dong Viet Nam. *Giai phap chinh tri bay diem va hai diem them chot noi ro them cua Chinh phu cach mang lam thoi cong hoa mien Nam Viet Nam* (Seven-Point Political Solution and Two-Point Clarification of the Provisional Revolutionary Government of South Vietnam). Thanh Hoa: Ty thong tin Thanh Hoa, 1972.

———. *Loi goi cua Ban chap hanh Trung uong Dang lao dong Viet Nam va Chinh phu* (Declaration of the Executive Committee of the Central Committee of the Vietnamese Workers' Party and the Government). Ha Noi: Nha xuat ban Su that, 1973.

———. *Nghi quyet Hoi nghi Trung uong lan thu 20* (Resolution of the 20th Plenum). Ha Noi: Nha xuat ban Su that, 1972.

———. *Nhiet liet huong ung Ban tuyen bo cua Chinh phu ta ngay 26-10, kien tri day manh cuoc khang chien chong My den thang loi hoan toan* (Welcoming the Government's Report of 26 October to Sustain and Strengthen the Anti-American Resistance until Total Victory). Lao Cai: Hoa thong tin Lao Cai, 1972.

———. *Nhung van kien co ban cua Hoi dong chinh phu ve tang cuong lanh dao cong tac quan su tai cac nganh, cac don vi co so cua Nha nuoc* (Essential Documents of the Council of Ministers on Increasing Leadership of Military Work in Basic Branches and Units of the State). Ha Noi: Nha xuat ban Su that. 1972.

———. *Tom tat Nghi quyet Hoi nghi lan thu 19 cua Ban chap hanh Trung uong Dang* (Summary of the Resolution of the 19th Plenum of the Party Central Committee). Ha Noi: Thoi su pho thong xuat ban, 1972.

Ho Chi Minh. *Tuyen Tap* (Collected Works). Ha Noi: Nha xuat ban Su that, 1960.

———. *Vi doc lap tu do vi chu nghia xa hoi* (For Independence, Freedom, for Socialism). Ha Noi: Nha xuat ban Su that, 1970.

Le Duan. *Cach mang xa hoi chu nghia o Viet Nam*. Tap II (The Socialist Revolution in Vietnam. Vol. 2). Ha Noi: Nha xuat ban Su that, 1976.

———. *Thu vao Nam* (Letters to the South). Ha Noi: Nha xuat ban Su that, 1985.

———. *Tiep tuc nghien cuu xay dung ly luan quan su Viet Nam* (Continuing to Study and Build Vietnamese Military Thought). Ha Noi: Nha xuat ban Su that, 1974.

———. *Ve chien tranh nhan dan Viet Nam* (On the Vietnamese People's War). Ha Noi: Nha xuat ban Chinh tri quoc gia, 1993.

Le Duan and Pham Van Dong. *Ve to chuc lai san xuat va cai tien quan ly nong nghiep theo huong san xuat lon xa hoi chu nghia* (On Reorganizing Agricultural Production and Management According to the Guidelines of Large Socialist Production). Ha Noi: Nha xuat ban Su that, 1974.

Pham Van Dong. *Bao cao chinh tri cua Chinh phu: Tai ky hop thu 6 cua Quoc hoi khoa III, thang 6-1970* (Political Report of the Government: At the 6th Meeting of the National Assembly, 3rd Session, June 1970). Ha Noi: Nha xuat ban Su that, 1970.

———. *Kien tri ra day manh su nghiep chong My cuu nuoc den thang loi hoan toan* (Sustaining and Strengthening the Cause of the Anti-American Resistance for National Salvation until Total Victory). Ha Noi: Nha xuat ban Su that, 1972.

Truong Chinh. *Ve cong tac Mat tran hien nay* (About the Front's Present Work). Ha Noi: Nha xuat ban Su that, 1972.

Uy ban kiem tra cua Ban chap hanh Trung uong Dang lao dong Viet Nam. *De cuong bao cao truoc dang vien trong dip thi hanh chi thi 192 CT/TW o cac to chuc co so Dang* (Draft Report before Party Members on the Execution of Instruction 192 CT/TW in the Base Organizations of the Party). Thanh Hoa: Uy ban kiem tra tinh uy Thanh Hoa–An Hanh, 1973.

Viet Nam Cong Hoa. *Tuyen bo cua tong thong Viet Nam Cong Hoa ngay 11-7-1969* (Declaration of the President of the Republic of Vietnam, 11 July 1969). Sai Gon: Bo ngoai giao, 1969.

Sources in English and French

Bases for a Settlement of the Viet Nam Problem. Hanoi: Foreign Languages Publishing House, 1971.

Biles, Robert E. *Bombing as a Policy Tool in Vietnam: A Staff Study Based on the Pentagon Papers*. Washington, D.C.: Government Printing Office, 1972.

Democratic Republic of Viet Nam Commission for Investigation of the U.S. Imperialists' War Crimes in Viet Nam. *The Late December 1972 US Blitz on North Viet Nam*. Hanoi: Department of Press and Information, 1973.

Herring, George C., ed. *Secret Diplomacy of the Vietnam War: The Negotiating Volumes of the* Pentagon Papers. Austin: University of Texas Press, 1983.

Hosmer, Stephen T., Konrad Keller, and Brian M. Jenkins. *The Fall of South Vietnam: Statements by Vietnamese Military and Civilian Leaders*. Santa Monica: RAND Corporation, 1978.

Laird, Melvin R. *The Nixon Doctrine*. Washington, D.C.: American Enterprise Institute for Foreign Policy Research, 1972.

Lavalle, A., et al. *The Tale of Two Bridges and the Battle for the Skies over North Vietnam*. Washington, D.C.: Government Printing Office, 1976.

Le Duan. *La révolution vietnamienne: problème fondamentaux, tâches essentielles* (The Vietnamese Revolution: Fundamental Problems, Essential Tasks). Hanoi: Éditions en langues étrangères, 1970.

Marolda, Edward, ed. *Operation End Sweep: A History of Minesweeping Operations in North Vietnam*. Washington, D.C.: Government Printing Office, 1993.

McCarthy, James R., and George B. Allison. *Linebacker II: A View from the Rock*. Washington, D.C.: Government Printing Office, 1979.

Momyer, William W. *Air Power in Three Wars*. Washington, D.C.: Government Printing Office, 1978.

National Archives and Records Administration. *Public Papers of the President of the United States: Richard Nixon, 1972*. Washington, D.C.: Government Printing Office, 1974.

Niehaus, Marjorie, and Robert Shuey. *Legislation Restricting Involvement of U.S. Military Forces in Indochina*. Washington, D.C.: Congressional Research Issue Brief IB 75022, 21 January 1975.

The Pentagon Papers: The Defense Department History of the United States Decision-Making in Vietnam. Senator Gravel Edition. Vol. 4. Boston: Beacon Press, 1971.

Pike, Douglas, ed. *The Bunker Papers: Reports to the President from Vietnam, 1967–1973.* Vol. 3. Berkeley: Institute of East Asian Studies, University of California, 1990.

Porter, Gareth, ed. *Vietnam: The Definitive Documentation of Human Decisions.* Vol. 2. Stanfordville, N.Y.: Earl M. Coleman Enterprises, 1979.

———. *Vietnam: A History in Documents.* New York: Meridian Books, 1981.

Republic of Viet-Nam. *Inaugural Address by President Nguyen Van Thieu, October 31, 1967.* Washington, D.C.: Embassy of Viet-Nam, 1967.

———. *Peace and Beyond: Official Statements and Communiqués on Peace and Postwar Development, July–September 1968.* Viet-Nam Document Series IV. Washington, D.C.: Embassy of Viet-Nam, 1968.

———. *On Peace and Manpower Requirements by Nguyen Van Thieu, April 10, 1968.* Washington, D.C.: Embassy of Viet-Nam, 1968.

République du Viêt-Nam. *Les négociations de paix et l'agression communiste* (Peace Negotiations and Communist Aggression). Saïgon: Ministère des affaires étrangères, 1969.

Rovine, Arthur W., ed. *Digest of United States Practice in International Law—1973.* Washington, D.C.: Government Printing Office, 1974.

Sharp, U. S. Grant, and William C. Westmoreland. *Report on the War in Vietnam as of 30 June 1968.* Washington, D.C.: Government Printing Office, 1969.

Truong Chinh. *Selected Writings.* Hanoi: The Gioi, 1994.

U.S. Congress. *Congressional Quarterly Almanac.* Washington, D.C.: Government Printing Office, 1971.

———. *Congressional Quarterly Weekly Report.* Washington, D.C.: Government Printing Office, 1972–75.

———. *Department of Defense Appropriations: Hearings before the Subcommittee of the Committee on Appropriations (House of Representatives).* 93rd Cong., 1st sess. Washington, D.C.: Government Printing Office, 1973.

———. *Statement of Information, Book XI: Bombing of Cambodia.* Washington, D.C.: Government Printing Office, 1974.

———. *Unauthorized Bombing of Military Targets in North Vietnam: Hearings before the Special Subcommittee on Armed Services Investigations.* Washington, D.C.: Government Printing Office, 1972.

———. *Unauthorized Bombing of Military Targets in North Vietnam: Report of the Special Subcommittee on Armed Services Investigations.* Washington, D.C.: Government Printing Office, 1972.

———. *United States–Vietnam Relations, 1945–1967: A Study Prepared by the Department of Defense.* Vol. 7. Washington, D.C.: Government Printing Office, 1971.

———. *The War Powers Resolution.* Washington, D.C.: Government Printing Office, 1976.

U.S. Department of State. *Aggression from the North: The Record of North Viet Nam's Campaign to Conquer South Viet Nam.* Washington, D.C.: Government Printing Office, 1965.

———. *The Department of State Bulletin.* Washington, D.C.: Government Printing Office, 1972–73.

———. *A Threat to the Peace: North Viet Nam's Efforts to Conquer South Viet Nam.* Washington, D.C.: Government Printing Office, 1961.

U.S. President. *Weekly Compilation of Presidential Documents—Richard Nixon.* Washington, D.C.: Government Printing Office, 1972–73.

U.S. Senate. *Hearings on the Paris Peace Accords: Hearings before the Select Committee on POW/MIA Affairs.* 102d Cong., 2d sess. Washington, D.C.: Government Printing Office, 1993.

Memoirs
Sources in Vietnamese

Hoang Van Khang. *Dang thang B-52: Hoi ky* (Defeating the B-52s: A Memoir). Ha Noi: Nha xuat ban Quan doi nhan dan, 1993.

Mai Van Bo. *Tan cong ngoai giao va tiep xuc bi mat* (Diplomatic Attacks and Secret Negotiations). Thanh pho Ho Chi Minh: Nha xuat ban Thanh pho Ho Chi Minh, 1985.

Sources in English and French

Bui Diem. *In the Jaws of History*. Bloomington: Indiana University Press, 1999.

Bui Tin. *Following Ho Chi Minh: Memoirs of a North Vietnamese Colonel*. Honolulu: University of Hawaii Press, 1995.

Colson, Charles. *Born Again*. Old Tappan, N.J.: Chosen Books, 1976.

Dobrynin, Anatoly. *In Confidence: Moscow's Ambassador to America's Six Cold War Presidents*. Seattle: University of Washington Press, 1995.

Ehrlichman, John. *Witness to Power*. New York: Simon & Schuster, 1982.

Ély, Paul. *L'Indochine dans la tourmente* (Indochina in Turmoil). Paris: Librairie Plon, 1964.

Haig, Alexander M., Jr., and Charles McCarry. *Inner Circles: How America Changed the World: A Memoir*. New York: Warner Books, 1992.

Haldeman, H. R. *The Haldeman Diaries: Inside the Nixon White House*. New York: Berkley Books, 1994.

Harriman, W. Averell. *America and Russia in a Changing World: A Half Century of Personal Observation*. Garden City, N.Y.: Doubleday, 1971.

Johnson, Lyndon B. *The Vantage Point: Perspectives of the Presidency, 1963–1969*. New York: Holt, Rinehart and Winston, 1971.

Kissinger, Henry A. *White House Years*. Boston: Little, Brown and Company, 1979.

——. *Years of Upheaval*. Boston: Little, Brown and Company, 1982.

Nguyen Cao Ky. *Twenty Years and Twenty Days*. New York: Stein & Day, 1976.

Nixon, Richard M. *RN: The Memoirs of Richard Nixon*. New York: Warner Books, 1978.

Truong Nhu Tang. *A Viet Cong Memoir*. New York: Vintage Books, 1985.

Van Tien Dung. *Our Great Spring Victory*. New York: Monthly Review Press, 1977.

Walters, Vernon A. *Silent Missions*. Garden City, N.Y.: Doubleday, 1978.

Westmoreland, William. *A Soldier Reports*. New York: Doubleday, 1976.

Newspapers and Miscellaneous Periodicals

Chinh luan
Doan ket
Ha Noi moi
London Sunday Express
Los Angeles Times
Le Monde
New York Times
Nhan dan
Peking Review
St. Louis Post Dispatch
Tin song
Wall Street Journal
Washington Evening Star
Washington Post
Washington Star-News

Secondary Sources
Books, Monographs, and Articles
Sources in Vietnamese

Ban chi dao tong ket chien tranh, Truc thuoc Bo chinh tri. *Tong ket cuoc khang chien chong My, cuu nuoc: thang loi va bai hoc* (Summarizing the Anti-American Resistance for National Salvation: Victory and Lesson). Ha Noi: Nha xuat ban Chinh tri quoc gia, 1995.

Ban nghien cuu lich su Dang Trung uong. *50 nam hoat dong cua dang cong san Viet Nam* (Fifty Years of Activities of the Vietnamese Communist Party). Ha Noi: Nha xuat ban Su that, 1979.

Bo Quoc phong, Vien lich su quan su Viet Nam. *Lich su nghe thuat chien dich Viet Nam trong 30 nam chien tranh chong Phap, chong My, 1945–1975* (History of Vietnamese Military Strategy in the Thirty-Year War against France, against the United States, 1945–1975). Ha Noi: Nha xuat ban Quan doi nhan dan, 1995.

Cao Van Luong. "Doc lap dan toc ket hop voi chu nghia xa hoi suc manh chien thang cua cuoc khang chien chong My, cuu nuoc" (Popular Independence Joins with Socialism to Strengthen the Victory of the Anti-American Resistance for National Salvation). *Nghien cuu Lich su*, no. 11 (1995): 1–14.

———. "Thang loi cua cuoc khang chien chong My, cuu nuoc: thanh qua tong hop suc manh cua ca nuoc cua doc lap dan toc va chu nghia xa hoi" (The Victory of the Anti-American Resistance for National Salvation: Fruit of the Combined Strength of the Country's Popular Independence and Socialism). *Nghien cuu Lich su*, no. 2 (1985): 1–10, 42.

———. "Ve cuoc tong tien cong va noi day dong loat Tet mau than, 1968" (On the Simultaneous General Offensive and Uprising of Tet, 1968). *Nghien cuu Lich su*, no. 1 (1993): 1–6.

Cuoc khang chien chong My cuu nuoc cua nhan dan Viet Nam (The Anti-American Resistance for National Salvation of the Vietnamese People). Ha Noi: Nha xuat ban Su that, 1987.

Dang cong san Viet Nam, Ban chap hanh dang bo thanh pho Ha Noi. *Lich su dang bo thanh pho Ha Noi, 1954–1975* (History of the Hanoi City Party Branch, 1954–1975). Ha Noi: Nha xuat ban Ha Noi, 1995.

Hiep Son et al. *Thu do Ha Noi: lich su khang chien chong My cuu nuoc, 1954–1975* (Hanoi the Capital: History of the Anti-American Resistance for National Salvation, 1954–1975). Ha Noi: Nha xuat ban Quan doi nhan dan, 1991.

Ho Khang. "Thu giai trinh 'My hoa' 'Viet Nam hoa' chien tranh" (Explaining the "Americanization" of "Vietnamization"). *Lich su Quan su*, no. 4 (1992): 16–19.

Ho Si Huu et al. *Lich su quan chung phong khong*. Tap II (History of the Air Defense Service. Vol. 2). Ha Noi: Nha xuat ban Quan doi nhan dan, 1994.

Hoang Dung. "Tim hieu ve chien luoc tien cong trong cuoc khang chien chong My, cuu nuoc" (Understanding the Offensive Strategy in the Anti-American Resistance for National Salvation). *Nghien cuu Lich su*, no. 2 (1985): 11–17, 70.

Hoang Minh Thao, "Nghe thuat biet nham thoi co" (The Art of Seizing Opportunity). *Tap chi Cong san*, no. 12 (1983): 23–29.

Hoang Van Thai. *Tran danh ba muoi nam: ky su lich su*. Tap II (The Thirty-Year Fight: Historical Developments. Vol. 2). Ha Noi: Nha xuat ban Quan doi nhan dan, 1995.

Hoc vien Quan su cao cap. *Cuoc khang chien chong My, cuu nuoc 1954–1975: nhung su kien quan su* (The Anti-American Resistance for National Salvation,

1954–1975: Military Events). Ha Noi: Nha xuat ban Quan doi nhan dan, 1980.

Hong Thai. "Lien minh cong nong trong cong nghiep hoa xa hoi chu nghia va dau tranh chong chien tranh pha hoai cua de quoc My (1961–1975)" (The Worker-Peasant Alliance in Socialist Industrialization and the Struggle against the American Imperialists' War of Destruction [1961–1975]). *Nghien cuu Lich su*, no. 2 (1976): 1–8, 18.

Khac Huynh. "Dam phan Pari va hiep dinh Pari ve Viet Nam voi phuong cham gianh thang loi tung buoc" (The Paris Talks and the Paris Agreement on Vietnam and the Guideline for Bringing About Decisive Victory). *Nghien cuu Quoc te*, no. 11 (1996): 22–28.

Kham Thien (Kham Thien). Ha Noi: Su van hoa thong tin Ha Noi, 1973.

Le Duc Tho. *Mot so van de ve tong ket chien tranh va bien soan lich su quan su* (Some Problems on Summarizing the War and Writing Military History). Ha Noi: Nha xuat ban Su that, 1989.

Le Mau Han. *Dang cong san Viet Nam: cac Dai hoi va Hoi nghi Trung uong* (The Vietnamese Communist Party: Congresses and Plenums). Ha Noi: Nha xuat ban Ching tri quoc gia, 1995.

Le Thi Nham Tuyet. *Phu nu Vietnam qua cac thoi day* (Vietnamese Women at Different Periods). Ha Noi: Nha xuat ban khoa hoc xa hoi, 1975).

Luu Van Loi. *50 nam ngoai giao Viet Nam, 1945–1995*. Tap I: *Ngoai giao Viet Nam, 1945–1975* (Fifty Years of Vietnamese Diplomacy, 1945–1995. Vol. 1: Vietnamese Diplomacy, 1945–1975). Ha Noi: Nha xuat ban Cong an nhan dan, 1996.

Luu Van Loi and Nguyen Anh Vu. *Cac cuoc thuong luong Le Duc Tho–Kissinger tai Paris* (The Le Duc Tho–Kissinger Negotiations in Paris). Ha Noi: Nha xuat ban Cong an nhan dan, 1996.

———. *Tiep xuc bi mat Viet Nam-Hoa Ky truoc Hoi Nghi Pa-ri* (The Secret Vietnamese-American Negotiations before the Paris Conference). Ha Noi: Vien quan he quoc te, 1990.

Mot so van kien cua Dang ve chong My, cuu nuoc. Tap II: *1965–1970* (Some Documents of the Party about the Anti-American Resistance for National Salvation. Vol. 2: 1965–1970). Ha Noi: Nha xuat ban Su that, 1986.

Muoi hai ngay dem chien thang co y nghia lich su (The Twelve Days and Nights Have a Historical Significance). Ha Noi: Nha xuat ban Su that, 1973.

Nguyen Co Thach. *Vi hoa binh va an ninh o Dong Nam A va the gioi* (For Peace and Security in Southeast Asia and the World). Ha Noi: Nha xuat ban Su that, 1984.

Nguyen Dinh Uoc. "Dau tranh ngoai giao phoi hop voi dau tranh quan su trong khang chien chong My, cuu nuoc" (The Diplomatic Struggle Combined with the Military Struggle in the Anti-American Resistance for National Salvation). *Lich su Quan su*, no. 1 (1993): 14–19.

Nguyen Duy Trinh. *Mat tran ngoai giao thoi ky chong My, cuu nuoc* (The Diplomatic Front in the Anti-American Period for National Salvation). Ha Noi: Nha xuat ban Su that, 1979.

———. *Mien Bac xa hoi chu nghia trong qua trinh thuc hien dai nhiem vu chien luoc* (The Socialist North in the Execution of Strategic Tasks). Ha Noi: Nha xuat ban Su that, 1976.

Nguyen Hung Phong et al. *Lich su doan 308 quan tien phong* (History of the Vanguard Troops of Unit 308). Ha Noi: Nha xuat ban Quan doi nhan dan, 1994.

Nguyen Huu Hop. "Tim hieu mat tran dau tranh ngoai giao va thang loi cua cuoc khang chien chong My, cuu nuoc (1954–1975)" (Understanding the Diplomatic Struggle and the Victory of the Anti-American Resistance for

National Salvation [1954–1975]). *Nghien cuu Lich su*, no. 221 (1975): 34–42.

Nguyen Phung Minh et al. *Nam Trung Bo khang chien, 1945–1975* (The Resistance in Southern Central Vietnam, 1945–1975). Ha Noi: Vien lich su Dang, 1992.

Nguyen Thanh Le. *Cuoc dam phan Pari ve Viet Nam* (The Paris Negotiations on Vietnam). Ha Noi: Nha xuat ban Chinh tri quoc gia, 1998.

Nguyen Thi Thap. *Lich su phong trao phu nu Viet nam* (History of the Vietnamese Women's Movement). Ha noi: Nha xuat ban Phu nu, 1981.

Nguyen Trong Phuc. "Tim hieu tu tuong Ho Chi Minh ve ngoai giao sau Hiep nghi Gio-ne-vo 1954" (Understanding the Thought of Ho Chi Minh on Diplomacy after the Geneva Conference of 1954). *Nghien cuu Lich su*, no. 11 (1995): 21–24.

Nguyen Tu Duong. *Duong mon tren bien* (The Sea Supply Trail). Ha Noi: Nha xuat ban Quan doi nhan dan, 1995.

Nhung su kien lich su Dang. Tap III: *Ve khang chien chong My, cuu nuoc, 1954–1975* (Historical Documents of the Party. Vol. 3: On the Anti-American Resistance for National Salvation, 1954–1975). Ha Noi: Nha xuat ban Su that, 1985.

Quan doi nhan dan Viet Nam. *1972: Mot nam vi dai* (1972: A Great Year). Ha Noi: Nha xuat ban Quan doi nhan dan, 1973.

Than Xuan Chung et al. *Quan doi nhan dan Viet Nam, 1944–1979* (The People's Army of Vietnam, 1944–1979). Ha Noi: Nha xuat ban Quan doi nhan dan, 1979.

Tong cuc hau can Bo quoc phong. *Lich su bo doi Truong Son–duong Ho Chi Minh* (History of the Truong Son–Ho Chi Minh Trail Soldiers). Ha Noi: Nha xuat ban Quan doi nhan dan, 1994.

Tran Minh Truong. *"Thu vao Nam*: Su hoan thien duong loi cach mang mien Nam" (*Letters to the South*: Perfect Blueprint of the Southern Revolution). In Vien nghien cuu Ho Chi Minh. *Le Duan va cach mang Viet Nam*, 273–84.

Tran Nham. *Nghe thuat biet thang tieng buoc* (The Art of Knowing How to Progress). Ha Noi: Nha xuat ban Chinh tri quoc gia, 1995.

Tran Van Tra. *Ket thuc cuoc chien tranh 30 nam* (Concluding the Thirty-Year War). Thanh pho Ho Chi Minh: Nha xuat ban Van nghe, 1982.

———. *Nhung chang duong lich su cua B2 thanh dong.* Tap I: *Hoa binh hay chien tranh* (History of the B2 Theater. Vol. 1: Peace or War). Ha Noi: Nha xuat ban Quan doi nhan dan, 1992.

Tran Vu. "1971: nam phan cong thang loi gianh quyen chu dong chien truong" (1971: Year of Successful Counteroffensives that Regained the Initiative on the Battlefront). *Lich su Quan su*, no. 4 (1991): 4.

Trung tam khoa hoc xa hoi va nhan van quoc gia, Vien su hoc. *Thang loi khang chien chong My va hai muoi nam xay dung dat nuoc sau chien tranh* (The Victory of the Anti-American Resistance and Twenty Years of Building the Country after the War). Ha Noi: Nha xuat ban Khoa hoc xa hoi, 1995.

Truong Chinh. "Cung co mien Bac, chieu co mien Nam" (Consolidating the North, Helping the South). *Hoc tap*, no. 1 (1963): 29–35.

———. *Viet Nam: 40 nam dau tranh va thang loi* (Vietnam: Forty Years of Struggle and Victory). Ha Noi: Nha xuat ban Su that, 1985.

12 ngay ruc ro chien cong lam nuc long the gioi (The Twelve Days of Flagrant Aggression Have Gained Us World Sympathy). Ha Noi: Nha xuat ban Su that, 1973.

Van Phong. "Quan he Trung-Viet va Viet-Trung" (Chinese-Vietnamese and Vietnamese-Chinese Relations). *Nghien cuu Lich su*, no. 6 (1979): 1–13.

Van Tao. "Chan ly 'Muon xay dung chu nghia xa hoi, truoc het can co nhung con nguoi xa hoi chu nghia' dang can duoc nhan thuc sau sac" (The Dictum "To Build Socialism, Above All One Needs Socialist People" Must Be a Profound Perception). *Nghien cuu Lich su*, no. 2 (1990): 9–15.

———. "Mien Bac xa hoi chu nghia: hau phuong lon cua mien Nam thang My" (The Socialist North: Great Rear Base for the South to Defeat the Americans). *Nghien cuu Lich su*, no. 4 (1986): 8–14, 25.

Van Tao and Nguyen Huu Dao. "Cong cuoc xay dung co so vat chat ky thuat cho chu nghia xa hoi trong dieu kien co chien tranh o Viet Nam (1955–1975)" (The Building of the Material and Technical Base for Socialism in War Conditions in Vietnam [1955–1975]). *Nghien cuu Lich su*, no. 2 (1984): 1–13, 37.

Van Tien Dung. *Buoc ngoat lon cua cuoc khang chien chong My* (The Great Turning Point of the Anti-American Resistance). Ha Noi: Nha xuat ban Su that, 1989.

———. *Cuoc khang chien chong My: toan thang* (The Anti-American Resistance: Total Victory). Ha Noi: Nha xuat ban Su that, 1991.

———. "Hai thang loi chien luoc 'danh cho My cut' " (Two Strategic Victories in the "Campaign to Expel the Americans"). *Lich su Quan su*, no. 5 (1992): 3–10.

Vien lich su. *Lich su cuoc khang chien chong My*. Tap II (History of the Anti-American Resistance. Vol. 2). Ha Noi: Nha xuat ban Su that, 1990.

Vien lich su quan su Viet Nam. *Lich su Quan doi nhan dan Viet Nam* (History of the People's Army of Vietnam). Ha Noi: Nha xuat ban Quan doi nhan dan, 1994.

Vien nghien cuu chu nghia Mac-Lenin. *Lich su Dang cong san Viet Nam, 1954–1975* (History of the Vietnamese Communist Party, 1954–1975). Ha Noi: Nha xuat ban Chinh tri quoc gia, 1995.

Vien nghien cuu Ho Chi Minh. *Le Duan va cach mang Viet Nam* (Le Duan and the Vietnamese Revolution). Ha Noi: Nha xuat ban Chinh tri quoc gia, 1999.

Sources in English and French

Aitken, Jonathan. *Nixon: A Life*. London: Weidenfeld and Nicholson, 1993.

Ambrose, Stephen E. *Nixon: Ruin and Recovery, 1973–1990*. New York: Simon & Schuster, 1991.

———. *Nixon: The Triumph of a Politician, 1962–1972*. New York: Simon & Schuster, 1989.

Amter, Joseph A. *Vietnam Verdict: A Citizen's History*. New York: Continuum, 1982.

Andradé, Dale. *Ashes to Ashes: The Phoenix Program and the Vietnam War*. Lexington, Mass.: Lexington Books, 1990.

"A B-52 Pilot Who Said No." *Newsweek*, 22 January 1973, 18.

Berman, Larry. *Lyndon Johnson's War*. New York: W. W. Norton & Company, 1989.

———. *No Peace, No Honor: Nixon, Kissinger, and Betrayal in Vietnam*. New York: Free Press, 2001.

Boudarel, Georges, Jean Chesneaux, and Daniel Hémery, eds. *Tradition et révolution au Viêtnam* (Tradition and Revolution in Vietnam). Paris: Éditions anthropos, 1971.

Boyne, Walter J. *Boeing B-52: A Documentary History*. London: Jane's Publishing Co., 1981.

Brigham, Robert K. *Guerrilla Diplomacy: The NLF's Foreign Relations and the Viet Nam War*. Ithaca: Cornell University Press, 1999.

———. "Vietnamese-American Peace Negotiations: The Failed 1965 Initiatives." *Journal of American–East Asian Relations* 4, no. 4 (1995): 377–95.

Bundy, William. *A Tangled Web: The Making of Foreign Policy in the Nixon Presidency.* New York: Hill and Wang, 1998.

Burchett, Wilfred G. *Grasshoppers and Elephants: Why Viet Nam Fell.* New York: Urizen Books, 1977.

———. *Vietnam North.* New York: International, 1966.

Buu Kinh. "Le Nord-Viêtnam et le conflit sino-soviétique" (North Vietnam and the Sino-Soviet Conflict). *Politique étrangère (suppl.)*, no. 6 (1972): 479–97.

Chen Jian. *Mao's China and the Cold War.* Chapel Hill: University of North Carolina Press, 2001.

Chen Min. "Myth and Reality of Triangulations: A Study of American Withdrawal from Vietnam." *Asian Profile* 18, no. 6 (1990): 515–31.

Chesneaux, Jean. "Les fondements historiques du communisme vietnamien" (The Historical Foundations of Vietnamese Communism). In Boudarel, Chesneaux, and Hémery, eds. *Tradition et révolution au Viêtnam*, 215–37.

Clodfelter, Mark A. "Culmination Dresden: 1945." *Aerospace Historian* 26, no. 3 (1979): 134–47.

———. *The Limits of Air Power: The American Bombing of North Vietnam.* New York: Free Press, 1989.

———. "Problems and Pitfalls in Researching the Air War against North Vietnam." *Air Power History* 38 (1991): 49–53.

Clodfelter, Michael. *Vietnam in Military Statistics: A History of the Indochina Wars, 1772–1991.* Jefferson, N.C.: McFarland & Co., 1995.

Cohen, Warren I. *America in the Age of Soviet Power, 1945–1991.* Vol. 4 of *The Cambridge History of American Foreign Relations.* New York: Cambridge University Press, 1993.

Colby, William, and James McCargar. *Lost Victory: A Firsthand Account of America's Sixteen-Year Involvement in Vietnam.* Chicago: Contemporary Books, 1989.

Crowley, Monica. *Nixon in Winter.* New York: Random House, 1998.

Dawson, Alan. *55 Days: The Fall of South Vietnam.* Englewood Cliffs, N.J.: Prentice Hall, 1977.

DeBenedetti, Charles, and Charles Chatfield. *An American Ordeal: The Antiwar Movement of the Vietnam Era.* Syracuse, N.Y.: Syracuse University Press, 1990.

De Borchgrave, Arnaud. "Exclusive from Hanoi." *Newsweek*, 30 October 1972, 26–27.

Dillard, Walter Scott. *Sixty Days to Peace: Implementing the Paris Accords, Vietnam 1973.* Washington, D.C.: National Defense University Press, 1982.

"Diplomacy by Terror." *Newsweek*, 8 January 1973, 10.

Divine, Robert A., ed. *LBJ at Home and Abroad.* Vol. 3 of *The Johnson Years.* Lawrence: University Press of Kansas, 1994.

Donelly, Dorothy C. "A Settlement of Sorts: Henry Kissinger's Negotiations and America's Extrication from Vietnam." *Peace and Change* 9, nos. 2–3 (1983): 55–79.

Drew, Dennis M. *Rolling Thunder 1965: Anatomy of a Failure.* Maxwell AFB, Ala.: Air University Press, 1986.

Duiker, William J. *The Communist Road to Power in Vietnam.* Boulder: Westview Press, 1996.

Ethell, Jeffrey, and Alfred Price. *One Day in a Long War.* New York: Berkley Books, 1989.

Face aux bombes (Against the Bombs). Hanoi: Éditions en langues étrangères, 1969.

Fitzgerald, Frances. *Fire in the Lake.* New York: Vintage Books, 1972.

Friedman, Leon, and William F. Levantrosser, eds. *Cold War Patriot and Statesman: Richard M. Nixon.* Westport, Conn.: Greenwood Press, 1993.

Gaddis, John Lewis. *Strategies of Containment: A Critical Appraisal of Postwar American National Security Policy.* New York: Oxford University Press, 1982.

Gaiduk, Ilya V. *The Soviet Union and the Vietnam War.* Chicago: Ivan R. Dee, 1996.

Galluci, Robert L. *Neither Peace nor Honor: The Politics of American Military Policy in Vietnam.* Baltimore: John Hopkins University Press, 1975.

Gardner, Lloyd C. "Lyndon Johnson and Vietnam: The Final Months." In Divine, ed. *LBJ at Home and Abroad*, 198–238.

Garthoff, Raymond. *Détente and Confrontation: American-Soviet Relations from Nixon to Reagan.* Washington, D.C.: Brookings Institution, 1985.

Gelb, Leslie H., and Richard K. Betts. *The Irony of Vietnam: The System Worked.* Washington, D.C.: Brookings Institution, 1979.

Gibson, James W. *The Perfect War: Technowar in Vietnam.* Boston: Atlantic Monthly Press, 1986.

Gilks, Anne. *The Breakdown of the Sino-Vietnamese Alliance, 1970–1979.* Berkeley: Institute of East Asian Studies, University of California, 1992.

Glines, Carroll V. *The Compact History of the United States Air Force.* New York: Arno Press, 1980.

Goodman, Allan E. *The Lost Peace: America's Search for a Negotiated Settlement of the Vietnam War.* Stanford, Calif.: Hoover Institute Press, 1978.

———. *The Search for a Negotiated Settlement of the Vietnam War.* Berkeley: Institute of East Asian Studies, University of California, 1986.

Gurtov, Melvin. *Hanoi on War and Peace.* Santa Monica: RAND Corporation, 1967.

Hai Thu. *Le Nord Viêtnam contre la guerre aérienne U.S.* (North Vietnam against the U.S. Air War). Hanoi: Éditions en langues étrangères, 1967.

Haley, P. Edward. *Congress and the Fall of South Vietnam and Cambodia.* East Brunswick, N.J.: Associated University Presses, 1982.

Herring, George C. *America's Longest War: The United States and Vietnam, 1950–1975.* New York: Knopf, 1979.

Hersh, Seymor M. *The Price of Power: Kissinger Inside the Nixon White House.* New York: Summit Books, 1983.

Hertz, Martin F., and Leslie Rider. *The Prestige Press and the Christmas Bombing, 1972: Images and Reality in Vietnam.* Washington, D.C.: Ethics & Public Policy Center, 1980.

History of the Communist Party of Vietnam. Hanoi: Foreign Languages Publishing House, 1986.

Hoang Van Thai. *How South Vietnam Was Liberated.* Hanoi: The Gioi, 1992.

Hoff, Joan. *Nixon Reconsidered.* New York: Basic Books, 1994.

Hoopes, Townsend. *The Limits of Intervention.* New York: David McKay Company, 1969.

Hunt, Richard A. *Pacification: The American Struggle for Vietnam's Hearts and Minds.* Boulder: Westview Press, 1995.

Huynh Kim Khanh. *Vietnamese Communism, 1925–1945.* Ithaca: Cornell University Press, 1986.

Hyland, William G. *Mortal Rivals.* New York: Random House, 1987.

Hy Van Luong. *Revolution in the Village: Tradition and Transformation in North Vietnam, 1925–1988.* Honolulu: University of Hawaii Press, 1992.

Indochina Resource Center. *Viet-Nam: What Kind of Peace?: Documents and Analysis of the 1973 Paris Agreement on Viet-Nam.* Washington, D.C.: Indochina Resource Center, 1973.

Isaacs, Arnold. *Without Honor: Defeat in Vietnam and Cambodia.* Baltimore: John Hopkins University Press, 1983.

Isaacson, Walter. *Kissinger: A Biography.* New York: Simon & Schuster, 1992.

Johnson, Alexis U., and Jeff McAlister. *The Right Hand of Power.* Englewood Cliffs, N.J.: Prentice-Hall, 1984.

Kahin, George McT. *Intervention: How America Became Involved in Vietnam.* New York: Knopf, 1986.

Kahin, George McT., and John W. Lewis. *The United States in Vietnam.* New York: Dell Publishing, 1969.

Kalb, Marvin, and Bernard Kalb. *Kissinger.* Boston: Little, Brown and Company, 1974.

Kaplan, Morton A., et al. *Vietnam Settlement: Why 1973, Not 1969?.* Washington, D.C.: American Enterprise Institute for Public Policy Research, 1973.

Karnow, Stanley. *Vietnam: A History.* New York: Viking Press, 1983.

Kiernan, Ben. *How Pol Pot Came to Power.* London: Verso Press, 1985.

———. *The Pol Pot Regime: Race Power, and the Genocide in Cambodia under the Khmer Rouge, 1975–1979.* New Haven: Yale University Press, 1996.

Kimball, Jeffrey. *Nixon's Vietnam War.* Lawrence: University Press of Kansas, 1998.

Kissinger, Henry A. *Diplomacy.* New York: Simon & Schuster, 1994.

———. "The Viet Nam Negotiations." *Foreign Affairs* 47, no. 2 (1969): 211–34.

Knappman, Howard, ed. *South Vietnam: U.S.-Communist Confrontation in Southeast Asia.* Vol. 1, no. 1. New York: Facts on File, 1973.

Kohloff, Arthur L. "The BUFs Go Downtown." *Vietnam,* no. 2 (1990): 46–53.

Kolko, Gabriel. *Anatomy of a War: Vietnam, the United States, and the Modern Historical Experience.* New York: Pantheon Books, 1985.

Komer, Robert W. *Bureaucracy at War: U.S. Performance in the Vietnam Conflict.* Boulder: Westview Press, 1986.

Kraslow, David, and Stuart A. Loory. *The Secret Search for Peace in Vietnam.* New York: Random House, 1968.

Lacouture, Jean, and Phillipe Devillers. *La fin d'une guerre* (The End of a War). Paris: Librairie Plon, 1959.

Lawson, Eugene K. *The Sino-Vietnamese Conflict.* New York: Praeger, 1984.

Le Gro, William E. *Vietnam from Cease-Fire to Capitulation.* Washington, D.C.: U.S. Army Center of Military History, 1981.

Lehman, John. *The Executive, Congress, and Foreign Policy: Studies of the Nixon Administration.* New York: Praeger, 1976.

Levinson, Jeffrey L. *Alpha Strike Vietnam: The Navy's Air War, 1964 to 1973.* New York: Pocket Books, 1990.

Lewy, Guenter. *America in Vietnam.* New York: Oxford University Press, 1978.

Logevall, Fredrik. *Choosing War: The Lost Chance for Peace and the Escalation of War in Vietnam.* Berkeley: University of California Press, 1999.

Lomperis, Timothy J. *The War Everyone Lost—And Won: America's Intervention in Vietnam's Twin Struggles.* Baton Rouge: Louisiana State University Press, 1984.

Lorell, Mark, Charles Kelley Jr., and Deborah Hensler. *Casualties, Public Opinion, and Presidential Policy during the Vietnam War.* Santa Monica: RAND Corporation, 1985.

Luu Van Loi and Nguyen Anh Vu. *Le Duc Tho–Kissinger Negotiations in Paris.* Hanoi: The Gioi, 1996.

Maclear, Michael. *Vietnam: The Ten Thousand Day War.* London: Thames Methuen, 1981.

Marr, David G. "Bringing the National Liberation Front Back into the History of the Vietnam War." *Diplomatic History* 25, no. 2 (2001): 525–28.

Marr, David, and Jayne Werner, eds. *Tradition and Revolution in Vietnam.* Berkeley: Indochina Resource Center, 1975.

Moïse, Edwin E. *Tonkin Gulf and the Escalation of the Vietnam War.* Chapel Hill: University of North Carolina Press, 1996.

Morris, Roger. *An Uncertain Greatness: Henry Kissinger and American Foreign Policy.* New York: Harper & Row, 1977.

Morris, Stephen J. *Why Vietnam Invaded Cambodia.* Stanford, Calif.: Stanford University Press, 1999.

Morzek, Donald J. *Air Power and the Ground War in Vietnam: Ideas and Actions.* Maxwell AFB, Ala.: Air University Press, 1988.

"The New Air War in North Vietnam." *U.S. News & World Report,* 24 April 1972, 15–17.

Ngoc Ha. *Viêtnam: destructions et dommages de guerre* (Vietnam: War Destructions and Damages). Hanoi: Éditions en langues étrangères, 1977.

Ngo Quang Truong. *The Easter Offensive of 1972.* Washington, D.C.: U.S. Army Center of Military History, 1980.

Ngo Vinh Long. "The Tet Offensive and Its Aftermath." In Werner and Hunt, eds. *The American War in Vietnam,* 23–45.

Nguyen Cao Ky. *How We Lost the Vietnam War.* New York: Stein & Day, 1976.

Nguyen Duy Hinh. *Lam Son 719.* Washington, D.C.: U.S. Army Center of Military History, 1979.

———. *Vietnamization and the Cease-Fire.* Washington, D.C.: U.S. Army Center of Military History, 1980.

Nguyen Hoang et al. "Indochine: le tournant 1972–1973" (Indochina: The Turning Point, 1972–1973). *Études vietnamiennes,* no. 39 (1974): 236–56.

Nguyen Khac Vien. *Vietnam: A Long History.* Hanoi: Foreign Languages Publishing House, 1987.

Nguyen, Gregory Tien Hung. *Economic Development in Socialist Vietnam, 1955–80.* New York: Praeger, 1977.

Nguyen, Tien Hung, and Jerrold L. Schecter. *The Palace File.* New York: Harper & Row, 1986.

Nichols, John B., and Barrett Tillman. *On Yankee Station: The Naval Air War over Vietnam.* Annapolis: Naval Institute Press, 1987.

Nixon, Richard M. *No More Vietnams.* New York: Warner Books, 1985.

"Nixon's Blitz Leads Back to the Table." *Time,* 8 January 1973, 12–14.

Nolan, Keith W. *Into Laos: The Story of Dewey Canyon II/Lam Son 719: Vietnam 1971.* Novato, Calif.: Presidio Press, 1986.

O'Ballance, Edgar. *The Wars in Vietnam, 1954–1980.* New York: Hippocrene Books, 1981.

Oberdorfer, Don. *Tet!* New York: Da Capa Press, 1971.

Palmer, Bruce, Jr. *The Twenty-Five-Year War: America's Military Role in Vietnam.* Lexington: University Press of Kentucky, 1984.

Papp, Daniel S. *Vietnam: The View from Moscow, Peking, Washington.* Jefferson, N.C.: McFarland & Company, 1981.

Pike, Douglas. *Viet Cong: The Organization and Techniques of the National Liberation Front of South Vietnam.* Cambridge, Mass.: Massachusetts Institute of Technology Press, 1966.

———. *Vietnam and the Soviet Union.* Boulder: Westview Press, 1987.

Porter, Gareth. *A Peace Denied: The United States, Vietnam, and the Paris Agreement.* Bloomington: Indiana University Press, 1975.

Portes, Jacques. *Les Américains et la guerre du Viêtnam* (Americans and the Vietnam War). Paris: Éditions complexes, 1993.

Prados, John. *The Hidden History of the Vietnam War.* Chicago: Ivan R. Dee, 1995.

Qiang Zhai. *China and the Vietnam Wars, 1950–1975.* Chapel Hill: University of North Carolina Press, 2000.

———. "Opposing Negotiations: China and the Vietnam Peace Talks, 1965–1968." *Pacific Historical Review* 68, no. 1 (1999): 21–49.

Reichley, A. James. *Conservatives in an Age of Change: The Nixon and Ford Administrations*. New York: Brookings Institution, 1981.

Rodman, Peter W. *More Precious Than Peace: The Cold War and the Struggle for the Third World*. New York: Charles Scribner's Sons, 1994.

Safire, William. *Before the Fall*. Garden City, N.Y.: Doubleday, 1975.

Schlesinger, Arthur M. *The Imperial Presidency*. Boston: Houghton Mifflin Company, 1976.

Schulzinger, Robert D. *Henry Kissinger: Doctor of Diplomacy*. New York: Columbia University Press, 1989.

Sen Gupta, Bhabani, "The Soviet Union and Vietnam," *International Studies* (New Delhi), no. 4 (1973): 559–76.

Serong, Francis P. "Vietnam's Menacing Cease-Fire." *Conflict Studies*, no. 51 (1974): 1–16.

Sharp, U. S. Grant. *Strategy for Defeat: Vietnam in Retrospect*. San Rafael, Calif.: Presidio Press, 1978.

Shawcross, William. *Sideshow: Kissinger, Nixon and the Destruction of Cambodia*. New York: Simon & Schuster, 1979.

Sheehan, Neil. *A Bright Shining Lie: John Paul Van and America in Vietnam*. New York: Random House, 1988.

Smith, John T. *Rolling Thunder: The American Strategic Bombing Campaign against North Vietnam, 1964–1968*. Surrey: Air Research Publication, 1994.

Smith, Welden E. "The Strategic Bombing Debate: The Second World War and Vietnam." *Journal of Contemporary History* 12, no. 12 (1977): 175–91.

Smyser, W. R. *The Independent Vietnamese: Vietnamese Communism between Russia and China, 1955–1969*. Athens: Ohio University Press, 1980.

Snepp, Frank. *Decent Interval: An Insider's Account of Saigon's Indecent End Told by the CIA's Chief Strategy Analyst in Vietnam*. New York: Random House, 1977.

Spector, Ronald H. *Advice and Support: The Early Years of the U.S. Army in Vietnam, 1941–1960*. New York: Free Press, 1985.

——. *After Tet*. New York: Free Press, 1991.

Summers, Anthony. *The Arrogance of Power: The Secret World of Richard Nixon*. New York: Viking Press, 2000.

Summers, Harry G., Jr. *On Strategy: A Critical Analysis of the Vietnam War*. New York: Dell Books, 1982.

Szulc, Tad. *The Illusion of Peace: Foreign Policy in the Nixon Years*. New York: Viking Press, 1978.

Thies, Wallace J. *When Governments Collide: Coercion and Diplomacy in the Vietnam Conflict, 1964–1968*. Berkeley: University of California Press, 1980.

Thompson, Robert. *Peace Is Not at Hand*. New York: David McKay Company, 1974.

Thornton, Richard C. *The Nixon-Kissinger Years: Reshaping America's Foreign Policy*. New York: Paragon House, 1989.

Tilford, Earl H., Jr. *Setup: What the Air Force Did in Vietnam and Why*. Maxwell AFB, Ala.: Air University Press, 1991.

Tran Van Don. *Our Endless War: Inside Vietnam*. San Rafael, Calif.: Presidio Press, 1978.

Tran Van Tra. "Tet: The 1968 General Offensive and General Uprising." In Werner and Luu Doan Huynh, eds. *The Vietnam War: Vietnamese and American Perspectives*, 37–65.

Turley, G. H. *The Easter Offensive: Vietnam, 1972*. Novato, Calif.: Presidio Press, 1985.

Turley, William S. *The Second Indochina War: A Short Political and Military History, 1954–1975*. Boulder: Westview Press, 1986.

Turner, Allan E. "Pave Strike." *Vietnam*, no. 1 (1990): 62–65.

Ulsamer, Edgar. "Airpower Halts Invasion." *Air Force*, no. 12 (1972): 58–64.

Valentine, Douglas. *The Phoenix Program*. New York: William Morrow and Co., 1990.

Van der Kroef, Justus. *Communism in Southeast Asia*. Berkeley: University of California Press, 1980.

Van Dyke, Jon. *North Vietnam's Strategy for Survival*. Palo Alto, Calif.: Pacific Books, 1972.

Vo Nhan Tri. *Croissance économique au Viêtnam, 1945–1965* (Economic Growth in Vietnam, 1945–1965). Hanoi: Éditions en langues étrangères, 1967.

Vu Quoc Tuan and Nguyen Xuan Lai. "Politique économique et guerre de libération nationale: La seconde résistance (1965–1972)" (Economic Policy and War of National Liberation: The Second Resistance [1965–1972]). *Études vietnamiennes*, no. 44 (1976): 198–220.

Werner, Jayne S., and David Hunt, eds. *The American War in Vietnam*. Ithaca: Southeast Asia Program, Cornell University, 1993.

Werner, Jayne S., and Luu Doan Huynh, eds. *The Vietnam War: Vietnamese and American Perspectives*. Armonk, N.Y.: M. E. Sharpe, 1993.

Whiting, Allen S. "Sino-American Détente." *China Quarterly*, no. 82 (1980): 330–42.

Wich, Richard. *Sino-Soviet Crisis Politics: A Study of Political Change and Communication*. Cambridge, Mass.: Harvard University Press, 1985.

Yenne, Bill. *SAC: A Primer of Modern Strategic Air Power*. London: Arms & Armour Press, 1984.

Index

The New Cold War History

Pierre Asselin
*A Bitter Peace: Washington, Hanoi, and the
Making of the Paris Agreement* (2002).
Jeffrey Glen Giauque
*Grand Designs and Visions of Unity: The Atlantic Powers and the
Reorganization of Western Europe, 1955–1963* (2002).
Chen Jian
Mao's China and the Cold War (2001).
M. E. Sarotte
Dealing with the Devil: East Germany, Détente, and Ostpolitik, 1969–1973
(2001).
Mark Philip Bradley
*Imagining Vietnam and America: The Making of Postcolonial Vietnam,
1919–1950* (2000).
Michael E. Latham
*Modernization as Ideology:
American Social Science and "Nation Building" in the Kennedy Era*
(2000).
Qiang Zhai
China and the Vietnam Wars, 1950–1975 (2000).
William I. Hitchcock
*France Restored: Cold War Diplomacy and the
Quest for Leadership in Europe, 1944–1954* (1998).